Public Procurement:
Global Revolution

International Economic Development Law

VOLUME 8

Series Editor

J.J. Norton
Centre for Commercial Law Studies
Queen Mary and Westfield College
University of London
London, UK

This titles published in this series are listed at the end of this volume.

SMU, School of Law
Dallas, Texas

Centre for Commercial Law Studies
Queen Mary and Westfield College
University of London

Public Procurement:
Global Revolution

Editors

Sue Arrowsmith,
Public Procurement Research Group,
School of Law, University of Nottingham

Arwel Davies
Public Procurement Research Group,
School of Law, University of Nottingham

KLUWER LAW INTERNATIONAL
LONDON – THE HAGUE – BOSTON

Published by
Kluwer Law International Ltd
Sterling House
66 Wilton Road
London SW1V 1DE
United Kingdom

Sold and distributed in
the USA and Canada by
Kluwer Law International
675 Massachusetts Avenue
Cambridge MA 02139
USA

Kluwer Law International incorporates
the publishing programmes of
Graham & Trotman Ltd,
Kluwer Law & Taxation Publishers
and Martinus Nijhoff Publishers

In all other countries, sold and distributed by
Kluwer Law International
PO Box 322
3300 AH Dordrecht
The Netherlands

© Kluwer Law International 1998
First published 1998

ISBN 90-411-9662-5

British Library Cataloguing in Publication Data is available

Library of Congress Cataloging-in-Publication Data
Public procurement: global revolution / editors, Sue Arrowsmith,
    Arwel Davies.
        p.   cm.—(International economic development law: 8)
    Includes index.
    ISBN 9041196625
    1. Government purchasing—Law and legislation—European Union
countries.   2. Public contracts—European Union countries.
3. Government purchasing—Law and legislation.   4. Public contracts.
I. Arrowsmith, Sue, 1962–   . II. Davies, Arwel, 1973–   . III. Series.
KJE5632.P828   1998
341.7′53—dc21   98–29820
                                                                                 CIP

Typeset in Palatino 10/11 pt by EXPO Holdings, Malaysia
Printed and bound in Great Britain by Athenaeum Press Ltd., Gateshead, Tyne
and Wear.

Table of Contents

    Armaments: Towards a European Defence Procurement Code?**
    Martin Trybus   71

    1. Introduction   71
    2. The Current State of European Defence Procurement
        Regulation   73
    3. National Influences on the Regulation of Defence
        Procurement   76
    4. Suggestions for a European Defence Procurement Code   87
    5. Conclusion   92

              PART II   PUBLIC PROCUREMENT REFORM IN DEVELOPING
                            AND TRANSITION ECONOMIES

5. **The UNCITRAL Model Law on Procurement of Goods, Construction
    and Services and its Impact on Procurement Reform**
    Robert R. Hunja   97

    1. Introduction   97
    2. Main Features of the Model Law   98
    3. The Impact of the Model Law on Procurement Reform   104
    4. Conclusion   108

6. **Procurement Regulation and Emerging Economies: The
    Examples of Laos and Bhutan**
    Peter Trepte   111

    1. Introduction   111
    2. The Context   112
    3. The Economic Background   115
    4. Realisation of Economic Objectives   116
    5. Conclusion   124

7. **Corruption in Developing Countries and in Countries in
    Transition: Legal and Economic Perspectives**
    John Linarelli   125

    1. Introduction   125
    2. Is Corruption Good or Bad?   126
    3. Do Institutions Matter?   130
    4. Conclusion   137

8. **A Critical Analysis of the Procurement Procedures of the World
    Bank**
    Tim Tucker   139

    1. Introduction   139
    2. The Origins and Development of World Bank Procurement
        Procedures   141

Preface

In 1995 Professor Don Wallace Jr remarked that the changes taking place in public procurement could be considered to add up to a "global revolution" or "reformation".[1] These changes have their origin both in domestic reform programmes designed to promote national objectives such as value for money and social policy, and in the spread of trade agreements which seek to open up public procurement to international competition. This collection of essays examines various aspects of this "global revolution" in public procurement, from both the domestic and international perspectives.

The first part of the book is concerned with the international liberalisation of public procurement, and also looks at the relationship between international agreements and domestic laws. The essays in this section are by European authors and focus primarily on the European Union but the section is of wider interest, since the European liberalisation programme is the earliest of the major international programmes, and the knowledge and experience gained will be invaluable in developing successful programmes elsewhere.

The second part of the book considers issues of special concern to developing economies and those in transition from socialism and communism, where the development or reform of public procurement systems has been – and continues to be – of particular importance. This section includes, *inter alia*, an overview of the UNCITRAL Model Law on procurement, which has been used as a reform model by many of these states. It also includes an examination of World Bank procurement procedures, since major projects in many of these countries are financed by the Bank and must be run in accordance with the Bank's procedures.

The third and final part looks at a range of topical subjects which are relevant to both national and international procurement systems. Issues covered include the use of procurement to promote social, environmental and industrial policies; the challenges presented by the increased use of information technology in public procurement; and the problem of post-tender negotiations.

In general there has been heavy reliance on legal rules to achieve the objectives of procurement policy, and this collection reflects this legal focus.

---

[1] D. Wallace Jr, 'The Changing World of National Procurement Systems: Global Reformation' (1995) 4 *Public Procurement Law Review* 57.

However, we have sought to include a broad range of perspectives on legal regulation, with contributions from economists, purchasing professionals and officials from the international institutions, as well as from legal specialists. We hope that the book will be a useful source of information and ideas for all those involved in public procurement, in whatever capacity, and that it may stimulate further debate and discussion of a subject on which there is still a dearth of published material.

Sue Arrowsmith
Arwel Davies
May 1998

List of Contributors

Sue Arrowsmith is Professor of Law and Director of the Public Procurement Research Group at the University of Nottingham, and a consultant for Achilles Information, the specialist procurement consultancy. She is also editor of the *Public Procurement Law Review* and a member of the European Commission's Advisory Committee for the Opening Up of Public Procurement.

Harvey Gordon is a Director of EuroStrategy Consultants, London, a policy and strategy boutique specialising in advising government and corporations on European issues. He has worked extensively on the economic implications of public procurement, including being responsible for the subject's core references – the *Cost of Non-Europe in Public Procurement* and the recently published *Public Procurement Single Market Review*.

Auke Haagsma is currently Head of the Unit responsible for various aspects of public procurement policy in the Directorate-General for the Internal Market and Financial Services of the European Commission in Brussels. He formerly held the post of Head of the Unit responsible for General Competition Policy and International Aspects.

Keith Hartley is Professor of Economics and Director of the Centre for Defence Economics at the University of York. He is founding editor of the journal *Defence and Peace Economics*; Adviser to National Audit Office for its studies of defence and a consultant to the Ministry of Defence, the United Nations and the EC.

Robert R. Hunja is currently working as Counsel, Procurement and Consultant Services in the Legal Department of the World Bank. Previously, he worked with the United Nations Commission on International Trade Law (UNCITRAL).

Stephen Kahn was, for the last 15 years, responsible for procurement regulations and procedures at the European Space Agency, where he is now engaged in training staff in procurement rules and practices.

Kai Krüger is Professor of Private Law at University of Bergen, teaching contract law, legal method and European public procurement law.

Peter Kunzlik is Professor of European Business Law and the Head of the Centre for Legal Research at the Law School, The Nottingham Trent University. He is a Barrister and the editor of the Common Market Law Reports.

John Linarelli is Lecturer in Law at the University of Wales, Aberystwyth. Mr. Linarelli has extensive experience as a practising lawyer in Washington, DC in public procurement law and litigation. He is formerly Senior Fellow and Director of Procurement Programmes at the International Law Institute in Washington, DC, and an Adjunct Professor of Law at Georgetown University Law Centre, where he taught courses in international procurement and global infrastructure projects.

Christopher McCrudden is Reader in Law, Oxford University, a Fellow of Lincoln College, Oxford and a Visiting Professor at Michigan Law School. He is also a member of the European Commission's Network on Gender and Law.

Shane Rimmer is a Director of EuroStrategy Consultants, a policy and strategy boutique specialising in advising government and corporations on European issues. He has worked extensively on the economic implications of public procurement, including being responsible for the subject's core references – the *Cost of Non-Europe in Public Procurement* and the recently published *Public Procurement Single Market Review*.

Peter Trepte is barrister specialising in European and international law with particular reference to competition, procurement and the utilities. His practice includes advising foreign governments, notably in Eastern and Central Europe and Asia, on the introduction and implementation of procurement regulations.

Martin Trybus is Rechtsreferendar at the Oberlandesgericht Hamm (Germany) and book reviews editor of the *Public Procurement Law Review*. During the work on his Ph.D.-thesis on European defence procurement law he was Deputy Director of the Public Procurement Research Group.

Tim Tucker is a freelance procurement consultant, with purchasing experience in agriculture and fisheries, mining, defence, electronics, banking, and pulp and paper. Having started his buying career in industry, he has specialised over the last 12 years in Aid-related procurement.

Part I
Global and Regional Arrangements on Public Procurement

1. National and International Perspectives on the Regulation of Public Procurement: Harmony or Conflict?

Sue Arrowsmith*

1. INTRODUCTION

Public procurement refers to the government's activity of purchasing the goods and services which it needs to carry out its functions – ranging from paper to missiles, from construction to street cleaning, from vehicle maintenance to information technology services. Such procurement is of huge economic importance in most countries, and this is particularly so for economies in transition from a socialist system to a free market, such as those of Central and Eastern Europe and the former Soviet Union, in which government spending continues to account for a large proportion of national output.

In the last decade or so there has occurred what has been described as a "global reformation" or "revolution"[1] in the area of public procurement, as a large number of countries have revised their systems for the regulation of public procurement, or have introduced legal regulation for the first time. This revolution has two main aspects. In the first place, states have introduced reform in order to promote their own domestic agendas in procurement. These are concerned mainly with achieving value for money and the effective delivery of public services, but also often involve other objectives such as preventing corruption and the support of national industrial development. Secondly, with the growth of international efforts to create free trade between states there have developed an increasing number of international agreements designed to eliminate discrimination in government procurement, thus ensuring that free trade extends to public as well as private markets. These agreements normally require national governments to adopt detailed legislation governing the award of their

---

* Director, Public Procurement Research Group, University of Nottingham. This chapter first appeared in H. Olszewskiego and B. Popouskiej (eds.), *Gospodarka Administracja Samazad* (1997).

[1] D. Wallace, Jr, "The Changing World of National Procurement Systems: Global Reformation" (1995) 4 *Public Procurement Law Review* 57.

major procurement contracts. For many countries, reform efforts have been directed simultaneously at both "domestic" and "international" objectives. This is the case, in particular, with the European and former Soviet "transition" economies which, as will be explained further below, have sought both to implement effective national procurement systems, and at the same time to create a free trade area between themselves and to prepare for future accession to the European Union.

These parallel developments raise interesting questions concerning the relationship between the domestic and international perspectives on public procurement regulation, which, in the author's view, has sometimes been a source of confusion. To what extent are the objectives of domestic and international regulation in harmony with each other, and to what extent do they conflict? Do the two aspects of the reform movement support each other, or does one detract from the other? This chapter will seek to elucidate the precise relationship between these different perspectives on procurement regulation, and to explore the questions raised above.

To examine these issues it is necessary to understand clearly the different objectives which may lie behind the regulation of public procurement. This chapter will thus begin by explaining the reasons for, and development of, both domestic procurement reform and international regulation. The questions posed above concerning the relationship between the two developments will then be considered. It will be seen that, to a very large extent, the parallel developments of domestic and international procurement reform are not merely consistent with but also reinforce and support each other. Nevertheless, there is potential for some conflict, which may become more acute as national procurement and administrative systems become more sophisticated, and this may ultimately demand the simplification of international procurement regulations to ensure a more judicious balance between the competing demands of national and international policies.

2. DOMESTIC REGULATION OF PUBLIC PROCUREMENT

2.1 The movement towards regulation and reform

The domestic procurement policy of most states has a number of objectives, as elaborated in section 2.2 below, the most important of which is generally to obtain value for money. These domestic objectives are sometimes implemented by non-legal means, such as by internal administrative circulars directing the actions of procurement officers – this, for example, has been the traditional approach of the United Kingdom government towards the control of the procurement activity of central government,[2] and has traditionally also been followed by a number of countries whose legal

---

[2] See generally C. Turpin, *Government Procurement and Contracts* (Longman, 1989). The United Kingdom now has legal regulations governing major central government contracts, however, to implement the international requirements of the European Union procurement rules, discussed further below. See further S. Arrowsmith, *The Law of Public and Utilities Procurement* (Sweet & Maxwell, 1996).

and administrative systems have been influenced by the United Kingdom, such as Malaysia. However, many other states regulate the award of procurement contracts by formal rules which have a legal status (although, as explained below, this does not necessarily mean that the rules in question are enforceable by affected individuals). This approach has been followed in France and by many European and non-European states which have been influenced by the French system of administrative law, as well as by the United States, which has a detailed regulatory system for the award of federal contracts.[3] Over the last decade issues relating to the regulation of procurement through legal means have been put increasingly under the spotlight, as a significant number of states have either adopted legal rules on procurement for the first time or have undertaken extensive programmes to reform their existing procurement provisions.

One important aspect of this trend has been the extensive development of procurement regulation in the "transition" countries – those countries which are undergoing a transition from central planning towards the creation of a free market economy. Whereas previously production and acquisition were determined largely by central planning, the new market framework in these states has necessitated the development of public procurement systems for the first time. The implementation of effective procurement systems is vital for these states, especially since public expenditure often accounts for a high proportion of economic output. The new procurements systems will be used for the acquisition of assets and services – ranging from public works to major information technology systems – which will be of key importance for the general economic development. Effective public procurement can also potentially contribute to the economic development of private sector business, and help foster confidence in administrative institutions. Such domestic concerns have led most of the states of Central and Eastern European and of the former Soviet Union to implement formal rules to govern the procurement process.[4] In addition, impetus to reform in many of the European states has been provided by the ambition of accession to the European Union, and in general it has been sought to ensure that the new procurement rules are consistent with the European Union regime: this is the case, for example, with the Polish law on procurement which was the first comprehensive procurement law adopted in Central and Eastern Europe.[5] Outside Europe and the former Soviet Union, countries which are also currently implementing public procurement regulation as part of a

---

[3] See J. Whelan, *Understanding Federal Government Contracts* (Commerce Clearing House, 1993); J. Cibinic, Jr and R.C. Nash, *Formation of Government Contracts* (2nd edn, Government Contracts Programme, George Washington University, 1986).

[4] For an overview of developments in Central and Eastern Europe, see E. Hupkes, "Public Procurement in Central and Eastern Europe" (1997) 6 *Public Procurement Law Review* 49; and C. Servenay and R. Williams, "Introduction of a Regulatory Framework on Public Procurement in the Central and Eastern European Countries: The First Step on a Long Road" (1995) 4 *Public Procurement Law Review* 237.

[5] See Office of Public Procurement, Republic of Poland, *The Act on Public Procurement with Implementing Laws, Forms and Commentary*, p. 1. It is also stated here that the Act is intended to be consistent with the World Trade Organization Government Procurement Agreement (GPA), which is described further in the text below.

transition prqcess (albeit a limited one) are Laos and the Republic of China. In the case of the latter it is probably true to say that the procurement reform process has been motivated more by a desire to join the World Trade Organisation than by purely domestic considerations,[6] although another strong influence may be the desire of the central government to assert greater control over national policy.

Many other states throughout the world have also recently undertaken reform in the procurement field. Often this has occurred as one aspect of more general administrative reform. Frequently – as, indeed, is also the case with the transition economies referred to above – reform has been funded by regional or bilateral aid or aid from the international development institutions such as the International Bank for Reconstruction and Development (the World Bank), which provides both a carrot (financial assistance for reform programmes) and a stick (the possibility of losing other financial aid in the absence of governmental reform). Pakistan, for example, has recently implemented a reform programme with assistance from the World Bank, while Indonesia is conducting a major reform of public procurement as part of a wider project (the Economic Law and Improved Procurement Systems project or ELIPS) assisted by the United States Agency for International Development (USAID) and has already adopted a series of regulatory provisions on procurement award procedures as well as relevant structural reforms.

These developments across the globe have been supported by the adoption by the United Nations Commission on International Trade Law (UNCITRAL) of a Model Law on the Procurement of Goods, Construction and Services. Adopted first for goods and construction in 1993 and extended to cover other services in 1994, the Model Law is designed as a guide for states seeking to reform or promulgate regulatory systems for procurement,[7] in particular for transition economies and developing countries.[8] It provides a suggested framework for a national procurement law, which states may draw on, reject or modify as they think fit, and is designed to be supplemented by regulations dealing with matters of

---

[6] At the time of writing, China is preparing a law to regulate government procurement. A major reason for this decision seems to be that the United States is anxious for China to accede to the GPA if it becomes a WTO member and is more likely to agree to Chinese membership of the WTO if China offers accession to the GPA, or at least to a WTO interim agreement on transparency in procurement (which is discussed further in the text below).

[7] A Guide to Enactment has also been issued, which provides general background to the Model Law and an article-by-article commentary. On the Model Law, see further chapter 5 of this volume and D. Wallace, Jr. "UNCITRAL Model Law on Procurement of Goods and Construction" (1994) 3 *Public Procurement Law Review* CS2; D. Wallace, "The UNCITRAL Model Law on the Procurement of Goods, Construction and Services: the Addition of Services" (1994) 3 *Public Procurement Law Review* CS 218; G. Westring, "Multilateral and Unilateral Procurement Regimes: to which Camp does the Model Law Belong?" (1994) 3 *Public Procurement Law Review* 142; D. Wallace, "The UN Model Law on Procurement" (1992) 1 *Public Procurement Law Review* 406; and J.J. Myers, "UNCITRAL Model Law on Procurement" (1993) 21 *International Business Lawyer* 179.

[8] UNCITRAL Model Law, Guide to Enactment, paragraph 3.

detail. Since its promulgation it has been used in practice to guide reform in a number of states, in particular in Central and Eastern Europe and the former Soviet Union – in Poland, for example, the influence of the Model Law has been clearly acknowledged by the Office of Public Procurement.[9]

2.2 The objectives of domestic regulation

National procurement regulations may be concerned with a variety of objectives, but the main concern is normally with obtaining "value for money" (or "economy") in procurement – that is, successfully acquiring the goods or services required, on the best possible terms. This involves a number of aspects. Thus, it must first be ensured that the goods, works or services being acquired are appropriate to the requirements: for example, an information technology system must, on the one hand, be capable of handling all the relevant information at the required speed, while, on the other hand, it is important that money is not wasted on features that are unnecessary. Secondly, value for money entails that the specified requirements are obtained on the best possible terms. This does not, of course, necessarily mean the lowest price: total life cycle costs, running costs, maintenance etc. will also often be relevant, as well as non-financial considerations such as the quality of the product or service and speed of service delivery. Finally, value for money involves ensuring that the chosen contractor has the financial and technical capability to fulfil the contract on the agreed terms. Not surprisingly, this objective is prominent in the UNCITRAL Model Law, which places the objective of "maximising economy" in procurement at the top of the list of objectives in its preamble, and most of the provisions of both the Model Law and of actual national procurement systems are primarily concerned with this objective.

However, other objectives are also pursued in government procurement, and these also are frequently the subject of regulatory provisions. Thus one important objective which influences the content of most national procurement legislation is the maintenance of "probity", or "integrity". This has two related aspects: first, preventing actual fraud or corruption, such as bribery, the award of contracts based on personal or family interests, or collusion or misrepresentation by bidders; and, secondly, securing the appearance of probity, by ensuring, for example, that procurement officials and politicians do not have personal interests in government contracts, regardless of

---

[9] See Office of Public Procurement, Republic of Poland, *The Act on Public Procurement with Implementing Laws, Forms and Commentary*, p. 1, where it is stated by Josef Zuk, Chairman of the Office of Public Procurement: "The Act on Public Procurement is a Polish law. It follows legal traditions embodied in pre-World War Two Polish code, but also reflects the influence of contemporary procurement laws in modern democratic societies, in particular, the Model Procurement Code developed by the United Nations Commission on International Trade Law." On the influence of the Model Law, see further Hupkes, note 4 above, p. 54.

whether these interests have any actual effect on procurement decisions. The appearance of probity is important both to limit opportunities for actual corruption, and for maintaining confidence in the procurement process. Both aspects of probity are reflected in the preamble to the UNCITRAL Model Law which states that "promoting the integrity of, and fairness and public confidence in, the procurement process" is another of the Model Law's objectives (paragraph (e) of the preamble). To a great extent, maintenance of probity can be regarded simply as one means towards the end of value for money, but it can also be considered an "objective" of procurement policy in its own right, for a number of reasons. First, as has been pointed out by Westring and Jadoun, "corruption can undermine the whole fabric of economic and political life",[10] and addressing corruption in public procurement can help to raise general moral standards; secondly, integrity in procurement is important for maintaining general public confidence in government; thirdly, corruption can cause political damage which goes beyond its financial importance; and, finally, corruption in procurement may provide a source of funds for those involved in criminal activity. Such concerns may be invoked to justify expenditure on anti-corruption measures which exceeds any possible financial savings in terms of improved "value for money" in obtaining particular goods and services.

Another important aspect of procurement procedure in many states is the use of the economic muscle provided by government procurement to support wider industrial, social or other policies which are not directly connected with the procurement itself. Thus, so far as industrial policy is concerned, in order to boost domestic industry and employment, general preferences have sometimes been given to national industry in awarding procurement contracts, either by reserving particular contracts for domestic products or suppliers only although more commonly by operating a preference for bids meeting specified domestic content requirements, in terms of use of domestic products or labour in the contract, or for firms which are deemed "national" firms in terms of their location or ownership. As well as providing for general national preferences, procurement is also frequently used to support more strategic industrial objectives, such as the support of industry in disadvantaged or declining regions, preservation of a national industrial capability in certain products for security reasons, or the creation or development of new, competitive industries ("infant industries"), especially in high-technology sectors, which might not be viable without initial government support because of, for example, inadequacies in capital markets or the inability of firms to retain for themselves all the benefits of technological innovation. Procurement contracts are also sometimes placed in a strategic manner to influence the structure of industry in a state – either to encourage restructuring through mergers or, conversely, to ensure that more than one firm is kept active in a particular market sector to ensure future competition – or because of balance of payments concerns.

---

[10] G. Westring and G. Jadoun, *Public Procurement – Manual for Central and Eastern Europe* (International Training Centre for the ILO, 1996).

The UNCITRAL Model Law recognises that states may seek to pursue industrial objectives in procurement and makes some provision for this possibility.[11]

Governments have also used the market power which they possess by virtue of their procurement activities to support a variety of policies of a non-economic nature, such as equal opportunities and fair wages and working conditions.[12] This may be done again either through strategic placement of contracts (for example, limiting contract awards to certain disadvantaged ethnic groups), or through a system of preferences; or the government may use its contractual bargaining power to induce contractors to comply with government policy – for example, by refusing contract awards to firms which do not employ a certain percentage of persons from disadvantaged ethnic groups. Where procurement is used to promote such "secondary" industrial and social objectives, legal rules may often be promulgated to establish the ambit of such policies – for example, the extent of preferences to be given and the type of contracts to which they are to apply – as well as to deal with issues of implementation such as methods of enforcement and the publicity to be given to such policies.

This list of reasons for the regulation of procurement at a domestic level is by no means exhaustive – other goals sometimes implemented through procurement legislation include, for example, the equitable distribution of opportunities for government business (which might suggest, for example, that firms should be issued with invitations to tender in rotation), and the effective implementation of market testing policies, which is an important area of procurement regulation in the United Kingdom, for example.[13] However, the pursuit of best value, the maintenance of integrity and the implementation of "secondary" industrial and social policies are in general

---

[11] See, in particular, Article 34. There is no explicit provision dealing with social policy objectives, perhaps because such objectives are of less concern in those countries to which the Model Law is mainly directed or perhaps because the Model Law does not wish to encourage the use of procurement to pursue social goals, because of the perceived adverse effect on transparency.

[12] See S. Arrowsmith, *The Law of Public and Utilities Procurement* (Sweet & Maxwell, 1996), chapter 16, and the works cited there; and S. Arrowsmith, "Public Procurement as a Tool of Policy and the Impact of Market Liberalisation" (1995) 111 *Law Quarterly Review* 237.

[13] "Market testing" refers to the process of comparing the relative effectiveness of service provision "in-house" (using an authority's own labour force), on the one hand, and service provision by an external contractor on the other. Many developed countries, including both the United Kingdom and the United States, have increasingly engaged in market testing, and as a result have greatly increased the extent of contracting-out (or outsourcing) of service provision to the extent that functions such as prison management and provision of welfare services are now often entrusted to private contractors. In the United Kingdom, detailed legislation has been adopted to regulate the market testing process of local authorities, because of the initial refusal of these authorities to implement market testing on a voluntary basis in accordance with policy set by the central government. On the United Kingdom legislation, see S. Arrowsmith, *The Law of Public and Utilities Procurement* (Sweet & Maxwell, 1996), chapters 12–14; S.D. Cirell and J. Bennett, *Compulsory Competitive Tendering: Law and Practice* (Longman, 1990); S.D. Cirell and J. Bennett, *Compulsory Competitive Tendering for Professional Services (Longman)*; A. Sparke, *The Compulsory Competitive Tendering Guide* (2nd edn, Butterworths, 1996).

the main concerns of domestic procurement legislation, and are objectives which are implemented to some extent in most domestic procurement regimes.

Finally, it hardly needs to be mentioned that, whatever the goal pursued, rules on procurement will always take account of the objective of efficiency – that is, ensuring that the award process itself is conducted in a timely and cost-effective manner. Benefits to be obtained from particular procurement procedures, whether in terms of better value for money, reduced corruption or the enhanced effectiveness of "secondary" objectives, will always need to be balanced against the costs of more complex and time-consuming procedures. For example, it is obviously not appropriate to use an open tendering procedure to purchase standard items of small value, since the costs of running such a procedure would outweigh any possible savings.

3. THE INTERNATIONAL PERSPECTIVE

As explained in the introduction, the second major reason for the recent wave of procurement legislation has been the growth of international agreements to regulate public procurement. These have arisen out of the more general global movement towards international free trade, which is now reflected in numerous bilateral, regional and global arrangements, many of them concluded, or substantially improved, over the last decade. Although diverse in the extent of their ambition and concrete commitment towards free trade, most of these recent trade agreements share the common objective of enhancing overall global economic welfare by promoting specialisation and trade based on the theory of comparative advantage.[14] As has already been observed above, governments have traditionally discriminated in their procurement in favour of national industry, and such discrimination constitutes a significant barrier to the attainment of free trade, particularly in those sectors of commerce and industry – such as construction, telecommunications and power generation – in which the government is a major player in the market. As the most general and visible barriers to trade (at least to trade in goods), such as tariffs and quotas, have been increasingly reduced or eliminated by trade agreements, so attention has turned increasingly towards more subtle and sophisticated protectionist practices such as discriminatory government procurement (which some might even say has increased over the last decades to compensate for the loss of other tools of protectionism).

The resulting international agreements have required that governments should put aside their traditional practices of using procurement to promote domestic industry, including through strategic development

---

[14] For a concise and clear explanation of this basic economic theory underlying trade liberalisation agreements, see J. Jackson, *The World Trading System* (first paperback edn, MIT Press, 1992), pp. 8–17.

policies, since these policies invariably involve discrimination in favour of national industry (although exceptions may sometimes be made for particular policies[15]). It should also be mentioned that the UNCITRAL Model Law also has as one of its objectives the opening up of procurement markets to international competition, by encouraging states to open their procurement procedures unilaterally to foreign competition unless there is some specific reason not to do so,[16] and also by creating the transparent procurement regimes necessary for states to accede to international market-opening agreements.

The impetus towards global regulation of public procurement from a free trade perspective has come largely from developments at a regional level. The earliest significant attempt to eliminate barriers to trade in public procurement, and currently the most developed system of regulation from this perspective, is found in the European Union.[17] Discrimination in public procurement is outlawed in principle by the EC Treaty,[18] which has applied to procurement in general (with the exception of procurement of military equipment) for over 25 years, and this basic principle is also supported through a programme of secondary legislation, taking the form of directives, which regulate the award procedure for major contracts in all Member States to ensure that discrimination cannot be concealed. These directives, which applied originally to public sector works and supplies contracts, go back to the 1970s,[19] but the policy really gained force and credibility from the late 1980s, when measures were adopted to ensure that the policy on procurement was truly effective in the run-up to 1992 andthe regime was also extended to embrace services contracts as well

---

[15] In particular, agreements sometimes allow procurement to be used to support objectives which are considered to override the free trade principle, such as regional development or national security. Under the GPA, for example, some states have specific exemptions for their regional developments, and Article XXIII provides for general exemptions for national security. Exceptions may also be given to enable the less developed countries, in particular, to use procurement to promote new, competitive industries.

[16] Thus Article 8 of the Model Law suggests that as a general rule procurements should be open to all participants regardless of nationality, unless otherwise specified. Provision is made, however, for preferences in bid evaluation based on national industrial considerations, where these are considered appropriate: see Article 34 of the Model Law.

[17] For details of the European regime, see S. Arrowsmith, *The Law of Public and Utilities Procurement* (Sweet & Maxwell, 1996), chapters 3–11 and 15–18; J.M. Fernández-Martín, *The EC Procurement Rules: a Critical Analysis* (Clarendon Press, 1996); A. Cox, *The Single Market Rules and the Enforcement Regime after 1992* (Earlsgate Press, 1993); P. Lee, *Public Procurement* (Butterworths, 1992); P. Trepte, *Public Procurement in the EEC* (Bicester: CCA Europe, 1993); F. Weiss, *Public Procurement in European Community Law* (European Community Law Series, 1993); C. Bright, *Public Procurement Handbook* (Wylie Chancery, 1994); and L. Digings and J. Bennett, *EC Public Procurement: Law and Practice* (Longman Law, looseleaf).

[18] See, in particular, S. Arrowsmith, "The Application of the EC Treaty Rules to Public and Utilities Procurement" (1995) 4 *Public Procurement Law Review* 255; and S. Arrowsmith, *The Law of Public and Utilities Procurement* (Sweet & Maxwell, 1996), chapter 4.

[19] Directive 71/305/EEC, OJ 1971, No. L185/1 on works; Directive 77/62/EEC, OJ 1977, No. L113/1 on supplies. The latter was slightly amended by Directive 80/767/EEC, OJ 1980, No. 215/1 to bring it into line with the new GATT Government Procurement Agreement.

as the previously excluded sectors of water, energy, transport and telecommunications.[20] The same rules now also apply to regulate access to public procurement between the European Union Member States and non-members Norway, Iceland and Liechtenstein, by virtue of the European Economic Area Agreement concluded in 1992.[21] Outside Europe, a fairly comprehensive programme on procurement has also now been implemented in the North American Free Trade Agreement, chapter 10.[22] All these regional agreements involve regulation of a significant proportion of government procurement. They require the parties to adapt their existing legal rules on procurement to give effect to the requirements of the agreements, and, significantly, to provide formal national procedures to allow aggrieved firms to challenge procurement decisions. This has resulted in a significant flurry of legislative activity in the procurement field. For example, as a consequence of the introduction of the European Union regime, many European states which did not have a significant tradition of legal regulation in procurement – such as the United Kingdom, Ireland and Denmark – have been required to implement extensive legal rules in this area for the first time.

Another interesting development is the fact that the broad Asia–Pacific Economic Co-operation Forum (APEC) recently announced its intention to create a programme on public procurement for its diverse membership of eighteen states spread across the Asia–Pacific region.[23] However, this differs in an important respect from the European Union and NAFTA regimes in that it envisages that the programme will be of a non-binding nature. Within Central Europe the Central European Free Trade Agreement (CEFTA) of 1995 between the Czech Republic, Hungary, Poland and the Slovak Republic provides in Article 24 for the opening up of public procurement between these states as part of a general free trade programme, at first limited to central government supplies in accordance with the 1979 GATT Agreement on procurement (considered further below), but with the prospect of later expanding coverage.

From a global perspective, the impetus of the achievements at regional level, in particular within the European Union and NAFTA, gave a significant boost to efforts to liberalise procurement on a more international

---

[20] For a summary of the reforms undertaken in this period, see the works cited in note 17 above. The current directives are Directive 93/36/EEC on public supply contracts, OJ 1993, No. L199/1, Directive 93/37/EEC on public works contracts, OJ 1993, No. L199/54, and Directive 92/50/EEC on services contracts, OJ 1992, No. L209/1. Procurement in the sectors of water, energy, transport and telecommunications (utilities) are governed by a separate Directive 93/38/EEC, OJ 1993, No. L199/84, and remedies by Directive 89/665/EEC, OJ 1989, No. L395/83 (public sector) and Directive 92/13/EEC, OJ 1992, No. L76/14 (utilities).

[21] OJ 1994, No. L1/1. See further C. Bock, "The EEA Agreement: Rules on Public Procurement" (1993) 2 *Public Procurement Law Review* 136.

[22] For an overview, see S. Greenwold, "The Government Procurement Chapter of the North American Free Trade Agreement" (1994) 3 *Public Procurement Law Review* 129.

[23] APEC, Osaka Declaration, November 1995, section 9. See further S. Arrowsmith, "Public Procurement within the Asia–Pacific Economic Co-operation Forum" (1996) 5 *Public Procurement Law Review* CS71.

basis, and led to the conclusion of a comprehensive Government Procurement Agreement (GPA) during the Uruguay Round of GATT negotiations.[24] The new agreement is one of several agreements to be administered by the new World Trade Organisation. Prior to the Uruguay Round, there already existed an agreement on procurement (commonly referred to as the GATT Government Procurement Agreement, although it was never part of GATT proper), concluded in 1979, under which a number of states agreed not to discriminate against each other in awarding major central and federal supply contracts. However, this agreement was very limited in scope. The new GPA covers works and services as well as supplies, and applies not only to contracts of central government but also to those of state and provincial governments, including municipal authorities, and to many utility activities and entities not covered by the old agreement. The approach to liberalisation under the GPA is similar to that of most of the regional agreements – discrimination against products and suppliers from other states is prohibited and this prohibition is supported by detailed rules governing the award of contracts to ensure that such discrimination does not take place. States signing the GPA must adopt formal rules governing contract award procedures in order to give effect to their obligations under the GPA, and – an important innovation in the new GPA – must provide for national challenge procedures for firms affected by a breach of the GPA.[25]

At present, the GPA is one of the "plurilateral" agreements of the WTO, which means only those WTO members which choose to sign the GPA are parties to it. The signatories at present are the European Union and its

---

[24] For reading on the GPA in general, see further Jones, "The GATT–MTN System and the European Community as International Frameworks for the Regulation of Economic Activity: the Removal of Barriers to Trade in Government Procurement" (1984) 8 *Maryland Journal of International Law and Trade* 53; J.H. Bourgeois, "The Tokyo Round Agreements on Technical Barriers and on Government Procurement in International and EEC Perspective" (1982) 19 *Common Market Law Review* 5; G. de Graaf and P. Trepte, "The Revised GATT Procurement Agreement" (1994) 3 *Public Procurement Law Review* CS70; G. de Graaf and M. King, "Towards a More Global Government Procurement Market: The Expansion of the GATT Government Procurement Agreement in the Context of the Uruguay Round" (1995) 29 *International Lawyer* 435; B. Hoekman and P.C. Mavroidis, "The WTO's Agreement on Government Procurement: Expanding Disciplines, Declining Membership?" (1995) 4 *Public Procurement Law Review* 63; A. Brown and C. Pouncey, "Expanding the International Market for Public Procurement: the WTO's Agreement on Government Procurement" (1993) 3 *International Trade Law Review* 69; S. Arrowsmith, "The World Trade Organization Agreement on Government Procurement: Obstacles and Opportunities" (1997) 1 *Malaysian Journal of Law and Society* 15; A. Low, A. Mattoo and A. Subramaniam, "Government Procurement in Services" (1996) 20 *World Competition* 5; A. Blank and G. Marceau, "The History of the Government Procurement Negotiations since 1995" (1996) 5 *Public Procurement Law Review* 77; V. Kulacoglu, "The WTO Government Procurement Agreement: Current Opportunities in United Kingdom Association for Regulated Procurement" in *Global Business Opportunities in Public Procurement* (conference papers of the UK Association for Regulated Procurement, 1996).

[25] Article XX. See, in particular, M. Footer, "Remedies under the New GATT Agreement on Government Procurement" (1995) 4 *Public Procurement Law Review* 80.

Member States, Aruba, Norway, Canada, Hong Kong, Israel, Japan, South Korea, the United States and Switzerland.[26] However, a priority of the WTO is to increase the number of states participating in open international markets. To this end, it was announced in the Ministerial Declaration[27] following the first WTO Ministerial Conference in Singapore in December 1996 that it is intended to establish a working party to study the transparency of public procurement procedures (a concept which is discussed further below) and, on the basis of this study, to develop principles to be included in an agreement on transparency.[28] It is hoped that states not ready to accede to the full rigours of the GPA may be willing to sign up to a more limited agreement of this kind. Such an agreement will not necessarily even involve any prohibition on discrimination in public procurement, in recognition that many countries may not yet feel ready to give up sovereignty in this area; but it may nevertheless facilitate international competition in procurements, first, in that enhanced transparency will internationalise participation in procurement even when a state does not undertake any obligations not to discriminate, by ensuring at least that foreign contractors are aware of the applicable rules and can make informed bidding decisions; and, secondly, in that acceptance of limited transparency obligations may be a first step towards accession to the GPA itself.

Finally, in addition to the regional and global arrangements mentioned above there is a large web of bilateral arrangements under which particular states have agreed between themselves to open their markets. A number of important agreements of this kind have been concluded between GPA members, dealing with areas of procurement which are not covered under the GPA – for example, a recent agreement between the European Union and Israel covering telecommunications procurement, an area which is currently totally outside the GPA.[29] The European Union has also concluded a series of bilateral agreements for opening up procurement in states of Central and Eastern Europe, as part of wider association

---

[26] These are the same as the parties to the old agreement except that South Korea was not formerly a party. As of February 1997 Singapore (a party to the old procurement agreement) and Liechtenstein had also completed accession negotiations, and their accession was awaiting ratification. Taiwan (not yet a WTO member) was negotiating for accession. Several other countries not referred to above have "observer" status, which entitles them to attend meetings of the Government Procurement Committee set up under the GPA: as of February 1997 the other countries were Argentina, Australia, Bulgaria, Colombia, Iceland, Latvia and Turkey.

[27] World Trade Organization, WT/MIN(96)/DEC/W, 13 December 1996, Article 21. Work is also being undertaken under Article XIII of the General Agreement on Trade in Services to develop limited rules on services procurement, which may apply to all WTO members.

[28] See further S. Arrowsmith, "The WTO Singapore Ministerial Declaration and Transparency" (1997) 6 *Public Procurement Law Review* CS49.

[29] See COM (96) 148 final. Another bilateral agreement contained in the same document is concerned with expanding the scope of the GPA, and also with opening up certain other procurement not covered by the GPA award rules or bid challenge procedures.

agreements which envisage the ultimate accession of these states to the European Union, as well as accession to the GPA.[30]

4. DIFFERENT OBJECTIVES: IN HARMONY OR CONFLICT?

4.1 Similarities in national and international procurement principles

Having considered the objectives of domestic and international procurement rules, we can now turn to consider the relationship between these different perspectives on procurement regulation. The starting point of this consideration is inevitably to note that, despite the differences in objectives and focus, the procedures put in place to achieve the international opening up of markets under most global, regional and bilateral arrangements are very similar to those adopted by most national governments to promote, in particular, the goals of value for money and integrity. In particular, both domestic and international rules on public procurement have usually emphasised the same key principles of *competition, publicity, use of commercial criteria* and *transparency*.

The principle of *competition* means simply that contracts are normally awarded by holding a competition between a number of contractors, to establish which can offer the most favourable terms for delivering the government's requirements. This is the usual method for governments to secure value for money in their domestic procurement, and, as explained further below, is also generally considered important in maintaining the integrity of public procurement, since competition is an effective means of achieving the transparency which prevents abuse of discretion. Thus the UNCITRAL Model Law, reflecting the practices of most national systems, provides for competitive award procedures to be used for procurements as a general rule, whether for works, supplies or services.[31] Under international liberalisation arrangements, the use of a competition which is open to contractors from other states ensures that domestic contractors are not favoured when contractors from other states are able to fulfil the contract more effectively. An obligation to hold a competition to award contracts is thus a general requirement of the GPA[32] as well as of the major regional agreements.

---

[30] See Council and Commission Decisions 93/742/Euratom, ECSC, EC, OJ 1993, No. L347 (approving the Europe Agreement with Hungary); 93/743/Euratom, ECSC, EC, OJ 1993, No. L348 (Poland); 94/907/Euratom, ECSC, EC, OJ 1994, No. L357/1 (Romania); 94/908/Euratom, ECSC, EC, OJ 1994, No. L358/1 (Bulgaria); 94/909/Euratom, ECSC, EC, OJ 1994, No. L359/1 (Slovak Republic); 94/909/Euratom, ECSC, EC, OJ 1994, No. L360/1 (Czech Republic); OJ 1994, No. L3735/2. (Lithuania); OJ 1994, No. L374/2. (Latvia) and OJ 1994, No. 373/2 (Estonia).
[31] See UNCITRAL Model Law, Article 18 (works and supplies) and Article 37 (services).
[32] See GPA, Articles VII–XV.

Under both domestic and international rules, only limited exceptions to the use of competition are normally permitted, which apply either where the reasons for competition are outweighed by other concerns, or where competition would be futile or clearly ineffective. The grounds recognised for derogating from competitive procedures are, in general, very similar under domestic and international rules covering, for example, cases of urgency, national security, where a previous competition has produced no tenders from qualified persons or where there is only one contractor able to fulfil the contract because of, for example, intellectual property rights.[33]

The principle of *publicity* supplements that of competition, ensuring that contractors who might be able to win contracts are able to find out about those contracts and put themselves forward. Both domestic and international rules generally stipulate particular forms of publicity for procurement opportunities, which in the first case are aimed at ensuring interest from a sufficient number of suitable firms to obtain value for money, and in the second case at ensuring that foreign contractors, in particular, are aware of these opportunities. Both types of rules also generally contain a variety of other detailed requirements designed to ensure that the competition is as fair and effective as possible.

Features found in many domestic systems, in the UNCITRAL Model Law and in the GPA and European Union rules, for example, include obligations for specifications to be drawn up so as not to artificially exclude certain products; rules requiring authorities to reject non-responsive bids (those which do not conform with the specifications or fail to meet other fundamental requirements); and minimum time limits for potential bidders to respond to contracting opportunities. The authority is thus able to select the "best" contractor under the criteria mandated by the relevant norms. The precise nature of the competition to be held does differ, however, both as between different domestic regimes and between different international agreements, largely according to differences of emphasis given to the need for transparency at different stages of the procedure, as will be discussed further below. Thus, while for supplies and works contracts, in particular, a form of tendering in which all qualified persons are permitted to bid is the normal procedure in many states (such as Spain and Portugal, for example)[34] and under the UNCITRAL Model Law, many countries prefer to place greater emphasis on restricted procedures under which only pre-selected firms are permitted to bid, sacrificing some transparency for greater efficiency in running the procurement process. The GPA and European regimes reflect this reality by allowing a free choice between open and restricted procedures for the public sector.

Another principle which underlies many of the specific rules of both international and domestic origin is the requirement to use *commercial*

---

[33] The list of grounds for using "sole-source" procurement given in Article 22 of the UNCITRAL Model Law are very similar to the grounds for use of "limited tendering" under Article XV of the GPA.

[34] See the statistics concerning the use of open procedures under the European rules in *The Single Market Review, sub-series III: Dismantling of Barriers*, vol. II, *Public Procurement* (Kogan Page Earthscan, 1997).

criteria in making procurement decisions. Thus, in particular, decisions on which contractors should be treated as eligible to bid are generally required to be based on the ability of firms to undertake the contract,[35] and in choosing which bid to accept authorities are required to consider only the merits of each bid (price, product quality etc.).[36]

In a domestic context, these criteria are aimed at the value for money objective and at the same time preclude improper influences, such as personal interest, from being taken into consideration. Of course, as has already been explained, other considerations sometimes limit or override value for money considerations in national systems. Thus protection of national industry or support for social policies, for example, may involve excluding some competitive firms from participation or giving a margin of preference to certain contractors. But while some exceptions may be made, the application of commercial criteria in decision-making is the starting point for most procurement systems in view of the fact that value for money is the primary objective.

Under international regimes the specific requirement to use commercial criteria is aimed at ensuring that domestic firms or bids are not favoured above non-national firms or bids where the latter provides a more commercial offer, on the assumption that value for money is indeed the primary aim of the domestic procurement process in national systems. While such international regimes are normally concerned to prevent support for national industry against foreign competition – which is the *raison d'etre* of these regimes[37] – they do not necessarily exclude the possibility of basing procurement decisions on other non-commercial criteria where otherwise allowed by national systems, in particular where such non-commercial criteria do not discriminate between domestic and non-domestic industry: thus the GPA, for example, allows procurement policies designed to support the enterprises of the handicapped or of prison labour[38] even where discriminatory, and certain states, including the United States, Canada, Japan and Korea have also taken specific exemptions in their individual annexes of the GPA for established preference policies such as regional preference systems. However, as the present author has described elsewhere,[39] in practice such agreements may have the effect of

---

[35] See, for example, UNCITRAL Model Law, Article 6; and GPA, Article VIII(b).

[36] See, for example, UNCITRAL Model Law, Article 34(4); and GPA, Article XIII(4)(b).

[37] Exceptions may be made even to this principle: for example, the GPA contains special provisions allowing developing countries to use procurement to support their industry including by imposing offset requirements under Article XVI (see further B. Hoekman and P.C. Mavroidis, "The WTO's Agreement on Government Procurement: Expanding Disciplines, Declining Membership?" (1995) 4 *Public Procurement Law Review* 63; and S. Arrowsmith, "The World Trade Organization Agreement on Government Procurement: Obstacles and Opportunities" (1997) 1 *Malaysian Journal of Law and Society* 15. Further, as explained above, a new WTO "interim" agreement is now envisaged which will contribute to opening international procurement markets through transparency without even prohibiting states from using procurement to support national industry.

[38] GPA, Article XXIII(2).

[39] S. Arrowsmith, "Public Procurement as a Tool of Policy and the Impact of Market Liberalisation" (1993) 111 *Law Quarterly Review* 235.

limiting the possibility for pursuing such policies,[40] either because they are considered unacceptable where discriminatory in their effect, or because the possibility for taking account of non-commercial criteria is considered too significant a limitation on transparency.

The concept of *transparency*, already mentioned several times above, refers to the idea that procurement procedure should be "characterised by clear rules and by means to verify that those rules were followed".[41] As already noted, it is a key feature of many domestic procurement regimes, and is a means to support all national procurement objectives, including those of value for money and probity. It is expressly mentioned as one of the goals of the UNCITRAL Model Law (see the preamble to the Model Law, item (f)), and has significantly influenced the content of the Model Law. It is also an important principle underlying all the major international agreements on procurement, and is highlighted in the preamble to the GPA.[42] In particular, under existing international agreements, notably the GPA, the European Union rules and NAFTA, transparent procedures provide a means of preventing and detecting purchasing decisions influenced by national industrial objectives rather than value for money or other legitimate national concerns such as authorised social policy objectives. In addition, however, as already observed above, transparency may contribute to the opening up of international markets even in states which do not accept a "national treatment" obligation, and for this reason the WTO has set up a working party to develop an interim agreement concerned only with transparency.

Transparent procurement regimes, whether domestic or international, all tend to share the following characteristics:

(i) All participants and potential participants in government procurement procedures should be aware of the applicable rules of the procedure. Both the UNCITRAL Model Law and the GPA, for example, first, provide for publication of all laws and general rulings on public procurement,[43] and, secondly, ensure that rules established for a particular procurement (such as criteria for qualification and contract award[44]) are publicised to potential bidders and are not changed during the procedure.

---

[40] Conversely, it can be pointed out that international free trade agreements – unlike domestic rules – do not normally contain provisions to *require* the use of procurement for non-commercial goals, given that such agreements are limited to the concern of opening up markets. However, some organisations concerned with trade, notably the European Union, also have other objectives, and these objectives (such as concern with the environment, equality and labour protection) could lead to social policy clause provisions being included in the European Union's procurement legislation.

[41] G. Westring and G. Jadoun, *Public Procurement: Manual for Central and Eastern Europe* (International Training Centre for the ILO, 1996), p. 6.

[42] The third paragraph to the preamble reads: "Recognising that it is desirable to provide transparency of laws, regulations, procedures and practices regarding government procurement ..."

[43] Model Law, Article 5; and GPA, Article XIX.

[44] See Model Law, Articles 6(3) and 34(4)(b); GPA, Articles IX(6)(f) and XIII(iv)(b).

(ii)   The discretion of procurement officers in achieving the goals of the procurement process should be structured and subject to formal rules. This reduces the possibility of errors of judgment and of decisions made through apathy (for example, a tendency to deal with previous contractors because this is less effort than seeking out new sources of supply), which may prejudice both domestic and international objectives. It also limits the opportunities for deliberate abuse of discretion, whether for personal gain or – of particular concern under international agreements – to favour national industry. As has already been noted, the emphasis placed by both national and international systems on competitive tendering to a set deadline is a reflection of the importance of transparency. The way in which such procedures must be conducted will depend very much on the importance attached to transparency: systems which place particular emphasis on this concept may, for example, prefer open rather than restricted or selective tendering procedures, since the latter provides an opportunity to favour or discriminate against particular suppliers in the course of the "shortlisting" process (that is, choosing firms to bid), and may also be more concerned to prohibit negotiations with potential contractors at various stages in the tendering process.

(iii)   Compliance with the applicable rules should be verifiable. Provisions to support this aspect of transparency may include, for example, requirements for the publication of the results of award procedures, public opening of tenders, the keeping of detailed records of decisions (for example, on why firms were considered un-qualified and why a particular bid was chosen) and the furnishing of reasons to firms participating in a procurement procedure.

(iv)   Mechanisms should exist for scrutinising decisions to ensure compliance with legal norms. Some verification mechanisms are normally provided in both domestic and international systems. Under domestic systems provision is often made for certain types of discretionary decisions by procurement officials, in which a potential for error or abuse exists – such as a decision to use a procedure other than open tendering, or to derogate completely from competition requirements[45] – to be subject to approval by, or at least notification to, a higher administrative person or entity within the state. Similar requirements are not normally found in international systems, although it is interesting to note that under the European Union regime certain limited decisions (such as to reject a bid as abnormally low in a procedure based on the "lowest price" award criterion[46]) must be notified to the European Commission, which has an important role in ensuring adherence to the rules by the Member States. External monitoring is, on the other hand, often provided in

---

[45] See, for example, UNCITRAL Model Law, Articles 20 and 22.
[46] See S. Arrowsmith, *The Law of Public and Utilities Procurement* (Sweet & Maxwell, 1996), pp. 244–6.

international systems at a more general level through requirements
to provide statistical information to an external monitoring
authority, such as the WTO Government Procurement Committee
under the GPA.[47] Under both international and domestic regimes,
responsibility for detecting and remedying breaches, and hence
providing some incentive to compliance, is frequently placed on
participating firms, through a formal complaints procedure, or even
a system of enforceable legal remedies; we have already observed
above that this is an important feature of the GPA and the
procurement arrangements of the European Union and NAFTA.

In general, it can be been that, to a great extent the formal rules on
procurement procedures considered appropriate for opening international
markets are similar to those often adopted to implement national objectives
of value for money and probity. One consequence of this is that the parallel
developments which have occurred in procurement regulation at the
domestic level, on the one hand, and the international plane, on the other,
have to a certain degree supported and reinforced each other. Thus the
development of formal systems to regulate procurement from a domestic
perspective can make a valuable contribution to opening markets to
international competition, both simply by increasing the transparency of the
procurement process (even in the absence of national treatment obligations)
and as a first step towards the implementation of a system which corresponds precisely with the procedural requirements (as well as the non-
discrimination requirements) of the WTO or other relevant international
norms, such as those of the European Union. It should also be mentioned
that the existence of procurement obligations under domestic law may have
the effect of strengthening the protection given to non-domestic firms under
international agreements, since where these agreements include national
treatment clauses, the procedural rules governing the rights and remedies of
domestic firms in contract award procedures must also be extended to non-
domestic firms. Thus, for example, while Article XX of the GPA provides for
quite minimal remedies for aggrieved contractors – damages, for example,
may be limited to costs of participating – those signatory states which
provide for domestic remedies systems which go beyond these minimal
requirements – for example, providing damages for loss of profits – must
extend the benefit of these more generous rules on remedies to firms from
GPA signatory states seeking to enforce the GPA, by virtue of Article III of
the GPA on national treatment.

Conversely – as appears to be occurring in China, for example –
international concerns to regulate procurement with a view to market
opening may stimulate a process of reform which may be extended to
aspects and contracts of purely domestic significance; and, related to this,
such concern has also probably played a part in encouraging states and
international institutions to make available the technical and financial aid
necessary to facilitate procurement reform in less developed and transition

---

[47] GPA, Article XIX.

economies. International agreements have also sometimes had a more direct impact on domestic procurement law, by encouraging states to adapt their purely domestic rules to international standards – either to simplify the procurement system, or because international rules are considered to reveal inadequacies in the national approach. This has occurred to quite a considerable extent within the European Union. For example, in France, domestic procurement rules embodied in the *Code des Marchés Publics* have traditionally been enforceable by contractors, but remedies were until recently very limited (annulment of procurement decisions was not a possibility) and the procedure for obtaining them in the administrative court unduly lengthy, taking one or two years. However, a new system of rapid and effective remedies[48] introduced to comply with the European Union Remedies Directive 89/665/EEC has been applied to breaches of purely domestic procurement, including for award procedures which are outside the scope of the European directives.[49]

4.2 The different scope of national and international regimes

On the other hand, while there are many procurement rules which tend to be common to both domestic and international procurement regimes, the different objectives of the two regimes mean that the subject-matters of the regimes are not co-extensive.

First, it should be mentioned that the scope of international procurement rules is normally limited in the light of the purpose of those rules, and in particular such rules normally apply only to contracts of cross-border interest. Thus, the detailed rules on contract award procedures contained in the GPA, NAFTA and the European Union regimes govern only contracts above certain financial thresholds, since cross-border interest in smaller contracts is considered to be too low to justify interference with national procedures. The GPA rules, for example, apply only to works contracts worth at least SDR5 million[50] and supply and services contracts worth at least SDR130,000.[51] For services, it is also usual to exclude specific types of services (for example, legal services) for which there appears to be little scope for cross-border trade, or little scope for savings to be made, although this kind of selective approach has not in general been applied to supply contracts under the EU rules or the GPA.

International rules also do not deal with many aspects of procurement activity with which national rules are concerned. An example is the area of

---

[48] See further P. Valadou, "Enforcing the Public Procurement Rules in France" in S. Arrowsmith (ed.), *Remedies for Enforcing the Public Procurement Rules* (1993), chapter 10; S. Ponsot, "Public Procurement in France: Transposition of the Remedies Directives" (1996) 5 *Public Procurement Law Review* 29, and the works and commentaries cited there; and J.M. Fernández-Martín, *The EC Public Procurement Rules: a Critical Analysis* (Clarendon Press, 1996), chapter 9.

[49] See Administrative Tribunals and Administrative Courts of Appeal Code, Article L22.

[50] The threshold is even higher than this for some signatories, who were unwilling to accept regulation at the SDR5 million figure.

[51] Again, a higher threshold applies for some types of contracts and for sub-federal government.

financial and technical capacity. As has been mentioned, in order to obtain value for money, governments need to ensure that selected firms have the financial and technical standing to carry out the contract, and national procurement rules generally contain provisions to ensure that this is so. Such rules will generally *require* procuring entities to examine the standing of firms for this purpose, and may often include provisions on how this is to be done (for example, what kind of references should be sought) in order to ensure that the examination is effective to establish the contractor's capability. Domestic provisions may also seek to ensure that contractors are not wrongly excluded, in a manner which could prejudice value for money (by inappropriate exclusion of a firm which might make the best offer) or the probity objective (by eliminating an improperly favoured firm's main competitors). The perspective of international rules on this issue, on the other hand, is rather different: such rules do not *require* an examination to be made of financial and technical matters, but are normally only concerned to ensure that any examination which is carried out is not used to exclude firms wrongfully, in particular in a way which might discriminate against non-domestic firms.[52]

It is sometimes said that national and international rules have a common objective of ensuring best value for money, but the above example shows that such statements oversimplify the issue: international rules are directed at value for money but only to the extent that this objective of the procurement process might be adversely affected by discriminatory behaviour. Thus these rules go only so far as is considered necessary to eliminate any potential for discrimination to influence the process. Once this is done, the way in which value for money is achieved is left as a matter for domestic procurement policy. Since the concern is with the possibility for discrimination and not best value in general, other rules commonly found in domestic procurement systems, such as requirements for contractors to submit procurement bonds, are also absent from international regimes.

This different perspective of national and international rules is also sometimes reflected in the provisions concerning entitlements to benefit from and (where applicable) to enforce procurement rules. In domestic systems, these entitlements invariably extend at least to domestic contractors and, where there is no policy of discrimination, often also to non-domestic firms. On the other hand, under the GPA it is generally considered that the right to benefit from and enforce the rules is limited to

---

[52] Under the GPA, see, in particular, Article VIII.

[53] On the assumption that the GPA does not confer rights on European Union firms in their own and other European Member States but concerns only the relations between the Member States and third countries, the European Union has proposed to amend its own directives on public procurement, which are in some ways less stringent than the GPA (for example, the thresholds for regulating central government services contracts are lower) to ensure that European Union contractors have the same rights against Member State governments as third country contractors: see Amended Proposal for a Directive Amending Directives 92/50/EEC, 92/36/EEC and 93/37/EEC, COM (96) 623 final of 13 December 1996; and Amended Proposal for a Directive Amending Directive 93/38/EEC, COM (96) 598 final of 20 November 1996.

non-domestic contractors from GPA signatory states: although, in practice, it would be unusual if the same rights were not also extended to domestic contractors, this does not appear to be required.[53] It is interesting, however, that the same position does not apply under the European Union rules where domestic as well as non-domestic contractors may benefit from and enforce the rules, even when only domestic bidders are involved in the procurement procedure.[54] The possibility of actions by domestic contractors does provide a greater deterrence to breach of the rules, since in practice it is these contractors which are most likely to seek participation in award procedures and to initiate legal proceedings.

4.3 A potential for conflict?

The different ambit of international and domestic procurement rules does not of itself present any problems, and, as we have seen, where these rules deal with the same aspects of procurement they tend to establish similar requirements, and thus to support and reinforce each other. However, it needs to be acknowledged that there is some potential for conflict between domestic and international regimes, which may become more acute in future. This derives, in particular, from divergent practices which are developing in different countries in establishing the optimum balance between transparency and other concerns.

So far as the objective of best value is concerned, it has been explained above that transparency is seen in government procurement systems as the most appropriate means of ensuring best value in general, as well as an essential means of ensuring that procurement is not influenced by protectionist considerations in contravention of international rules prohibiting discrimination. However, the extensive limitations on the discretion of procurement officials which the concept of transparency demands may prevent officials from maximising value for money, particularly in complex and high-value procurement transactions.[55] For example, while formal tendering procedures which forbid negotiations with suppliers may help to remove opportunities for improper influences on the selection process, it may be difficult to elicit the most appropriate proposals from bidders without such negotiations.

At another level, emphasis on competitive tendering for each individual contract means that a procuring entity does not have the option of developing a "partnering" relationship with a particular supplier which goes beyond the life of one contract. The development of such relationships is, however, now widely regarded as "best practice" in some fields in the private sector, on the basis that it may produce more effective results than competitive tendering – for example, by providing a partner with the incentive for co-operation and optimum performance on existing contracts, by facilitating joint research and pooling of skills, and by enabling partners to build up knowledge of each other's business. The management of

---

[54] As confirmed by the ECJ in Case C-87/94, *Commission of the European Communities* v. *Belgium* [1996] ECR I-2043.
[55] See, in particular, S. Kelman, *Procurement and Public Management* (AEI Press, 1990).

partnering relationships is, however, a relatively non-transparent process compared to competitive tendering.

From a domestic perspective, the optimum balance between transparency and flexibility in obtaining value for money is something which will differ between states in the light of factors such as the motivation, skills and training of procurement personnel, and the extent of corruption. It will also be affected by the prominence of other objectives in procurement – in particular, a state which places a strong emphasis on probity and the appearance of probity in the procurement process is more likely to insist on transparency even if this may in some cases have an adverse effect on the value for money goal. In recent years some countries, such as the United Kingdom, have sought increasingly to replicate private sector best practice in public sector procurement, by conferring a wide discretion on procurement officers, and focusing on the development of purchasing skills and measurement of outcomes as a method of securing value for money, rather than on formal regulation.[56] In these cases, the ability to implement the preferred approach is limited to some extent by the requirements of international rules which emphasise transparency and competition as a means of preventing discrimination.[57]

The actual and potential conflict between international and domestic rules in this respect should not, however, be exaggerated. Most states of the world do not have a particularly sophisticated structure for the procurement activity, and the transparent award procedures of the GPA, at least, and the general requirement for a competition are to a large extent consistent with the procedures which would naturally be adopted by domestic law in order to achieve best value for money and integrity in the procurement process. Since global and regional procurement regimes must deal with states with widely differing cultures and structures, it appears inevitable that the rules will have an adverse impact on the preferred policies of a few of the signatory states.

The emphasis placed by international agreements on transparency has also created some tension with other domestic objectives. First, it is relevant to mention here that controversy has arisen both under the European Union regime and the GPA as to how far states should be permitted to use procurement as a tool of social policy. Under the European Union rules, the European Commission and the European Court of Justice appear to have come down in favour of a strict approach, according to which even non-discriminatory policies cannot be taken into account in deciding who is eligible for contracts, in shortlisting firms and in evaluating bids.[58] This has

---

[56] The United Kingdom policy is set out most recently in the White Paper, *Setting New Standards: a Strategy for Government Procurement* (London: HMSO, Cm 2480, 1995).

[57] The author has discussed this issue in more detail in the context of the constraints imposed by the European Union procurement rules in another article: see S. Arrowsmith, "The Way Forward or a Wrong Turning? An Assessment of European Community Policy on Public Procurement in Light of the Commission's Green Paper" (1997) 3 *European Public Law* 389.

[58] For explanation and discussion, see Arrowsmith, note 39 above, and chapters 11 and 12 of this volume.

been justified by the potential of such considerations for adversely affecting the transparency of the process and presenting opportunities for abuse of discretion to favour national industry. The position under the GPA, where no specific derogations have been given for such policies, is less clear,[59] but may be elucidated as a result of a controversy which has recently arisen over the decision of certain states of the US to refuse to do business with firms having business interests in Myanmar.[60] The requirements of international procurement regimes have also sometimes been criticised as imposing too many detailed requirements in relation to matters such as record-keeping and statistical reporting, which may undermine the efficiency of the procurement process and deter states from acceding to these agreements.

In future, there probably needs to be some further consideration given to the appropriate balance between transparency and the legitimate domestic concerns of signatory states. On balance, it is submitted that international agreements have in general placed too much emphasis on transparency at the expense of these other objectives, and that some simplification is needed. Since some discretion inevitably remains in any procurement procedure, there is always room for discrimination by a determined purchaser, and international rules should focus on eliminating systematic discriminatory policies, changing the outlook of signatory states and eliminating structural obstacles such as differing national standards, rather than on policing isolated incidents of discrimination. Thus while the basic principles of competition, publicity and equality should continue to be applied – even if these do inhibit those states aspiring to emulate private sector best practice – a case can be made for simplifying the detailed award procedures laid down in the agreements to introduce more flexibility. It is submitted, for example, that, provided that a competition is held and all firms are treated equally, negotiations should be permitted with suppliers throughout the award process. (This is permitted under the GPA after receipt of tenders where stated in advance, and is possible throughout the procedure under the European utilities rules but not generally under the public sector rules). As has been argued elsewhere,[61] states should also be given freedom to implement social policy goals where there is no discrimination against non-domestic industry.

Such flexibility will become more acceptable as states' existing protectionist practices are slowly eliminated, and the benefits of open competition become apparent. There has been considerable discussion within the European Union on the possibility of simplifying procurement legislation to emphasise the general principles of equality, transparency, competition etc. as opposed to detailed rules, as the above developments occur and as states become more sophisticated in their procurement practices. The development of an interim agreement on procurement under

---

[59] For discussion, see Arrowsmith, note 39 above, and chapters 11 and 12 of this volume.

[60] See "The Mass that Roared" *Economist*, 8 February 1997.

[61] See S. Arrowsmith, "Public Procurement as a Tool of Policy and the Impact of Market Liberalisation" (1995) 111 *Law Quarterly Review* 237.

the WTO, initially designed for states outside the GPA, presents an opportunity for a more simple global procurement regime, and it is not inconceivable that this regime – while originally planned as a stepping-stone to full GPA membership – may ultimately come to represent the "general" WTO approach to procurement, and take over from the more complex and bureaucratic GPA.

5. CONCLUSION

The last two decades have certainly seen a revolution – or, rather, the beginnings of a revolution – in public procurement, as across the globe states have begun to reform their government purchasing systems. As we have seen, these developments have been prompted both by domestic objectives, and by the international community's increasing concern with opening up procurement markets to international competition. This chapter has sought to explain the way in which these developments have reinforced each other, in view, in particular, of the fact that both domestic and international objectives have been pursued by implementing the same general principles of competition, publicity, use of commercial criteria and transparency.

We have also, however, highlighted the potential for some conflict between the requirements of international rules and the concerns of domestic policy. This is particularly so in those states which are seeking to move away from the bureaucratic approach which is traditional in government procurement towards a more flexible, but less transparent, regime which is more closely modelled on private sector best practice. However, a certain conflict between international and domestic perspectives may also be seen even in those countries with a more traditional approach to procurement in so far as the fairly stringent transparency requirements seen as necessary to curb discrimination in procurement may impede the flexibility needed to obtain best value for money, as well as impinging on states' abilities to use procurement for social goals and imposing significant transaction costs. The future is perhaps likely to see an effort to adjust current international rules to take more account of these domestic concerns, especially as national procurement becomes more sophisticated, and this may result in a greater emphasis on principle rather than detail in international procurement rules.

2. The Economic Impact of the European Union Regime on Public Procurement: Lessons for the WTO*

*Harvey Gordon,*** Shane Rimmer,*** and Sue Arrowsmith****

1. INTRODUCTION

Discriminatory public procurement constitutes an important barrier to trade and the opening up of public markets has increasingly been a target of regional trade agreements. In Europe measures designed to tackle this problem have been applied by the European Union,[1] the European Economic Area[2] and the Central European Free Trade Agreement (CEFTA).[3] In the Americas the North American Free Trade Agreement (NAFTA) includes a significant programme on procurement,[4] and agreement has recently been reached to move towards a non-binding open procurement regime within the Asia–Pacific Co-operation Forum (APEC).[5] On a global level, from 1980 public procurement was the subject of a side

---

* A version of this chapter first appeared as an article in (1998) 21 *The World Economy* © Blackwell Publishers. This material is reproduced by permission of the copyright holder.
** EuroStrategy Consultants.
*** Director, Public Procurement Research Group, Nottinghham.

1 For details of the European regime, see S. Arrowsmith, *The Law of Public and Utilities Procurement* (Sweet & Maxwell, 1996), chapters 3–11 and 15–18; J.M. Fernández-Martín, *The EC Procurement Rules: a Critical Analysis* (Clarendon Press, 1996); A. Cox, *The Single Market Rules and the Enforcement Regime after 1992* (Earlsgate Press, 1993); P. Lee, *Public Procurement* (Butterworths, 1992); P. Trepte, *Public Procurement in the EEC* (Bicester: CCA Europe, 1993); F. Weiss, *Public Procurement in European Community Law* (European Community Law Series, 1993); C. Bright, *Public Procurement Handbook* (Wylie Chancery, 1994); and L. Digings and J. Bennett, *EC Public Procurement: Law and Practice* (Longman Law, looseleaf).
2 See C. Bock, "The EEA Agreement: Rules on Public Procurement" (1993) 2 *Public Procurement Law Review* 136.
3 Article 24 of CEFTA.
4 Chapter 10 of NAFTA. For an overview, see K.E. Troy, "Chapter 10: New Opportunities in North American Government Procurement Markets" in J.H. Bello, A.F. Holmer and J.J. Norton (eds.), *NAFTA: a New Frontier in International Trade and Investment in the Americas* (1994), chapter 7; and S. Greenwold, "The Government Procurement Chapter of the North American Free Trade Agreement" (1994) 3 *Public Procurement Law Review* 129.
5 See S. Arrowsmith, "Public Procurement within the Asia–Pacific Economic Co-operation Forum" (1996) 5 *Public Procurement Law Review* CS71.

agreement to the GATT, and a much-expanded version of this GATT procurement agreement now constitutes one of the plurilateral (optional) agreements administered by the new World Trade Organisation.[6]

The most long-standing and most developed regime is that of the European Union, which has adopted stringent measures on public procurement – on paper at least – since 1971.[7] This European regime has to a large extent served as a model for subsequent procurement regimes, and has had a significant influence on the development of the current World Trade Organisation Government Procurement Agreement (GPA). In 1995 the European Commission commissioned a study from EuroStrategy Consultants to assess the economic impact of the European rules.[8] In view of the similarities in their approach to regulation, the results of the European Union efforts are of considerable interest for the GPA and other regional arrangements. This chapter outlines the key findings of the study, and examines its implications for regulatory strategy, in particular in the context of the GPA.

The first section of the chapter provides a brief introduction to the European and GPA rules. The second section then sets out the main findings of the European Commission study on the European rules. The third section considers the implications of the findings for the GPA. It is suggested, in particular, that there is a need for clear rules, for more effective enforcement,

---

[6] For reading on the GPA in general, see further M.L. Jones, "The GATT–MTN System and the European Community as International Frameworks for the Regulation of Economic Activity: the Removal of Barriers to Trade in Government Procurement" (1984) 8 *Maryland Journal of International Law and Trade* 53; J.H. Bourgeois, "The Tokyo Round Agreements on Technical Barriers and on Government Procurement in International and EEC Perspective" (1982) 19 *Common Market Law Review* 5; G. de Graaf and P. Trepte, "The Revised GATT Procurement Agreement" (1994) 3 *Public Procurement Law Review* CS70; G. de Graaf and M. King, "Towards a More Global Government Procurement Market: The Expansion of the GATT Government Procurement Agreement in the Context of the Uruguay Round" (1995) 29 *International Lawyer* 435; B. Hoekman and P.C. Mavroidis, "The WTO's Agreement on Government Procurement: Expanding Disciplines, Declining Membership?" (1995) 4 *Public Procurement Law Review* 63; A. Brown and C. Pouncey, "Expanding the International Market for Public Procurement: the WTO's Agreement on Government Procurement" (1993) 3 *International Trade Law Review* 69; S. Arrowsmith, "The World Trade Organization Agreement on Government Procurement: Obstacles and Opportunities" (1997) 1 *Malaysian Journal of Law and Society* 15; A. Low, A. Mattoo and A. Subramaniam, "Government Procurement in Services" (1996) 20 *World Competition* 5; A. Blank and G. Marceau, "The History of the Government Procurement Negotiations since 1995 (1996) 5 *Public Procurement Law Review* 77; V. Kulacoglu, "The WTO Government Procurement Agreement: Current Opportunities in United Kingdom Association for Regulated Procurement", *Global Business Opportunities in Public Procurement* (conference papers of the UK Association for Regulated Procurement, 1996).

[7] This date is selected as significant as the date of adoption of the first harmonisation directive on public procurement, which regulated contract award procedures. However, basic prohibitions on discriminatory procurement within the European Economic Community date back even further: for a history, see C. Turpin, "Public Contracts in the EEC" (1972) *Common Market Law Review* 411; and Arrowsmith, note 1 above, pp. 50–7.

[8] European Commission, *The Single Market Review, sub-series III: Dismantling of Barriers*, vol. II, *Public Procurement* (Kogan Page, Earthscan, 1997). The results of the project are summarised in a Communication from the Commission to the European Parliament and the Council, *The Impact and Effectiveness of the Single Market* COM (96) 520 final (see pp. 16–17 on public procurement).

for efforts to tackle differences in technical specifications and other general market obstacles, and for greater attention to the problems of the supply-side.

2. THE EUROPEAN UNION AND GPA RULES ON PUBLIC PROCUREMENT

2.1 Public procurement in the European Union[9]

Within the European Union discrimination in public procurement against firms and products from other Member States is prohibited by the general EC Treaty provisions on free movement, in particular Article 30 (free movement of goods), Article 52 (freedom of establishment) and Article 59 (freedom to provide services). These provisions govern all contracts awarded by public bodies, however small. However, it is generally recognised that a general prohibition on discrimination is insufficient to secure a free market. This arises because it is difficult to prove discrimination and also because the difficulties of access of foreign bidders are due not merely to intentional discrimination but also to the inertia of public purchasers in seeking out new sources of supply. Competition is also hindered by market obstacles in the form of differing technical specifications.

To tackle these problems the European Union adopted a series of directives that regulate in detail award procedures for major contracts. The first directives, adopted in the 1970s, dealt with public sector works and supply contracts. These early rules were largely ignored in practice and were ineffective. From 1985, however, procurement was made one of the main priorities in the drive towards the 1992 European single market, resulting in an intensive legislative programme in this field. This involved tightening the provisions applying to public sector works and supplies, extending the regime to services and to the utilities sectors of water, energy, transport and telecommunications (which were formerly excluded) and improving enforcement.

The current directives fall into two groups – the public sector directives, and the directives on utilities. The directives for the public sector are Directive 93/36/EEC[10] on supply contracts (the Supplies Directive), and Directive 93/37/EEC[11] on works contracts (the Works Directive) and Directive 92/50/EEC[12] on services contracts (the Services Directive). Purchasing in the utilities sectors is governed by Directive 93/38/EEC.[13] Coverage is the same for all Member States: they may not take derogations for particular entities or sectors in order to protect national economic or other interests.

---

[9] See further the materials cited in note 1.
[10] OJ 1993, No. L199/1.
[11] OJ 1993, No. L199/54.
[12] OJ 1993, No. L199/1, OJ 1993, No. L199/54 and OJ 1992, No. L209/1. There is currently a Proposal to make some minor amendments to these directives to align them with the GPA: see COM (96) 623 final.
[13] OJ 1993, No. L199/84.

Unlike the Treaty, the directives apply only to contracts above certain financial thresholds[14] – those likely to be of interest to firms from other Member States. Entities are expressly prohibited from splitting contracts to avoid the directives. In addition, the amounts of smaller contracts awarded over a period of time for the same type of product or service must be added together, and if their total value exceeds the thresholds the directive will apply (the aggregation rules[15]). This ensures that contracts which are split to avoid the directives will be covered even if an intention to avoid the directives cannot be proven, and also that contracts must be aggregated in situations where it is commercially reasonable to do so.

The directives lay down specific procedures for contract awards, which need not be described in detail here.[16] Obligations include a requirement to award contracts by competition, following an advertisement in the *Official Journal of the European Communities*; provision of adequate time limits for firms to respond; and the use of commercial criteria to select the winning bidder. An underlying principle is transparency, implying that contracts must be awarded according to clear rules, the application of which can be verified. This ensures that discriminatory decisions cannot be concealed. Provisions supporting transparency include, for example, requirements to state precise qualification and contract award criteria in advance, an obligation to keep records, and (at present for the public sector only) a requirement to state reasons for decisions on request. In general, the public sector procedures are more rigid than those for the utilities and place greater emphasis on transparency.

The primary enforcement method is through remedies for aggrieved firms,[17] and specific directives – Directive 89/665/EEC for the public sector and Directive 92/13/EEC for the utilities[18] – lay down minimum standards for these. It is required, *inter alia*, that remedies should be rapid and effective; that review fora should be independent, and that specific remedies should be available, namely damages, setting aside of decisions and correction of unlawful provisions in documents, and interim measures to suspend award procedures.[19] The other main way of securing compliance is

---

[14] For works contracts ECU5 million; for public sector supply contracts ECU200,000 or SDR130,000 for contracts covered by the old GATT Agreement on procurement; for public sector services contracts ECU200,000; for utilities supply and services contracts ECU600,000 (telecommunications) or ECU400,000 (other utilities); for works contracts in all sectors ECU5 million.

[15] For a detailed analysis, see S. Arrowsmith, *The Law of Public and Utilities Procurement* (Sweet & Maxwell, 1996), pp. 167–75 and 447–51. For works contracts there is a rule requiring separate contracts which relate to the same "work" to be added together.

[16] On these, see the works cited in note 1 above.

[17] See, in particular, S. Arrowsmith, "Enforcing the Public Procurement Rules: Legal Remedies in the Court of Justice and the National Courts" in S. Arrowsmith (ed.), *Remedies for Enforcing the Public Procurement Rules* (Earlsgate, 1993), chapter 1; J.M. Fernández-Martín, *The EC Public Procurement Rules* (Clarendon Press, 1996), chapters 7 and 8.

[18] OJ 1989, No. L393/33; OJ 1992, No. L76/14.

[19] The last two remedies need not apply for utilities; another system of sanctions such as financial sanctions can be used instead. These two remedies also do not need to be available where the contract has already been concluded.

through the European Commission, which ensures that the directives have been implemented and also follows up complaints about breaches.[20] If not satisfied, the Commission can take action against Member States in the ECJ under Article 169 of the EC Treaty.

2.2 The World Trade Organisation Government Procurement Agreement[21]

The World Trade Organisation (WTO) Government Procurement Agreement (GPA) is the successor to the old GATT Government Procurement Agreement. This was negotiated under the auspices of GATT (not strictly part of the GATT but a "side agreement" to it) during the Tokyo Round between 1973 and 1979, and came into force on 1 January 1981.[22] This original agreement was narrow in scope, covering only supplies contracts (not works or services), and only central or federal government entities (not, for example, regional bodies or local authorities). In parallel with the Uruguay Round, however, a more extensive agreement was concluded, which has become one of the agreements administered by the World Trade Organisation. This took effect for most signatories on 1 January 1996.

The GPA's approach broadly follows that of the European rules. Thus it contains both general provisions prohibiting discrimination (see Article III[23]) and also detailed award procedures. These are quite similar to those under the European regime involving, for example, competition and the use of formal tendering, although the procedures are generally more flexible than under the European rules, particularly for the public sector.

Scope of coverage is set out in Appendix 1 to the GPA. The coverage of the new agreement is much wider than the old in that it covers works and other services as well as supplies; it embraces certain activities in the utilities sector; and it applies to many sub-federal entities and certain public undertakings, as well as to central or federal government. As a result, procurement subject to the GPA regime will increase tenfold.[24] In contrast with the European rules, however, the scope of the GPA is not uniform for the different signatories: its precise application for each state is set out in a series of separate annexes. This situation has arisen because of the vast differences in the nature and amount of procurement which different states were willing to regulate. A consequence of these divergences is that many

---

[20] See further S. Arrowsmith, "Enforcing the Public Procurement Rules: Legal Remedies in the Court of Justice and the National Courts" in S. Arrowsmith (ed.), *Remedies for Enforcing the Public Procurement Rules* (Earlsgate, 1993), pp. 4–43; J.M. Fernández-Martín, "The European Commission's Centralised Enforcement of Public Procurement Rules: A Critical View" (1993) 2 *Public Procurement Law Review* 40; S. Arrowsmith, *The Law of Public and Utilities Procurement* (Sweet & Maxwell, 1996), pp. 920–32.

[21] See further the material cited in note 6 above.

[22] The Agreement was slightly amended in 1987 by a Protocol that came into force on 14 February 1988.

[23] Article III contains a national treatment clause and a most-favoured-nation clause.

[24] European Commission Press Release, Memo/94/29, *EU–US Negotiations on Public Procurement* (21 April 1994), p. 1.

states have insisted on derogations for their own application of the GPA, based mainly on the principle of sectoral reciprocity. The approach thus adopted marks a significant departure from the "Most Favoured Nation" (MFN) principle as regards scope of coverage. As with the European directives, the GPA contains "aggregation" rules to ensure that smaller contracts which could have been packaged together to make larger contracts do not escape the application of the rules because individually they fall below the relevant thresholds.[25]

As with the European regime, it was considered necessary to give individuals the right to enforce the rules in order to make the regime effective. Article XX of the GPA on "challenge procedures" lays down minimum standards for these. The other mechanism for securing the application of the agreement is through the World Trade Organisation's intergovernmental dispute-settlement mechanism.[26]

The GPA is a plurilateral agreement which means that WTO members may choose whether to accede.[27] The present parties are the European Union and its Member States, Aruba, Norway, Canada, Israel, Japan, Liechtenstein, South Korea, the United States and Switzerland.[28] Singapore has completed accession negotiations and is likely to accede in September 1998.[29] The WTO has recently sent up a working group to consider the possibility of a new agreement on procurement involving less onerous obligations based around transparency, with a view to attracting wider membership or, perhaps, application to all WTO members. Similar discussions are taking place in relation to services procurement under the General Agreement on Trade in Services.[30]

3. THE EUROSTRATEGY CONSULTANTS STUDY OF THE ECONOMIC IMPACT OF THE EUROPEAN RULES

3.1 The approach of the EuroStrategy study

In 1995 the European Commission commissioned from EuroStrategy Consultants a study to examine the impact that the European procurement

---

[25] GPA, Article II(3) and (4).

[26] See M. Footer, "Remedies under the New GATT Agreement on Public Procurement" (1995) 4 *Public Procurement Law Review* 80; A. Davies, "Remedies for Enforcing the WTO Agreement on Government Procurement from the Perspective of the European Community: a Critical View" (1997) 20 *World Competition* 113.

[27] However, the existing GPA members have adopted a policy of insisting that potential new members of the WTO, such as China, Russia and Saudi Arabia, should accede to the GPA also.

[28] These are the same as the parties to the old agreement except that South Korea was not formerly a party.

[29] Argentina, Australia, Bulgaria, Colombia, Iceland, Latvia and Turkey have observer status.

[30] Such negotiations are required under Article XIII. The meetings of the GATS and the transparency working group are taking place in tandem and largely involve the same personnel from member countries.

rules have had between 1987 – when the revision of the directives began – and 1994.[31] This formed part of a wider study to assess the impact and effectiveness of the European single market programme. The study focused on procurement-sensitive products and sectors – that is, those products and sectors for which the public sector and utilities are major, often dominant, purchasers.[32] The study sought to determine the effectiveness of policy by considering:

(i)   the extent to which purchasing entities have opened up their markets to international firms (in particular to firms from other Member States);

(ii) the extent and nature of any savings in the period under review;

(iii) the extent of improvements in the competitiveness of the supply-side; and

(iv) the extent to which such savings and improvements can be attributed to the directives.

A distinction was made between, first, direct impacts, which considered the extent to which interested suppliers have equal opportunity to tender and are treated equally (addressed at 3.2 below), and, secondly, the changes that have taken place on the demand and supply-sides as a result of the direct impacts, in terms of supplying industries having responded to new opportunities and (where appropriate) restructuring, and purchasing entities having experienced a reduction in their purchasing costs (addressed at 3.3 below).

The study's overall methodology was driven by the limited availability of reliable and complete statistical data on the public procurement market. As a result, considerable importance was placed on two pieces of primary research, namely (i) a survey of suppliers to the public sector or utilities, which was structured to allow inferences to be made about the *total* supply-side population; and (ii) a survey of a cross-section of regulated purchasers.

For purchasers, the survey sample was drawn on a constrained pareto basis, targeting purchasers representing 80 per cent of procurement at each level of government and utility type in each Member State. In total, some 698 purchasing entities were targeted, covering for any Member State: (i) central government ministries representing an estimated 80 per cent of central government procurement, covering in the main ministries responsible for defence, public works, transport, education, interior or home office, health and post and telecommunications; (ii) purchasing

---

[31] Note 8 above.

[32] More precisely, the characteristics of the sectors selected for study were that they account for a large share in total public purchasing; depend heavily on public sector purchases; are tradeable (can be transported long distances within and between Member States); were not freely traded in 1987, due to nationalistic purchasing; and were supplied in 1987 by a few dominant suppliers in each Member State.

entities at a regional level accounting for an estimated 80 per cent of total regional procurement, representing 80 per cent of national GDP; (iii) bodies representative of total local government procurement, within sub-regions representing 80 per cent of the GDP of the regions described at (ii); and (iv) the largest utilities representing 70–80 per cent of procurement in each of the sub-sectors as defined in Annexes I to X of the Utilities Directive. As a result, the survey covered a wide range of entity sizes, ranging from large spending central government ministries, such as the Ministry of Defence, to local authorities and local fire services and, in a number of cases, independent purchasing units within local bodies. Purchasers focusing on works, supplies and services were also covered.

For the supply-side, the sample focused on procurement-sensitive supplying sectors, which account for some 62 per cent of the value of procurement. It also ensured that the large Member States and major supplying sectors had adequate representation for the purposes of making inferences about the total population. Quota samples were drawn on a 4:1 basis from *Tenders Electronic Daily* (TED, Contract Award Notices) and *Kompass* and other business directories to ensure representation of all Member States and procurement-sensitive sectors. Random samples were drawn in each cell (Member State and supplying sector). In total 6,000 companies were drawn. This approach yielded an effective sample of 1,608 companies, representative of the size of firms selling to the public sector or utilities within quotas.

In addition to this primary research, the study considered the public procurement market from all key perspectives using a wide range of sources. For example, information contained in the TED database was used to obtain data on publication of notices, and price data from previous European Commission studies and *Eurostat* were used to ascertain the extent of price convergence (as described further below). Thus it was possible to take into account the results of a number of qualitative, quantitative and quali-quantitative analyses to arrive at an assessment of the impact of the legislation which was consistent, plausible and coherent. It should also be emphasised that no one individual analysis provided the answer to whether the public procurement legislation had achieved its aims. It was only the combination of the results of all individual analyses (which themselves reflect a range of information sources) that was able to provide this overall assessment.[33]

3.2 Direct impacts: openness and fairness

3.2.1 Publication of notices

The most easily measured indicator of non-compliance with the directives is failure to publish notices. The study revealed that as a result of the procurement legislation, there has been an increase in the number of entities

---

[33] Comprehensive technical descriptions of the methodology are contained in Annex I (Technical Information) to the study.

publishing, reflecting, in particular, implementation of the Utilities Directive, and a recent increase in publication by sub-central bodies. The total number of notices published in the *Official Journal* has risen from around 12,000 in 1987 to over 95,000 in 1995. Entry into force of the Utilities and Services Directives resulted in a step change in the number of notices published by the utilities, which increased from 0 per cent in 1992 to 14.7 per cent of all notices published in 1995, and services notices published, which rose from 11.3 per cent of all notices published by central and sub-central government in 1993 to 28 per cent of the total number of notices in 1995.

Despite this, the number of entities subject to the legislation, and which might reasonably be expected to be publishing some tenders falls far short of those which do publish. The European Commission's own – as yet incomplete – database contains over 100,000 entities, but in 1995 only just over 15,000 bodies published notices – a mere 14 per cent of the total. These findings are supported by an earlier study for the European Commission, which showed that in one of the EU's largest Member States almost 10 per cent of towns with more than 100,000 inhabitants did not report any procurement in 1993. Further, 28 per cent of towns of 10,000–50,000 inhabitants, and over 30 per cent of towns of 50,000–100,000 reported no contracts *at all*. It was concluded to be inconceivable that these entities did not have any purchases covered by the Directives. Likewise, a Commission analysis highlighted considerable variation between notice publication by similarly sized (major) sub-central government bodies with similar responsibilities in other Member States. An equally low level of publication was also found in a study of Dutch municipalities undertaken by Telgen and de Boer: it was estimated that only between 77 and 83 per cent of procurements covered by the European rules were actually advertised.[34] That there is under-publication of tender notices is also illustrated by the continuing increase in the number of supplies notices being published by public sector entities,[35] and by the reported differences in above-threshold procurement in statistical returns by Member States, with central government in some Member States claiming above threshold procurement at a mere 16 per cent. This is inconceivable in terms of the size of aggregated budgets on supplies and services.[36] Although there is significant under-publication, entities which have been publishing are, in general, complying with the Directives in terms of the type of procedure used, with central and sub-central government principally using the open and restricted procedures, and utilities primarily using the negotiated and restricted procedures.

---

[34] J. Telgen and L. de Boer, "Experience with the EC Directives on Public Procurement: A Survey of Dutch Municipalities" (1997) 6 *Public Procurement Law Review* 121.

[35] Since the legislation has been in force since 1989 for the largest Member States, publication levels might reasonably have been expected to have levelled off, or, at a minimum, be growing at a lower rate.

[36] It can also be noted that the EuroStrategy study revealed that for every two tender notices only one Contract Award Notice was published. This finding is similar to that of other studies: see, for example, S. Martin and K. Hartley, "Public Procurement in the European Union: Issues and Policies" (1997) 6 *Public Procurement Law Review* 92 at 102.

In some instances clearly entities have quite simply not been complying at all. However, the study revealed that in other instances non-publication or under-publication reflected a varied understanding of the directives' requirements. For example, in some cases a contract-based approach to purchasing was employed, resulting from a misinterpretation of the aggregation rules; in others different definitions of what constitutes a "discrete operating unit" for the purpose of applying the rules on aggregation were used;[37] and in yet others there was a misunderstanding of entity coverage, leading to non-compliance.

Non-publication was exacerbated by a number of factors, which will be considered further below, including inadequate policing and enforcement, with a reluctance to sue potential customers, and a lack of awareness of the legislation's requirements by suppliers, particularly small and medium-sized enterprises (SMEs).

3.2.2 Use of the Official Journal

To the extent the required notices were being published in the *Official Journal*, the study revealed that the *Official Journal* has been a very valuable source of information, but only *for those who read it*. It is regarded as the single point of focus for business in the public sector, domestically and in other Member States. This was particularly the case with suppliers committed to entering new markets. This was illustrated by the survey of suppliers. This found that an estimated 41 per cent obtain information from the *Official Journal*, although SMEs have only a 30 per cent readership, suggesting that larger companies are the main beneficiaries of this information. The survey also found that an estimated 14–20 per cent of all suppliers to the public sector had identified additional opportunities in their domestic markets, and an estimated 9–13 per cent in other EU markets, and that over two-thirds of *Official Journal* readers considered information provided in notices to be adequate for business purposes. These findings were supported by the views of major European purchasers surveyed, the majority of which reported that their only change in the publications they used to advertise contracts since the directives came into force was the use of the *Official Journal*. This implied that the directives have led to greater openness both within Member States and in other EU Member States.

On the other hand, it was found that there is still a lack of knowledge among potential suppliers on the extent of information on public sector opportunities available in the *Official Journal* due to both limited promotion of the *Official Journal* at Member State level, and the relatively high subscription fees for the *Official Journal* and the TED database, especially for SMEs.

---

[37] While all the purchases of a legal entity must generally be aggregated for the purpose of the directives' threshold requirements, it is probably not required to include purchases by independent purchasing units, under certain conditions: see further European Commission, *Policy Guidelines on Contracts Awarded by Separate Units of a Contracting Entity under Directive 90/531/EEC*, CC/92/87 final.

It was also possible to infer that SMEs have benefited least from the legislation since the vast majority of smaller contracts are still being let locally to broadly the same suppliers without publication in the *Official Journal*, as they are not being aggregated. Even when notices are published a smaller proportion of SMEs actually knows about them, due to their lower awareness of the *Official Journal*.

3.2.3 Fairness of procedures

Compliance in relation to other aspects of the rules is harder to measure. As regards specifications, it was, however, found that those entities which are publishing notices do – or try to – issue functional, rather than detailed or discriminatory specifications. For many purchasers this has required a major reassessment of their approach to procurement definition. However, the definition and application of qualification and award criteria is an area where entities – albeit unintentionally – can be, and are, "unfair". In particular, the lack of clarity in the rules on shortlisting in restricted and negotiated procedures (that is, the selection of bidders from among a number of candidates who meet minimum qualification criteria)[38] increases the scope for misuse and the favouring of traditional suppliers.

It was also found, as confirmed by both suppliers and purchasers, that purchasing authorities often introduce competition and award an occasional contract to a new supplier to force traditional players to reduce prices, even though the latter would have won under the strict application of "most economically advantageous".

When considering these issues, it was recognised that in all regulated environments there always remains a degree of potential for unfairness. However, this can be minimised by having clear and unambiguous rules, and effective policing and efficient enforcement.

3.2.4 Clarity of the rules

However, one of the study's key findings was that the current rules are far from clear and unambiguous in a number of key areas, giving significant scope for unintentional breaches. Lack of clarity can also increase the possibilities for deliberate non-compliance, in that effective policing of the rules becomes more problematic. Some of the key areas in this respect include permissible criteria for shortlisting in the public sector (as already indicated above); the extent to which renewals, extensions or amendments to existing contractual agreements constitute new contracts;[39] and the extent to which alterations to bids are permitted in open and restricted procedures.[40] Most importantly of all, there is significant uncertainty over

---

[38] On this problem, see S. Arrowsmith, *The Law of Public and Utilities Procurement* (Sweet & Maxwell, 1996), pp. 217–22.

[39] *Ibid.*, pp. 119–22; and for a more detailed analysis, see S. Arrowsmith, "Amendments to Specifications under the European Public Procurement Directives" (1997) 6 *Public Procurement Law Review* 128.

[40] Arrowsmith, note 38, pp. 247–50.

the application of the "aggregation rules", both regarding the level at which products or services should be aggregated and the treatment of discrete operating units within the same entity. As already explained above, there is a significant degree of non-compliance with even the most basic publication requirements, especially by smaller entities, which to a large extent is due to misunderstanding of these rules on aggregation.

The situation has not been helped by the fact that national transposing legislation has, in general, merely repeated the directives' rules.[41] As a consequence, ambiguous European rules have become equally ambiguous national rules. This has led to some entities having genuine difficulties complying, while giving others the opportunity to circumvent them. The problem is exacerbated by the lack of any definitive European-level guidance and interpretation dealing with the "grey" areas of the rules.

3.2.5 Enforcement

Another matter of concern was the inadequacy of the enforcement system. There was revealed to be little active policing of compliance at Member State level. As indicated above, the primary method of enforcement was intended to be through the possibility of aggrieved firms bringing actions against procuring entities before national review bodies. However, the effectiveness of national arrangements in relation to remedies was generally revealed to be inadequate, due in particular to an inability to obtain remedies with sufficient rapidity. This was so despite the obligation, already explained, to provide rapid and effective remedies, which is set out in the Remedies Directive and the Utilities Remedies Directive. While some states, such as France (where procurement cases must normally be decided within 20 days of the application) have made serious efforts to meet this obligation, many others, such as the United Kingdom, Spain and Portugal, have relied on existing national review fora which are too slow and cumbersome to meet the directives' requirements.[42]

3.3 Downstream impacts

3.3.1 Changes in competition and import penetration

It was estimated that between 14 per cent and 20 per cent of all suppliers to the public sector had identified additional (new) opportunities in their *domestic* markets from notices published in the *Official Journal*, with between 9 per cent and 13 per cent having won new business as a result. In terms of *non-domestic* markets, between 9 per cent and 13 per cent of all suppliers to the public sector had identified additional opportunities from notices published in the *Official Journal*, with 3 per cent to 4 per cent having won

---

[41] On the national transposition, see Annex II to the study.
[42] On the implementation of the remedies directives, see Annex II of the study, and also S. Arrowsmith (ed.), *Remedies for Enforcing the Public Procurement Rules* (1993); S. Arrowsmith, "Public Procurement: Example of a Developed Field of Community Remedies Established by Community Law" in H. Micklitz and N. Reich (eds.), *Public Interest Litigation before European Courts* (Nomos, 1996), p. 125.

additional business as a result. In both cases, this level of success was *directly* attributable to the directives' publication requirements and their impacts. Yet although firms of all sizes have been successful in winning additional business using the *Official Journal*, large companies had been far more successful, particularly for non-domestic business, which reflected their higher readership of the *Official Journal* – 69 per cent of all large companies compared to 53 per cent for medium-sized and 34 per cent for SMEs – and greater presence in non-domestic markets. These changes on the supply-side were corroborated by the views of purchasers that there had been *some* increase in non-domestic suppliers tendering for opportunities and the mix of their supplier bases (in the latter instance, large and multinational companies were highlighted, particularly by utilities and sub-central government bodies).

The study also examined the extent of public sector import penetration, and the data here supported the evidence of supply-side changes given above. Public sector import penetration was defined as:

$$\frac{\text{public sector purchases of foreign origin}}{\text{total public sector purchases}}$$

Public sector purchases of foreign origin equal the sum of direct and indirect imports by the public sector. A direct import is a purchase from a supplier from outside the purchaser's national territory. An indirect import is a purchase of foreign origin from a supplier operating inside the purchaser's national territory.

The methodology applied to estimate total public sector import penetration was based on making separate estimates by supplying sector and Member State of (i) intra-EU direct public sector import penetration; (ii) intra-EU and extra-EU indirect public sector import penetration; and (iii) extra-EU direct public sector import penetration. Since there is no systematic recording or analysis of the national origin of purchases by entities, it was not possible to use demand-side data to make sound estimates of import penetration by supplying sector or in total for each Member State. A more reliable source of information was private sector companies supplying the public sector or utilities, since they keep detailed records of their exports and imports. In general, this information is published in their annual reports at regional level permitting identification of exports to other EU states and to third countries.

The supply-side survey provided data on a representative sample of 1,608 suppliers to the public sector (broken down by Member State, supplying sector and company size). The data covered total turnover; percentage of turnover supplied to the domestic public sector; percentage of turnover exported to the public sector in other EU Member States; and percentage of domestic public sector sales imported. Using the supply-side sample data, estimates of intra-EU direct and total indirect import penetration by supplying sector and Member State were made, based on the assumptions (i) that the value of intra-EU public sector exports in a sector is equal to that of intra-EU public sector imports; and (ii) that the total value of sales to the public sector in the EU provides a good estimate of the value of EU public sector consumption.

The estimates of extra-EU direct import penetration were based on a selection of Member State returns as required by the current directives. The problem of limited availability was considered to be of less importance when estimating direct extra-EU import penetration, since overall levels of direct extra-EU imports into the public sector were reported to be very low and any inaccuracies would thus have little impact on the total estimates.

It was found that public sector import penetration had increased from the Cecchini report's 6 per cent estimate in 1987 to 10 per cent in 1994. Within this, direct imports had increased from 1.4 per cent to 3 and indirect imports from 4.5 per cent to 7 per cent. See also Figure 2.1 below. On this basis, it was concluded that the minimal change in nationality of suppliers perceived by purchasers in the supply-side survey, as outlined above, reflected the small and uneven nature of the increase in direct public sector import penetration, and the fact that the majority of the increase in public sector import penetration comprises purchases from locally based firms, including subsidiaries of foreign companies, which have imported the products in question.

There were differences between the levels of public sector import penetration for "commodity" purchases (low-tech standard purchases, such as office furniture, paper, stationery, etc.), and high-cost strategic products. "Commodity" purchases had seen a general significant increase in intra-EU trade, and this was reflected in a rise in public sector *indirect* import penetration. For example, there has been a significant increase in intra-EU trade consistent with a high level (18 per cent) of indirect public sector imports for paper. This was supported by a reported lack of success by paper suppliers in winning new *direct* (cross-border) business in other Member

Figure 2.1   Estimated change in public sector import penetration for selected countries between 1987 and 1994

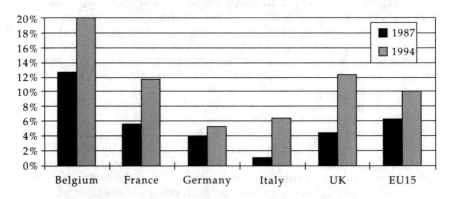

Note: Estimates for 1994 are based on the average of the upper and lower limits; comparative figures for individual products or sectors are not available, since public sector import penetration was not researched by this level of detail in the original Cecchini study in 1987

Sources: European Commission Publication, *Cost of Non-Europe in Public Sector Procurement*, Tables 1.6.2.9 and II, p. 175, Table 4.8 (see Annex I.1.7.4).

States (Table 2.1). Since both public and private sectors procure these commodity products from the same intermediate local suppliers, by inference public sector import penetration equals private sector import penetration.

Procurement of strategic products had experienced increases in both intra-EU and extra-EU trade, albeit at a lower level than the changes for "commodity" purchases. However, the level of direct purchases from non-domestic suppliers for strategic products is, today, more important than for that of "commodity" purchases. This was supported by the experiences of suppliers of strategic products, such as railway rolling stock and telecommunications equipment, which reported the highest levels of new business in other Member States.

For works and services, public sector import penetration was, in general, far lower, with any public sector trade in the main related to a small number of large international construction projects and closely related services, such as architecture and consulting engineering. The case studies indicated a perceived continued existence of general barriers to trade in these areas, which the public procurement legislation could not be expected to overcome.

3.2.2 *Price convergence*

It was assumed that opening up public procurement would lead to price convergence between different Member States in tradable sectors, due to improvements in competitiveness,[43] and the extent of price convergence was investigated in order to determine whether the procurement rules had achieved their objectives. The main data sources for this analysis were price data created by DRI McGraw Hill for a European Commission study on price convergence (1995), Eurostat and several other European Commission studies.[44] It was found that price convergence had occurred only in a very limited number of sectors, indicating that in most sectors the directives had not had the expected effects. Apart from the limited extent of compliance already referred to above, a number of factors relating primarily to the structure of the markets concerned had contributed, individually and collectively, to this state of affairs. These included the following:

(i) Imperfect market competition. The demand and supply-side surveys and other analyses indicated that often only a minority of purchasers and suppliers are aware of the opportunities in the marketplace.

(ii) Supply chain structure. The nature of national supply chain structures often restricts price savings to intermediaries, rather than end purchasers.

---

[43] A depreciating currency can make the concerned country's exports price competitive. However, this price advantage is usually eroded by higher inflation and lower productivity. The situation is also complicated when dealing with technologically complex products, such as some telecommunications equipment, by the fact that a price advantage may result from innovative design, such that competitors' products are technologically different though, possibly, functionally similar.

[44] *The Cost of Non-Europe in Public Sector Procurement* (1987); *The Implications of Opening Up Public Procurement in Greece, Italy, Portugal and Spain* (1990).

Table 2.1 Supplier response and public sector import penetration

Sector/product	NACE	Percentage Official Journal readership	Percentage winning new domestic business	Percentage which won new other EU direct business	Public sector import penetration (per cent) 1994	
					direct	indirect
Low-tech products						
Office furniture	316	34	9	2	5	8
Uniforms	453	47	12	4	3	13
Printing and paper	471/2	26	6	0	<1	17–19
High-tech products with common technical specifications						
Office machinery	33	45	17	3	4	22–29
Motor vehicles	351	41	12	3	3–4	16–19
Medical equipment	37	26	10	2	5–6	19–21
High-tech products with different technical specifications						
Boilers	315	31	12	4	4	9–10
Power-generating equipment	341/2	42	10	4	6–7	11–14
Telecommunications equipment	344	42	13	7	6–8	18–22
Railway rolling stock	362	49	12	10	10–11	19–21
Works						
Construction/civil engineering	502	44	11	4	3	4–7

Table 2.1 (Contd)

Sector/product	NACE	Percentage *Official Journal* readership	Percentage winning new domestic business	Percentage which won other new EU direct business	Public sector import penetration (per cent) 1994	
					direct	indirect
Services						
Consulting engineering	83	52	22	4	1	5–6
EU average		41	9–13	3–4	2–4	5–9

Source: EuroStrategy Consultants study

(iii) Differences in national technical standards resulting in incompatibilities or modification costs for suppliers wishing to supply non-domestic markets.
(iv) Use of detailed technical specifications. The use of detailed rather than functional specifications mitigates against the use of non-traditional solutions.
(v) Exchange rate movements. These create artificial price advantages of a temporary or permanent nature and result in a climate of commercial uncertainty.

For commodity products, the underlying problem was largely the supply chain structure, with such products almost exclusively purchased locally from national suppliers. These suppliers are normally intermediaries, which themselves source their purchases internationally on the basis of (ex-factory) prices – as illustrated by the increases in trade since 1987 – and sell at *national* price levels. These observations were consistent with the high levels of *indirect* import penetration for commodity products, as already outlined above. This point is illustrated by the example of filing cabinets, which were 36 per cent more expensive in the United Kingdom than the cheapest Member State. However, the United Kingdom was the largest exporter of filing cabinets to the rest of Europe in 1994, reflecting the change in the terms of trade due to exchange rate movements. In addition, lack of price convergence was explained to some extent also by the fact that there had been little competition for some commodity products, resulting from mis-interpretation of the aggregation rules and other factors as explained above.

In the case of strategic products, a distinction was made between those with common technical specifications, such as medical equipment, vehicles and office machinery, and those with significantly different technical requirements due to incompatibility of systems, as with railways and power-distribution systems. Although there had been recession-induced price reductions for strategic purchases, no real price convergence had occurred, with the exception of cardiac monitors, buses and office machinery. The price convergence observed for these three products could be explained by their relatively more transparent markets with few European players, and the fact that the products themselves require little to no adaptation for different markets. The fact that there had been no price convergence for the other strategic products largely reflected the fact that they are manufactured to different national technical standards. In addition, these products' suppliers (generally in response to purchaser preference) normally have a local presence resulting in a national cost base and price to national markets. This state of affairs was supported by the fact that for such purchases, *direct* public sector import penetration was low compared to *indirect* imports.

3.3.3 Employment and the structure of industry

In all procurement-sensitive sectors there has been significant supply-side rationalisation, reflected in reduced employment and productivity improvements (Table 2.2).

Table 2.2 Economic indicators

Sector/product	Public sector import penetration (per cent) 1994		Price convergence	Trade change	Production percentage change	Employment change
	Direct	Indirect	1987–93	1988–92	1988–92	1988–92
Low-tech products						
Office furniture	5	8	none	large increase	+2.3	+1
Uniforms	3	13	n/a	large increase	+1.2	–17
Printing and paper	<1	17–19	none	increase	+3.5	–3
High-tech products with common technical specifications						
Motor vehicles	3–4	16–19	none/some[a]	large increase	+0.1	–18
Office machinery	4	22–29	some	large increase	+6.5	–13
Medical equipment	5–6	19–21	none/some[b]	large increase	n/a	n/a
High-tech products with different technical specifications						
Telecommunications equipment[c]	6–8	18–22	none	increase	–1.5	–18
Power-generating equipment[c]	6–7	11–14	none	large increase	+2.7	–19
Power-distribution equipment[c]	6–7	11–14	none	large increase	+2.7	–19
Railway rolling stock[c]	10–11	19–21	none/some	large increase	+6.6	–5
Boilers	4	9–10	none	decrease		–9
Works						
Construction/civil engineering	3	4–7	n/a	increase	+1.2	+7

Table 2.2 (Contd)

Sector/product	Public sector import penetration (per cent) 1994		Price convergence 1987–93	Trade change 1988–92	Production percentage change 1988–92	Employment change 1988–92
	Direct	Indirect				
Services Consulting engineering	1	5–6	n/a	increase	decrease	n/a

Notes:
a buses
b cardiacmonitors
c single market (public sector) induced restructured industries
Source: EuroStrategy Consultants Study

In commodity areas, there had been significant recession-induced price reductions in national markets. These changes could not, however, be attributed to the procurement legislation since, as already mentioned, there had been no price convergence and there had also been significant non-publication.

In the strategic areas, there had not only been a recession-induced reduction in employment, but also a (public sector) market-induced restructuring, which has resulted in the creation of a small number of global players in telecommunications, power-generation equipment and railway rolling stock and significantly increased intra-EU and extra-EU trade. The bulk of this has been in indirect imports reflecting the strategies of these global players to have local assembly capabilities in key European markets. The apparent lack of price convergence observed, however, indicates this restructuring has not been due to any creation of a single European market by the directives.

Despite the lack of price convergence, since 1990 suppliers in high-cost strategic product areas have been forced by public purchasers to reduce their prices by 20–40 per cent, reflecting the recession and squeeze on public spending. Interviews with market leaders suggested that the public sector has used the procurement legislation to bring down price levels in national markets by threatening traditional suppliers that they would award contracts to new, lower priced competitors. In practice, there have been occasional contracts awarded to non-domestic players, resulting in lower prices but no appreciable change in market shares. In the case of telecommunications, savings had resulted from the impact of liberalisation and globalisation.

3.4 Downstream impacts: a cost–benefit analysis

The extent of benefits arising from the European procurement legislation has been outlined above. As explained, for some strategic products with common specifications (cardiac monitors, buses and office machinery) the identified price convergence between 1987 and 1994 implied the achievement of savings in the less competitive Member States. For other strategic products some price savings were found but the absence of price convergence implied that any savings which did exist could only be attributed to factors other than the directives, such as the recession.

Some price savings were also seen for commodity products. Thus 9–13 per cent of all suppliers to the public sector reported winning *at least one new contract, which would not have been identified otherwise.* Since both purchasers and suppliers confirmed that contracts in these areas are in the main awarded on the basis of price, this implied that the public sector had experienced *some* price savings due to the legislation, and this conclusion was consistent with the survey of purchasers where a minority claimed some degree of price savings from opening markets. However, such price savings were the exception rather than the rule. The absence of significant benefits from the directives is in any case indicated by the lack of price convergence between Member States.

Despite an overall lack of success, however, it is important to note that, as a consequence of the implementation of the public procurement legislation there *have been* instances where purchasing entities have achieved considerable savings on individual procurements. This, coupled with the continued existence of substantial intra-EU price differences, supports the hypothesis that there *is* potential for significant public sector savings. When new suppliers have responded positively to public sector opportunities, a high proportion *was* successful, implying that purchasing entities have benefited from improved offers.

As the Utilities Directive has only been in force for the majority of Member States since January 1993 (for supplies and works) and the Services Directive for the public sector since July 1993 and for utilities since July 1994 (in most Member States), it could be argued that the time scales are too short to expect the legislation to have fully achieved its objectives. However, as explained above, legislation on public sector supplies and works has been in force since the 1970s, and the revisions to strengthen it came into force in January 1989 and July 1990 respectively in the majority of Member States. However, the combination of related demand-side, supply-side and legal factors that have been identified above – such as imperfect markets, technical obstacles, and lack of enforcement and compliance – have all conspired to hampered the achievement of such gains.

On the cost side, there was a consensus of opinion among purchasers surveyed that the application of the legislation has created additional administrative costs. For example, in many cases an increased number of interested suppliers had emerged, without this translating into any change to the supplier base and any consequent efficiency savings. The costs of applying the rules were exacerbated by the fact that, in view of the potential threat of legal action, purchasers tend to adopt a cautious and defensive approach in applying the legislation. This can increase the costs of procurement both by reducing the flexibility needed to obtain value for money, and by increasing the administrative costs of running the procedure. On balance, purchasers in general felt that the costs of applying the legislation outweighed any benefits that they received – although this is not, of course, conclusive evidence that this is the case, since it tends to be the natural reaction of administrators faced with increased restrictions. Nevertheless, it is clear that costs, as well as benefits, have been experienced as a result of the legislation.

4. THE IMPLICATIONS FOR THE GPA

As explained above, the approach to the opening up of public procurement markets under the GPA is similar to that of the European Union and the findings of the EuroStrategy Consultants study are thus significant for the GPA. It is submitted that the findings of the study raise a number of key issues that need to be considered in the context of the future development of the GPA.

4.1 Clarity of the rules

As has been explained, one important reason identified by the study for the lack of compliance and consequent lack of success was the lack of clarity in the European rules on matters such as aggregation, shortlisting in the public sector and the application of the directives to renewals and amendments. Numerous other illustrations could be given.

For the most fundamental matters, such as shortlisting, and the most straightforward, it is submitted that the European legislation itself requires amendment. However, legislative clarification of every small matter is not appropriate, especially in complex areas where it is impossible to anticipate every eventuality. Many of the rules will eventually be clarified by the ECJ, either on the request of national review bodies under Article 177 of the EC Treaty, or in actions by the European Commission against Member States that breach the rules. In the meantime, however, the practical needs of purchasers and suppliers and the supply industry need to be met by detailed and reasoned guidance from the European Commission. While this would not provide a conclusive interpretation, it would provide operators with a framework to think in a constructive way about the problems of inter-pretation and to make intelligent judgments. In 1987 the Commission published a brief *Guide to the Community Rules on Open Procurement*,[45] covering the original Supply Directive 71/305/EEC and Works Directive 77/62/EEC, and which is to be updated. However, this barely goes beyond paraphrasing the directives and provides little useful interpretative guidance. More useful is a series of Commission guidelines on specific pro-blems (discussed and, in some cases, approved by the procurement Advisory Committees[46]), and Commission Communications,[47] but these cover only very limited areas and, moreover, are not easy for the public to obtain.

The GPA is in general more clearly drafted than the European rules, and also more flexible, which reduces the scope for disputes (for example, the rules on qualification of firms are much less prescriptive than the European public sector rules). However, there are still many important areas of potential difficulty. Examples include the following:

(i)   the rules on aggregation (discussed further below);
(ii)   the extent to which amendments and renewals of existing contracts are caught by the rules. This is important since the revision of contracts once awarded can present an important opportunity for collusion between public authorities and favoured bidders;

---

[45]   OJ 1987, No. C358/1.
[46]   *Policy Guidelines on the Interpretation of the Obligation to Refer to European Standards in the Framework of the Public Procurement Directives*, CC/91/61 (Rev. 2) final; *Draft Policy Guidelines on Defining the Term "Product Area" in Periodic Indicative Notices for Directive 90/531/EEC*, CC/92/22 (Rev. 1); *Policy Guidelines on Standards Having Currency in the Community*, CC/92/80 final; *Policy Guidelines on Contracts Awarded by Separate Units of a Contracting Entity under Directive 90/531/EEC*, CC/92/87 final; *Policy Guidelines on non-Relevant Airport Activities under the "Utilities Directive" 90/531/EEC*, CC/92/24 (Rev. 1) final.
[47]   See in particular *Public Procurement: Regional and Social Aspects*, COM (89) 400 final; Commission Communication of 22 September 1989, OJ 1989, No. C311/7.

(iii)   the application of the GPA to concession-type arrangements, where
        the successful bidder is paid by being permitted to exploit a work
        or asset (for example, toll roads and bridges); these sort of arrange-
        ments – sometimes referred to as "privately financed" transactions
        or Build-Operate-Transfer etc. – are increasingly important and
        present some of the main opportunities for cross-border trade; and
(iv)   the possibility for implementing social, political and environmental
        policies through the use of public procurement; this has arisen as a
        topical issue, following the decision of several state governments in
        the United States to refuse to deal with firms which have business
        interests in Myanmar.

Clarification of the GPA will be difficult to obtain, since there is no
mechanism for national review bodies to refer questions of interpretation to
a central authority; the intergovernmental dispute-resolution panels,
composed of experts in public procurement, can only consider issues of
interpretation in the context of intergovernmental disputes.

Detailed interpretative guidance from the WTO on these and other issues
would thus be extremely welcome. This could be invaluable for assisting
signatories to implement the agreement; for helping individual purchasers
to apply them; and to enable bidders to know their rights. It can also assist
potential signatories to make a decision on accession, and may encourage
accession by reducing the difficulties of applying the agreement. Previous
guidance on the old GATT Agreement lacks the required detail and, in any
case, has not yet been updated.[48]

It has been explained that, in particular, lack of understanding of the
rules on aggregation has resulted in many smaller entities failing to apply
the European rules at all. The aggregation rules under the GPA (Article II(3)
and (4)) are not worded in exactly the same way as the EU rules but are
very similar, and may give rise to the same problems. In particular,
difficulties arise in interpreting Article III(4) which requires the aggregation
of separate contracts (over, roughly speaking, a 12-month period) if "an
individual requirement for a procurement results in the award of more than
one contract or in contracts being awarded in separate parts". The problem
arises in determining what is an "individual requirement". How similar do
products need to be to be part of an individual requirement? What about,
for example, different stationery products normally purchased from the
same supplier? Are goods of the same type obtained partly on lease and
partly by purchase an individual requirement? An important question of
principle, also, is how far the definition of an individual requirement
depends on the purchasing practices of the particular authority, and how
far it is an objective requirement that certain types of product be aggregated
for the purpose of these rules.

It is difficult to see an easy solution to the problems caused by the misunderstanding of the aggregation rules, particular as the problem mainly
affects large numbers of smaller authorities. However, there is at the very

---

[48]   GATT Secretariat, *Practical Guide to the Agreement on Government Procurement*.

least a need to (i) publish very clear guidance on the issue, which contains a range of detailed examples of when aggregation appears to be required, and (ii) to ensure that this guidance is properly distributed to the purchasing entities concerned.

4.2 Enforcement

The EuroStrategy Consultants study concluded that the European enforcement system was still deficient, a finding which raises important questions relating to the development of effective mechanisms for enforcing international procurement rules.

As explained above, the current European system places considerable reliance on national review actions by aggrieved firms, and a similar national review system has been adopted under the GPA. However, as has also been explained, many European Union Member States have failed to implement a truly effective system of remedies, and, in particular, to provide redress that is *rapid*. It is submitted that an adequate system can only exist where disputes are resolved within a few weeks, at most. When this is not the case, review bodies are – rightly – reluctant to suspend a procurement because of the inconvenience to the government and third parties, and it is not then possible to correct breaches. Damages alone often cannot provide a suitable remedy because of the difficulties of proving damage, especially in those cases – for example, non-publication of a notice – where the aggrieved firm has not had any opportunity to tender. It is submitted that the European remedies system would be greatly improved if a maximum time limit were to be set for resolution of actions in national review fora. This might also minimise the problems noted earlier of defensive purchasing resulting from the fear of litigation: if cases are speedily resolved, litigation will be less disruptive. It should also reduce vexatious threats to litigate.

It seems unlikely that the GPA will avoid the enforcement problems which have arisen in Europe: indeed, more than half the signatories to the GPA are the European Union Member States themselves, which will apply their own inadequate remedies systems to GPA procurements. The introduction of a maximum time limit for review by national review bodies would therefore be a valuable reform for the GPA also, ensuring that review bodies can in practice exercise the right to suspend a procurement, which they are required to be given under Article XX of the GPA.

The GPA also suffers from the same uncertainty as the European Union rules as to what damages must be made available. Article XX states that damages may be limited to tender costs, but does not make it clear what conditions can be placed on the recovery of those costs. For example, can firms be required to prove both that they would have won the contract (probably won? or certainly won?), and would have made profits sufficient to cover their costs? If so, it will be difficult to obtain damages. Like the European Union Member States, other GPA signatories might fail to clarify these issues, and such uncertainty may be a significant deterrent to legal actions.

It can also be pointed out that the GPA remedies requirements are not in any case as stringent as those under the European rules.[49] In particular, signatories are not required to provide for both set aside of unlawful decisions and compensation, and, further, damages may be limited to tender costs only. However, the possibility for effective remedies under the GPA is strengthened by the Article III obligation to treat "GPA firms" as favourably as national firms and as favourably as firms from other signatory states. Thus where states have existing national remedies systems which are more favourable than those required by the GPA (as in the European Union), these systems must be made available to GPA bidders.

The question has also been raised as to whether remedies for aggrieved firms should be strengthened by allowing recovery of financial penalties as well as damages. The European Commission has raised this possibility for the European procurement regime in its recent Green Paper[50] on public procurement, and it is understood that the United States proposed a similar approach for the GPA during negotiations. It is submitted, however, that this would be a retrograde step; in particular, the problem of cautious and defensive procurement would be exacerbated. A better approach in enhancing the role of aggrieved bidders would be to speed up the dispute resolution process, as recommended above.

The above discussion has been focused on the effectiveness of the remedies provided for aggrieved firms, but another issue is whether it is adequate to rely on these as the primary enforcement mechanism. It seems likely that the inherent limitations of this approach, as well as the inadequacy of remedies currently provided, may be a factor in explaining the current extent of non-compliance in Europe. One deterrent to litigation may be fear of "biting the hand that feeds", although in some countries, such as Denmark and Sweden, there has been a lot of litigation, suggesting this factor is not always important. In this respect, the culture of the state concerned may play a role. Problems of proving breaches in court – for example, that a purchaser did not use the bid evaluation criteria stated – can also be significant, although the importance of this problem is to some extent dependent on the standards of scrutiny of the review body. Further, for some breaches legal actions are not very useful – for example non-publication of notices, which may not be discovered in time.

For truly effective enforcement it is probably necessary to develop other policing mechanisms. In Europe the European Commission plays some role, as explained earlier, and the recent Green Paper raises the possibility of strengthening its role and powers, including by providing the Commission with investigatory powers and more effective sanctions.[51] The Green Paper also seeks comments on the idea of setting up independent national enforcement authorities in Member States,[52] which could undertake general compliance audits as well as reacting to complaints.

---

[49] The weakness of GPA remedies is also highlighted by A. Mattoo, "The Government Procurement Agreement: Implications of Economic Theory" (1996) 19 *World Economy* 695.

[50] European Commission, Green Paper, *Public Procurement in the European Union: Exploring the Way Forward*, 27 November 1996, COM (96) 538 final, paragraphs 3.3.7 and 3.38.

[51] *Ibid.*, 3.31.

[52] *Ibid.*, 3.33–3.34.

There is no equivalent to the Commission under the GPA; the only alternative to national litigation is the intergovernmental dispute resolution system, which is purely reactive and likely to be invoked only for major breaches. If the GPA is to be seriously applied and enforced in future, consideration may need to be given to further enforcement mechanisms. For the present, however, the concept of remedies for aggrieved firms is itself a radical one – the GPA is one of only a few WTO agreements providing for national remedies for affected individuals to enforce governmental obligations.

An interesting issue is whether any provisions on enforcement, in particular by suppliers, will be included in any interim agreement on transparency, which may be developed. Transparency is generally considered to demand not only that procurement be conducted according to clear rules, but that adequate provision should be made for verifying their application. Provision of legal remedies may deter states from signing up to the agreement, but it is to be hoped that at least some form of complaints procedure will be incorporated, in order to give potential bidders confidence that they will be fairly treated.

4.3 Structural obstacles: standards, investment and competition

The EuroStrategy study has clearly highlighted the importance for open government procurement of common product standards.[53] Article VI of the GPA requires purchasers to base their technical specifications on international standards, where appropriate, but such standards are yet to be developed for many products. For many areas the success of the GPA will depend on progress within the WTO and other international organisations (such as the ISO) in developing common standards and mutual recognition agreements for products and services which are important in government procurement.

Another important issue for government procurement is the extent to which firms are permitted to establish subsidiaries and agencies in other states, and to invest in companies already established there. As explained, the EuroStrategy study has highlighted the importance of a local presence for winning public contracts, and of indirect as opposed to direct imports. The importance of a local presence is also supported by a study by Hartley and Uttley of United Kingdom public contracts in four procurement-sensitive fields,[54] which found that while 99.5 per cent of successful bidders were based in the United Kingdom, only 64 per cent of these were United Kingdom-owned companies.[55] In this context, an important provision of the

---

[53] Further, for the services sector, absence of rules on the mutual recognition of qualifications was an important barrier to market opening. Rules on these will also be needed to open markets. Article VI of the General Agreement on Trade in Services deals with this issue but in general merely by providing for development of rules in the future.

[54] Medical products, shipbuilding, paper products and textiles.

[55] K. Hartley and M.R.H. Uttley, "The Single European Market and Public Procurement Policy: the Case of the United Kingdom" (1994) 3 *Public Procurement Law Review* 114.

GPA is Article III(2) prohibiting discrimination against locally established firms on the basis of foreign affiliation or ownership or the origin of goods or services. However, firms will only be able to take full advantage of the GPA if they are guaranteed rights to set up in the first place in other states, and if wider obligations are put in place to guarantee the fair treatment and security of foreign investors. At present, the World Trade Organisation itself has only very limited rules to tackle establishment and investment issues.[56] However, it was agreed at the 1996 Singapore Ministerial Conference to undertake a further study on such matters.[57]

Imperfect structures in supply industries is another problem which has significantly reduced the potential impact of government procurement rules in opening up markets (and which also affects the private sector, as illustrated by the study of commodity markets in the EuroStrategy study). This is a difficult problem to tackle even for a relatively well-developed system of competition law such as exists within the European Union.[58] At present, this is a field into which the WTO has not ventured,[59] although it was again agreed at Singapore to establish a working group to study competition issues.[60]

4.4 The need to address supply-side problems

Many purchasers who had complied with the European rules were disappointed with the response from the supply-side. As explained, the EuroStrategy study indicated that awareness of the European rules was low among public sector suppliers, and that use of the *Official Journal* was limited, because of lack of awareness or expense.

The results suggest a need for attention to be given to supply-side problems, which is equally applicable to the GPA. The development of an accessible and cheap information system is vital, and the opportunity for this may be provided by the development of the internet: in the future this may be used to provide free access to information in both the European Union and the GPA. Training programmes to raise supplier awareness of opportunities and to instil confidence in suppliers that they will receive fair treatment may also be important. Improvement in the enforcement system as recommended above can also, of course, play an important part in instilling this confidence.

---

[56] For goods, these are found mainly in the TRIMs (Agreement on Trade-related Investment Measures); and, for services, under GATS (General Agreement on Trade in Services). See further P. Sauvé, "A First Look at Investment in the Final Act of the Uruguay Round" (1994) *Journal of World Trade* 5; and World Trade Organization, *Annual Report 1996*, vol. I, chapter 4.

[57] Singapore Ministerial Declaration, paragraph 20.

[58] Some aspects of these problems are discussed by D. Konstadakopulos, "The Linked Oligopoly Concept in the Single European Market: Recent Evidence from Public Procurement" (1995) 4 *Public Procurement Law Review* 213.

[59] On the issues, see E. Fox, "Toward World Anti-Trust and Market Access" (1997) 91 *American Journal of International Law* 1.

[60] Singapore Ministerial Declaration, paragraph 20.

5. CONCLUSION

The European Union regime on procurement represents the most long-standing and rigorous attempt to open up competition in public markets. The recent study by EuroStrategy Consultants on the impact of the regime shows, however, disappointing results, with the objectives sought being achieved only in a very few sectors. Key reasons include the problem of effective enforcement, lack of clarity in the rules, the existence of structural market obstacles and lack of response on the supply-side.

While obviously there are some important differences between the European Union and other international arrangements, the information provided by the study is relevant also for the GPA and for other regional groupings. From the point of the view of the GPA, the study indicates that it would be helpful to pay greater attention to the problem areas indicated above. It is submitted that the issue of clarification can easily be dealt with and ought to be made a priority. Attention should also be paid to ensuring effective implementation of national remedies, and in particular to ensuring that they are rapid. In the longer term, consideration should be given to improving the GPA enforcement mechanisms. It will also be simple to take basic measures to assist the supply-side, such as improving electronic information flows. These are all matters that may be addressed in the review of the GPA being undertaken in 1997.

More problematic are the general market obstacles such as differing national specifications, limitations on foreign direct investment and imperfect supply structures, which must be tackled in the long term if the procurement rules are to be truly effective. The extent to which the anticipated benefits from open government procurement are reduced as a result of these market obstacles may have been underestimated, and needs to be taken into account by potential GPA signatories in weighing up the costs and benefits of signing the agreement. However, it is submitted that it is important for work to continue on procurement in parallel with efforts to tackle these structural obstacles, in order to prevent delay to the ultimate attainment of open procurement markets. In this context the proposed interim agreement, which will impose less significant procedural burdens and other costs but will familiarise all states with basic transparency concepts and bring some improvements in market access and participation, is likely to make a valuable contribution to the ultimate goal.

3. Defence Procurement, the Single Market and the European Armaments Agency

*Keith Hartley**

1. INTRODUCTION: THE POLICY ISSUES

Currently, European Union nations pursue national defence policies, with each nation providing a range of independent armed forces and each pursuing an independent policy for the procurement of its defence equipment. Traditionally, collective military action by European states has been organised through the North Atlantic Treaty Organisation (NATO). However, during the 1990s, the Western European Union (WEU, which comprises European members of NATO and other European states) became the defence component of the European Union: it developed a European defence identity and capability for smaller-scale peace-keeping, human-itarian and crisis-management operations. Within the WEU, the Western European Armaments Group (WEAG) is the body with responsibility for promoting armaments co-operation, the harmonisation of operational requirements and moves towards the liberalisation and rationalisation of European defence equipment markets. A further development occurred with the formation in late 1996 of the Quadrilateral Armaments Agency involving France, Germany, Italy and the UK (also known as the Organisation for Joint Armaments Co-operation or OCCAR).[1]

The bewildering variety of national and international institutional and organisational arrangements for both European armed forces and defence procurement provides scope for returning to basic principles. The existing national arrangements involve major inefficiencies resulting from the duplication of costly armed forces, their facilities (for example, training and support) and defence industries. This chapter focuses on the opportunities for improving the efficiency of European defence procurement. Questions arise about the aims of defence procurement policy, the causes of the policy

---

* Centre for Defence Economics, University of York. The research for this chapter was funded by the ESRC as part of its Single European Market Programme (L113251028). Thanks are due to Dr S. Martin for his comments and assistance.
[1] Statement on the Defence Estimates, 1995 (London: HMSO, Cmnd 2800, 1995); Statement on the Defence Estimates, 1996 (London: HMSO, Cmnd 3223, 1996).

problem and the possible solutions. Answers to these questions will depend on whether a national, an EU or a NATO perspective is taken. Since a number of EU states are members of NATO, they might regard the creation of a Single European Market and a European defence industrial base as a precondition for the eventual formation of a NATO free trade area in defence equipment. A broad cost–benefit approach will be used to evaluate alternative policies and identify which groups are the likely winners and losers.

The chapter proceeds by outlining the economics of defence procurement and defence industries, followed by a specification of the policy problem. Alternative scenarios for creating a Single European Market for defence equipment and the various roles for a European Armaments Agency are assessed. The conclusion explores the possible development of a NATO free trade area for defence equipment.

2. THE ECONOMICS OF DEFENCE MARKETS

Defence markets have both demand and supply-sides. The demand side is dominated by government in its role as a purchaser of all the inputs of labour, capital, land and other resources and services needed for its armed forces. Some of these items are purchased from industries which might be specialist suppliers of defence equipment (for example, missiles, submarines or tanks) or which are suppliers of civil goods and services (for example, food and office equipment).[2]

2.1 Defence procurement

Government is central to understanding defence equipment markets. It is a major buyer (for some equipment, it is the only buyer) and regulator of the market. Governments purchase a variety of equipment, goods and services for their armed forces. Equipment purchases range from simple items such as motor cars, batteries and clothing to highly complex and high-technology items such as combat aircraft, missiles and nuclear-powered warships. These items might be purchased from state-owned or privately-owned firms. Within Europe state-owned defence companies characterise France, Greece, Italy and Spain; while privately-owned defence industries are characteristic of Germany, the UK and the US.

In defence procurement, government can use its buying power to determine all the major features of its national defence industries, namely, industry size, structure, ownership, location, conduct and performance. For example, disarmament following the end of the Cold War has resulted in major "downsizing" of defence industries in NATO and the former Warsaw Pact. Governments can promote or prevent entry and exit (for example, support for national champions); they can support or prevent

---

[2] K. Hartley and N. Hooper, *Study of the Value of the Defence Industry to the UK Economy* (DTI, London).

mergers; and they can influence the form of competition (that is, conduct reflected in price or non-price competition). The government can also use its buying and regulatory powers to determine industry performance reflected in technical progress (for example, via the performance requirements of weapons), exports (for example, via licences) and profitability (for example, via profit controls).[3]

2.2 Defence industries

A number of economic features are important for understanding defence industries:

2.2.1 *The importance of research and development*

The requirements of the armed forces for high-technology and high-performance equipment has resulted in high and increasing R&D costs. For example, the total development costs for the four-nation Eurofighter 2000 combat aircraft were estimated at almost £13 billion (1996–7 prices)[4] and development costs for the American F-22 combat aircraft were estimated at almost US$23 billion (1997 prices).[5] As a result, it is important to spread such total fixed costs over a large output.

2.2.2 *The importance of quantity*

Quantity is a determinant of average costs through the spreading of R&D costs and its impact on unit production costs. Greater output leads to economies of scale and learning and hence lower unit production costs. For example, learning economies in the aerospace industry result in a reduction of about 10 per cent in unit production costs for each doubling of cumulative output (for example, from 200 to 400 units).[6] There are also relationships between development and unit production costs. For example, the ratio of development to unit production costs is 100–200 for combat aircraft and 1,500–5,000 for missiles.[7]

2.2.3 *US competitiveness and domination*

Large American defence companies able to achieve economies of scale and scope are a major competitive threat to European and other countries defence industries. Following the end of the Cold War, there has been major

---

[3] S. Martin and K. Hartley, "Comparing Profitability in the Public Utilities, Defence and Pharmaceuticals" (1997) 17(1) *Journal of Public Policy* 81; and T. Sandler and K. Hartley, *The Economics of Defense* (Cambridge University Press, 1995).

[4] *Major Projects Report 1996* (National Audit Office, London: HMSO, House of Commons Paper 238, 1997).

[5] *A Look at Tomorrow's Air Forces* (Congressional Budget Office, Washington, DC: 1997).

[6] T. Sandler and K. Hartley, *The Economics of Defense* (Cambridge University Press, 1995), p. 124.

[7] D. Kirkpatrick, "The Rising Cost of Defence Procurement" (1995) 6(4) *Defence and Peace Economics* 263; P. Pugh, "The Procurement Nexus" (1993) 4(2) *Defence Economics* 179.

restructuring in the US defence industry resulting in a smaller number of larger firms, especially in the aerospace and electronics industries (for example, Boeing takeovers of Rockwell and McDonnell Douglas; and Lockheed Martin acquisitions of Loral and Northrop-Grumman). However, achieving efficient scale in world markets involves domestic monopoly in the US market with implications for higher prices and profits and reduced pressure to innovate.

2.2.4 *Defence industries as economically strategic industries*

In addition to their military-strategic significance, defence industries have the features of an economically strategic industry. Such industries are characterised by decreasing costs reflecting economies of scale and learning, high-technology reflected in major and costly R&D, together with technical spill-overs to the rest of the economy (for example, aerospace, electronics and nuclear). Typically, competition in these industries is imperfect based on national monopolies and oligopolies leading to monopoly profits. As a result, they are the focal point for government strategic trade policy whereby government support for these industries (for example, via subsidies or anti-competitive behaviour) is seen as a means of promoting technical spill-overs for the economy and of enabling a nation to obtain a share of monopoly profits in world markets.[8]

3. THE NEED FOR DIFFICULT CHOICES

Economic pressures from falling defence budgets and rising equipment costs means that defence policy-makers cannot avoid the need for some difficult choices. UK and US evidence suggests that, for a variety of equipment, cost growth has averaged about 10 per cent per annum in real terms, so that unit for unit, new military equipment costs far more than the old items which they replace.[9] As the unit costs of defence equipment rise faster than national defence budgets, smaller numbers of each type will be bought and new programmes will be funded less frequently: trends which have led some analysts to speculate about an eventual one-ship navy and a one-aircraft air force (Starship Enterprise).[10] These developments will affect the future size and range of forces which nations will be able to afford, with implications for equipment procurement policy and support for a domestic defence industrial base.

---

[8] K. Hartley, "National Defence Policy and the International Trade Order" in H. Siebert (ed.), *Towards a New Global Framework for High Technology Competition* (Tubingen; J. Mohr, 1997).

[9] D. Kirkpatrick,, "The Rising Unit Cost of Defence Procurement" 1995 6(4) *Defence and Peace Economics* 263; P. Pugh, "The Procurement Nexus" (1993) 4(2) *Defence Economics* 179.

[10] D. Kirkpatrick, "The Rising Unit Cost of Defence Procurement" 1995 6(4) *Defence and Peace Economics* 263.

Governments will be forced to review their traditional procurement policies: will they be willing to continue paying the price of independence through supporting a national defence industry, or are there significantly cheaper methods of obtaining defence equipment? There are alternatives to buying from domestic industry and these include importing foreign equipment or international collaboration where two or more nations agree to share both development and production costs and work. In each case, choices are required about the foreign supplier and the partner nations for collaboration (for example, Europe *versus* US). Often, when a nation buys foreign equipment it demands that some of the work be undertaken by its domestic industry. Work-sharing can take the form of an offset arrangement (industrial participation) where the foreign supplier offers to place some work in the buying nation; or work-share might take the form of the buying nation undertaking the licensed or co-production of the foreign equipment. International collaboration also involves work-sharing between the partner nations, but the members of the "club" determine the type of equipment to be developed. The work-sharing associated with the different procurement policies is often justified in terms of its support for the national defence industrial base, together with its industrial and wider economic benefits (for example, jobs and technology)[11]

Economists can contribute to the debate about alternative procurement and industrial policies by assessing the benefits and costs of the alternatives and by providing evidence on the magnitudes involved. Myths, emotion and special pleading in procurement choices need to be identified and critically evaluated, as well as identifying those who benefit, those who lose and those who pay. Table 3.1 presents a broad *illustrative* cost–benefit framework for evaluating projects and alternative industrial policies. Project evaluation requires reliable evidence on both costs and benefits. All too often, procurement choices are based on vague criteria and special pleading. For example, references are made to how *vital and important* equipment is for the forces, local industry and for the national economy; but vital to whom, at what cost and would the forces be willing to pay extra for such benefits? Similarly, policies which *appear* attractive often have their limitations. The fact that a national equipment project will support domestic jobs is not a convincing argument, since alternative public spending might well create more jobs than domestic defence procurement. Similarly, it has to be asked whether industrial and wider economic objectives are the proper concern of defence ministries or of other ministries (for example, employment or industry). A further example of the need for critical assessment in procurement choices arises with offsets. These appear attractive, but how much new business and new technology is involved; does the work benefit defence or civil industries; how many new jobs are created and how highly skilled are these jobs?[12]

---

[11] T. Sandler and K. Hartley, *The Economics of Defense* (Cambridge University Press, 1995), p. 124.
[12] S. Martin (ed.), *The Economics of Offsets* (Harwood, 1997).

Table 3.1 Policy Options: A Framework for Procurement Choices

POLICY OPTIONS	COST				BENEFITS								
	Acquisition price		Life cycle costs		Military/satrategic features					National economic benefits			
	Unit	Total fleet	Unit	Total fleet	Per-form-ance	Number	Delivery schedule	Defence Industrial Base	Others (eg NATO) Standard-isation	Jobs	Techno-logy	Balance of payments	Others
1. National project (independence)													
2. Collaborative project (two or more nations)													
3. Licensed or Co-production													
4. Imported equipment:													
i. Off-the-shelf													
ii. With offset													

4. A SINGLE EUROPEAN MARKET FOR DEFENCE EQUIPMENT

A search for efficiency improvements in procurement policy will lead EU nations to review the traditional support for their national defence industries. The inefficiencies of the existing fragmented and national defence markets and industries increases the attractiveness of creating a Single European Market for defence equipment. After all, the economic benefits of the single market for *civil* goods and services, namely, competition and scale effects, indicate that similar benefits are likely from extending the single market to embrace defence procurement.[13] Article 223 of the EC Treaty forms a barrier to extending the single market to defence procurement. This Article allows Member States to take any necessary action for the protection of the essential interests of its security which are connected with the production of, or trade in, arms, munitions and war material (for example, nuclear arms, combat aircraft, missiles and tanks). As a result, Member States can use their procurement policies to protect substantial parts of their domestic defence industrial base. The results are costly.

4.1 The problem: inefficiency in EU defence markets

Compared with the US, European nations have too many rival projects and short production runs reflecting the small scale of national procurement. The result is a duplication of costly R&D projects and a failure to obtain economies of both scale and learning (the costs of non-Europe in defence procurement). There is considerable duplication of industrial development and production facilities for combat aircraft, helicopters, missiles, tanks and warships. For example, EU nations are developing three different types of advanced combat aircraft and the aggregated production order for about 1,200 units will be spread over the three types. Sweden with the Gripen will order some 300 aircraft; France with the Rafale requires about 300 aircraft; and for the four-nation Eurofighter 2000, Germany, Italy, Spain and the UK require a total of some 600 aircraft. Total development costs for Eurofighter 2000 are estimated at almost £13 billion (1997 prices).[14] If the six nations could agree on one type of aircraft, there would be savings in R&D costs and an order for 1,200 units of one type would lead to reductions in unit production costs of 10–20 per cent. In contrast, over the period 2005–2030, the US plans to buy about 3,000 units of its new Joint Strike Fighter for the Air Force, Navy and Marine Corps (that is, a combined order from three services) with development costs estimated at US$22 billion and flyaway costs at almost US$50 million per aircraft (1997 prices).[15]

The economic benefits from creating a Single European Market in defence equipment are expected to result from *increased competition* both within and

---

[13] K. Hartley, "The Single Market" in P. Barbour (ed.), *The European Union Handbook* (Fitzroy Dearborn, 1996).

[14] *Major Projects Report 1996* (National Audit Office, London: HMSO, House of Commons Paper 238, 1997).

[15] *A Look at Tomorrow's Air Forces* (Congressional Budget Office, Washington, DC: 1997).

between nations, from *savings in R&D costs* (through less duplication of costly R&D projects) and from *economies of scale and learning* due to longer production runs. There might also be additional *dynamic benefits* from innovations due to competition and the creation of the single market. However, dynamic benefits are difficult to measure and give rise to the possibility of "double-counting" the impacts of competition. One solution is to recognise that if dynamic benefits exist they are a "bonus" to be added to the estimated benefits of competition and greater scale. Nor can it be assumed that a single market will lead to the end of all duplication of costly R&D programmes. Some duplication might be required to maintain competition in the development stage and avoid the costs of monopoly.

4.2 The scenarios

There are opportunities for improving the current inefficient arrangements for defence procurement in non-Europe. Economists can contribute to policy formulation by estimating the benefits and costs of various methods of creating a single market for defence equipment. Four scenarios for a single market are analysed, each with a possible role for a European Armaments Agency. The scenarios were based on a study undertaken for the European Commission with the scenarios specified by the Commission.[16] For each scenario, there was assumed to be a non-discriminating liberalised competitive market either restricted to Member States or open to the world. This assumption requires the national or centralised purchasing agency to act as a non-discriminating competitive buyer. The four scenarios are (see Table 3.2).

(i)   Scenario one comprised a liberalised competitive market with national procurement by national defence ministries and agencies. If the market were restricted to EU Member States, firms in each state would be able to bid for defence contracts in other Member States. Alternatively, if the market were open to the world, firms in countries outside the EU would be allowed to bid for defence contracts in EU states. Under this scenario, a European Armaments Agency would act as a competition agency ensuring that Member States abided by the procurement rules for the opening up of their national defence markets.

(ii) Scenario two comprised an EU centralised procurement agency buying standardised equipment with the agency replacing national defence ministries. A European Armaments Agency would have a major role in this scenario and it would be expected to achieve significant savings from competitive purchasing, from less duplication of R&D and from large-scale production orders. Effectively, this scenario assumed a single EU army, navy and air force similar

[16] K. Hartley and A. Cox, *The Cost of Non-Europe in Defence Procurement* (EC DG III, Brussels, unpublished, July 1992).

to the US model: hence, economically this is the most attractive option but the most challenging politically.

(iii) Scenario three involved limited liberalisation. This was a modified version of scenario one under which certain equipments were excluded, namely, nuclear systems, anti-toxic radio-active agents and cryptography. As in scenario one, a European Armaments Agency would act as a competition agency promoting competition and policing the restrictions.

(iv) Scenario four was the twin-track model. This involved competition for small and medium-sized projects (for example, small arms such as rifles and ammunition, artillery and small missiles) with large projects undertaken on a collaborative basis and collaboration extended to major air, land and sea systems (for example, aircraft, missiles, tanks and warships). Two assumptions were applied to collaborative projects, namely, work allocated on the traditional basis of *juste retour* and work awarded on the basis of competition. Under this scenario, a European Armaments Agency would have responsibility for ensuring competition for small to medium-scale projects and for developing and managing collaborative programmes.

The four scenarios can be ranked in terms of their expected cost savings. Scenario two is expected to offer the greatest cost savings, followed in order by scenarios four, one and three. There are overlaps between some of the scenarios. For example, scenario one might involve elements of scenarios two and four. This could arise where two or more nations voluntarily agree to buy the same equipment (standardisation) either on a collaborative basis or from a foreign supplier. An example occurred in 1975 when four European nations reached a co-production agreement for the purchase of US F-16 aircraft: hence, standardisation does not require centralised procurement.

Similarly, the scenarios could be modified. Scenario two, for example, might involve the creation of a centralised purchasing agency (a European Armaments Agency) which would not replace national defence ministries, which would not impose standardisation and which would operate on a voluntary basis. Such an agency would obtain economies from the use of its large-scale ordering and buying power. It would assemble national orders for equipment, parts and components and invite firms to bid for large orders and long-term contracts (for example, national orders for different types of tank track could be offered as one large order over, say, a ten-year period). The agency might also obtain cost savings by aggregating different national orders for the same equipment or components and by identifying products where standardisation might be worthwhile (that is, by acting as an information and education agency).

4.3 Estimating the benefits

Estimating the benefits of the four scenarios involved two approaches. First, a case study approach based on the estimated cost savings from reduced duplication in R&D and from longer production runs for specific weapons. For example, increasing the output of a combat aircraft with a unit production cost of ECU50 million from 250 to 1,000 units might reduce unit costs by 20 per cent to ECU40 million. This assumes the production of 1,000 units of an identical type of aircraft with no modifications. Such examples provide persuasive illustrations of the cost savings from equipment standardisation.

Secondly, the different scenarios are expected to lead to cost and price savings reflecting the impact of both competition and economies of scale from larger orders. Greater competition from within the EU or from the rest of the world results in alternative estimates of the *competition effect*; while longer production runs lead to lower unit costs and prices which provide estimates of the *scale effect*. It is assumed that cost savings are reflected in lower prices. The lack of publicly available data required a company interview study to estimate competition and scale effects. The competition effect was estimated at 10–20 per cent for the EU-wide market and 15–25 per cent for the EU market open to the world. Similarly, the scale effect was estimated at a 12 per cent unit cost reduction for a doubling of output (alternative estimates were used as sensitivity tests). These estimates of competition and scale effects were applied to the EU's total spending on defence equipment and procurement, so indicating the likely magnitude of the aggregate savings from the various scenarios. There are also possible dynamic benefits which would increase the estimated savings.

The estimated cost savings from the various Single European Market scenarios are summarised in Table 3.2. With all the difficulties and uncertainties involved in this estimation procedure, the reported figures are lower bound estimates and should be regarded as broad orders of magnitude. The estimated budget savings are based on 1990 defence procurement budgets. Disarmament following the end of the Cold War has

Table 3.2 Benefits of a single market

Scenarios	Annual savings in ECU billion (1990)	Percentage of annual defence procurement
Liberalised market	5.5 to 7.0	8.5 to 11.0 per cent
Centralised procurement	9.4 to 10.9	14.5 to 17.0 per cent
Limited liberalisation	5.3 to 6.6	8.0 to 10.0 per cent
Twin-track: version A	6.5 to 7.6	10.0 to 12.0 per cent
Twin-track: version B	7.4 to 9.3	11.0 to 14.0 per cent

Notes:
(i)   Figures are for annual savings based on 1990 defence procurement budgets of ECU65 billion. Alternative estimates resulted in lower equipment spending figures (i.e. based on Article 223 items and NATO definitions). The original study was based on the EC and the budget savings are for EC Member States in 1990.
(ii) Twin-track A assumes collaboration based on *juste retour*; version B assumes collabortion based on competition for work-sharing.
Source: K. Hartley and A. Cox, *The Cost of Non-Europe in Defence Procurement* (EC DG-III, Brussels, unpublished, July 1992); and House of Commons Paper 333 (1995), p. 100.

resulted in lower equipment budgets, but the estimates of the percentage competition and scale effects remain unchanged. In fact, budget cuts will increase the intensity of competition in the short to medium term, so that the percentage competition effect is likely to be higher than the lower bound estimates used in the study.

Table 3.2 shows that all the scenarios for a single market offer substantial cost savings. Centralised procurement (scenario two) offers the greatest annual savings, reflecting the economies of scale and learning from the large-scale purchase of common and standardised equipment.

4.4 The costs of a single market

Creating a single market for defence equipment involves costs as well as benefits. Typically, the costs will be incurred in the short to medium term and the benefits will arise over the longer term. For such a change to be socially desirable, the benefits have to exceed the costs. The costs of change will be reflected in job losses, plant closures and exits from the defence market; and these costs will be additional to those resulting from disarmament following the end of the Cold War. The most vulnerable sectors include firms in developing defence industries; firms which have not been exposed to competition; and the smaller companies, although some of these might survive through specialisation (for example, in niche markets). It is also likely that the opening up of the EU market, especially to the rest of the world, will shock some firms into improving their efficiency and hence their chances of survival.

However, some problems remain. Difficulties will arise in creating a level playing field, especially where there is competition between state and privately owned firms. Mergers will result in a smaller number of larger defence contractors and the possibility of cartels, collusive tendering and monopoly within the EU. As a result, to maintain competition in the EU defence market will require that the market be opened up to firms from the rest of the world. Effectively, this means US competition with implications for maintaining the EU defence industrial base. However, it has to be recognised that a European defence industrial base does not yet exist; but its creation could be one of the tasks for a European Armaments Agency.

4.5 A European Armaments Agency?

While a comprehensive European Armaments Agency involving all EU Member States remains to be created, a possible start has been made with the formation of the four-nation Organisation for Joint Armaments Co-operation (OCCAR). This Organisation will focus on achieving a more efficient, effective approach to the management of collaborative programmes: this is an area where there is considerable potential for efficiency improvements.

European collaborative programmes have been characterised by *juste retour* where work is allocated on the basis of equity, bargaining and fair shares and not on the basis of efficiency criteria (that is, competition and comparative advantage). The result has been cost penalties and the belief that collaboration takes longer than similar national projects.[17] For example, the cost increases and delays on the collaborative Eurofighter 2000 project partly reflected the rigid work-sharing arrangements and the requirement to provide a "balanced spread of technology" between the partner nations.[18] The Flight Control System (FCS) for the EF 2000 is a classic example of all the worst features of collaborative work-sharing and a major source of programme delays. One view was that the industrial work-sharing arrangements for the FCS had all the characteristics of an "accident waiting to happen. Even though British companies ... had demonstrated their competence to carry out the work, other companies became involved who were either not up to the job or whose involvement made arrangements unduly cumbersome."[19] GEC-Marconi estimated that a solo bid for the work would have been one-third cheaper than the consortium bid.

Nor are partner governments in collaborative programmes models of efficient decision-making. Governments and their civil servants create elaborate and complex committee structures which seek consensus at every level and require unanimity for major decisions (there is no majority voting based on each nation's financial commitment to the project). Further complications arise from extensive monitoring arrangements as partner nations seek to police progress and costs on projects which, because of their complexity, are inevitably associated with incomplete contracts. On the EF 2000 project there is a four-level hierarchy of committees (originally 39 committees were established), with a steering committee providing overall guidance and meetings attended by national officials and other interested parties. Up to 60 people might be present at a meeting and in 1994, there were over 500 meetings.[20] The result of government programme management is excessive bureaucracy and slow decision-making which is a further source of delays and inefficiency in collaboration.

Efficiency on collaborative programmes can be improved by applying three policy rules. First, abandon *juste retour* and allocate work on the basis of competition. Secondly, select a prime contractor with total responsibility for the programme and ensure that the prime contractor is subject to an incentive contract placing it at risk. Thirdly, introduce adequate compensation for those firms, workers and regions which are likely to lose from efficiency improvements in collaborative programmes (for example, via manpower policies for training and mobility). The UK supports the introduction of some of these principles for the new Organisation for Joint Armaments Co-operation. There are, however, alternative pressures for a "Fortress Europe" policy with all the worst features of protectionism resulting in the absence of competition, subsidies and inefficiency.

---

[17] S.T. Sandler and K. Hartley, *The Economics of Defense* (Cambridge University Press, 1995).

[18] *Ministry of Defence: Eurofighter 2000* (National Audit Office, London: HMSO, House of Commons Paper 724, 1995).

[19] *Progress on Eurofighter 2000 Programme* (Defence Committee, House of Commons, London: HMSO, House of Commons Paper 222, 1994).

[20] *Ministry of Defence: Eurofighter 2000* (National Audit Office, London: HMSO, House of Commons Paper 724, 1995).

5. A NATO FREE TRADE AREA?

A Single European Market for defence equipment might be viewed by European nations as a precondition for the eventual creation of a NATO free trade area. The scenarios for such a NATO free trade area could be similar to those outlined in Table 3.2, but with higher estimated cost savings than if the single market were restricted to EU Member States. A NATO Armaments Agency could be created with the task of promoting both competition and collaboration. Such an agency would be responsible for ensuring free entry into all member nation's markets, for monitoring government contract decisions, for policing cartels and collusive tendering and for preventing governments behaving anti-competitively (that is, favouring their national champions).

A NATO free market will involve both winners and losers. Potential gainers will be US firms which will have open access to all NATO EU markets: such firms are likely to benefit in high-technology equipment and where there are significant economies of scale and learning. However, NATO EU firms will benefit from access to the US market and they are likely to gain from small-volume equipment and in specialist (niche) markets. Potential losers will be those NATO EU firms which fail to restructure to match the size of US contractors and those European firms which have operated in protected markets with no experience of competition. On the other hand, the EU nations can offset their possible losses by combining their orders to create a major buying power to counteract the monopoly power of large US firms (countervailing power).

There is a possible alternative to a NATO free market, namely, managed competition. Such a solution would comprise some limited competition (workable competition) and fair work-shares so that no nation's defence industries are required to make major adjustments due to the competitive shocks of a free market. Once again, managed competition and fair work-shares would be organised by a NATO Armaments Agency. While such a solution is politically attractive to governments and their defence industries, there would be a price to pay in the form of cost penalties and delays from limited competition and work-sharing.

6. CONCLUSION

Within the EU, independence through supporting a domestic defence industrial base is costly. Each Member State's support for its national defence industry has resulted in the duplication of costly R&D programmes and relatively short production runs, reflecting small national orders. Non-Europe in defence procurement is costly and a single market offers opportunities for achieving significant cost savings. Questions have to be asked about non-Europe: who is maximising what for the benefit of whom?

4. National Models for the Regulation of the Acquisition of Armaments: Towards a European Defence Procurement Code?

*Martin Trybus**

1. INTRODUCTION

Nearly all European countries support their own national armed forces and even the relatively small Grand Duchy of Luxembourg has an army of about 600. These forces need standard services and supplies, works and, above all, expensive armaments. In 1993–4 the United Kingdom expenditure on defence equipment, for example, was estimated to be £9.4 billion,[1] thereby supporting about 300,000 jobs.[2] The defence industries employ approximately 1 per cent of the workforce in most European countries.[3] Thus defence procurement is a significant part of public procurement.

Defence spending can be separated into two categories. The first category consists of the standard supplies and services bought by all public authorities, in the United Kingdom about 7 to 8 per cent of expenditure.[4] The second category, armaments, is the more important, not only because of its economic share but also for its high-technology nature. This high-technology aspect makes defence procurement particularly interesting for a Europe-wide public procurement regime.

Procurement of armaments is characterised by high prices, long procurement cycles involving expensive and time-intensive research and

---

* *Rechtsreferendar am Oberlandesgericht Hamm.* The author wishes to thank Professor Sue Arrowsmith for comments on this chapter.
[1] Statement of the Defence Estimates (London: HMSO, Cmd 2550, 1994), p. 53.
[2] Ministry of Defence, *Frontline First – Defence Costs Study* (London: HMSO, 1994), p. 29, paragraph 412.
[3] According to a recent Communication of the Commission, "The Challenges Facing the European Defence-Related Industry: A Contribution for Action at European Level" COM (96) 10 final, the annual output of the European defence industries is worth ECU5 billion, or 2–3 per cent of Europe's total industrial output. Job losses were about 37 per cent (from 1.6m to 1m) between 1984 and 1992.
[4] *Britain's Defence Procurement* (MoD, Chief of Information, Defence Public Relations (E & P), July 1993).

development, a highly politicised procurement process and national security considerations. The most important recent development in defence procurement, not only in Europe, is the decline of defence expenditure.[5]

Within the European Union civil procurement is regulated on the European level by the European Community directives on public works, supplies and services and on utilities,[6] and on the international level by the Government Procurement Agreement of the World Trade Organisation (GPA) and also a number of bilateral agreements. The procurement of military equipment, such as tanks, missiles and fighter aircraft, is, however, excluded from the application of these regimes. For Europe, as explained in chapter 3 by Professor Keith Hartley, the establishment of a common procurement regime for military materials is a particularly pressing issue in an environment of decreasing defence budgets and increasing unit costs. National defence markets are too small to produce economies of scale and to remain competitive. At present the European situation is characterised by widespread discrimination and low levels of market penetration of equipment from other European countries.

Chapter 3 considered the options for developing a European single market in armaments.[7] Such a market may involve a centralised agency or, alternatively, work on the basis of separate national procurement authorities. Whatever the approach, a common market will need common procurement rules. The main aim of this chapter is to consider what the nature and content of such common procurement rules might be.

Section 2 of this chapter is concerned with the current state of the regulation of defence procurement within the European Union. It will explain that little has been achieved so far, and will consider what developments are likely in the future. Section 3 deals with the approach to the regulation of defence procurement that is found in national systems of the economically and militarily most important European countries, France, Germany and the United Kingdom. Clearly, their existing systems are likely to have an important influence on the development of a common European regime. This section will consider which of these national systems, offering essentially three different models, is most suitable for such a common European regime. The fourth and final section will outline some brief recommendations for the contents of a possible European Defence Procurement Code.

---

[5] W. Walker and S. Willett, "Restructuring the European Defence Industrial Base" (1993) *Journal of Defence Economics* 141 at 143; and T. Taylor, "West European Defence Industrial Issues for the 1990s" (1993) *Journal of Defence Economics* 113 at 114. For the United Kingdom, for example, there has been a decline from £25.437 million (1990–1) to 21.307m (1994–5) according to GSS, *UK Defence Statistics* (London: HMSO, 1994).

[6] Works Contracts Directive 93/37/EEC, OJ 1993, No. L199/54; Supply Contracts Directive 93/36/EEC, OJ 1993, No. L199/1; Services Contracts Directive 92/50/EEC, OJ 1992, No. L209/1; Public Sector Remedies Directive 89/665/EEC, OJ 1989, No. L395/33; Utilities Directive 93/38/EEC, OJ 1993, No. L199/84; and the Utilities Remedies Directive 92/13/EEC, OJ 1992, No. L76/14.

[7] Chapter 3 of this book.

2. THE CURRENT STATE OF EUROPEAN DEFENCE PROCUREMENT REGULATION

The European Commission has a very weak position in the area of defence procurement.[8] For hard defence material such as tanks, missiles or fighter aircraft, the Commission has no jurisdiction, as hard defence equipment is explicitly excluded from the common market according to Article 296(1)(b) of the EC Treaty. In 1958, as is provided by Article 296(2) of the EC Treaty, the Council drew up a list of products to which the provision of Article 296 of the EC Treaty applies. This list has never been officially published although it is part of the public domain. In 1978 new interpretations to the list of 1958 were issued to take technical progress into account, but there have been no alterations since then. Thus there is no single market for hard defence equipment within the EU and the national governments have total control over this market.

Soft defence material or dual-use material which can be used for both civil and military purposes, such as cross-country vehicles, transport ships or tents, is subject to the normal civil procurement rules as Article 296 of the EC Treaty is not applicable. This material can, however, be subject to the national security derogations of the EC Treaty, such as Article 30, 39 or 46 of the EC Treaty, or of the civil directives themselves.[9] It was held by the ECJ in *Richardt*[10] that the Treaty derogations cover internal and external security and in *Campus Oil*[11] that they allow the security objectives contained in them to be implemented by economic means. This allows governments to award contracts strategically to protect a national industrial capability for defence purposes for both hard defence material and dual-use materials. If these derogations do not apply, this material is subject to the open market in the usual way, including possible enforcement through the Commission.

So far within the EU nothing has been achieved by way of liberalisation of hard defence procurement.[12] However, there have been many proposals to change that, especially from the European Parliament,[13] and above all involving the deletion of Article 296 of the EC Treaty;[14] and in a recent

---

[8] T. Stormanns, "Europe's Defence Industry – Single Market, Yes – But How?" (1992) *EC Public Contract Law* 74; D. Lasok, *The Law of the Economy in the European Communities* (Butterworths, 1990), p. 73.

[9] Article 4(b) of the Works Directive 93/37/EEC; Article 2(1)(b) of the Supplies Directive 93/36/EEC; Article 4(2) of the Services Directive 92/50/EEC; and Article 10 of the Utilities Directive 93/38/EEC. For an analysis, see S. Arrowsmith, *The Law of Public and Utilities Procurement* (Sweet & Maxwell, 1996), chapter 17.

[10] Case C-367/89, *Ministre des Finances v. Richardt* [1992] 1 CMLR 61.

[11] Case 72/83, *Commission v. Ireland* [1994] ECR 2727.

[12] T. Stormanns, Europe's Defence Industry – Single Market, Yes – But How?" (1992) *EC Public Contract Law* 74 at 74–5.

[13] See the Klepsch Report, E. Klepsch, *European Armaments Procurement Co-operation* (Luxembourg: EC Document 3/78, 1978); Greenwood Report, D. Greenwood, *European Technological Co-operation and Defence Procurement* (Brussels: EC, 1979); Tindemanns Report, L. Tindemanns in J.D. Drown *et al.*, *A Single European Arms Industry? European Defence Industries in the 1990s* (London, 1990), pp. 77–8; and the Maastricht Treaty Declaration on Defence, taken from the Treaty on European Union Provisions on a Common Foreign Policy – Annex (1990), p. 77.

[14] EU Commissioner Sir Leon Brittan QC, speech on 30 October 1991.

Communication the European Commission suggested that the liberalisation of the market ought still to be pursued in the future through the framework of the EU.[15]

While the EU has not yet taken any firm measures in this area, procurement of hard defence material is, however, subject to some regulation within the Western European Union (WEU), a regional international organisation formed of the European Member States of the North Atlantic Treaty Organisation (NATO) and Turkey. The defence ministers of these states agreed in 1976 to create the Independent European Programme Group (IEPG), in 1992 renamed the Western European Armaments Group (WEAG), with a small secretariat in Brussels. They also agreed in 1988 on the creation of a European Defence Equipment Market (EDEM) to achieve harmonisation of defence procurement procedures, the main principles of which are set out in a Common Policy Document (CPD) of 1990.[16] In November 1996 the ministers created the Western European Armaments Organisation (WEAO) with its own charter as a subsidiary body of the WEU, but only to supervise common research and development projects.[17]

In relation to the harmonisation of defence procurement, the ministers agreed to open up all development, procurement and maintenance contracts for hard defence material with a value over ECU1 million according to paragraph 7 of the CPD. It was agreed that they would publish tenders in other European countries through national bulletins, according to paragraph 8 of the CPD. Contracts covered include all hard defence material apart from material such as nuclear missiles, ship hulls, and toxic and radioactive substances listed in paragraph 7 of the CPD. Contracts must be awarded to the bid representing the most economic solution, meaning either the lowest or the most advantageous tender.[18]

However, the principle of open competition is, in theory, qualified by the principle of *juste retour*. This provides that a participating nation can expect an equitable industrial return in proportion to the extent of its own purchasing in the market and that measures should be taken to correct unacceptable imbalances as stipulated in paragraph 13 of the CPD.[19] The

---

[15] "The Challenges Facing the European Defence-Related Industry" Communication COM (96) 10 final, 13 February 1996 (Brussels: 1996); see the press release of the European Commission, 25 January 1996, IP/96/77 and for reactions B. Tigner, "EU Official Call for End to National Industry Preference" *Defence News*, 29 January–4 February 1996, p. 10; and M. Trybus, "The Challenges Facing the European Defence-Related Industry – COM (96) 08 of the Commission" (1996) 5 *Public Procurement Law Review* CS99. On the reaction of the defence industries, see M. Rogers, "EU Group Moves Ahead on Common Arms Policy" *Jane's Defence Weekly* 3 July 1996, p. 3; *The European Defence Industries' Views on the Communication from the Commission on the Establishment of a European Defence Domestic Market* (Brussels: European Defence Industries Group (EDIG), 24 April 1996).

[16] WEU Council of Ministers, 1990 Policy Document (CPD) attached to the Copenhagen Communiqué, 16 November 1990 (unpublished).

[17] See WEU Council of Ministers, Ostend Declaration, 19 November 1996, p. 9, point 33 (unpublished).

[18] Brussels: WEAG publication, 1996, looseleaf.

[19] On the political importance of this principle, see WEAG publication, 1996; WEU Council of Ministers, Copenhagen Communiqué, 16 November 1990 (unpublished), p. 2; and WEU Council of Ministers, Oslo Communiqué, 6 March 1992 (unpublished), p. 3.

support for the so-called DDI (developing defence industry) countries[20] is the most important special case of *juste retour*.[21] Apart from these requirements the participating nations continue to apply their existing national rules on defence procurement.

In contrast to the civil procurement regime of the Community, the regime of EDEM does not require the participating nations to provide for legal redress for contractors for violations of the rules, although there is an informal complaints system. This is all that has been achieved so far. EDEM suffers from a lack of detail and depth, fails to address the main problems of a functional procurement regime including enforcement, and does not commit the participating nations to any enforceable legal structure. In practice it is widely considered a failure because it is not followed seriously.

In February 1997 the defence ministers of France, Germany, Italy and the United Kingdom signed an agreement to establish the Organisation for Joint Armaments Co-operation (OCCAR), and Belgium, the Netherlands and Norway have expressed their interest in joining the new structure. The legal status of OCCAR will not be decided before 1998. It might become a part of the WEAG as a subsidiary body of the WEU, a part of the WEAO, a separate international governmental organisation or an organisation integrated into the second pillar of the Treaty on European Union (TEU). The "founding structure" is based in Bonn. The primary objective of the organisation is the management of joint armament programmes, but work on procurement rules will follow. OCCAR is currently preoccupied with establishing its administrative functions and with defining its precise objectives. It is still too early to ascertain the precise legal nature or any other details of the common procurement rules that may be implemented through the yet developing structures of OCCAR.

The participating nations have established a set of five principles that have to be accepted by any new members as *acquis communautaire*. These principles are:

(i)   the priority of lowering the costs of defence and increasing efficiency in the participating nations;

(ii) the long-term harmonisation of standards and requirements including a common policy in the field of technology;

(iii) the preservation of a competitive European defence industrial base;

(iv) the abolition of *juste retour*; and

(v)   openness of the organisation to other participating nations of the WEAG, provided these states accept the five principles and intend a real participation in the structure.[22]

---

[20] Countries with a developing defence industry such as Portugal or Greece.

[21] On the political importance of this aspect see WEAG publication, 1996, WEU Council of Ministers, Copenhagen Communiqué, pp. 2 and 3 and attachment (CPD and EUCLID paper); WEU Council of Ministers, Brussels Communiqué, 3 July 1991 (unpublished), p. 2; WEU Council of Ministers, Oslo Communiqué, p. 3; Vredeling Report, *Towards a Stronger Europe*, points 17 and 64 to 68.

[22] Information given by Marc Prévôt, Director of OCCAR, Bonn, 9 April 1997.

It needs to be stressed, however, that these principles lack any legal quality so far. Decisive developments can be expected during the next couple of years.

3. NATIONAL INFLUENCES ON THE REGULATION OF DEFENCE PROCUREMENT

At present, the development of a common defence procurement regime for Europe is still in its infancy. Whatever system is adopted is likely to be influenced to a large extent by the current regimes applied by the major European defence powers, and it is thus appropriate to consider the main features of these existing national systems. Since France, Germany and the United Kingdom account for 90 per cent of the defence industries[23] in Europe and are also the main military powers the following explanations will concentrate on these countries.

3.1 France: defence procurement on a regulated basis

France follows a regulated approach to defence procurement. This means that the procurement process is based on an enforceable legal framework similar to the regime for civil goods embodied in the EC procurement directives, which were themselves mainly influenced by this traditional French approach. The law relevant to defence procurement is part of the French administrative law.

This law can be divided into five main categories:[24]

(i)   the Government Procurement Code *Code des Marchés Publics* (CMP)[25] that provides the basic rules that have to be respected by all public authorities;

(ii) the Government Directives on Prices[26] representing a major part of the relevant pricing law;

(iii) the Books of General Administrative Clauses;[27]

(iv) the Books of Auditing Clauses;[28] and

(v)   the General Clauses (DGA)[29] in particular dealing with the matter of quality assurance of the contracts of the French defence procurement agency.

---

[23] K. Hartley and A. Cox, *The Costs of Non-Europe in Defence Procurement-Executive Summary* (study carried out for the Commission of the European Communities, DG III, July 1992, released December 1994).

[24] According to a document of the DGA, *Les Achats de la Défence en France* (DGA, 1995) kindly forwarded to the author by Mr L. Barthélemy of the French embassy in London, p. 8.

[25] *Official Journal*, édition mise à jour en 21 février 1996.

[26] *Directives Gouvernementales sur les Prix.*

[27] *Cahiers des Clauses Administratives* (CCA G).

[28] *Cahiers des Clauses Comptables.*

[29] *Clauses Générales "DGA"* (the DGA is the *Délégation Générale pour l'Armement*, the French defence procurement authority).

The main legal framework is the CMP, which applies to *all* public procurement including hard defence material and contracts below the thresholds of the EC directives. This is divided systematically into five books. The books of the CMP relevant to defence procurement are Book 1 on general provisions and Book 2. The award procedures to be followed are listed in Article 83 of the CMP.[30] These procedures are the allocation procedure, the competitive bidding procedure and private negotiation.

Articles 84 to 92 of the CMP provide for the allocation procedure.[31] There are two different kinds of allocation procedure: the open allocation procedure[32] according to Articles 85 to 90 of the CMP and the restricted allocation procedure[33] according to Articles 90 and 91 of the CMP. Under the allocation procedures contracts are awarded according to the prescribed procedures after a public announcement accessible to an unlimited number of companies.

There are two different kinds of competitive bidding[34] procedures provided for in Articles 93 to 100 of the CMP: the open competitive bidding procedure[35] in Articles 94 to 95*ter* of the CMP; and the restricted competitive bidding procedure[36] in Articles 96 to 97*quater* of the CMP. Public authorities have a free choice between the allocation and competitive bidding procedures.[37] The main characteristics of the item to be procured must be set at the beginning and published.[38] In the open competitive bidding procedure any contractor may submit a bid after a call for tender[39] by the contracting authority in question.[40] In the restricted competitive bidding procedure the contracting authority publishes the call for tender prior to creating a list of candidates that are eligible to submit a bid[41] so that the actual solicitations are preceded by the initial screening of candidates.

Article 103 of the CMP provides for the private negotiation procedure[42] which is allowed only in specified circumstances as listed in Article 104 of the CMP. This limitation of private negotiation to specified circumstances can also be found in the European Community directives and, of course, in most other procurement systems, and is necessary to ensure competition

---

[30] As amended by Decree No. 92-1310 of 15 December 1992 (Article 42), *Official Journal*, 18 décembre 1992, p. 17326; for an overview of French procurement law see, C. Goldman, "An Introduction to the French Law of Government Contracts" (1987) 20 *George Washington Journal of International Law and Economics* 461.

[31] *Adjudication.*

[32] *Adjudication ouverte.*

[33] *Allocation restreinte.*

[34] *Appel d'offres.*

[35] *Appel d'offres ouvert.*

[36] *Appel d'offres restreinte.*

[37] Instruction of 29 December 1972, reprinted in *Instruction pour l'Application du Code des Marchés Publiques* (Livres I et II) (*Official Journal* No. 2000, 1985), p. 80.

[38] Article 38 II(2) of the CMP.

[39] *Appel public de candidature.*

[40] Article 93(2) of the CMP.

[41] Articles 96(1) and 97(1) of the CMP.

[42] *Marchés négociés.*

and transparency in the award of contracts wherever possible. As the CMP is applicable to military procurement, it contains grounds for using private negotiation procedures that are specifically designed for the military sector, as well as the kind of grounds also to be found in other systems such as extreme urgency or absence of any tenders in a previous tendering procedure. In this respect, Article 104(1) point 1(a) of the CMP allows the negotiated procedure in times of mobilisation and Article 104(1) point 6(b) of the CMP to protect predetermined national defence industrial capabilities. Using this procedure the person responsible for the contract may enter freely into any contract with the company of its own choice.[43] There are two variations of the private negotiated procedure which are possible: one with a prior call for tender, which means that there will be some competition for the contract, and one which does not involve any prior call for tender.

For the allocation procedure the lowest-price argument is the only criterion allowed for the evaluation of bids.[44] For the open competitive bidding procedure and the restricted competitive bidding procedure the criteria are stipulated in Article 95II(2) of the CMP. The basic principle is the selection of the most advantageous bid, in particular taking into account especially price, utility, technical merit and the time limits to execute the contract.[45] Other criteria have to be specified in the tender documents.[46] It is always prohibited to include criteria that are not justified by the nature of the contract or its conditions of deliverance. For the private negotiated procedure the CMP does not provide for any fixed award criteria. Information to be given to unsuccessful and successful bidders is regulated (or not regulated) according to the special procedure used by the public authority.

As far as the implications of the French enforcement system for a common European enforcement system for defence contracts are concerned, it can be said that, due to the well-developed nature of the system, it could have a strong impact on a future common regime.

It is also notable that the stringent enforcement system set up in France applies, in theory, to the military sector as well as the civil sector. This system provides for summary proceedings under Articles L22 and L23 of the Code of Administrative Tribunals and Appellate Administrative Courts.[47] These provisions enable any person who can demonstrate that he or she has been harmed or risks being harmed by an infringement of the legislation on public procurement rules to take action before the contract is awarded in order to obtain rapidly (usually within 20 days) from a single judge, a ruling on temporary or substantive measures against that award

---

[43] Article 103 of the CMP.
[44] Articles 84 and 89 of the CMP.
[45] Article 95II(2) of the CMP.
[46] Article 95II(3) of the CMP.
[47] *Code des Tribunaux Administratifs et des Cours Administratifs d'Appel* (CTA–CAA), translation by P. Martin, "New Developments in Public Procurement in France" (1995) 4 *Public Procurement Law Review* CS53–4.

procedure.[48] In order to speed up the proceedings, no appeal is provided.[49] These rapid procedures were introduced in order to implement the requirements of EC law, which requires certain minimum remedies to be given in national courts for enforcing the European procurement rules, and there is already a considerable body of case law concerning their application.[50] The Act on Preventive Measures Against Corruption 1993[51] later extended the scope of the remedy to cover enforcement of *all* national French rules on advertising and open competition in public procurement[52] including, for example, rules on the choice or the operation of the tendering procedure as well as the European rules for which it was originally introduced.[53] Thus it appears that this remedy can be used against unlawful award procedures concerning defence contracts, although a case has yet to be brought in the defence sector.

Another remedy that can be awarded by judges under French law is damages. This power has long been recognised in French law[54] and is the main remedy available after the contract is signed since, because of the principle of the stability of contracts, it is not possible to annul the contract afterwards,[55] especially in public law.[56] Defence contracts are normally

---

[48] See on these proceedings, S. Ponsot, "Public Procurement in France: Transposition of the Remedies Directive" (1996) 5 *Public Procurement Law Review* 29; P. Martin, "France – The Contractual 'Référé' Procedure under Article L22 of the Administrative Tribunals and Administrative Court of Appeal Code: Application in Practice" (1994) 3 *Public Procurement Law Review* CS112; P. Gouzinet, La Loi No. 92-12 du 4 janvier 1992: les nouveaux pouvoirs du juge en matière de passation des marchés" (1992) *Revue Marchés Publics*, No. 269, 45; R. Vandermeeren, "Le référé administratif précontractuel" (1994) AJPI, special issue, July, 91; M. Roncière, "L'article 22 du Code des tribunaux administratifs et des cours d'appels administratives: innovation et interrogation" (1994) LPA, 12 August, 7 *et seq.*; S. Lasvignes, "L'entendue des pouvoirs du juge en matière de référé précontractuel" (1994) *Revue Française du Droit Administratif* 741; R. Chapus, *Droit Contentieux Administratif* (Editions Montchrétien, 1994), No. 1134 *et seq.*; and P. Valadou, "Enforcing the Public Procurement Rules in France" in S. Arrowsmith (ed.), *Remedies for Enforcing the Public Procurement Rules, Public Procurement in the European Community* (Earlsgate Press, 1993), vol. IV, p. 327 at p. 334.

[49] P. Valdou, "Enforcing the Public Procurement Rules in France" in S. Arrowsmith (ed.), *Remedies for Enforcing the Public Procurement Rules, Public Procurement in the European Community* (Earlsgate Press, 1993), vol. IV, p. 327 at p. 334; S. Ponsot, "Public Procurement in France: Transposition of the 'Remedies Directive'" (1996) 5 *Public Procurement Law Review* 29 at 32 and 33.

[50] *Scmeltz*, TA Pau, 7 March 1994 (1994) LPA No. 64, 3; *Sté Routière Chambard*, TA Grenoble (1994) RFDA 741; *Sté Polytec*, TA Grenoble, 17 March 1994 (1994) RFDA 751; *Gpt. d'entreprises Gigoni SMBTP-Livera*, TA Besançon (1994) RFDA 747.

[51] Law No. 93-122 of 23 January 1993, *Official Journal*, 30 January 1993, p. 1588; see also P. Martin, "The Act on Corrupt Practices (29 January 1993) and Public Procurement Law" (1994) 3 *Public Procurement Law Review* CS41.

[52] S. Ponsot, "Public Procurement in France: Transposition of the 'Remedies Directive'" (1996) 5 *Public Procurement Law Review* 29 at 31.

[53] See note 49 above.

[54] S. Arrowsmith, "France – Actions to Enforce Community Rules in France: Decree No. 92-994 of 7 September 1992" (1993) 3 *Public Procurement Law Review* CS12.

[55] A. de Laubadère *et al.*, *Traité des Contrats Administratifs* (Librairie Générale de Droit et de Jurisprudence, 1983) vol. 2, sections 1817 *et seq.*

[56] P. Valdou, "Enforcing the Public Procurement Rules in France" in S. Arrowsmith (ed.), *Remedies for Enforcing the Public Procurement Rules, Public Procurement in the European Community* (Earlsgate Press, 1993), vol. IV, p. 327 at p. 339.

subject to administrative law, and thus compensation cases in this area are heard by the administrative courts.

From a European perspective the regulation of competition in defence contracting in France through legal rules of a formal nature which are subject to a strict enforcement regime is likely to have an impact on a future common European defence procurement regime. The French are likely to push for formal rules as this follows the concept of the directives and their legal tradition. The CMP could be a major influence for any future defence regime, as it has been in the past for the existing civil regime of the directives.

3.2 Germany: defence procurement on a semi-regulated basis

Germany[57] follows a second, semi-regulated approach to defence procurement. This means that there is a formal procurement regime with detailed rules, but this regime is not generally enforceable.

The main national regulations are stipulated in the Terms and Conditions for Placing Public Orders – Excluding Construction Contracts, Part A (VOL/A)[58] without the "a-paragraphs" (the "a-paragraphs" represent a part of the German implementation of the EC public procurement directives and are only relevant to civil and dual-use goods). As hard defence material is excluded from the EC public procurement regime these provision have not been applied by the German government to contracts for military material, and the VOL/A has to be read without these paragraphs when dealing with defence contracts. Therefore defence procurement is German public procurement in its original form, before the implementation of the relevant EC directives. This means that it contains the main characteristics of this old German public procurement law, which include the lack of any enforceable rights for the bidder.

The most interesting paragraphs in the VOL/A are sections 1, 2, 3 and 25. Section 1 of the VOL/A describes performances that are covered by the VOL/A. There are four principles of contract awards. The first principle is that contracts for supplies and services shall be awarded as a rule by way of competition.[59] The second principle is that any anti-competitive and unsound practices should be prevented.[60] The third principle is that contracts shall be awarded to competent, efficient and reliable competitors

---

[57] For a detailed analysis of the German system, see M. Trybus, "An Overview of Defence Procurement in the Federal Republic of Germany" (1996) 5 *Public Procurement Law Review* 217.

[58] *Verdingungsordnung für Leistungen ausgenommen Bauleistungen – VOL/A*, published as "Neufassung der VOL/A, Ausgabe 1990" ("New Version of the VOL/A, edition 1990") in the *Bundesanzeiger* (*Federal Gazette*) BAnz. No. 45a, 6 March 1990; for a detailed, section-by-section analysis of the VOL/A, see H.S. Kulartz and N. Portz, *Verdingungsordnung für Leistungen (ausgenommen Bauleistungen) – VOL/A* (Deutscher Gemeindeverlag: W. Kohlhammer, 1993).

[59] Section 2 No. 1(1) of the VOL/A.

[60] Section 2 No. 1(2) of the VOL/A.

on the basis of fair and reasonable prices.[61] A fourth and final principle is
that national and international bidders must be treated equally.[62]

Section 3 of the VOL/A describes the detailed procedures for hard
defence contracts and contracts below the thresholds of the EC directives.
These procedures are the public advertising procedure, the restrictive
advertising procedure and the non-competitive advertising procedure.
Using the public advertising procedure, contracts are awarded according to
the prescribed procedure after a public announcement to an unlimited
number of companies.[63] The restrictive advertising procedure is as a rule
applicable if supplies and services can only be provided by a limited
number of companies,[64] and not at the free choice of the authority. Using
the restrictive advertising procedure, contracts are awarded according to
the prescribed procedure after a public call for tender to a limited number
of companies.

The non-competitive procedure[65] is allowed only in limited circumstances stipulated in section 3 No. 4 of the VOL/A including not only the
usual grounds also listed in the directives but also circumstances relating to
secrecy or the lack of precise specifications. Using this procedure contracts
are awarded without a prescribed procedure, but bids must still be sought
on the market if possible. The non-competitive procedure can also be used
with a prior public call for tender when considered appropriate.[66] In the
case of this variation of the non-competitive procedure, companies have to
be called for tender through publications in periodicals, etc.

The bids are evaluated according to criteria stipulated in section 25 No. 2
of the VOL/A.[67] The final award must be given to the most economic
tender; the lowest price is not to be decisive. From a European perspective
the regulation of competition in defence contracting in Germany through
detailed rules like the VOL/A is likely to have an impact on a future
common European defence procurement regime. The Germans are likely to
accept the existence of formal rules as this follows the concept of the
directives and their legal and administrative tradition. However, problems
that have arisen in connection with the implementation of the EC directives
into German law[68] show a certain reluctance to accept rules which are of an
enforceable nature.

---

[61] Section 2 No. 2 of the VOL/A.
[62] Section 7 No. 1(1) of the VOL/A.
[63] Section 3 No. 1(1) of the VOL/A: *öffentliche Ausschreibung.*
[64] Section 3 No. 1(2) of the VOL/A: *beschränkte Ausschreibung.*
[65] Section 3 No. 1(3) of the VOL/A: *freihändige Vergabe.*
[66] Section 3 No. 1(4) of the VOL/A.
[67] H.S. Kulartz and N. Portz, *Verdingungsordnung für Leistungen (ausgenommen Bauleistungen) –
VOL/A* (Deutscher Gemeindeverlag: W. Kohlhammer, 1993), p. 9.
[68] On this discussion, see Case C-433/93, *Commission v. Germany* [1995] ECR I-2303 and case
note by M. Trybus (1996) 5 *Public Procurement Law Review* CS44–5; H.J. Priess, "New
Infringement Proceedings Regarding the Transposition of the Remedies Directives" (1996) 5
Public Procurement Law Review CS48; H. Brinker, "Public Procurement in Germany" (1995) 9
International Trade Law and Regulation 205; and W. Heiermann and T. Ax, "The New German
Procurement Law?" (1997) 14 *International Construction Law Review* 318.

3.3 United Kingdom: defence procurement on a non-regulated basis

The United Kingdom[69] follows a third, non-regulated approach to defence procurement. This means that in the United Kingdom defence contracts are not awarded according to fixed and legally binding contract award procedures; there is no set of legally enforceable rules like the French CMP nor even a formal and mandatory framework like the VOL/A in Germany. Rather, each case has to be handled individually, on the basis of mere administrative guidelines, the Chief of Defence Procurement Instructions (CDPIs), set up by the ministry itself. The sources of these guidelines are, on the one hand, the contracting experience of the Procurement Executive of the Ministry of Defence (MoD) and, on the other hand, government policy,[70] which means that the government can change these guidelines if it wishes to do so. The principles are also referred to as "principles of contracting" and are normally followed, in practice furnishing a consistent set of administrative guidelines.[71] However, these principles do not significantly reduce the margin of discretion of the MoD; traditionally they have been drafted in a flexible manner which provides the contracting authority with a large margin of manoeuvre.[72]

However, these guideline offer some consistency, and in general reflect policies and practices comparable to those of France and Germany. Thus, not surprisingly, the available award procedures are similar to those of the French and German systems: (i) the open competitive procedure where any firm is permitted to bid; (ii) the selective competitive procedure where participation is limited to invited firms; and (iii) the direct negotiation procedure for single-source procurement. The last, involving direct negotiations with only one provider, is limited to prescribed situations which are similar to the grounds allowing the negotiated procedures in the French and German systems. However, as the United Kingdom regime is not binding, the MoD can in practice use non-competitive procedures whenever it considers that appropriate. Apart from the underlying criterion of value for money, the criteria for the evaluation of bids are different depending on the kind of procedure used in the award process. For the open competition procedure, the lowest price is the only award criterion in the evaluation of bids.

The United Kingdom approach to defence procurement is based on the general procurement regime applicable in the United Kingdom before implementation of the European Community directives – a non-legal

---

[69] See in general, K. Hartley, "Competition in Defence Contracting in the United Kingdom" (1992) 6 *Public Procurement Law Review* 440; M. Trybus, "Die Beschaffung von Rüstungsgütern im Vereinigten Königreich" (1997) 3 *Vergaberecht* 35; and S. Arrowsmith, *The Law of Public and Utilities Procurement* (Sweet & Maxwell, 1996), chapter 17.

[70] J.M. Fernández-Martín, *The EC Public Procurement Rules – A Critical Analysis* (Oxford University Press, 1996), p. 98.

[71] C. Turpin, *Government Procurement and Contracts* (London, 1989), pp. 73 *et seq.*

[72] J.M. Fernández-Martín, *The EC Public Procurement Rules – A Critical Analysis* (Oxford University Press, 1996), p. 99.

approach, which still also applies in the United Kingdom to civil procurement contracts of central government outside the ambit of the directives. The lack of legal quality has major implications: economical, political and legal. Economically it has implications because, as far as contracts of a European interest are concerned, the MoD is always free to award the contract to whomever it considers convenient. This case-by-case award policy makes the MoD an unpredictable partner. Suppliers from other European countries can never be sure about their chances and whether their tendering costs are worthwhile. This might defeat the objective of competition. Legally this has implications, because the lack of legal nature of the guidelines excludes unsuccessful suppliers from any form of redress. Finally the approach has political implications as this policy might alienate the European partners in the long run.

This regime, allowing maximum flexibility to the MoD, shows no commitment of the United Kingdom for defence integration and could nourish suspicions that Whitehall wants to open foreign markets for the British defence industries without opening her own market. 90 per cent by value of United Kingdom defence equipment is bought from United Kingdom companies.[73] Nevertheless, the British defence procurement regime offers some interesting points for a European model. In particular, the priority of operational requirements over defence industrial considerations which has been applied in practice over the last decade has shown convincing results with regard to competition and military capability.[74] This has gone hand in hand with the privatisation of the defence industries which has increased the competitiveness of the British defence industrial base.[75]

3.4 A regulated procurement model for Europe

The main question about a future European defence procurement system is which type of regime the participating states should adopt. As has been explained, the national systems offer essentially three models: (i) the United Kingdom non-regulatory model without any formal or enforceable regulation; (ii) the German semi-regulated model with non-enforceable but

---

[73] Britain's Defence Procurement, Chief of Information, Defence Public Relations (E & P), MoD, July 1993, p. 12; K. Hartley, "Competition in Defence Contracting in the United Kingdom" (1992) 1 *Public Procurement Law Review* 440 at 445 (75 per cent directly plus 16 per cent in collaborative programmes with United Kingdom participation); although these figures do not prove discrimination, they do not indicate an open market either.

[74] T. Taylor, "British Defence Policy" in T. Taylor (ed.), *Reshaping European Defence* (Royal Institute of International and Security Studies, 1994), p. 76 at p. 79; Pierre de Vestel, *Defence Markets and Industries in Europe: Time for Political Decisions?* (Paris: Institute for Security Studies of the Western European Union, November 1995), p. 36.

[75] Defence Committee, First Report; and Trade and Industry Committee, First Report, "Aspects of Defence Procurement and Industrial Policy" (reports together with the proceedings of the Committees, ordered by the House of Commons to be printed 23 November 1995) HC 61 and 62 (session 1995–6), p. IX; Defence Committee – Third Special Report, "Government Reply to the First Reports from the Defence and Trade and Industry Committees on Aspects of Defence Procurement and Industrial Policy" (ordered by the House of Commons to be printed 7 February 1996) HC 209 and 210 (session 1995–6), p. IX.

formal procurement orders and (iii) the French regulated model with an enforceable procurement code. The French model is also followed in the European Community procurement directives whereas the WEAG regime follows the British non-regulatory model.

It is submitted that historical experience has shown that the non-regulatory approach to defence procurement is not an appropriate model for a European defence procurement market. Before the adoption of the European Community procurement directives, the procurement activities of public authorities and utilities were not regulated by detailed rules. They were merely governed by the broad principles of the EC Treaty and national laws, where in force. The results were widespread discrimination on the grounds of nationality within the EC, even with the prohibition of that kind of discrimination by virtue of Article 12 of the EC Treaty (then Article 7 of the EEC Treaty), and other relevant provisions such as Articles 28, 43 and 49 of the EC Treaty. Even with the broad principles of the EC Treaty in force, the discriminatory procurement reality represented a significant barrier to trade within the single market.

This was due to two main reasons. First, it was difficult to prove discriminatory treatment. Secondly, trade barriers also arise because of the inefficient sourcing practices and not only because of discrimination.[76] In addition, structural obstacles such as the lack of common specifications have to be mentioned. Only with the adoption of detailed rules through directives did this start to change, as the directives could take these specific problems into account. Discrimination became harder to disguise with specifically prescribed procedures and award criteria, European-wide publicity allows for more efficient sourcing practices and the issue of standards is dealt with as well. Nevertheless, the rules are still inefficient in many respects.[77] The reality of defence procurement today is similar to the situation pre-1977 for civil public supply and services contracts: there are no supranational regulatory frameworks. Discrimination against foreign bidders, especially from European countries, is the rule as well as inefficient sourcing practices and different standards.

The policy guidelines in the Common Policy Document (CPD) establishing the EDEM of the WEAG represent another non-regulated approach. As explained before, the regime of the CPD is widely considered a failure. This failure is due to the non-binding nature of the rules: there is no enforcement system and the regime is not followed seriously. However, even if the regime was binding, it would represent an insufficient approach as the

---

[76] S. Arrowsmith, *The Law of Public and Utilities Procurement* (Sweet & Maxwell, 1996), p. 52.

[77] On the inefficiencies of the rules, see S. Arrowsmith, *The Law of Public and Utilities Procurement* (Sweet & Maxwell, 1996), pp. 71–4; J.M. Fernández-Martín, *The EC Public Procurement Rules – A Critical Analysis* (Oxford University Press, 1996), especially pp. 121–46; A. Cox, *The Single Market Rules and the Enforcement Rules after 1992* (Earlsgate Press, 1993); "Implementing 1992 Public Procurement Policy: Public and Private Obstacles to the Creation of a Single European Market" (1992) 1 *Public Procurement Law Review* 139; K. Hartley and M. Uttley, "The Single European Market and Public Procurement Policy: the Case of the United Kingdom" (1994) 3 *Public Procurement Law Review* 114 and the citations in endnote 83 therein.

rules are not detailed enough: the system lacks detailed provisions on procedures, principles of contract awards and, again, enforcement and remedies. The current regime's efforts since 1990 to achieve an open market, involving advertising, broadly defined award criteria and a monitoring system, have been insufficient, an account clearly proven by the current situation. Historical experience clearly shows that non-regulation will not achieve an open market for defence goods.

In the United Kingdom the lack of regulation goes along with a lack of transparency causing disadvantages to foreign bidders who are less familiar with the policies of the United Kingdom government than are domestic suppliers. This discourages foreign bidders right from the start. The lack of enforcement raises the risk of wasted investments by foreign bidders. Although it is true that it is possible to have greater transparency without legal enforcement, for example through formal rules without enforcement mechanisms as in Germany, enforcement is nevertheless widely considered an important aspect of a transparent system and will greatly enhance confidence in it. Furthermore, a non-regulated regime or policy system does not represent a serious and convincing commitment to an open European defence equipment market.

The semi-regulated German regime is also not an appropriate model for Europe. Again, the historical experience is the main argument against it. Just like the United Kingdom model, this regime lacks an enforcement system and does not represent a sufficiently committed approach to the open market, although it does involve greater transparency. Lack of adequate enforcement was an important reason for the failure of the old Directive 71/305/EEC[78] for works and Directive 77/62/EEC[79] for supplies.[80] Moreover, lack of an adequate enforcement system is also considered a reason for the failure of the current regime.[81]

It should be noted, however, that this German model, in a modified and extended form, could represent a compromise between the regulated model of France and the European Community directives, on the one hand, and the non-regulatory policy model of the United Kingdom, on the other. As the negotiations towards an integrated regime will take place in a highly politicised environment, a compromise might become necessary. Therefore a model of a European Defence Procurement Code that is not enforceable

---

[78] OJ 1971, No. L185/1.

[79] OJ 1977, No. L13/1.

[80] So the European Commission in COM (84) 717 final; COM (84) 747 final; and the White Paper from the Commission to the Council on Completing the Internal Market COM (85) 310 final.

[81] It has been argued that it is doubtful whether the enforcement system of the remedies directives encourages legal action of providers, who are very often reluctant to take action against contracting authorities to preserve their chances for the next contract and thus to deter breaches of the rules. This is due to several reasons: there are problems with a sufficient implementation, lack of clarity and flexibility and a reluctance of courts to grant interim relief, to name but a few. For details, see S. Arrowsmith, *The Law of Public and Utilities Procurement* (Sweet & Maxwell, 1996), chapter 18, especially pp. 917–18; A. Cox, *The Single Market Rules and the Enforcement Regime after 1992* (Earlsgate Press, 1993), pp. 241–54; and P. Trepte, *Public Procurement in the EC* (CCH Europe, 1993), chapter 7.

along the lines of the German VOL/A but is more formal and detailed than EDEM could offer a solution to reconcile the two extreme British and French models and would at least offer greater transparency. Such a compromise might at least be necessary for a transitional period. However, a transitional period with a transitional regime could also prove to be fatal for the industry with regard to the urgency of making unambiguous political decisions soon.

The only possibly successful solution in the long run, however, is the regulatory model existing in France, through something similar to the procurement directives of the European Community. It encourages foreign bidders as, through some kind of enforcement, at least their investments might be recovered. It shows a serious commitment, signalling a true chance to foreign bidders to win a contract. It ensures transparency of procedures and may end the current state of hesitation considered so unfavourable by industry and parts of the Member State governments. It also has to be mentioned that this approach has produced limited results in the civil sector,[82] so anything less than this is extremely unlikely to be successful. It will be necessary to introduce adequate legal remedies and mechanisms to prevent evasion to create an effective regime for Europe.

The special features of the military sector such as monopsony, research and development, long development phases, national security and secrecy, to name but a few, do not provide an argument against regulation in general. Countries like France, Germany or Austria have such regulation in one form or another. However, it is submitted that these special features of military procurement are so significant that the modifications which are needed to take account of them would change the directives beyond recognition. Therefore it seems more appropriate to propose a European Defence Procurement Code (EDPC). The special features of the utilities sector justified the adoption of a separate directive for that sector, and similarly the special features of the defence sector certainly justify the adoption of a separate EDPC.

The different memberships of EU, WEU, WEAG and OCCAR are another argument for a framework separate from the directives. With a regime outside the EU – which still appears a distinct possibility – neither the directives nor the EC Treaty would be applicable. The analysis in section 2 of the possible content of a common system of rules will be based on the assumption of such an EDPC either within or outside EU law.

---

[82] On the limited impact of the rules, see, in particular, EuroStrategy Consultants, *The Single Market Review: Series III: Dismantling of Barriers*, vol. 2, *Public Procurement* (Kogan Page, 1997). See also chapter 2 of this volume; and A. Cox, "Implementing the 1992 Public Procurement Policy: Public and Private Obstacles to the Creation of a Single European Market" (1992) 1 *Public Procurement Law Review* 139; J. Telgen and L. de Boer, "Experience with the EC Directives on Public Procurement: A Survey of Dutch Municipalities" (1997) 6 *Public Procurement Law Review* 121; K. Hartley and M. Uttley, "The Single European Market and Public Procurement Policy – the Case of the United Kingdom" (1994) 3 *Public Procurement Law Review* 194; J.M. Fernández-Martín, "The European Commission's Centralised enforcement of Public Procurement rules: A Critical View" (1993) 2 *Public Procurement Law Review* 40 and the citations in endnote 78 therein.

4. SUGGESTIONS FOR A EUROPEAN DEFENCE PROCUREMENT CODE

The precise nature of any EDPC will depend partly on the organisational structure that will be the basis of the code.

A minimal solution would be the separate procurement of defence equipment through the existing national defence procurement authorities on the basis of limited common defence procurement rules aimed at ensuring an open market. These common rules could have the form of minimum standards which would only have to accommodate the objectives of equal treatment and transparency. These objectives are similar to the objectives of the EC directives which only aim at establishing a common competitive procurement market without discrimination on grounds of nationality. Other objectives, such as value for money and probity are not a direct concern of international procurement regimes of this kind. These objectives can be integrated into the national laws implementing international regimes, but only as a matter of national law.

Another solution could be a rather mixed model combining the separate procurement through national procurement authorities described in the last model with common procurement in limited areas on the basis of common rules for both these types of procurement. Common procurement would be exercised in prescribed areas where this procurement is appropriate or necessary. Two different sets of rules would be needed in this model. The first set for the national procurement authorities would comprise of minimal standards as in the first model, aimed simply at securing transparency and equality of treatment. The second would comprise of a code of detailed rules to be followed by the agency, to govern all aspects of the process.

A far-reaching solution would be the introduction of a common procurement agency[83] simultaneously with the abolition of the national procurement authorities. An EDPC that is drafted for a centralised procurement agency would have to accommodate additional objectives to equal treatment and transparency. Probity and value for money need to be a part of the code as national legislators do not play a part in the regulation of the procurement process as they do, for example, at the implementation level of EC directives. All aspects of the procurement process would have to be regulated by the EDPC which in this case is not merely a minimal framework. Lower thresholds, precise common requirements on technical capacity and financial standing – which, for example, require assessments of standing rather than merely regulating the way in which any assessments are carried out – common registration requirements, and provisions covering auditing and monitoring are examples of concerns of such an EDPC that are not normally dealt with by international regimes such as the EC directives. National armies would send

---

[83] See for details, A. Cox, "The Future of European Defence Policy: The Case of a Centralised Procurement Agency" (1994) 3 *Public Procurement Law Review* 65.

their orders and requirements to the authority that would then procure material for them.

Whatever the organisational structure, there would, as explained, have to be at least a core of common minimal standards comparable to the EC directives for civil procurements, and it is this set of rules designed to secure minimum standards of transparency and equality that will be dealt with in the analysis in the remainder of this chapter. As indicated above, it will have to take into account the special characteristics of the military sector, such as the need for secrecy, national security concerns, the defence procurement process and industrial policy considerations.

First, so far as coverage is concerned, it is submitted that the example of the EC directives, by giving a general definition of the entities covered followed by an illustrative list.[84] If the code is designed for national purchasing authorities, the definition could refer to an "authority governed by public law involved in defence purchasing" and an annex could list most of the existing authorities considered to be covered. This broad definition will exclude the possibility of creating new defence agencies to avoid the application of the rules. In an organisational model including a centralised procurement agency this agency should be expressly named. Apart from some specific exclusions, such as nuclear and cryptographic equipment,[85] all hard-defence materials in the sense of Article 223 of the EC Treaty should be covered by the code. It is submitted that national security exclusions, as provided in the directives,[86] should not be included: considerations of national security can be accommodated at later stages within the code, for example as grounds allowing the use of the negotiated procedure or as contract award criteria, as will be explained below.

In an EDPC only establishing minimal standards, it is submitted that there should be only one legally binding principle of contract awards following the example of the EC directives. This should be the principle of equal treatment as established by the ECJ in the *Storebaelt* case[87] ruling out, in particular, discrimination on the grounds of nationality. This principle is obviously essential to establish a common market for defence goods and all procurement decisions will have to comply with the requirement of equal treatment.[88] A non-binding statement of objectives at the beginning of the code could stipulate other objectives like competition. However, principles like competition should rather be accommodated in

---

[84] See Title I (especially Article 1(1)(b)) of the Supplies Directive 93/36/EEC and Annex I; Title 1 of the Utilities Directive 93/38/EEC and Annex 1; section 1 of the VOL/A; and Article 1 of the CMP.

[85] See paragraph 7(a) of the CPD.

[86] Article 2(1)(b) of the Supplies Directive 93/36/EEC; Article 4(b) of the Works Directive 93/37/EEC; Article 4(2) of the Services Directive 92/50/EEC and Article 10 of the Utilities Directive 93/38/EEC.

[87] Case 243/89, *Commission* v. *Denmark* [1993] ECR I-3353; see case note by J.M. Fernández-Martín in (1993) 2 *Public Procurement Law Review* CS153–7.

[88] See also Article III of the General Procurement Agreement (GPA) of the World Trade Organization and Article 8 of the UNCITRAL Model Law on Procurement of Goods, Construction and Services, adopted 17 June 1994.

the detailed rules on competitive procedures. A centralised European procurement agency would also have to include additional principles like value for money and probity, but, as explained, these aspects of the procurement process will not be considered further here.

Offsets are a common feature in international defence procurement. They require the industry of the country of a foreign supplier to compensate the industry of the buying country for the business of the contract, normally in the form of sub-contracts or other contracts. As they represent a significant barrier to trade and discrimination on grounds of nationality they will need to be abolished between the participating nations of a common market for defence goods, although they may have to be included for contracts awarded to industries outside that market.

The main area where the special needs of the defence sector have to be accommodated in a EDPC is in relation to the rules on award procedures. The experience of the defence procurement authorities in Germany, France and the United Kingdom shows that the open and restricted procedures of the EC directives (or their national equivalents), with formal tendering and only very limited possibilities for negotiating with firms, are only suitable for simple off-the-shelf equipment and hardly used for defence purchases.[89] As these procedures offer the highest level of competition and transparency, they should be included in a code to be used at least as often as possible, but they are clearly unsuitable for many defence purchases.

The criteria to be taken into account for the evaluation of bids in these competitive procedures will depend on the procedure used. For the various national and international forms of the open and restricted procedures the deciding criterion is normally the lowest bid. For more complex procurements the criterion will normally be the economically most advantageous tender. In the area of defence procurement, where more complex procurements are dominant, this allows a purchaser to take various other aspects into account. These will usually include, for example, delivery date, running costs, cost-effectiveness, quality, aesthetic and functional characteristics, after-sales service, technical assistance,[90] competition in sub-contracting and military operational requirements.

As noted above, however, the larger part of defence procurement activity will need to be conducted by using some form of negotiated procedure. Negotiated procedures are provided in all national and international procurement systems. In the national defence procurement systems of France, Germany and the United Kingdom there are basically two different types of the negotiated procedure, one with and one without competition.[91] It is submitted that the free use of the competitive version of the negotiated

---

[89] For example in Germany 5.5 per cent of procedures use the open advertising procedure and 7.5 per cent use the restricted advertising procedure, *Finanzbrief* 9/1985, as cited by J. Rogmanns, *Öffentliche Aufträge: Leitfaden für die Vergabe und Abwicklung von Öffentlichen-, einschließlich Bauaufträgen (VP PR/30/53 und VO PR 1/72)* (Erich Schmidt Verlag, 1993), p. 20.

[90] See, for example, Article 26(1) of the Supplies Directive 93/36/EEC.

[91] The UNCITRAL Model Law provides a sophisticated selection of negotiating procedures, including competitive tendering according to Article 49(1) and request for proposals according to Article 48.

procedure, allowed in the EC Utilities Directive, is clearly necessary for the EDPC to allow sufficient flexibility in making complex purchases.[92]

In addition, in many circumstances which occur in the defence sector, the use of the negotiated procedure without competition, in other words single-sourcing, is necessary. As this procedure offers the lowest level of transparency and competition it is, however, limited to prescribed circumstances in most procurement regimes and this should also be the case under a defence regime.

On what grounds should this single-sourcing procedure be available? It is first important to note that situations that are sometimes currently dealt with by single-sourcing, or even by a total exclusion from the rules on award procedures, can in fact often be accommodated in some form of negotiated procedure with competition. In particular, secrecy concerns may prohibit a public call for tender, but it will still be possible to negotiate with more than one reliable supplier. All national defence procurement systems described in this chapter follow this approach.[93] In the EC directives, on the other hand – for example in Article 2(1)(b) of the Supplies Directive 93/36/EEC – secrecy is not a ground to justify the use of the negotiated procedure without prior call for tender but a reason for a general exclusion from the application of the directives. The EDEM system of the WEAG contains a similar provision. A general exclusion on the basis of secrecy would render the whole code useless. This applies especially when the interpretation of secrecy is not clear, thus leading to the possibility of abuse. Theoretically all purchases of a defence procurement authority can come under this heading, especially hard defence material but also dual-use material. It has to be noted, however, that, as hard defence material is excluded from the application of the directives anyway, an exclusion such as Article 2(1)(b) of the Supplies Directive 93/36/EEC is mainly aimed at dual-use goods. Nevertheless, an EDPC that aims at regulating the procurement of hard defence material would defeat its purpose if it contained such a broad security exclusion. Secrecy also does not appear to offer a general justification for single-sourcing. Instead, it is submitted that secrecy concerns should generally be dealt with by providing for a form of negotiation with competition, but without imposing an advertising requirement.

Situations in a state of mobilisation or close to war, on the other hand, may justifiably lead to single-sourcing as due to urgency it may not be possible to negotiate with more than one supplier. The state of war or mobilisation is an exceptional situation where the interest of national security may override many other interests having a more important status in times of peace. National security would certainly override the interest in competition and transparency in such a situation. The use of a competitive

---

[92] A. Brown, "The Extension of the Community Public Procurement Rules to the Utilities" (1993) 30 *Common Market Law Review* 721 at 746; R. Boyle, "EC Public Procurement Rules – 'A Purchaser Reflects on the Need for Simplification'" (1994) 3 *Public Procurement Law Review* 101 at 103.

[93] Germany: section 3(d) of the VOL/A; France: Article 104(1) point 5 of the CMP; and the respective practice in the United Kingdom.

procedure, even without any advertising requirements, would not be sufficient due to the especially tense level of urgency and the national security
implications involved in such situations. Therefore such a mobilisation
ground allowing for single-sourcing should be included in an EDPC. The
state of mobilisation or crisis, however, has to be clearly defined to prevent
abuse. The French system contains such a ground in Article 104(1) point
6(a) of the CMP and the United Kingdom regime includes a similar
practice.

The protection of the defence industrial base for strategic purposes can
also be a good reason for using a single-source procedure, which may be
needed to protect a particular capability of strategic importance. The French
system includes such a circumstance for the protection of the national
defence industrial base in Article 104(1) point 6(b) of the CMP. To accommodate the principle of equal treatment, however, it is the preservation of
the European defence industrial base rather than a national defence
industrial base that should be a reason for the use of single-sourcing.[94]
Otherwise the open market within Europe would be put into question. The
national defence industries are so small that many items can only be
produced by a single national supplier. Large parts of the requirements of
the armed forces would be procured by single-sourcing to keep this
strategically important provider afloat. On a European level there can be
products that can only be procured from one supplier but it is less likely
and cross-border trade would not be affected in these cases. It is perhaps
even doubtful whether the concept of protecting even a European defence
industrial base is viable in a world of interdependent security concerns
within NATO and the WEU where most defence equipment will contain at
least some components from other countries. Nevertheless, political reality
will probably lead to single-sourcing in these circumstances.[95] To prevent
abuse the areas of strategic importance should be carefully predetermined.

Another possible ground for single-sourcing may be the award of a
contract for production to the firm that has done the research and development work for the product. In innovative projects the procurement cycle
can be separated into different phases, most notably a separate research and
development phase and a production phase. As far as the choice of a
procurement procedure for these phases is concerned there are essentially
three possibilities. First, the two phases can be treated as one contract and
awarded on the basis of competitive bidding before the start of the research
phase. Secondly, the phases can be treated as separate contracts awarded
on the basis of separate competitive bidding procedures. Finally, the phases
can be treated as separate contracts with the research and development

---

[94] In COM (96) 10 final, pp. 17–19, the protection of the defence industrial base is seen as one of
the special features of the defence sector, a system, otherwise "largely motivated by the EC
directives" had to take into account.
[95] Stephen Kahn, discussing European preference in the European Space Agency (ESA), states:
"Nevertheless it is only realistic to assume that many international or regional organisations
will continue to operate such constraints": S. Kahn, "Advanced Technology Projects and
International Procurement: the Case of the European Space Agency" (1993) 2 *Public
Procurement Law Review* 13 at 19; on the ESA system, see also chapter 13 this volume.

phase awarded on the basis of competitive bidding and the production phase awarded on the basis of single-sourcing with the same contractor. The last option strikes a balance between the objectives of competitiveness and the commercial interest of prospective contractors. In contrast to the second option the contractor can plan on the basis of both contracts. In contrast to the first option there is still some commercial pressure, as the contract for the production phase of a particular project is not awarded automatically with the award of the research and development contract and a production contract can be negotiated on the basis of the results of the research and development phase.

In addition, both the three national systems discussed and the EC directives have certain other grounds for single-source negotiations which are common to most procurement regimes. These grounds, which include, for example, extreme urgency, the existence of exclusive rights or the absence of any offers in a previous competitive procedure, could easily be agreed for a common defence regime.

Finally, the possibility of an enforcement and remedies system of an EDPC must be considered briefly. As mentioned above, the rules need to be enforceable to ensure compliance and to encourage foreign bidders to participate. The system should consist of elements of non-financial relief, damages and other means to ensure compliance with the code. Non-financial relief through set aside should be allowed in a form similar to the French summary proceedings procedure with a single judge sitting in an internal judicial body (see 3.1 above). This should only be available before the conclusion of the contract. After the conclusion of the contract damages should be available if there is a wrongful breach of duty by the contracting authority and a loss to the bidder caused by that breach of duty. Damages consisting of the tender costs should be available to the bidder who had a real chance of winning the contract. Damages consisting of the profits of a contract should also be available to a bidder who would almost certainly have been awarded the contract. In an EDPC outside the EU there should also, ideally, be an enforcement mechanism similar to Article 226 of the EC Treaty allowing enforcement by a centralised authority representing all the participating states, although the possible models for such an authority cannot be discussed in detail here. Finally there should be monitoring and reporting requirements, auditing and a complaint system.

5. CONCLUSION

The European nation states will continue to support armed forces for their defence. In an environment of decreasing defence budgets after the end of the Cold War these forces will be smaller and less and less money will be spent to purchase new equipment for them. The integration of these national armies on the basis of the EU or the WEU is still set in an unforeseeable future and may not happen at all. The integration of the national defence equipment markets of Europe, however, is a certain and urgent necessity to ensure the survival of the European defence industries and to keep defence affordable.

The central element of this integration is the creation of a common set of rules regulating the procurement process similar to the civil procurement directives of the European Union. Important models for such a set of rules, apart from the EC directives, are the national systems of the most important European countries, France, Germany and the United Kingdom. These systems offer essentially three models. Of these, it has been argued in this chapter that the French system based on formal enforceable rules is the only viable option: the example of the EC directives has shown that only detailed rules representing a serious commitment to a common market will ensure compliance and encourage foreign bidders to participate. In particular, an effective enforcement system will be a crucial element of a common system.

It has also been suggested in this chapter that the many special characteristics of the military sector, such as national security concerns, the need for secrecy, monopsony or the defence procurement cycle, make it necessary to create a completely separate set of rules for defence procurement, rather than just adapting the civil procurement directives to the military sector. In particular, it will be important to introduce new forms of the negotiated procedure with competition, and to include more grounds allowing the use of single-source negotiations, such as during a state of mobilisation, to protect strategic industrial capabilities and to accommodate the defence procurement cycle.

So far the European decision-makers seem to be stuck in a constitutional debate over the political basis of common defence and common defence procurement. It is clearly time, however, to start the discussion on a common set of rules to create a single market for defence goods within Europe. Decreasing defence budgets, technological progress and an increasingly competitive US defence industry make the integration of the European defence equipment markets an urgent priority.

Part II
Public Procurement Reform in Developing and Transition Economies

5. The UNCITRAL Model Law on Procurement of Goods, Construction and Services and its Impact on Procurement Reform

*Robert R. Hunja**

1. INTRODUCTION

The United Nations Commission on International Trade Law (UNCITRAL) is an intergovernmental body created by the United Nations General Assembly in 1966[1] with the aim of enabling the United Nations (UN) to play a more active role in reducing or removing obstacles to the flow of international trade. The Commission was charged with the mandate of furthering the progressive harmonisation and unification of the law of international trade and of enhancing broader participation by, in particular, developing states, in this process.[2] The Commission meets annually, but also works through working groups, each dealing with a specific subject. The International Trade Law Branch of the UN Office of Legal Affairs serves as the substantive secretariat of the Commission.

In pursuance of its mandate, the Commission has formulated a number of legal texts including conventions, model laws and legal guides.[3] Work on the Model Law on Procurement of Goods, Construction and Services began in 1989 and was carried out by the Commission's Working Group on the New International Economic Order. A study carried out by the Commission Secretariat had revealed that in many countries, the existing legislation governing procurement was inadequate or outdated.[4] This inadequacy resulted in inefficiency and ineffectiveness in the procurement process and

---

* Counsel, Procurement and Consultant Services, Legal Department, World Bank. The author was formerly Chairman and then Secretary of the UNCITRAL Working Group that prepared the Model Law. The views expressed here are his own and do not represent those of UNCITRAL or the World Bank.
[1] General Assembly Resolution 2205(XXI) of 17 December 1966.
[2] *Ibid.*, Section II, paragraph 8.
[3] Among the better known of these are International Conventions on Contracts for the International Sale of Goods (the Sales Convention); On Carriage of Goods by Sea (Hamburg Rules); Model Laws on International Commercial Arbitration and International Credit Transfers; and the UNCITRAL Arbitration Rules.
[4] UNCITRAL Document A/CN-9/WG V/WP22.

led to uneconomic results whereby the public purchaser failed to get "value for money". Furthermore, the report revealed that many of these laws did not promote international competition in procurement and were therefore a hindrance to international trade. The Commission therefore decided to prepare a model law setting out what would be considered as transparent, competitive and efficient procurement procedures. These efforts culminated in the adoption by the UN General Assembly of the UNCITRAL Model Law on Procurement of Goods, Construction and Services[5] (hereinafter referred to as the Model Law).

Being a model law, and not a binding legal text, it is intended to "serve as model for states for the evaluation and modernisation of their procurement laws and practices and the establishment of procurement legislation where none presently exists".[6] Having been prepared under the auspices of the UN, the Model Law is not only a widely acceptable legal text but has already had a significant impact on procurement legislation, in particular in those states where no procurement legislation previously existed, but also in states which are in the process of reforming existing procurement legislation. This chapter first discusses the main characteristics of the Model Law and then describes the impact the Model Law has had on procurement reform.

2. MAIN FEATURES OF THE MODEL LAW

2.1 Objectives and scope

The Model Law contains 57 Articles divided into six chapters.[7] It begins with a preamble which states the main objectives of the Model Law. These objectives include maximising competition and efficiency, promoting fair and equitable treatment of all suppliers and contractors and promoting integrity and fairness in the procurement process mainly by bringing about increased transparency in procurement procedures. All the procedures in the law are therefore geared towards achieving the objectives as stated in the preamble. While it is recognised that a preamble may not be common legislative practice in many states, it was agreed that it would be useful to have a statement setting out what would be considered as the minimum criteria that good procurement legislation should aim to achieve.

---

[5] Official Records of the General Assembly, Forty-Ninth Session, Supplement No. 17 (A/49/17). For further readings on the Model Law, see J.J. Myers, "UNCITRAL Model Law on Procurement" (1993) 21 *International Business Lawyer* 179; D. Wallace, Jr. "The UN Model Law on Procurement" (1992) 1 *Public Procurement Law Review* 406; and G. Westring, "Multilateral and Unilateral Procurement Regimes: To Which Camp Does the UNCITRAL Model Law on Procurement Belong?" (1994) 3 *Public Procurement Law Review* 406.

[6] *Guide to Enactment of UNCITRAL Model Law on Procurement of Goods, Construction and Services* (New York: United Nations, 1995), paragraph 1.

[7] These are: Chapter I, General Provisions; Chapter II, Methods of Procurement and their Conditions for Use; Chapter III, Tendering Proceedings; Chapter IV, Principal Method for Procurement of Services; Chapter V, Procedures for Alternative Methods of Procurement; and Chapter VI, Review.

As to scope, it is expected that legislation enacted on the basis of the Model Law will be applicable to the procurement of all goods, construction and services that are financed by public funds. This should also include procurement by municipalities and regional governments. However, Article 1(2) recognises that some states may wish to exempt procurement involving national defence or national security from the application of the law. It is also recognised that procurement financed by external resources may often be subject to procurement procedures established by the sources of the funds.[8] It is expected, however, that any exemptions from the law would be narrowly proscribed and publicly notified either in the law itself or in procurement regulations.

2.2 Procurement methods

The Model Law establishes a number of procurement methods which the procuring entities can use. For procurement of goods and construction, the Model Law prescribes the use of public tendering as the main method of procurement and as the method that is best able to promote the objectives stated in the preamble.[9] Recognising that there are significant differences between procurement of goods and construction and procurement of some services, the Model Law also prescribes a separate "principal method for procurement of services".[10]

For those instances where tendering, in the case of goods or construction, or the "principal method for procurement of services" in the case of services, may not be appropriate or feasible, the Model Law establishes alternative methods of procurement. These other methods may only be used when the conditions for their use are met. Such conditions for use of the other methods are clearly stated. The methods of procurement as set out in the Model Law are as follows.

2.2.1 Tendering

It is expected that tendering proceedings will be used in most cases for the procurement of goods or construction. The procedures for tendering in the Model Law are therefore crafted so as to maximise the advantages of competition, transparency, and fairness in the procurement process. The objective of promoting competition is achieved by the provisions mandating the widest possible advertisement of upcoming procurement so as to enable as many potential bidders as possible to take part in the procurement.[11] The opportunity to participate in the procurement process should be afforded to all those who express an interest in so doing. A number of articles are also geared towards promoting transparency, in particular by means of pre-disclosure to all bidders of all relevant information regarding the tendering

---

[8] Article 3 of the Model Law.
[9] Article 18(i) of the Model Law.
[10] Chapter IV of the Model Law.
[11] Article 24 of the Model Law.

process in the solicitation documents.[12] Particularly important in this regard is the pre-disclosure of all the criteria that will be used in the evaluation of the successful tender;[13] the corollary of which is that only the criteria that have been pre-disclosed can be used during the actual evaluation.[14] The other important clause in promoting transparency is the requirement that all tenders shall be opened in public at which point the tender prices will be announced[15] and a record kept of the proceedings.[16]

These main features of tendering for goods or construction are also found in the principal method for procurement of services. The main reason for establishing a separate method for procurement of services is that, unlike the procurement of goods or construction, procurement of services involves the supply of intangible products whose quality and exact content may be difficult to quantify.[17] The skill and expertise of the service provider may therefore be a more dominant factor than price in the evaluation process. Thus, the main difference between tendering and the main method for procurement of services is in the means of evaluating the successful proposal where, in the case of services, account is given to the predominant weight accorded to the qualifications and expertise of service providers.[18]

2.2.2 *Other methods of procurement*

While the Model Law recommends tendering as the method of procurement to be used in most cases, a number of other methods are provided for use in those instances when tendering may not be appropriate or feasible. For example, in those cases where it might not be feasible to formulate specifications to a degree of finality necessary to enable comparison of tenders, the Model Law provides three optional methods. These are two-stage tendering,[19] a request for proposals[20] and competitive negotiations.[21]

With two-stage tendering, the procuring entity uses the first stage to seek various proposals relating essentially to the technical characteristics of the goods or construction to be provided. The procuring entity may then hold negotiations with the various suppliers or contractors with a view to clarifying the quality and technical specifications. At the second stage, the procuring entity issues a single set of specifications on which tenders can then be submitted. Regular tendering procedures are then used after this. With the request for proposals, the procuring entity approaches a number of bidders, solicits various proposals on how best to meet its needs and negotiates with these bidders to arrive at a closer understanding of the

---

[12] Articles 25, 26 and 27 of the Model Law.
[13] Articles 25(d) and 27(b) of the Model Law.
[14] Article 34(4)(a) of the Model Law.
[15] Article 33 of the Model Law.
[16] Article 11 of the Model Law.
[17] Paragraph 11 of the Guide to Enactment.
[18] Articles 42, 43 and 44 of the Model Law.
[19] Articles 19 and 46 of the Model Law.
[20] Articles 19 and 48 of the Model Law.
[21] Articles 19 and 49 of the Model Law.

specifications. Following this process, the bidders are requested to submit their best and final offer. The successful proposal is then chosen from these best and final offers on the basis of pre-disclosed criteria.

These two methods are very useful, particularly in circumstances when the procuring entity wishes to benefit from technical knowledge and innovation that bidders may possess. This would be the case, for example, with the procurement of sophisticated information technology systems where the procuring entity would use the first stage to seek technical proposals from the industry and to discuss the possible solution to its needs on the basis of the technical proposals presented.

Competitive negotiation is different from these other methods in that the Model Law provides few structured rules on how it should be carried. It is merely stated that, after negotiations with a number of bidders, the successful bidder will be chosen on the basis of a "best and final offer". It is therefore a rather open-ended method that may be considered as fraught with the opportunity for abuse.

For cases where the goods, construction or services are so technically complex as to be available only from a limited number of suppliers, or in a case of procurement of such low value that economy or efficiency are best served by restricting the number of tenders, the procuring entity may use restricted tendering.[22] Except for the requirement of wide advertising, all the other procedures for open tendering apply to restricted tendering. In restricted tendering, the procuring entity is permitted to extend the invitation to tender to a limited number of suppliers or contractors only.[23]

For the procurement of goods or services of a low value and which are standardised in nature, the Model Law provides for the use of request-for-quotations[24] whereby the procuring entity solicits quotations based essentially on price from a number of suppliers and makes an offer to the responsive supplier with the lowest bid.

Finally, for exceptional circumstances such as urgency or catastrophic events or whether the goods, construction or services may only be available from one supplier, the Model Law provides for single-source procurement.[25]

2.3 Participation by foreign bidders in the procurement process

One of the findings of the UNCITRAL Secretariat's research on existing procurement practices was that many procurement laws are a hindrance to participation by foreign suppliers. As an entity whose mandate includes the promotion of international trade, UNCITRAL aimed to encourage a change by urging states to set up procurement systems that encouraged participation by foreign contractors and suppliers. Therefore, one of the basic tenets of the Model Law is that participation in the procurement proceedings

---

[22] Article 20 of the Model Law.
[23] Article 47 of the Model Law.
[24] Articles 21 and 50 of the Model Law.
[25] Articles 22 and 51 of the Model Law.

should be open to all bidders without discrimination on the basis of nationality. The rationale underlying this position is that wider competition will ultimately enable the procuring entities to get better value for money.

However, recognising that there may exist legitimate situations where restrictions on the basis of nationality could be imposed,[26] the Model Law aims to make such restrictions as transparent and rational as possible by stating that any such restrictions, and the grounds on which they are imposed, should be notified in the law or in procurement regulations.

As a means of circumventing the negative effects of blanket exclusion of foreign bidders, the law allows for the use of a "margin of preference" in favour of local bidders during the evaluation process.[27] The benefit of using a "margin of preference" is that it provides local bidders with the chance to enhance their competitiveness against foreign bidders, while also providing them with an improved opportunity of being awarded some contracts.

Concern has been expressed that, while it ensures greater transparency, the emphasis of the Model Law on openness and non-discrimination on the basis of nationality and the preference for open over restricted tendering may impinge on the interest of economy and efficiency.[28] However, a case can be made that, while the Model Law leans heavily towards promoting transparency, there are also provisions that mitigate against excess pursuit of any one of the objectives stated in the preamble to the detriment of the others. For example, while the principle of non-discrimination on the basis of nationality as expressed in Article 8 may seem rather extreme, Article 23(b) allows for domestic tendering in cases where the procuring entity decides that, in view of the low value of the goods, construction or services to be procured, only domestic suppliers or contractors are likely to be interested in submitting bids. With regard to the preference for open over restricted tendering, Article 20(b) also provides that the procuring entity may resort to restricted tendering where the time and costs required to examine a large number of tenders would be disproportionate to the value of goods, construction or services to be procured. Thus, in both cases, the procuring entity is provided the opportunity to balance the benefits that accrue with more transparent procedures with the interests of cost, economy and efficiency.

2.4 Review procedures

One of the key features of the Model Law is that it provides for procedures through which bidders can seek review of the decisions of the procuring entity which are in violation of the Model Law.[29]

---

[26] These may include, for example, primary trade boycotts or sanctions imposed by organisations such as the United Nations.

[27] Article 34(4)(d) of the Model Law.

[28] See, for example, G. Westring, "Multilateral and Unilateral Procurement Regimes: To Which Camp Does the UNCITRAL Model Law on Procurement Belong?" (1994) 3 *Public Procurement Law Review* 406.at 148.

[29] Chapter VI of the Model Law.

Enabling bidders and potential bidders to have recourse against wrong-ful decisions of the procuring entity not only encourages the procuring entity to make the right decisions but also makes the law largely self-policing since bidders have an opportunity to enforce compliance with the law. It is, however, recognised that in some states, such procedures may already exist as part of the larger body of administrative law or the law relating to review of the decisions of governmental entities. States are therefore provided with a number of options on how to implement the review procedures. It is also provided that some of the decisions of the procuring entity that do not directly impact negatively on the treatment accorded to suppliers or contractors are not open to review. These include decisions such as the selection of the method of procurement.[30]

The provisions state that in the first instance, and if the procurement contract has not already entered into force, a complaint should be lodged with the procuring entity itself.[31] Under this procedure, a complaint can only be entertained if it is brought before the procuring entity within 20 days of the time that the supplier or contractor became aware (or should have become aware) of the circumstances giving rise to the complaint. Upon the lodging of a complaint, the head of the procuring entity has 30 days within which to issue a written decision indicating any corrective measures taken if the complaint is upheld. An appeal on the decision of the procuring entity (or the failure of the procuring entity to act on a complaint) may be made under administrative review[32] or through judicial review.

The provisions on review also provide for suspension of the procurement proceedings.[33] However, to guard against abuse of the complaint mechanism, which can lead to costly disruption to the activities of the procuring entity, suspension of the procurement proceedings only takes place under closely circumscribed circumstances. These safeguards include the requirement that the bidder have a *prima facie* case, a declaration by the bidder that irreparable injury would be caused in the absence of a suspension and the limitation of any suspension to seven days. Further-more, the procuring entity is provided with the opportunity to circumvent suspension by a certification that urgent public interest considerations require the procurement to proceed.

2.5 Other provisions

The Model Law contains other provisions that are worthy of note, including those on pre-qualification proceedings and on record-keeping. On pre-qualification proceedings, the Model Law provides that the procuring entity must pre-disclose to all potential bidders the qualification criteria

---

[30] Article 52(2) of the Model Law.
[31] Article 53 of the Model Law.
[32] The provisions on administrative review are only of relevance to those states where hierarchical review of administrative actions and decisions are a feature of the legal system. In states where such a review is not available, recourse might only be available through judicial review.
[33] Article 56 of the Model Law.

and the manner in which the evaluation of the qualified contractors or suppliers will be carried out.[34] During the pre-qualification evaluation, only such criteria as are necessary to establish the bidders' qualifications to perform the contract should be applied. In addition, only those criteria pre-disclosed in the pre-qualification documents can be used. All bidders who are qualified should then be granted an opportunity to submit tenders or proposals. The opportunity for post-qualification is also provided.

The provisions on the necessity to keep a record are key to increasing the transparency of the procurement process.[35] The two aspects that are of particular importance in this regard are the need to keep a record of bid-opening including the prices that are read out during bid-opening, and the requirement to maintain a record of the evaluation process. The necessity of keeping a record of the entire procurement process should, like the possibility of review, focus the procuring entity on the need to make correct decisions. Record-keeping is also important for purposes of facilitating review of decisions.

2.6 The Guide to Enactment

During the early stages of work on the Model Law, the Commission recognised that the text to be finally adopted would need to be accompanied by a commentary to provide an explanation on the considerations that had been taken in arriving at a particular formulation in the Model Law. Earlier drafts of the Model Law were therefore accompanied by a commentary for each article. However, as the Commission finalised its work, it was decided that it would be more useful to prepare a Guide to Enactment which would provide background and explanatory information for those drafting or enacting legislation based on the Model Law.

A Guide to Enactment was thus produced, which is intended to explain the rationale underlying the provisions of the Model Law. In addition to the materials on each article, the Guide also contains other useful information. For example, recognising that the Model Law states the possibility of enactment of procurement regulations to provide further details on some aspects of the Model Law's provisions, the Guide discusses possible issues that such regulations could cover. Another important subject covered in the Guide is the type of administrative structures that states might need to put in place to oversee proper implementation of the Law.[36]

3. THE IMPACT OF THE MODEL LAW ON PROCUREMENT REFORM

Among the advantages of the Model Law, and one that has greatly contributed to its general worldwide acceptability, is the fact that it was

---

[34] Articles 6 and 7 of the Model Law.
[35] Article 11 of the Model Law.
[36] Paragraphs 36–40 of the Guide to Enactment.

prepared under the auspices of the UN. Since UNCITRAL is an organ of the UN General Assembly, participation in its work is open to states at all levels of economic development and with different legal and political systems. With regard to the Model Law, participation in the meetings of the Working Group, where most of the substantive work was carried out, involved not only many different states, but also multilateral lending agencies, other international organisations and even non-governmental organisations.[37] The Model Law received the *imprimatur* of the UN General Assembly which urged that all states "give favourable consideration to the Model Law" when reforming their procurement systems.[38]

This wide acceptance has enabled the Model Law to have a significant impact on reform in the area of procurement. Wide participation in its preparation has ensured that the Model Law constitutes what are internationally recognised as the fundamental components of good procurement practice for most states, and sets the threshold by which good procurement legislation should be measured. It establishes that a modern procurement system will normally promote openness, competition and transparency and also fairness and accountability to the public. Further, the Model Law states a view on some of the more controversial issues in public procurement. One such issue is the manner in which procurement legislation should address the issue of participation in procurement by foreign suppliers and contractors and to what extent states should encourage international competition. The Model Law resolved that issue by establishing a system based on open international competition, thereby discouraging indiscriminate use of public procurement for protectionist purposes.

One specific issue on which the Model Law has had an impact concerns decentralisation of procurement and the administrative or institutional framework needed to oversee implementation of a procurement system based on the Model Law. By providing that procurement shall be organised and carried out by the procuring entity, the Model Law proposes establishment of a procurement system that is decentralised and where decisions and accountability lie with the entity that is carrying out procurement to meet its own needs. In such a system, as opposed to one with a central agency that carries out procurement on behalf of other public agencies, the public agencies are themselves provided the responsibility for carrying out the procurement and ensuring compliance with the provisions of the Law. Further, while the Model Law itself does not deal with the issue of an institutional structure, the Guide to Enactment does mention that states may find it desirable to provide an institutional mechanism to oversee proper implementation of the law. In line with the structure of decentral-

---

[37] Among the multilateral lending agencies that consistently participated were the World Bank and the Inter-American Development Bank. Other organisations that actively participated included the International Bar Association and the European Space Agency. Consistent and active participation by the World Bank in the preparation of the Model Law has enabled the World Bank to recommend adoption of legislation based on the Model Law when the Bank provides finances for procurement reform.

[38] Paragraph 2 of the UN General Assembly Resolution 49/54.

ised procurement that the Model Law proposes, the functions that are suggested for such an institution do not involve operational procurement but are mainly of an overall supervisory nature.

Adoption of the Model Law took place at a time when a significant number of states were in the process of reforming their procurement systems. There have essentially been three reasons why procurement reform has increased. One is the large number of states that are undergoing the transition from centrally planned socialist economies into market-based economies. The second is the need to modernise public expenditure management in emerging market economies. The third is the need felt by some states to update procurement systems that were adopted essentially during the colonial era and have therefore become outdated.

In the former socialist economies, the concept of competitive public procurement did not exist. The transition to a market-based economy necessitated the change from a system where the state essentially supplied itself through a system of "state orders" into a system where public entities purchased from the private sector through a competitive process. Many of these states have therefore had to enact procurement legislation so as to put in place a competition-based procurement system.

The other objective that has motivated these states in enacting procurement legislation is the desirability of complying with the World Trade Organization Government Procurement Agreement (GPA). The GPA mandates that each government acceding to the GPA should ensure that its procurement legislation conforms with the rules, procedures and practices contained in the GPA.[39] Enactment of legislation based on the Model Law ensures such conformity because the procedures contained in the Model Law are closely related to the provisions of the GPA. In addition, many states (including former socialist states) have signed association agreements with the European Union. These call for progress towards harmonisation with the European Union's procurement regime, and this has necessitated enactment of procurement legislation that is transparent and promotes competition.[40]

The need to modernise public sector financial management has also been a factor in the enactment or review of procurement legislation of a significant number of states. In some of these states, in particular the emerging economies of Asia and Latin America, procurement reform is part of a larger effort aimed at increasing transparency in governmental functions and enhancing efficiency in the public and private sectors. In some other states, particularly in Africa, procurement reform is motivated by the need to update outdated procurement systems that were put in place during the colonial era and is also normally part of larger reforms in public sector financial management.

---

[39] Article XXIV, paragraph 5(a) of the WTO Government Procurement Agreement.
[40] See E. Hupkes, "Public Procurement in Central and Eastern Europe" (1997) 6 *Public Procurement Law Review* 49 for a fuller discussion on this subject.

3.1 State practice

Many of these states that are reforming their public procurement systems have implemented legislation based on the Model Law. Among the countries that have legislation based on the Model Law are the following:

3.1.1 Poland

Poland was the first of the former socialist states of Eastern Europe to enact procurement legislation based on the Model Law. It was also the first to put in place a comprehensive procurement system with a fully fledged and professional Office of Public Procurement. The Polish Act on Public Procurement was enacted by the Polish Parliament on 10 June 1994. The Act closely reflects the principles and concepts of the Model Law and also reflects some aspects of the European Community directives, in particular with regard to applicable thresholds. The draft had been widely discussed within Poland and views were sought from a number of international organisations including the World Bank, which financed some of the technical assistance activities for the preparation of the law.[41]

3.1.2 Russia

A decree on "Priority Measures to Combat Corruption and Reduce Budget Expenditures Through Organising Auctions to Procure Products for State Needs" was signed by the President of the Russian Federation on 8 April 1997.[42] The decree states that procurement of goods and works and services shall be carried out by means of competitive bidding.[43] The decree also approved a set of "Regulations on the Organisation of Procurement of Goods, Construction, Works and Services for State Needs". These Regulations, which are appended to and were approved together with the decree, form the substantive procurement law for Russia. The Regulations are closely modelled, both in substance and structure, on the Model Law. The main departure from the Model Law is that the Regulations do not contain separate provisions dealing with services. The terms of the decree are that it shall remain effective until the coming into force of a law on the "Organisation of Auctions to Procure Goods, Construction, Works and Services for States Needs".[44]

3.1.3 Latvia

The Law on Government and Municipal Procurement was passed by the Latvian Parliament on 24 October 1997 and came into effect on 1 January 1997. The law is largely based on the Model Law. The main difference is

---

[41] See "The Act on Public Procurement with Implementing Laws, Forms and Commentary" (Polish Office of Public Procurement).
[42] Decree No. 305, 8 April 1997.
[43] *Ibid.*, paragraph 1.
[44] *Ibid.*, paragraph 7.

that it does not contain separate provisions on services. The law also does not contain some of the procurement methods found in the Model Law such as two-stage tendering and restricted tendering. It does, however, contain the key principles found in the Model Law that are geared towards transparency, competition and fairness.

3.1.4 Albania

In 1993, a decree was passed in Albania which governed all procurement by public entities and provided that such procurement shall be carried out on a competitive basis.[45] With technical assistance from the World Bank, Albania then embarked on preparation of comprehensive procurement legislation. Such legislation was passed on 26 July 1995.[46] This law is closely modelled on the Model Law. However, rather than create an extra method of procurement for services, this law provides that "request for quotations" shall be used as the method to "obtain consulting services or other services for which tendering is not a suitable" method. This law entered into force on 1 November 1995.[47]

Other countries which have passed legislation based on the Model Law include Kazakhstan[48] and the Kyrgyz Republic.[49] Many of these states that have already adopted such legislation were those where no competitive procurement systems had existed in the past. Other such states that are in the process of preparing legislation based on the Model Law include Tajikistan, the Ukraine, Turkmenistan, Croatia, Uzbekistan and Slovakia.

3.1.5 Other countries

There are also a number of states that have had competition-based procurement systems which are in the process of reforming their procurement legislation and are in the process of enacting legislation based on the Model Law. These include Pakistan, Ghana, Ecuador, Tanzania and Malawi.

4. CONCLUSION

The UNCITRAL Model Law has established the minimum threshold that good procurement legislation should meet. It has codified the common understanding that the public purchaser will most likely get the best value for money when the procurement procedures are characterised by

---

[45] Procurement Decree No. 467 of 18 August 1993.
[46] Public Procurement Law, No. 7971, 26 July 1995.
[47] *Ibid.*, Article 21.
[48] Law on State Procurement, enacted by the Parliament in June 1997 and to come into force on 1 January 1998.
[49] Law on State Procurement of Goods, Construction and Services, adopted by the Legislative Assembly in April 1997 and entered into force on 1 July 1997.

transparency, wide competition and economy and efficiency. Adoption of legislation based on the Model Law will not only enable states to put in place such modern and up-to-date procurement systems but will also have an impact on the institutional mechanisms that states will need to put in place to ensure compliance with the law. It is expected that many states will take up procurement reform as the push for greater transparency in the management of public resources becomes even more widespread. Further, as more states become parties to the WTO Government Procurement Agreement, the necessity to enact legislation that is in conformity with the GPA will lead states to use the Model Law as a readily available model for such legislation. The influence of the Model Law will, therefore, continue to be enhanced by these developments.

6. Procurement Regulation and Emerging Economies: The Examples of Laos and Bhutan

*Peter Trepte**

1. INTRODUCTION

This chapter addresses some of the issues involved when considering the development of domestic procurement rules in emerging economies. The examples of Laos[1] and Bhutan[2] have been chosen for opportunistic reasons and not because they shed any particular light on the processes involved: the author was retained by the Asian Development Bank to draft appropriate procurement rules for these countries.[3] They do, however, in their different ways, offer an insight into some of the issues and imperatives which characterise the need for procurement regulation. This chapter is necessarily of a general nature and does not seek to offer a detailed analysis of all the principles and objectives which underlie the recent exponential emergence of regulated procurement systems. Those principles are manifold and the nature and scope of any particular system is entirely dependent on its context. There is no universally appropriate system[4] since each system, domestic, regional or international, is the result of a whole series of economic, social and political considerations which prevail at a given moment in the geographical area in which procurement is regulated. For example, a national system cannot always be used as a model for a regional system based, as is at least partly the case with the European Community, on the integration of the regional markets, nor can a

---

* Barrister, Littleton Chambers, London.
[1] The Lao People's Democratic Republic.
[2] The Kingdom of Bhutan.
[3] The views expressed in this chapter are personal to the author and do not represent the views of the Asian Development Bank.
[4] The UNCITRAL Model Law on Procurement of Goods, Construction and Services comes closest. It is a model and not a blueprint to be applied, as has sometimes been the case, automatically without discretion and without regard to the local practical, legal and political constraints.

system based on free trade necessarily be used as a model for systems to be used in developing countries.[5]

2. THE CONTEXT

Both Laos and Bhutan are economies in transition. Laos was and remains for the foreseeable future a country with a communist ideology. It is, as is the case with many other former communist countries,[6] slowly abandoning its reliance on the command economy where the requirements of the government in terms of goods and works were met by way of internal resource allocation rather than by way of procurement which implies the existence of a market from which such requirements may be purchased. The move towards such liberalisation faces a number of difficulties in a formerly centrally planned economy. In particular, there is a problem of a lack of suppliers who have been largely ignored by the central government. For its part, Bhutan is a kingdom which has traditionally been subject to significant central control. Its economic policies have tended to follow the pattern of planned economies such as India and, indeed, Bhutan's five-year economic plans run in parallel with those of India. Further, Bhutan is an isolated country, both geographically and politically. The result has been heavy dependence on its Indian neighbour for goods and construction services and a poor domestic supply base. With a greater contemporary emphasis on liberalisation and decentralisation, the Bhutanese government is seeking to diminish its dependency and improve its own domestic supply base. In both cases, the government is by far the largest buyer of goods and services, both economies having poorly developed private markets.

In their own way and for markedly different reasons, both Laos and Bhutan are embracing the market economy. From a procurement perspective, there are two major concerns, similar in both contexts, which arise from this transition.

In the first place, the move from the central control of the economy places more control or increased discretion in the hands of the bureaucracy – the ministries and departments responsible for meeting the requirements of the government. They are given more power to deal with finances, though they usually remain closely controlled by a central audit unit operated by the Ministry of Finance or Auditor's Office. This move towards decentralisation is not only of ideological inspiration: it is a practical necessity. The size of

---

[5] There is no reason why developing countries should not aspire to membership of free-trade-based rules such as the World Trade Organization (WTO) Government Procurement Agreement and there may be many good reasons why they should: A. Mattoo, "The Government Procurement Agreement: Implications of Economic Theory" (1996) 19 *World Economy* 695. However, such a move would be foolish where they have not yet developed an appropriate domestic system which will enable them to benefit from such a framework. The relationship between domestic and international procurement rules is considered further in chapter 1 of this volume.

[6] Though not necessarily those in Central and Eastern Europe whose transition has been far quicker.

modern government, the increase in the demands made on it and the breadth of its involvement is such that its affairs cannot, as a matter of logistical possibility, be controlled by one person or one small group of persons. Gone is the idea that a central authority can be all-knowing and all-seeing;[7] there is simply too much information. This is particularly true for procurement, which covers all sectors of the economy. It is the tension between the need to decentralise government activities such as procurement and the need to ensure continued control over the finances of the government that gives rise, in this context, to the need to control or regulate[8] procurement.

In the second place, the transition to market economy is endangered by the absence of a critical component: a market. In the case of Laos, central control and internal resource allocation have deprived the nascent suppliers of any market: they had no buyers. In the case of Bhutan, its geographical isolation[9] and concomitant dependence on neighbouring states has produced a situation in which there is little developed supply base. The move towards a market economy is coupled with the need to create the market. While in developed market economies, it may be said that procurement rules are designed to preserve and enhance competition resulting from market failures, in the case of emerging market economies it would be truer to say that procurement rules assist in the creation of competition and of the competitive market.

It will be seen that, from this perspective, the objectives of procurement rules are almost entirely economic and that it is the transition to a market economy which is seen as desirable to these particular societies.[10] That is not to say that there is no economic objective to other procurement systems, such as the EC or WTO procurement rules; far from it. The point is that, whereas those systems have been developed on the basis of long (national) experience and in the context of societies long accustomed to the economics of the welfare state and the interplay of free trade, emerging economies do not and will not for some time have the luxury of such experience. For them, there are much stronger economic imperatives. There is little doubt

---

[7] F.A. Hayek's "synoptic delusion" wherein lies the belief that all relevant social facts are capable of being known to some one mind and that it is possible to construct from this knowledge of the particulars of a desirable social order: F.A. Hayek, *Law, Legislation and Liberty*, vol. 1, *Rules and Order* (London: 1973), p. 14.

[8] For our present purposes, I adopt Selznick's definition of regulation as "a sustained and focused control exercised by a public agency ... over activities that are generally regarded as desirable to society": "Focusing Organizational Research on Regulation" in Noll (ed.), *Regulatory Policy and the Social Sciences* (University of California Press, 1985). In this case, the public agency is likely to be the ministry of finance, rather than an independent agency. It is a question of self-regulation.

[9] Though its isolation has created a need for self-sufficiency, the supply base has developed in a piecemeal and parochial fashion concentrating on particular localities. This isolation has deprived the existing suppliers of the experience and technology which would have enabled it to develop as in a market economy. This, of course, has left the door open to foreign suppliers who may exploit the situation without, as a corollary, transferring their experience or technology.

[10] *Cf.* Selznick, note 8 above.

that, with time, such economies will recognise the potential of procurement rules for the pursuit of other goals, not only economic but social, industrial[11] and political as has been the case with Western governments;[12] but, for the moment, there are more pressing needs. It is also here that the emerging democracies of Central and Eastern Europe part company with those of, for example, Asia. While they are also concerned with introducing market economies, they must do so within particular constraints. Their desire to integrate speedily with Western Europe has led them to sign a series of agreements with the European Union which require them to take on board a number of legal provisions, including procurement provisions, which have been developed within and for the purposes of the European Union. If membership of the European Union is to follow association, this is necessary. This is not the place to assess the validity of such a course of action, although it is worth reflecting that, in terms of procurement, these countries have been obliged to adopt regulations which reflect those of the European Union in circumstances where their economies do not exhibit the failures such regulations were designed to address and where their economies have not always developed sufficiently to enable such comprehensive systems to have any meaningful economic effect.[13]

There is a further gloss in the case of emerging economies. They are often the beneficiaries of preferential loans and grants on a bilateral basis or from international finance institutions such as the World Bank or the Asian Development Bank. There is a danger that such institutions may come to be seen as a source of plenty and that the supply of funds is there for the asking. That is not so and the institutions are well aware of that, as are, to be fair, those in the beneficiary countries who are responsible for co-ordinating and administering those funds. From both donor and beneficiary comes the knowledge that such funds need to be spent wisely and in the most efficient way possible. Inefficient, injudicious or incompetent expenditure results not only in immediate hardship to the beneficiary in the sense that envisaged projects are either badly or incompletely accomplished but may also put in jeopardy the future readiness of the lending institutions to continue to offer such preferential loans. Explicit or not, the danger is ever present and the need recognised internally for efficient procurement is one that is encouraged and promoted by the lending agencies.[14]

---

[11] It could be said that the creation of a competitive market is an industrial policy, although that term is used more to describe a policy of protecting or developing a particular domestic industry. Here, it is more fundamental. It is a question of creating a competitive market *in toto*, not concentrating on any particular market segment for special consideration.

[12] See, for example, P.A. Geroski "Procurement Policy as a Tool of Industrial Policy" (1990) 4 *International Review of Applied Economics* 182; S. Arrowsmith "Public Procurement as an Instrument of Policy and the Impact of Market Liberalisation" (1995) 111 *Law Quarterly Review* 235.

[13] The requirement to adapt their legislation to conform with the *acquis communautaire* is, however, tempered by transitional periods which are designed to allow time for readjustment.

[14] It is no coincidence that these lending agencies offer beneficiary countries grants to assist in the preparation of appropriate procurement rules.

3. THE ECONOMIC BACKGROUND

Borrowing once again from Hayek, he argues that the formation of market exchange relations are self-generating structures which have a tendency to equilibrium. Markets are thus superior mechanisms to central planning systems because they have in-built discovery procedures through the ability of the pricing system to register preferences.[15] This corresponds fairly accurately to the basic tenets of neo-classical and liberal economics[16] which have had such a huge impact on the modern mixed market economies in which procurement regulations have been developed and have, dare it be said, flourished.

From an economic point of view, economic efficiency is the goal or, in terms of the Chicago School, the natural outcome of the free market. Such a natural outcome relies, however, for its achievement on the intellectual construct of perfect competition. At the risk of oversimplifying, it may be said that if all factors of production and goods and services pass through perfectly competitive structures, the outcome will be economically efficient.[17] Such perfection relies on a number of assumptions and it is the inadequacy of these assumptions, or market failures, which has led, in many cases, to the intervention of the state by way of regulation. It is also one of the reasons why procurement has been regulated. The pursuit of economic efficiency in procurement is the result of a recognition that market failures exist and the economic purpose of procurement rules is to correct such failures. In the case of emerging economies, the purpose is not only to correct such failures but also to promote and to seek to establish an environment in which competition may flourish.

The assumptions underlying the principle of perfect competition may be characterised as follows:

(i) many buyers motivated by self-interest and acting to maximise utility;
(ii) many sellers motivated by self-interest and acting to maximise profits in atomistic industries or contestable markets;
(iii) individual buyers and sellers are unable to exert any control over market prices and are thus price takers;
(iv) prices serve as guideposts for decision-makers in the market to communicate scarcity;
(v) products are standardised;
(vi) there are no barriers to entry or exit;
(vii) all buyers and sellers are fully informed as to the terms of all market transactions;

---

[15] Hayek, note 7 above.

[16] Largely espoused by the Chicago School of Economics.

[17] Such efficient outcomes are said to be *Pareto optimal*, after the economist Pareto, by which is meant that resources cannot be reallocated so as to make one individual better off without making someone else worse off. See, for a more detailed explanation, N. Mercuro and S. Medema, *Economics and the Law* (Princeton University Press, 1997).

(viii) resources are held in private property with all rights defined and assigned; and

(ix)   prevailing laws are fully enforced through the state.[18]

While most of these assumptions have an effect on procurement one way or another, from the point of view of emerging economies, it is those assumptions which concern the government as buyer which are relevant. The model of perfect competition assumes that the government is a buyer like any other (point (i) above), that it cannot exert control over market prices (point (iii) above) and that, as buyer, it is fully informed of market transactions (point (vii) above). The model ignores the role and status of government which is seen as some sort of "black box" and treated as an individual like any other. On the other side, emerging economies cannot merely assume that the sellers operate in contestable markets (point (ii) above) and their recent history demonstrates that prices do not always reflect the reality of the market (point (iv) above).[19] Their procurement rules are partially designed to create such contestable markets and not to correct failures in contestability.

4. REALISATION OF ECONOMIC OBJECTIVES

The government is not a buyer like any other. For present purposes, it is different to private buyers because (i) it is a government with the responsibility for the welfare of its people and (ii) it is a collectivity of individuals who hold hierarchical positions within that collectivity. The result of its responsibility for its people's welfare is that, even in terms of procurement, the pursuit of economic efficiency is unlikely to be its only function. It will have endowed itself with objectives of social as well as economic welfare; it will have political imperatives and priorities;[20] it will want to ensure its position in the international arena. These other imperatives have always coloured Western governments' approach to procurement policy[21] and may well find a role to play in the policies of emerging democracies. However, the development of their first procurement policy is dictated by the considerations consequent upon a move from a centrally controlled or planned economy to a decentralised one. Their immediate concern

---

[18] *Ibid.*, pages 13–14.

[19] The continuing use of schedules of rates and attempts to assess costs in a vacuum and in the absence of competition are perhaps the best indication of the difficulty of abandoning the comfort of a control economy. Prices were irrelevant when it was a question of internal resource allocation. Persuading suppliers in a newly created market economy to evaluate the real costs of production relative to scarcity is no mean feat.

[20] As a body of politicians it may well have other priorities, not the least of which will be the desire for re-election and this may well affect its regulatory policies: Buchanan, "Rent Seeking and Profit Seeking" in J.M. Buchanan, R.D. Tollison and G. Tullock (eds.), *Toward a Theory of the Rent-Seeking Society* (Texas, 1980). It may also be the (willing) victim of such "capture". These considerations are all outside the scope of this chapter.

[21] See, for example, note 14 above.

remains control over finances and imposing not only the objective but also the requirement of economic efficiency[22] on those responsible for government procurement.

The difficulties in this context arise from the nature of government itself. It is not an individual but is made up of politicians and bureaucrats. It is these latter that are usually responsible for procurement: they are the agents of government.[23] Agents, of course, may not share the aspirations of the politicians in their entirety and, if the objective is to keep sound control over finances, it is important that the agents should be made to comply with the principles of good financial husbandry. This becomes a necessity where financial resources are scarce and where inefficient spending and wastage will have a serious knock-on effect on other areas of government spending and the economy.

Perhaps the most obvious danger and one that the West[24] is quick to remark upon is that of corruption. It may be axiomatic to state that bureaucrats who earn US$100 a month may be tempted to accept bribes, but that does not make it any less of an issue. Taking the first assumption of the efficiency theory described above, the utility sought to be maximised by the agent is most likely to be his own personal utility, i.e. increased income, better working conditions and improved job prospects. It is not necessarily co-extensive with the utility sought by the government.[25] Add to that the fact that in many countries in transition there is a poor private market which gives a greater incentive for suppliers with poor alternative markets to resort to bribery of government purchasers and the danger of corruption looms large. However, corruption is a gamble,[26] a risk to the bribee, and the success of that gamble largely depends on the constraints within which the agent operates. There are essentially two areas in which the corrupt official could defeat the competitive process; he can influence the choice of supplier and he can manipulate the terms on which the contract is awarded. In both cases, the control exercised by the government as principal (for example, by way of audit or hierarchically superior internal control by the Ministry of Finance) can temper the potential lack of probity.

In terms of identity of the supplier, provisions relating to access to the procurement process, that is allowing only properly qualified bidders to participate and ensuring that the process of selection is open and transparent is a reliable means of preventing bids from bidders who would be

---

[22] At least, what is perceived to result in economic efficiency.

[23] It is in this recognition of the principle of agency that the new institutionalist economists have been most helpful in clarifying the role of procurement regulation.

[24] It is interesting that corruption is seen as an Asian problem whereas European countries can hardly come with clean hands themselves. It is perhaps only more sophisticated and concealed in the West. There is also a certain amount of hypocrisy with Western companies complaining that they need to bribe in order to get work; to such an extent that bribes paid for contracts outside the country are even tax-deductible (as for example, in Germany). That is not to suggest that there is not a problem but to remark that throwing stones in glasshouses is a dangerous activity.

[25] J. Gwartney and R. Stroup, *Economics: Private and Public Choice* (New York, 1980).

[26] O. Cadot, "Corruption as a Gamble" (1987) 33 *Journal of Public Economics* 223.

able to participate only by means of a bribe. However, it is not only incompetent bidders who may be tempted to bribe. Even where the bidder is certain of his ability to execute the contract on the best terms, he may be tempted to offer bribes in circumstances where it is known that the only means of obtaining any contract is by way of bribe. If price were the only factor in determining the award of a contract and in the absence of private markets against which prices may be compared, then a system of sealed bids by qualified bidders would suffice to avoid or at least alleviate corruption.[27] However, price is rarely the only factor other than in cases of mundane, off-the-shelf purchases. There is a need to consider other factors such as quality, durability, long-term economic benefits or contractual terms, for example is it the agent that is likely to possess greater information and knowledge than his principal and is it the agent who has the upper hand?[28] Procurement regulation can have an impact on diminishing this particular informational discrepancy by curbing the discretion of the agent. This is done by way of ensuring that the considerations taken into account are objectively verifiable. Thus, the bases upon which bids are evaluated must be clear and precise and must be capable of *ex post* assessment. There will still be discretion in the hands of the agent (the engineer must be able to decide what is necessary for a particular works) but it will be capable of verification, though that ability to verify will depend on the capacities of the monitoring authorities.[29]

Establishing such rules in the procurement process will certainly assist in curbing what may be called "opportunistic" corruption; that is, the exploitation made possible by the principal–agent relationship. More sophisticated forms of corruption may require more sophisticated forms of detection,[30] but the establishment of procurement rules is certainly an important weapon in the armoury.

This lack of a common identity of purpose between the principal and agent also gives rise to less obnoxious but hardly less damaging inefficiencies. If the buyer were a private firm, its objective would be to maximise profits. If similar economic objectives were assumed to exist in government buyers, the profit motive could be characterised as the need to save money on one transaction in order to be able to carry out further transactions in the public good. Where resources are scarce this becomes imperative. This

---

[27] S. Rose-Ackerman, "The Economics of Corruption" (1975) 4 *Journal of Public Economics* 187.

[28] This asymmetrical information in the hands of the agent is inherent in the concept of procurement agency and gives rise to a number of problems of inefficiency: see, for example, J.-J. Laffont & J. Tirole, *A Theory of Incentives in Procurement and Regulation* (MIT Press, 1993).

[29] In developing countries, control of the procurement process is usually carried out on the first level by hierarchically superior tender committees and, secondly, by auditors. Judicial review procedures are a rarity in developing countries, partly due to the unwillingness of the central government to cede authority over financial control. However, judicial review at the instance of disappointed tenderers is a way of relieving the government of the task and cost of monitoring the process and delivers into the hands of the government's constituents (its subjects) the ability to ensure that the goals of economic welfare are being pursued. See, for examples, J.J. Laffont & J. Tirole and A. Mattoo, notes 5 and 28 above.

[30] S. Rose-Ackerman, note 27 above.

government profit motive may not be shared by the agent whose objective may rather be to benefit his own position, as noted above. A reduction in his work effort or failures in his work may reduce the firm's or the government's profit but it does not directly affect the agent's profit (income). Inefficient procurement rarely leads to the closure of the department (whereas a private firm may well suffer to the extent of bankruptcy) and only in cases where the lack of probity is proven, will it lead to redundancy. Further, as noted, knowledge of the procurement market is likely to be in the hands of the agent, not the principal, so that it may be difficult for the principal to realise that there has been inefficiency. This is compounded by the fact that there is less likely to be in the case of a government purchaser than in the case of a private purchaser, a clear yardstick by which to measure economic performance. The cost–benefit analysis resulting in profits and losses for a private company is far less direct in the case of the government buyer.[31]

As a result, it is often the case that agents buy goods and services without regard for the "profit" the government may be assumed to need for the pursuit of other socially desirable objectives. Since the agent feels no direct benefit from the increased profit assumed to result from the application of economically efficient procurement, he may tend to ignore such efficiencies. Notwithstanding any lack of probity on his part, he may simply become careless for he has no incentive to be otherwise. Equally serious is the agent who, far from being careless, has the public good at heart. He sees it as his duty to get the best results; the problem is that the best result in his mind is the best product, invariably the most expensive. There is a danger here that contract specifications are overly optimistic and that the government obtains products which are far above what is needed with the concomitant over-expenditure and vulnerability to excessive long-term costs.

Procurement rules seek to alleviate both instances of such inefficiency by requiring goals to be set objectively. Thus, the desire to get the cheapest product is palliated by the ability to evaluate goods and services in a way that is suited to the requirements. The ability of the agent to take into account the quality and performance of what is to be purchased is similarly subjected to the need to obtain the best value for money. This is achieved by setting out the criteria to be used for evaluating and awarding contracts. Specifications are set according to the output that is required which will be as simple or as sophisticated as necessary and the offers which meet these specifications will be evaluated in terms of best value, either by reference to price or by reference to price in addition to other criteria such as quality, performance over the long term, costs of repair, availability of spare parts

---

[31] This proposition is based on the tensions inherent in the principal–agency relationship. It is not necessarily the case that public sector organisations are always less efficient and less "profitable" than their private counterparts: A. Boardman and A. Vining, "Ownership and Performance in Competitive Environments: A Comparison of the Performance of Private, Mixed and State-Owned Enterprises" (1989) *Journal of Law and Economics* 1; M. Uttley and K. Harper, "The Political Economy of Competitive Tendering" in Clarke and Pitelis (eds.), *The Political Economy of Privatization* (Routledge, 1993).

etc. The "most economically advantageous tender" of the EU system and the "lowest evaluated substantially responsive bid" of the lending institutions' systems each seek to fulfil this objective.

Agents in transitional economies face further practical obstacles to the achievement of such goals, however. The move from a command economy has placed pressure on procurement agencies to tackle these problems in a piecemeal fashion with each department dealing with the problems on an isolated basis. Coupled with the absence of permanent and properly trained procurement officers, the lack of a standardised procurement system throws up discrepancies and inconsistencies between government procedures and serves to compound existing difficulties, In addition, the result of the participation of so many aid and loan agencies (bilateral or otherwise), each with their own preferred system of procurement, merely adds to the confusion.[32] The purpose of domestic procurement rules in such circumstances is to standardise and streamline the national procurement policy and to persuade lending agencies, where possible, to rely on such procedures which will, ultimately reflect precisely the same concerns and offer substantially the same results as their own systems.

The difficulties of the emerging competitive markets pose more challenging difficulties. Suppliers accustomed to the traditional command economy have difficulty in adapting to the development of contestable markets required by the competitive bidding procedures envisaged by procurement regulation. They have been used to a situation in which prices are not an accurate indication of the real costs of supply. They have been used to calculating prices based on a schedule of rates published by the government. Such a schedule indicates the prices expected to be paid by the government (based largely on tentative and unsubstantiated market analysis or on comparative analyses) which do not, or rarely, reflect the true cost of production. Indeed, in the absence of a properly developed market such estimates are redundant and may well be the result of capture.[33] The practice is usually to accept the published rates and then to shave off a percentage from one rate or increase another in order to arrive at a final, cosmetic, price. For its part, the government tends to use the published rates as a guideline and exclude all bids which are below or above, say, 20 per cent of the rate. That does not leave it with bids which are any more likely to fulfil its requirements. A frequent complaint in such economies is that the successful suppliers and contractors fail to perform as expected and almost invariably seek further payment to complete the tasks. Such

---

[32] Most of these systems, it should be said, are identical in their objectives but are often different in their detailed provisions. The difficulty is more to do with different terminology than it is with substantively different procedures, though this does not prevent such agencies insisting on having their own systems applied, to the detriment of the already confused national procurement agencies.

[33] That is, where there is no competitive market, the government is obliged to make a survey of prices. The survey will be carried out using the existing suppliers who certainly have no interest, individually or collectively, in giving low estimates. Since the government is usually the only buyer, it may of course make its own low estimates which are wholly uneconomic and may lead to difficulties.

payments are necessary for, without it, the bidders will be unable to proceed and may simply vanish. This is not the undeniably frequent cost and time overruns experienced in other countries occasioned by inflation or exchange-rate fluctuations or unforeseen circumstances, it is a direct result of cosmetic pricing. The bidders have no real idea of the true costs of providing the service where they rely on published rates. In works contracts, for example, they assume that the government has done its work at the site and fail to make their own site visits. They rely instead on the published rates and calculate their costs and profit accordingly. It is no surprise, therefore, that they often cannot complete the project on time, at the agreed price or at all.

By requiring competitive bidding, the procurement rules seek to force suppliers to take account of the true costs of carrying out projects and base their bids on the reality of doing business. There will undoubtedly be casualties but this is a necessary part of creating a competitive market. Not all suppliers will survive in a competitive market but the government's interest is to benefit from the competitive market not waste its energies and scarce resources in supporting inefficient suppliers.

This attitude is tempered in one respect, however. Markets which have been closed to outside competition for long periods find themselves particularly vulnerable to competition from third countries whose suppliers have been able to develop in competitive markets and which are, by and large, more efficient than domestic companies. It is usually the case that such foreign firms have a comparative cost advantage, that is, as a result of their experience in the competitive market, they have succeeded in reducing costs. This will not normally be the case for domestic suppliers whose costs may be higher.[34] It is often thought advisable to grant a certain amount of limited protection to the domestic industry by giving local goods or local suppliers a certain preference. The aim is not to protect inefficient suppliers but to allow efficient suppliers to develop and emerge in the newly competitive market. To allow unrestricted access for third country suppliers to markets in the early stages of their development may give governments access to cheaper products but at the cost of the development of a domestic supply base and of impoverishing the national economy. It is a limited restriction based on a preference for purchasing the domestic firm's products provided the increased cost involved in buying the domestic product does not exceed the cost of buying the foreign product by a certain fixed percentage.[35] This benefits the domestic firms who have a cost disadvantage by allowing the government to opt for the higher-priced bid. The benefit to the government is that the profit made by the domestic supplier re-enters the national economy, thereby

---

[34] However, with labour costs and sometimes raw material costs lower in the domestic markets, it is perfectly possible for the domestic firms to hold a comparative advantage.
[35] See R.P. McAffee and J. McMillan, "Government Procurement and International Trade" (1989) 26 *Journal of International Economics* 291; F. Branco, "Favoring Domestic Firms in Procurement Contracts" (1994) 37 *Journal of International Economics* 65.

increasing social welfare.[36] To operate optimally, such price preferences should apply on an industry-by-industry basis according to the relative cost advantages between domestic and foreign suppliers. Such an analysis would be gargantuan, however, and most countries which operate such a system, evidently not only developing countries, have opted for single fixed preference levels.[37]

The use of a limited price preference avoids the dangers of other more direct import restrictions which may have the effect of sealing off the domestic market. Total insulation is of little assistance to emerging economies.[38] Small markets, even at government level, targeted by a number of domestic suppliers arrests the development of efficiencies of scale as well as development in terms of new technologies and experience. Collusion among this small band of suppliers is also a distinct possibility. Moreover, insulation from foreign suppliers provides them with mono- poly positions which reduces their incentive to reduce costs and maximise their efficiency. Limited price preference, though in practice incapable of multi-industry specificity, is a middle road which serves to offer limited protection to domestic industry and to assist the government in its objective of building its economy without closing off foreign competition.

There are undeniable merits to allowing international trade which may improve national output and the benefits of discrimination are far from proven;[39] but it is naive to suggest that procurement systems based on free trade principles are motivated purely by altruism. Countries are content to subscribe to such systems not because they seek to develop their own domestic markets through competitive forces but because they see advant- ages for their own suppliers in having access to the markets of third countries. That membership of such a system implies reciprocal access merely indicates the belief that their own domestic markets are sufficiently strong to withstand such competition. It is not only developing countries which may be permitted certain derogations from the GPA; the existing text contains a series of annexes which indicate very clearly those areas in which the existing signatories would prefer to maintain a certain amount of protection for their own markets.[40] Emerging economies are wise to

---

[36] In cases where the domestic firm has a cost advantage, however, this would simply serve to increase the cost to the government unnecessarily for, even without the price preference, the local supplier would have won the bid.

[37] For example, the US applies a basic 6 per cent price preference under the Buy America Act, Canada 10 per cent and Australia 20 per cent.

[38] A. Krueger, *Trade Policies and Developing Nations* (Brookings Institution, 1995).

[39] *Cf.* A. Mattoo, "The Government Procurement Agreement: Implications of Economic Theory" (1996) 19 *World Economy* 695; M. Herander, "Discriminatory Government Procurement with a Content Requirement: its Protective Effects and Welfare Costs" (1986) 14 *Atlantic Economic Journal* 20.

[40] A cynic might comment that the current debate concerning the maintenance of labour and environmental standards in international trade, albeit couched in terms of moral rectitude, and espoused by the developed countries has less to do with economic efficiency and global economic welfare than with the desire of those countries to protect themselves from the identifiable comparative cost advantages of some developing countries. A modicum of cynicism may be justified.

require initial protection, at least until they have a sufficiently strong domestic supply base to obtain bilateral advantage from free trade rules.

The existence of a single buyer has also shaped the attitude of suppliers. As mentioned above, it creates an incentive for such suppliers to engage in corrupt practices since, in the absence of alternative markets, they depend on government purchases. This situation also provides an environment in which supplier collusion may flourish. A single supplier may not be able to carry out all the contracts on offer and may decide, in collusion with other suppliers, to allocate the different contracts between the suppliers. In small societies where all market participants are on social terms, this practice becomes an attractive and socially necessary proposition. In addition, foreign suppliers, by virtue of their proximity and preferential access to those markets,[41] also have an incentive to co-operate both with each other and with domestic suppliers.[42]

This presents the procurement regulator with a difficulty since procurement regulation imposes duties and obligations on the buyer, not the seller. The seller responds to the requirements of efficiency imposed by the regulation; he is given the opportunity of participating on fair and equal terms. The impact of that regulation on the conduct of sellers is far more limited and is properly the domain of anti-trust legislation. Needless to say, the development of anti-trust legislation is also in its infancy in transitional economies but it is important that such legislation be pursued since procurement legislation is capable only of controlling one side of the equation; it cannot also effectively control collusion. The ability given to procurement agencies to reject bids where there has been no effective competition is a mechanism which enables the agency, to a limited extent, to reject bids in circumstances where there has been collusion. However, it will be a reaction based on supposition since collusion is an art form in itself and its effect will be commensurately reduced.

A further consequence of the absence of market experience is the lack of contracting experience; and the desire of emerging economies to elaborate an effective procurement system is accompanied by the desire to ensure adequate contract elaboration and responsibility. The problems associated with the inability of suppliers to complete their contracts on time or at all are not only the result of the long-standing comfort of standardised prices expected by the government, as explained above, but also the result of the failure of the procurement agent properly to draft the contract. While the mechanisms of bid security, performance bonds and liquidated damages are recognised, they are rarely properly understood. A bid security is often used after the award of a contract as a performance security for example and is, consequently, ineffective as a guarantee of the completion of the contract since its value is based on its use as a guarantee to see the bidding process through to its conclusion, not the contract.

---

[41] In the case of Bhutan, Indian suppliers, in the case of Laos, Thai suppliers, neither of whom, it is fair to say, are renowned for their high level of probity.

[42] This could, of course, be beneficial if such co-operation were accompanied by a transfer of technology and experience.

Such misunderstandings are common and it is inevitable that assistance is needed on the contracting front as well as on the primary need for procurement regulation. Naturally, most of the problems require solutions based on the applicable law of contract as well as the positions of the parties and have little to do with the regulation of procurement (though all to do with the procurement process) which, for its part, is concerned only with the process up to the award of the contract. Nevertheless, the issue of bidding documents will contain reference to the contract terms expected and the ability of the parties to comply with such terms may well have an effect on the pre-contractual procurement process. Procurement rules developed for emerging economies will, therefore, unlike their counterparts in developed countries, include a good deal of contract information which, while largely incapable of regulation,[43] will assist the agencies to administer their contracts effectively and encourage a more competitive reaction from the developing domestic supply base.

5. CONCLUSION

The objectives of reforming the procurement practices of emerging economies are manifold. They seek, *inter alia*:

  (i)   to streamline disparate purchasing practices;
  (ii)   to establish rules which require responsibility and accountability in procurement agencies;
  (iii) to encourage economic efficiency in procurement;
  (iv)   to avoid abuse of power and diversion of public funds;
  (v)   to assist in the creation of conditions under which competitive markets may be established and flourish;
  (vi)   to assist in the development of a domestic supply base;
  (vii) to encourage an understanding of effective contracting; and
  (viii) to develop expertise in the procurement process.

While the essential characteristics of such systems are identical to the bases on which international procurement systems are predicated, their immediate objectives may differ. It is the context of the procurement rules which must be appreciated. Recent procurement reforms in many developing countries have focused on the reform of procurement law from a domestic point of view. However, their implementation of efficient procurement procedures will mean that they are also well placed to accede to international agreements on public procurement.

---

[43] Where the applicable contract law is based on the freedom of contract which, following transition, it usually is.

7. Corruption in Developing Countries and in Countries in Transition: Legal and Economic Perspectives

John Linarelli[*]

1. INTRODUCTION

Corruption has ancient roots and is a global phenomenon.[1] This chapter examines the effects of corruption in developing countries and in countries in transition from socialism, with a focus on corruption in public procurement. Corruption and the incentives provided by laws and institutions are examined to assess whether there should be attempts to deter corruption because it is socially wasteful or whether corruption should be left alone as the "grease" that facilitates voluntary exchange and market equilibrium. On the whole, corruption results in numerous undesirable consequences, and governments should implement legal and institutional measures to detect it and penalise corrupt agents in both the public and private sectors.

Section 2 of this chapter examines arguments for and against corruption and sets forth a brief survey of the literature. Section 3 examines some of the significant legal and institutional approaches to stopping corruption. The conclusions that are reached are problematic. The elimination of corruption in public procurement in developing and transitioning countries depends on much more than good procurement rules. It will depend on long-lasting and credible reform of the executive, legislative and judicial organs of state that surround the procurement system and upon which a properly functioning procurement system depends for its viability. There are no easy solutions to combating corruption.

---

[*] Lecturer in Law, University of Wales, Aberystwyth.
[1] P. Bardhan, "Corruption and Development: A Review of the Issues" (1997) 35 *Journal of Economic Literature* 1320; P.M. Nichols, "Outlawing Transnational Bribery Through the World Trade Organization" (1997) 28 *Law and Policy in International Business* 305.

2. IS CORRUPTION GOOD OR BAD?

No consensus exists in the literature on whether corruption harms or facilitates social welfare. The conclusions depend on the discipline. The trend, however, is to condemn corruption as bad for economic growth and for the sustainability of institutions that facilitate development.

Legal scholars tend to *assume* that corruption is undesirable. Corruption as it is dealt with in the law probably can be traced to the origins of criminal law, to moral philosophy and to Judeo-Christian ethics and tenets.[2] In criminal law, a distinction exists between *malum in se* and *malum prohibitum*. Corruption is undesirable because it is a lie, results in a fraud and is an abuse of the public trust. In the common law generally, fraud and misrepresentation taint the integrity of the bargain process and in some cases make a contract void or voidable. Corruption in the law carries normative labels that are quite unfavourable. How could lawyers argue that violations of formal law (for example, of an anti-bribery statute), or fraud in the inducement of a contract, can be good? The normative issues associated with a legal analysis of corruption may have the effect of making it difficult for lawyers to do much more than condemn corruption and to formulate ways to stop it.

Economists have attempted to model the consequences of corruption in an economy and in transactions – to describe the effect of corruption on exchange and on industrial organisation.[3] Far fewer have been econometric studies of corruption, most likely because it is very difficult to obtain data on corruption.[4] No economic theories on corruption exist for which there is a broad consensus, and there are very few data-driven studies on corruption. Nevertheless, the literature sheds light on the operations of corruption and on its negative effects.

Some scholars have posited that corruption facilitates trade and voluntary exchange. "It is often argued that bribes serve as 'lubricants' in an otherwise sluggish economy and improve its efficiency."[5] Corruption has been said to facilitate the avoidance of cumbersome regulations by entrepreneurs. This position has been explained as follows:

Interference with the free market usually induces inefficiencies. However, bribes sometimes can partially restore the price mechanism and improve allocative efficiency. Corruption might be viewed as people's optimal response to market distortions. In this sense, corruption has some beneficial effects to society, but the resulting solution is only second-best.[6]

---

[2] This chapter refers to Western law.

[3] In the interest of brevity, descriptions of formal economic models are omitted.

[4] See P. Mauro, "Corruption and Growth" (1995) *Quarterly Journal of Economics* 681.

[5] F.T. Lui, "An Equilibrium Queuing Model of Bribery" (1995) 93 *Journal of Political Economy* 760.

[6] F.T. Liu, "Three Aspects of Corruption" (1996) 14 *Contemporary Economic Policy* 26. A standard graduate microeconomics text summarises the meaning of "second best" as the "best allocation of resources that is obtainable when various constraints preclude attaining true economic efficiency": W. Nicholson, *Microeconomic Theory: Basic Principles and Extensions* (Dryden Press, 1995), p. 878. For an extended treatment, see R.G. Lipsey and K.J. Lancaster, "The General Theory of Second Best" (1956–7) 24 *Review of Economic Studies* 11.

Political scientists have asserted that corruption could in appropriate circumstances promote development.[7] Nye, writing in 1967, catalogued the costs and benefits of corruption. In his analysis, corruption could benefit development in the following ways:

(i) by facilitating capital formation through bribes collected by political leaders;

(ii) by cutting red tape where cumbersome regulations have been promulgated as a reaction against colonialism;

(iii) by providing incentives for entrepreneurship, particularly among members of minority groups that would otherwise suffer discrimination and who lack political power;

(iv) by facilitating national integration; elites that control money and those that control politics may assimilate through corruption; moreover, non-elites, unaccustomed to modern government, may find it easier to integrate into society through low-level corruption of government officials; and

(v) by augmenting the capacity of weak governments to govern; legal incentives may have to be augmented by corrupt incentives.[8]

Each of these potential benefits has been debunked thoroughly or rendered irrelevant over the years. In fact, some of them, particularly the first potential benefit, strike us today as naïve.

Some contend that bribery may be a substitute for civil service wages. Bribes may make smaller or eliminate payments of salaries to government officials who, if they can be effectively supervised, will still carry out their functions on a fee-for-service basis.[9] There are significant limitations on this analysis. It assumes effective principal–agent monitoring and does not account for the costs of monitoring. Rent-seeking may result in exemptions from regulation only for bribers.[10] Indeed, regulations themselves may be promulgated or interpreted not with the public interest in mind but to create opportunities for enrichment of government officials through bribes.

[7] N. Leff, "Economic Development Through Bureaucratic Corruption" (1964) *American Behavioural Scientist* 8; and S.P. Huntington, *Political Order in Changing Societies* (Yale University Press, 1968).

[8] J.S. Nye, "Corruption and Political Development: A Cost–Benefit Analysis" (1967) *American Political Science Review* 417.

[9] G. Tullock, "Corruption: Theory and Practice" (1996) 14 *Contemporary Economic Policy* 6.

[10] "Rent-seeking" refers to the use of resources by private actors to attempt to capture the economic rent arising from excessive government intervention. Government intervention may take the form of such devices as permits, approvals, licences, quotas and foreign investment controls. Such rents would not be available in market transactions. Economic rent is the payment to a factor of production (capital, labour, land) in excess of its opportunity (economic) costs. G. Tullock, "The Welfare Costs of Tariffs, Monopolies, and Theft" (1967) 3 *Western Economic Journal* 224; and A.O. Krueger, "The Political Economy of the Rent-Seeking Society" (1974) 64 *American Economic Review* 291.

There are stronger arguments for the proposition that corruption is harmful. There is a statistically significant relationship between slow economic growth and corruption.[11] The problem of corruption is exacerbated in countries in transition from central to market economies. Corruption increases in transition states because of the loss of monopoly power over corruption by former autocratic elites. The weakness of central government allows various government agencies to impose independent bribes and, when entry into the market for corruption is free or relatively inexpensive, high levels of corruption result. Competing bureaucracies are costly to development.[12]

Bribes are similar to taxes but they are more distortionary because they are illegal and secret. The availability of goods in an economy will be determined by corruption opportunities rather than by demand or technological needs. Bureaucrats establish "roadblocks" to prohibit entry of firms in order to keep bribes at higher amounts from established corrupt suppliers. This is a classic situation in which officials may seek to sole-source in procurement. Alternatively, government officials attempt to induce substitution from goods that are genuinely required or preferred, into goods on which bribes may be relatively easier to obtain. The social costs of corruption through misallocation of resources can be quite substantial.[13] Shleifer and Vishny offer the following procurement example from a bottle-making factory in Mozambique:

In 1991 that factory had modern Western equipment for making bottles, but used a traditional process for putting paper labels on these bottles. Three old machines were used: one cut the labels from paper; one then glued the white label on the bottle; and finally one printed a red picture on the label. The bottles were moved manually between these machines. In roughly 30 per cent of the cases, the picture was not centered on the label. When this happened, the bottles were handed over to approximately twelve women, who sat on the floor near the machines and scraped off the labels with knives, so that the bottles could be put through this process again.

Apparently, the process of labelling bottles could be mechanized with a fairly simple machine that cost about $10,000 and could be readily bought with aid money from any number of Western or even Third World suppliers. The manager of the factory, however, did not want to buy such a machine, but instead wanted to have a $100,000 machine, that not only mechanized the existing process, but also printed labels in sixteen colors and different shapes, and put them on different types of bottles. Only one producer in the world made that machine, and the Mozambique government applied to the producer's home country for an aid package to buy it. Since that aid was not immediately forthcoming, the factory kept using the traditional technology.

The demand for equipment much fancier than the factory appeared to need seems irrational until one realizes that buying a fancier machine offered the manager (and ministry officials) much better opportunities for corruption. If the factory bought a

[11] P. Mauro, "Corruption and Growth" (1995) *Quarterly Journal of Economics* 681.
[12] A. Shleifer and R.W. Vishny, "Corruption" (1993) *Quarterly Journal of Economics* 599.
[13] *Ibid.*; and S. Rose-Ackerman, "The Economics of Corruption" (1975) 4 *Journal of Public Economics* 187.

generic machine, the manager would probably have to use international donor's guidelines and consider several offers. There would be very little in this deal for him personally. On the other hand, if he got a unique machine, he would not have to solicit alternative bids. The supplier in turn would be happy to over-invoice for the machine, and kick back some of the profits to the manager (and his ministerial counterpart). The corruption opportunities on buying a unique and expensive machine are much better than such opportunities on buying cheaper generic products.[14]

This is a bilateral monopoly situation – a sole-source procurement. In this example, government enterprise managers are acting rationally in their self-interest. It is the perverse system of incentives and the low risk of detection and punishment that results in the distortionary behaviour. Corruption stifles entrepreneurship and misallocates talent to unproductive rent-seeking activities:

Private rent-seeking takes the form of theft, piracy, litigation, and other forms of transfer between private parties. Public rent-seeking is either redistribution from the private sector to the state, such as taxation, or alternatively from the private sector to the government bureaucrats who affect the fortunes of the private sector. The latter kind of public rent-seeking takes the form of lobbying, corruption, and so on.[15]

Moreover:

Public rent-seeking attacks innovation, since innovators need government-supplied goods, such as permits, licenses, import quotas, and so on, much more than established producers.[16]

Corruption discourages innovation because it is secret and non-transparent. It requires that the numbers of persons involved in the corruption be kept at controllable levels. New entrants have the potential to undermine the system.[17]

In sum, corruption is undesirable and arguments that corruption is beneficial do not take into account a number of costs that far outweigh any occasional benefit in specific transactions. While corruption may facilitate some transactions, it is impossible to restrict it as if in some sealed container that can be easily opened only in certain cases.[18] Assertions on the benefits of corruption suffer from a malady akin to Hayek's "fatal conceit".[19] There is no way that a government can ever know all of the facts and circumstances, and be able to adapt quickly enough, to be able to properly plan such economic activity. Opportunities for corruption provide government

---

[14] A. Shleifer and R.W. Vishny, "Corruption" (1993) *Quarterly Journal of Economics* 599.
[15] K.M. Murphy, A. Shleifer and R.W. Vishny, "Why is Rent Seeking so Costly to Growth?" (1993) 82 *American Economic Association Papers and Proceedings* 409.
[16] *Ibid.*
[17] A. Shleifer and R.W. Vishny, "Corruption" (1993) *Quarterly Journal of Economics* 599.
[18] S. Rose-Ackerman, *Corruption: A Study in Political Economy* (Academic Press, 1978), p. 8.
[19] F.A. Hayek, *The Fatal Conceit: The Errors of Socialism* (University of Chicago Press, 1988).

officials and firm managers with incentives to engage in economically wasteful activities rather than in innovation and productive enterprise.

3. DO INSTITUTIONS MATTER?[19a]

Having briefly surveyed the consequences of corruption, we may turn to the question of how governments should go about stopping it. What measures can governments take to eliminate or at least mitigate corruption? The analysis below discusses (i) the US Foreign Corrupt Practices Act and the efficacy of methods of one government to control corruption in other countries; (ii) the efforts of the Organisation for Economic Co-operation and Development (OECD) to deter corruption; (iii) the efficacy of domestic enforcement regimes and the ability of governments to stop corruption within their own borders; and (iv) the efforts of the World Bank in controlling corruption in procurements that it finances.

3.1 The US Foreign Corrupt Practices Act

The Foreign Corrupt Practices Act, a federal law in the United States, makes it a crime for a "domestic concern", or "any officer, director, employee, or agent of such concern or any stockholder acting on behalf of such domestic concern", to make a payment to a foreign official for the purposes of influencing or inducing the foreign official to engage in corruption.[20] The US is only one of two countries that has such a law.[21] Some countries have even permitted a tax deduction for payment of foreign bribes, in effect subsidising companies that engage in international corruption.

Some legal scholars contend that the Foreign Corrupt Practices Act is effective in restricting the ability of US firms to engage in corruption outside of the US.[22] The Act may have only a limited effect however, in deterring corruption.[23] The law can be examined at both the macro-level of international trade policy between countries and at the micro-level of transactions between public and private enterprises.

[19a] The phrasing of this title is borrowed loosely from the literature on new institutional economics. For a basic discussion of new institutional economics see O.E. Williamson, "The Institutions of Governance" (1998) 88 *The American Economic Review Proceedings* 75. This chapter, however, does not strictly apply the techniques of new institutional economics.

[20] 15 USC 78dd-2. This is of course a summary of the statute. The statute is quite detailed and contains several exceptions.

[21] Sweden also has such a law but it is narrower in scope. OECD Actions to Fight Corruption, Note by the Secretary-General, Council at Ministerial Level, 26–27 May 1997.

[22] P.M. Nichols, "Outlawing Transnational Bribery Through the World Trade Organization" (1997) 28 *Law and Policy in International Business* 305; C.F. Dugan and V. Lechtman, "The FCPA in Russia and Other Former Communist Countries" (1997) 91 *American Journal of International Law* 378.

[23] The Foreign Corrupt Practices Act has two potential effects. First, it may bar US companies from engaging in corruption in other countries. Secondly, it may decrease the level of corruption in a country to the extent that US firms engage in substantial trade in the country. The legislative history of the Act has not been reviewed to determine the Congressional intent underlying the Act. Congress may have been concerned primarily with the first goal. In any event, the focus of the analysis in this chapter is not on intentions but on the effects of the Act.

At the trade policy level, the Act illustrates the classic prisoner's dilemma.[24] The governments of countries without such an anti-corruption law have no incentive to enact a law that restricts their nationals, since these nationals benefit from the restrictions imposed by the US government on US nationals. States in general may be better off if they co-operate and refuse to engage in corruption, including by attempts to combat it such as that adopted by the US, but there is inadequate incentive to engage in such co-operation.

In a competitive environment with corruption that is unlikely to be detected or punished by governmental authorities, US companies may have little choice but to engage in corruption.[25] Compliance with the Act can be examined from a transaction-cost perspective. Companies either incur the costs of retaining counsel to provide assurances of compliance, or incur the costs of paying the bribe and the costs associated with the risk of detection. Counsel and bribes are in this sense substitutes, although by no means perfect ones. In this context, corruption increases the costs of transacting with the corrupt government, regardless of the existence of the anti-corruption law.

3.2 OECD efforts

Some have argued that a multilateral treaty may prove to be the most effective way to require countries to adopt measures to stop or discourage corruption outside of their borders.[26] Such a treaty, however, is not a realistic possibility. Governments are unlikely to be willing to agree to a treaty obligation when they are unwilling to engage in the same behaviour without the treaty.[27]

Far from a treaty, the OECD has issued recommendations and declarations condemning bribery in international transactions. In 1994, the OECD issued a Recommendation on Bribery in International Transactions.[28] In 1996, it conducted a review of the Recommendation, and adopted a Recommendation on the Tax Deductibility of Bribes to Foreign Officials.[29] Also in 1996, the OECD Development Assistance Committee adopted a recommendation setting forth anti-corruption proposals relating to procurement financed by bilateral aid programmes.[30] In 1997, the OECD issued a Revised Recommendation on Combating Bribery in International Transactions.[31] The Revised Recommendation sets forth more specific

---

[24] Alternatively, the Foreign Corrupt Practices Act presents a free-rider problem.

[25] See A. Shleifer and R.W. Vishny, "Corruption" (1993) *Quarterly Journal of Economics* 599.

[26] I am indebted to Christian Walser for this point.

[27] Harvey Palmer suggested this general point to me in the review of another paper.

[28] OECD Document C(94)/75/final (1994); see P. Nichols, "Outlawing Transnational Bribery Through the World Trade Organization" (1997) 28 *Law and Policy in International Business* 305 at 356–7 for a short summary of OECD efforts.

[29] OECD Document C(96)27/final (1996).

[30] OECD Document DCD/DAC/(96)11/final (1996).

[31] OECD Document C(97)123/final (1997).

commitments on corruption in public procurement. Specifically, the Revised Recommendation recommends that:

(i)   Member countries should support the efforts in the World Trade Organisation to pursue an agreement on transparency in government procurement.

(ii)   Member countries' laws and regulations should permit authorities to suspend from competition for public contracts enterprises found to have bribed foreign public officials in contravention of that member's national laws. To the extent a member applies procurement sanctions to enterprises that are determined to have bribed domestic public officials, such sanctions should be applied equally in case of bribery of foreign public officials.

(iii) In accordance with the Recommendation of the Development Assistance Committee, member countries should require anti-corruption provisions in bilateral aid-funded procurement, promote the proper implementation of anti-corruption provisions in international development institutions, and work closely with development partners to combat corruption in all development co-operation efforts.[32]

The OECD measures illustrate the inability of countries to implement anything mandatory at the country level. The OECD recommendations do not, of course, qualify as treaties. There has been only a modest movement towards laws similar to the US Foreign Corrupt Practices Act,[33] and subsequent to the issuance of the Recommendation on tax deductibility, only one country, Norway, passed legislation disallowing the tax deductibility of bribes of foreign public officials.[34] The OECD measures may be evidence of the hypothesis that treaties will arise merely to confirm behaviour that countries would engage in without the treaty.[35] The OECD measures, moreover, suggest that the OECD operates like a private legislature, promulgating vague, open-ended prescriptions of limited value.[36] The structure and operation of the OECD as an international organisation may preclude it from serving as a catalyst for meaningful reform.

3.3 Domestic enforcement regimes

In contrast to unilateral measures such as the US Foreign Corrupt Practices Act, and multilateral measures such as OECD recommendations, enforcement of domestic anti-corruption laws by governments has the potential to

---

[32] *Ibid.* (footnotes omitted).

[33] *Ibid.*

[34] *Ibid.*

[35] Of course, one would have to rely on more than an anecdotal discussion to test the hypothesis.

[36] See P. Stephan, "Accountability and International Lawmaking: Rules, Rents and Legitimacy" (1996) 17 *Northwestern Journal of International Law and Business* 681 (describing attributes of private legislatures).

deter corruption significantly. Institutions do matter here. Weak governments facilitate corruption. Weak governments in a highly regulated state provide perhaps the best environment for corruption.[37]

Political competition through democracy will help to minimise corruption. Democratic institutions may respond to strong public pressure against corruption. Low bribes keep potential political competitors out. Conversely, in non-democratic states, there are no such incentives to keep bribes down.[38] This is borne out by two examples – Japan and the former Zaire. In Japan, the procurement of civil works has been characterised by significant sole-source procurements, conflicts of interest, cartelisation, the use of registration requirements to keep out overseas competitors and other forms of distortionary rent-seeking activity.[39] Public discontent with the procurement system may have had a great deal to do with recent reforms initiated by the Japanese government.[40] By contrast, in the former Zaire, it is widely accepted that corruption was widespread and that the former government participated in corruption on a massive scale.[40] The government of the former Zaire apparently was one of the more pure non-democratic kleptocracies, with no incentive to change.[41]

A number of conclusions may be drawn about the appropriate norms and institutions that govern public procurement. There are two models of procurement systems that exist today: the industrialised nation model and the developing or transitioning country model. These models are designed principally around the institutions available to governments and financing bodies to monitor and detect corruption and bad procurement practice.

In the industrialised nation model, a high degree of professionalisation of the government workforce exists, as well as good pay for public officials. The professionalisation of the workforce is due in substantial part to years of costly investment in the human capital of government workers. The industrialised nation model includes a substantial criminal and quasi-criminal investigative machinery that complements significant regulatory restrictions on procurement. For example, in the US, there are numerous levels of "checkers" or internal enforcement bodies whose functions are to detect corruption. There are the audit agencies, the most notable of which is the Defence Contract Audit Agency (DCAA). Although an agency of the US Department of Defense, the DCAA is the premier audit agency of the US government, and has a tradition of entering into inter-agency agreements to serve as auditors for civilian agencies. The DCAA performs cost audits. The US General Accounting Office (GAO), a legislative agency, also performs audits, but at a programme level. The GAO is an arm of Congress; Congress controls the appropriations power of the US government. If fraud is suspected on a federal contract, auditors may refer the suspected fraud to

---

[37] A. Shleifer and R.W. Vishny, "Corruption" (1993) *Quarterly Journal of Economics* 599.

[38] *Ibid*.

[39] M. Aihara, "The Reformation of the Japanese Public Procurement System in Construction" (unpublished, 1997, on file with the author).

[40] See Country Reports on Economic Policy and Trade Practices, S. Prt. 103-68, 103rd Cong., 2nd Session 30 (February 1994).

[41] *Ibid*.

the Inspector-General of the procuring agency, an official appointed by the President and whose mission is to ferret out "fraud, waste and abuse."

If the Inspector-General suspects criminal activity, he or she may refer the matter to the US Department of Justice or to a US Attorney for criminal prosecution. In addition, the US government may suspend and debar contractors that lack integrity. Suspension and debarment result in the inability of suspected wrongdoers to enter into further contracts with the entire federal government. The government may terminate contracts tainted by corruption as void *ab initio* and may recover all payments made to the contractor even if the contractor successfully performed the contract. Government officials also may be subject to various administrative and criminal penalties for corruption. In addition to such internal enforcement regimes, industrialised nations have developed bid challenge or bid protest systems that permit interested parties to protest procurement actions that violate procurement law.

In the industrialised nation model, governments have a significant degree of leverage over contractor compliance with procurement rules. Certifications in bids on compliance with a host of statutory or regulatory requirements can be enforced. Governments can require disclosure of substantial information by contractors. For example, in the US, the Truth in Negotiations Act requires contractors to disclose to the procuring agency all cost or pricing data that may affect price negotiations significantly in certain circumstances. Onerous civil and criminal penalties may apply to the contractor for failure to comply. Governments may have substantial market power, since they buy significant amounts of goods and services, and are sometimes a monopsony for a product.

In the industrialised nation model, procurement by open procedures or by sealed bidding is not emphasised. The enforcement regime and a well-trained and compensated bureaucracy make less transparency a worthwhile trade-off for enhanced discretion and flexibility.

Although many of these regulatory schemes have been criticised, they will be tinkered with but not substantially reformed, due primarily to the politics of regulatory reform. Notable features of the procurement model outlined above are its cost and complexity.[42]

Almost all of the characteristics of procurement regulation in the industrialised nation model either do not exist in the developing and transitioning countries, or exist in only the nascent stages. The implementation of the above model in these countries would require the fundamental reform of judiciaries, legislatures and bureaucracies, something that cannot be forthcoming immediately in developing and transitioning countries as enforcement machinery simply does not exist or is deficient. The developing country model relies on procurement procedures to facilitate monitoring of agencies and contractors. Open competitive bidding, which provides more transparency than methods of procurement based on requests for proposals

---

[42] The example from the United States provided above may differ significantly from Western European models, although the differences may lie primarily in the details and not in the fundamentals.

or negotiation, are preferred. Bidding promotes a number of procurement disciplines that are fundamental to good procurement practice and that should be mastered before taking on procurement through requests for proposals or negotiation.

Procurement procedures, however, cannot be a substitute for enforcement. Without enforcement capabilities, there may exist considerable risks of non-compliance and corruption by government agents. The Mozambique procurement discussed above reflects precisely the type of behaviour that would constitute "waste and abuse" in American parlance. It would reflect indisputably bad procurement practice in any properly functioning procurement system. But without the means for detection and imposition of penalties, corruption can continue without detection, regardless of strict requirements mandating the use of competitive bidding.

Indeed, legal and institutional reform outside of public procurement perhaps should precede procurement reform. As explained by Rose-Ackerman:

A corrupt judiciary, or one that is not independent of the executive and political branches, is a major problem because corruption cannot be reduced without credible legal sanctions. Once an honest, effective enforcement system has been established, the state can move on to the reform of political and bureaucratic institutions.[43]

Procurement reformers face a daunting task. Procurement reform often occurs in a vacuum, with little or no emphasis on fundamental institutional reform. It is an overlay on existing legal and administrative frameworks. If procurement reform cannot occur in the absence of such fundamental reform, however, then there would seem to be little that the improvement or tightening of procurement procedures alone will do.

3.4 The World Bank

Some commentators criticise the World Bank on a number of grounds, including that the Bank's procurement guidelines are too strict. While the Bank may deserve some criticism, some of the criticism directed against its procurement requirements largely miss the point. Although it is a development bank and not a commercial or merchant bank, the Bank is a *lender*. It is in the business of lending the money of the taxpayers of one country to the taxpayers of another country. It is a creditor that essentially takes the place of the taxpayer in a borrowing country. The Bank, in its role as a lender, faces a typical principal–agent problem: how can it ensure that borrowed funds will be spent in an appropriate manner and not end up siphoned into the personal bank accounts of a select few elites of the borrowing country?[44]

---

[43] S. Rose-Ackerman, "Corruption" (1995) *Annual World Bank Conference on Development Economics* 373.

[44] In addition, the World Bank finances project procurement, i.e. procurement for specific projects. It thus would have less of an incentive to promote procurement procedures that focus on long-run relationships.

The Bank itself is not totally immune from monitoring. The Bank is answerable to the governments of its board of directors on how it spends its money, although this monitoring may focus primarily on politics rather than on development policy. It is in the Bank's best interests to be conservative in its approach to procurement.

The World Bank relies on at least the following nine mechanisms to monitor loan disbursements and to promote efficient expenditure of loan proceeds:

(i) Country procurement assessment reports and appraisals. The World Bank conducts appraisals of the procurement systems of borrowing countries primarily for two reasons: (a) to assess the adequacy of procurement institutions for purposes of loan disbursement and to prepare adequate protections to be set forth in loan agreements; and (b) to determine a country's need for reform of procurement institutions as part of improving governance and to facilitate the transition to a market economy in the borrowing countries.

(ii) Loan conditions. The Bank will include in its loan agreements provisions that govern disbursement of loan proceeds through procurements. The loan agreement trumps domestic law.

(iii) International competitive bidding. The Bank is conservative in its approach to procurement in that it requires the use of international competitive bidding on major procurements. It generally forbids requests for proposals or negotiations for procurement of goods and works. Bidding facilitates monitoring, or at least that is the theory. The public opening of bids makes the procurement process more transparent to interested parties than other award procedures. Bidding is by no means a perfect deterrent of corruption, and there are ways that corruption can occur even in a bidding process. Open competitive bidding nevertheless does make corruption more difficult.

(iv) Loan disbursement procedures. The Bank uses a system of disbursement procedures that is designed to mitigate corruption opportunities. As part of the disbursement process, the Bank will review procurement information provided by the borrower and issue "no objection" notices at important junctures in the procurement process. This monitoring system is by no means foolproof. It is essentially a review – the lowest level that an accountant would take in the examination of the books of an institution. The Bank issues "no objection" notices on the basis of information provided by the borrower, with no independent review by the Bank.

(v) Informal complaints by bidders. The Bank will hear complaints of bidders in the appropriate circumstances. The Bank has been ambivalent in its promotion of bid challenge procedures in its procurement reform efforts.

(vi) Anti-corruption rules. The Bank recently incorporated anti-corruption rules in its guidelines. It remains to be seen how active the Bank will be in policing for corruption.

(vii)   Audits. The Bank has started to conduct programme audits of procurements. These audits are more than Operations Evaluation Department (OED) audits, which deal with the success of an entire project, but also different from a cost audit performed by a traditional auditor. They are audits to assess whether borrowers have conducted procurements with economy and efficiency and free of corruption. It is unknown whether these audits will continue with any vigour as it would be impracticable for the Bank to conduct audits of its numerous borrowers on a systematic basis.

(viii) The threat of misprocurement. In the event that the Bank finds that loan proceeds were spent in a manner inconsistent with its guidelines or with borrower's representations which form the basis of the "no objection" notice issued by the Bank, the Bank may declare a misprocurement and cancel the portion of the loan proceeds allocated to the procurement in question. This could have disastrous consequences for a borrower, particularly where the procurement is for an item that is integral to a project. The misprocurement may also be construed as an event of default under the loan. In practice, the Bank rarely declares misprocurement, although it may use the threat of such a declaration to obtain compliance from a borrower.

(ix)   Procurement reform. The Bank is financing procurement reform in various countries, with a particular emphasis on countries in transition.

4. CONCLUSION

The analysis and findings set forth in this chapter may leave the impression that governments that seek to mitigate corruption face dismal prospects, and that there are few tangible solutions. This is not the intent of the chapter. The "bottom line" of this chapter is straightforward and perhaps obvious: the level of corruption in public procurement does not depend on procurement laws and institutions alone. There are a number of domestic legal and bureaucratic institutions that play a major role. The legal and administrative systems have to generate credible threats of detection and enforcement. Deregulation should remove opportunities for corruption. Finally, professionalisation of the procurement workforce should help to combat corruption.

8.   A Critical Analysis of the Procurement Procedures of the World Bank

*Tim Tucker**

1. INTRODUCTION

Anybody who has worked as a buyer for most of the last 40 years must have noticed that his profession has changed. At the end of the last war, a buyer prided himself on his confrontational approach, and the aim of negotiation was to screw your opponent to the ground. One found solace in the large number of one's suppliers. The buyer was deskbound and put overwhelming emphasis upon price. Procurement was a trade learned by experience. All that has changed, and is still changing: buyers now seek for common ground and a less adversarial approach when dealing with suppliers. They tend to reduce their supplier base, and are now almost as mobile as salesmen. The cry now is for quality over price. Procurement is taught at colleges and universities.

This change would probably have happened anyway, but has been speeded up by the example of the Japanese. The fact that Japanese industry did not have to hold large stocks and could depend upon high-quality supplies arriving at the right time did wonders for cash flow. It gave the Japanese a competitive edge that played a major part in driving many enterprises in older industrial countries out of business. While Europe and America, however, have learned the importance of the profession of supply the World Bank has taken little part in the revolution of purchasing techniques.

On the other hand, it is a very important procurement organisation. It spends US$2.5 million every hour,[1] and since its inception has provided nearly US$250 billion in financing for some 5,000 development projects. In recent fiscal years average annual lending of US$22 billion has accounted for about 220 new projects.[2] As explained in an official text book on World Bank procurement:

---

* Procurement Consultant.
[1] S. George, *Faith and Credit, The World Bank's Secular Empire* (Penguin, 1995).
[2] http://www.worldbank.org/html/opr/procure/about.html.

The World Bank, with its own lending and that of its sister organisation, the International Development Association, has been in the forefront of development financing both in terms of volume and with respect to the formulation of operational policies, including procurement policy ... The Bank has established detailed procedures for procurement in connection with projects funded by itself ... The Bank has formulated and expressed in its procurement Guidelines a set of rules for international competitive bidding which have gained recognition in all areas of the world ... The Bank has also sponsored standard bidding documents for use by executing agencies in charge of Bank-funded projects. Regional development banks, and other international financing institutions, have adopted procurement directives modelled on those of the World Bank.[3]

By "regional development banks" is meant other huge lending organisations like the African and Asian Development Banks. Thus the direct and indirect influence of the World Bank's procurement policies is truly vast.

The aim of this chapter is to take a critical look at the procurement procedures that are adopted by the World Bank for Bank-financed projects. The chapter will first explain briefly the historical background to these procedures and outline the procedures that currently apply. The second part of the chapter will identify some of the main problems that these procedures and their application can cause for effective purchasing. The concluding section then makes some recommendations for changes to both structures and specific practices, which, in the author's view, could greatly improve the efficiency with which money is spent in Bank-financed projects.

The findings and suggestions in this chapter are the product of the author's practical experience as a consultant on World Bank projects, and the chapter focuses on those areas in which the author has perceived problems to exist through his own involvement in Bank projects. However, while the specific illustrations are drawn from the author's own experiences, they are typical of the sort of problems encountered.

It is surprising that World Bank procurement has not as yet been the object of more serious and detailed scrutiny. For example, George and Sabelli describe the Bank as a procurement organisation early on in their excellent book *Faith and Credit*, but hardly mention procurement thereafter. Similarly, Christian Aid, whose criticisms of the World Bank and International Monetary Fund are among the most trenchant of all, has not addressed the Bank's procurement systems as a major problem. It is to be hoped that this chapter will generate further discussion and debate on the issues that it raises.

---

[3] G. Westring and G. Jadoun, *Public Procurement Manual for Central and Eastern Europe* (International Training Centre for the ILO, 1996).

2. THE ORIGINS AND DEVELOPMENT OF WORLD BANK PROCUREMENT PROCEDURES

The nature of the existing World Bank procedures is to some extent a factor of the historical origin of World Bank procurement. It is therefore useful to highlight a few points relating to early World Bank procurement.

First, it can be noted that the World Bank's first ventures were into large-scale industrial projects, such as infrastructures, steel mills, dams and pulp and paper mills. These projects required set forms of bidding document and contract to cope with the very large size of these early projects: thus forms for the procurement of works, consultancies and goods were developed. Only the largest firms could undertake such projects; they were able to employ many of their own permanent staff.

Secondly, there was difficulty in communications after the Second World War, especially in Third World countries. There was little telex, scarce courier services and no computers. Airmail was a comparatively new phenomenon.

Thirdly, there was a very different procurement philosophy, as already mentioned in the introduction.

Finally, the World Bank was then a new concept: Early practitioners started with a clean sheet, as little was known about the first bidders. With a world in ruins, the Bank could not rely on the past performance of bidders. As a consequence the Bank was forced into treating all bidders as equal, and demanding that every bidder, however well known, should present themselves in a very formal and paper-heavy manner.

Present-day World Bank contractors live in a different atmosphere from when the World Bank was founded. Taking the points above in reverse order:

(i) Fund recipients can be certain that bidders are skilled at bidding, and that many would not even be in business without the World Bank. Most bidders will have had a past history and record of performance.

(ii) Procurement itself has changed, as has already been explained.

(iii) Within the last ten years worldwide communications have altered hugely. Whereas earlier projects were often located up-country, without telephones, with difficult access to telex, relying largely on postal services, and maybe the weekly visit of the courier, nowadays databases can be sourced from almost anywhere.

(iv) The World Bank's funds nowadays go less to the large-scale projects of the 1950s, 1960s and 1970s, and more to agricultural and small-scale projects. However, the documentation and the contract paperwork stay much the same, and has not been altered to suit present-day conditions. The author's experience has been that Bank officials put tighter restrictions on some of today's smaller projects than it did on larger contracts in the earlier days. Furthermore, a minority of staff on any project today are permanently on the contractor's payroll. Most are temporary employees, and all too often the contractor knows very little about them.

However, possibly the biggest difference since those early days is that the rate of change of technology has altered. Whereas in the past a buyer could put out an invitation to bid with some assurance that there would be little doubt about the description of the goods he was hoping to buy, today he is much less sure. This is not only the case with computers or with the many machines and pieces of equipment that depend upon microchips, but applies almost generally. New solutions are being sought, and research applied, in industries that had previously been thought static.

The main effect on procurement has been in negotiation: what had previously been a matter of comparing bids often now requires careful negotiation, either before or after the bidding process or both. If a bidding process is designed with no thought of negotiation, or when negotiation is considered likely to encourage corruption, then strains in the system will occur.

3. PROCUREMENT PROCEDURES OF THE WORLD BANK

3.1 The objectives of World Bank procurement rules

In procurement projects financed by the World Bank for client countries, the contracts for the goods, works and services that are needed in connection with the project are concluded between the client country and the contractors. However, as we have already noted above, the procurement procedures for these contracts are required to be conducted according to procurement policies and procedures specified by the World Bank itself.

There are four main concerns of these World Bank policies and procedures:

(i)   To ensure that the loan is used to buy only those goods and services needed to carry out the project, and that they are procured in the most efficient and economical manner possible. Few outside the Bank believe that the World Bank's systems are efficient or economical, and this viewpoint will be argued in this chapter; but World Bank staff are genuine in believing this assertion. There will be much opposition to any attempt to change the system.

(ii) To give all qualified bidders from the Bank's eligible countries an equal opportunity to compete for Bank-assisted projects. Effectively this means a reliance on advertisement as a method of finding suppliers, as well as a refusal to grade suppliers for quality of performance.

(iii) To encourage development of local contracts and manufacturers, in the area in which the project is undertaken. Developing a supplier is always a pleasure to a buyer, and the Bank allows buyers to build in a margin of preference for local buyers. However, as will be explained this aim can degenerate into the cultivation of extra and unnecessary middlemen.

(iv)   To promote transparency. This is a fundamental issue in all World
        Bank-financed procurement. It is too easy to believe that the
        production of an open paper trail is all that matters to the Bank's
        task managers. A perfectly transparent paper trail can conceal
        corruption, suppress awkward evidence and even protect the guilty.
        The word "transparency" often goes together with "objectivity",
        another noble aim. However, just as "transparency" tends to
        degenerate into a smokescreen of documentation, so "objectivity"
        becomes a refusal to accept any evidence that is tainted with the
        slightest whiff of subjectivity. The success of a World Bank project
        therefore is not judged by whether it performs well, as that
        judgment must contain a subjective element.

3.2 An outline of World Bank procurement procedures

3.2.1 Preliminary matters

The first openly available document concerning any World Bank project is
usually the staff appraisal report (SAR). This document is always carefully
detailed, and usually it is from these SARs that invitations are issued to
tender for the performance of the projects suggested in the SARs. The winning bid is the basis of the subsequent contract, though often the winning
contractor is invited to write an inception report shortly after starting the
project. This document is intended to clear up any misunderstandings that
may have come to light between issuance of the invitations to bid, and
signature of contract. If there is an inception report it normally takes
precedence over the winning tender. Both parties, the Bank's client and the
contractor, will sign the inception report.

Parallel with this process, the World Bank and its client will have been
negotiating the loan agreement. Although mainly concerned with financial
affairs, such as the amount of the loan, the methods of payment and timing
of repayment, the loan agreement will also highlight the main management
and procurement issues of the loan. The loan agreement takes precedence
over the SAR.

At the start of a project, the World Bank's project task manager will issue
a "General Procurement Notice" announcing the project, describing its aims
and outlining in general its likely purchases. This is published in the United
Nations' *Development Forum Business Edition*, and will elicit expressions of
interest by possible suppliers.

3.2.2 Contracts for consulting services

Many consultancy contracts are awarded in connection with World Bank
projects. At the start of a project, consultancies are more frequent than later
on. They can vary from pre-investment studies, through services for
implementation to smaller services by individual consultants. Usually the
contract for the running of the project is itself a consultancy. When the Bank
is acting as the agency for executing the work, the contract will be between
the Bank and the consultant. Otherwise, as noted above, the contracts will
always be between the client and the consultants. The Bank seeks to
encourage and develop domestic consulting firms. Therefore foreign consulting firms are encouraged to sub-contract as much work as possible to

domestic firms, and their bids are marked up for their efforts towards this end.

The Bank's procedures for awarding contracts for consultancy services are laid down in Bank guidelines, entitled *Use of Consultants by World Bank Borrowers and by the World Bank as Executing Agency* (Consultancy Guidelines). The most recent version was published in 1997.

Many projects are extremely intricate, and require attention to be focused on quality of work rather than price. In these cases bids are examined for quality only, and the winner is adjudged to be the one whose proposal is the best. Thus traditionally price often has not been considered in selecting the winning consultant, although the price will have been examined carefully in negotiations after award and before signature of the contract. Traditionally this has been the most common approach for awarding contracts. However, revisions to the Consultancy Guidelines in 1997 have now provided for a method that involves consideration of price – the "Quality and Cost-Based Selection" – as the main method for choosing consultants. Under this selection method, dealt with in Part II of the Consultancy Guidelines, there is first an evaluation of technical aspects of proposals. Those whose technical proposals reach a certain threshold score are then considered on the basis of both price and technical aspects, with the winner being the consultant with best combined score for these two aspects. This method is now expected to be used for most contracts, but a method based mainly on quality – "Quality-Based Selection" – is maintained for appropriate cases, such as where innovation is important or where the methods of carrying out the work may differ widely so that direct comparison of proposals is difficult (see paragraphs 3.1–3.4. of the Consultancy Guidelines).

There are also a number of other selection methods mandated in Part III of the Consultancy Guidelines. This includes sole-sourcing, which is permitted in expressly defined and limited circumstances such as in emergencies and for small contracts.

Prior to 1997 invitations to participate in contracts were issued to known firms generally without advertisement. However, the 1997 Consultancy Guidelines provide for larger contracts (those estimated to be worth more than US$200,000) to be advertised, with shortlisted firms being selected from those responding to the advertisement.

The bank maintains a register of consultants, the DACON Register, which its clients may use to draw up shortlists (see p. 149, below).

One striking feature of the Bank's procedures for procurement of consultancy services is that no real use is made of the concept of vendor rating, which has considerable importance in best practice procurement in the private sector. This concept refers to the process whereby those who have previously undertaken contracts will be rated for key aspects such as performance of the products or services supplied, reliability or response to emergencies. The rating received is then taken into account in deciding on the award of future contracts. While there is provision for exclusion from future contracts for really poor performance (as set out in paragraphs 1.23 and 1.24 of the current Consultancy Guidelines) the relative rating of different firms who pass the minimum eligibility test is not generally taken into account in choosing future consultants. This issue is returned to later below.

3.2.3 Contracts for goods and works

The detailed procedures for the award of goods and works contracts are laid down in the Bank guidelines *Procurement under IBRD Loans and IBRD Credits* (1995) (the Procurement Guidelines). As a general principle the Bank recommends international competitive bidding (ICB) as the best method of buying goods and works (see section 1.3 of the Procurement Guidelines), bearing in mind the principles of the necessity for economy and efficiency, the desire to give all eligible bidders an equal chance of bidding, an interest in developing domestic manufacturing and contracting capacity, and transparency. ICB refers to a formal tendering procedure in which the contract is opened to international competition, and awarded through a formal tendering procedure, where a clear specification is set and bids are submitted to a common set deadline. All bidders who are qualified to undertake the work are entitled to have their bids considered.

The Bank has several standard forms for this procedure. The main ones are for the procurement of goods, of works, and of smaller works. There are standard forms and contracts for the supply and installation of plant and machinery. There are also detailed forms for use in bid evaluation.

In some cases, which are specified as "turnkey contracts or contracts for large complex plants or works of a special nature", it is realised that complete technical proposals are undesirable or impractical to prepare. The same applies to the purchase of complex supplies such as computer and telecommunications systems. In these cases the Bank allows a two-stage bidding process (see section 2.6 of the Procurement Guidelines). In the two-stage bidding method, unpriced technical proposals are invited, which will then be followed after clarification, by a more detailed proposal with an accompanying priced bid.

In both variations, bidding opportunities must be advertised in timely fashion (see section 2.7–2.8 of the Procurement Guidelines). Borrowers have to submit a draft general Procurement Notice, which the Bank then places in *Development Business*.[3a] This notice should include details of the borrower, the scope of procurement under ICB, pre-qualification (when pre-qualification is required) and the dates when pre-qualification and bidding documents will be available. The borrower has to maintain a list of answers to the notice, and a minimum delay of eight weeks must elapse between publication of the notice and the release of pre-qualification and bidding documents.

In addition the borrower must advertise its bidding opportunities in at least one leading newspaper in the borrower's country, and in the country's official gazette. It should inform all those who have showed an interest in the General Procurement Notice, and also preferably advertise specific contracts in *Development Business*. Embassies and trade representatives of countries likely to contain suitable suppliers and contractors should be

---

[3a] *Development Business* is published 24 times a year by the United Nations Department of Public Information. *The World Bank Operational Summary*, a component of *Development Business*, is published 12 times a year, and may be bought separately. (*Development Business*, P O Box 5850, Grand Central Station, New York, NY 10163–5850.)

informed. Direct invitation to known suppliers is not specified as a method of contacting suppliers, although it is not forbidden if the other steps have been taken first.

Prospective bidders must be given time to pre-qualify or bid: a minimum of six weeks is advised for normal tenders, but a minimum of 12 weeks is recommended for complex goods or large works.

The stated aim of this notification process is to give access to World Bank-funded contracts to the widest possible number of suppliers. However, it is realised that on some occasions, firms might bid which were not capable of performing under the contract. In these cases, a process of pre-qualification may be required (see sections 2.9–2.10 of the Procurement Guidelines). Pre-qualification is used for large or complex works, to make sure that bidders have the capacity to perform, and also to determine eligibility for domestic preference. There is a standard pre-qualification document available, which requires potential bidders to list their experience and past performance on similar contracts, their capabilities in personnel and facilities, and their financial position. The pre-qualification process has to be notified in much the same way as is required for the actual bidding, outlined above.

Rules concerning the bidding documents are set out in sections 2.11 and 2.12 of the Procurement Guidelines, and require use of the Bank's standard bidding documents where relevant, although these may be altered by including special conditions. The bidding documents will state the closing time and date and the precise place for their submission. They will also announce the time and place of bid-opening. The time allowed for submission must be at least six weeks in the case of simpler bids, but 12 weeks at least are recommended for more complex offers (section 2.43 of the Procurement Guidelines).

There are also rules on drawing up specifications. The general principle is that "standards and specifications quoted in bidding documents shall promote the broadest possible competition" while assuring that critical performance requirements are met (section 2.19 of the Procurement Guidelines). To this end, it is stated that accepted international standards such as those of the International Standards Organization must be used "as far as possible". When such standards are not available – which is the case in practice for most products and services – national standards may be used. However, bidders must indicate that performance to other standards that offer "substantial equivalence" will also be accepted (section 2.19 of the Procurement Guidelines). There is also a general requirement to use either specifications referring to characteristics, or performance requirements. One implication of this is that "brand names, catalog numbers, or similar classifications" may not be used unless necessary, in which case a willingness to accept "equivalent" products or services must again be made clear (section 2.20 of the Procurement Guidelines). In this case also, the Bank specifies that the test is whether the alternative is a *substantial* equivalent.

Rules on bid-opening are contained in section 2.44 of the Procurement Guidelines. Bid-opening must be conducted in public, and bidders and their representatives are invited to attend. As each bid is opened, the bidder's name and the amount(s) quoted are read out aloud, and recorded, a copy of this record being sent to the Bank. Bids submitted after the closing time will not be read out or evaluated but sent back unopened. Evaluation is dealt with in sections 2.48 to 2.53 of the Procurement Guidelines. After opening, bids are examined in several stages. In the first, bids are examined for arithmetical accuracy, completeness, for signature, the presence of the requisite securities, whether all items are quoted as being from eligible countries, and whether the bids are substantially responsive (whether or not the bid contains material deviations or reservations to the conditions of the bidding documents). This is often difficult to decide, and the evaluation team will often require the assistance of technical experts to verify this point. Bids that are not considered substantially responsive will not be considered further, and the bidder may not correct material deviations or withdraw reservations after bid-opening.

The subsequent commercial evaluation will take into account the price and other considerations. To ensure transparency, any non-price factors to be considered (including any permitted domestic preference) must be mentioned in the bidding documents, along with the method in which they will be taken into account (section 2.51 of the Procurement Guidelines).

It is not permitted for bidders to make any alterations to the bids after the deadline for receipt (section 2.45 of the Procurement Guidelines). While clarifications of bids may be sought and arithmetical errors corrected by the purchaser, in order to maintain transparency it is not permitted to conduct post-tender negotiations under which, for example, bidders are asked to lower their prices.

Once a decision has been made, a process of post-qualification may be necessary to make sure that the bidder meets the terms of the bidding documents. If the winner fails, then the next lowest evaluated bidder should be approached for post-qualification. The eventual winner must be the one who is both substantially responsive to the bidding documents and who offers the lowest evaluated cost.

Sometimes the World Bank will allow a simplified ICB procedure for "Quick Disbursement Operations" (sections 2.63 and 2.64 of the Procurement Guidelines). This allows for a faster advertising procedure, and the period of bid submission can be as little as four weeks. A variation of this faster procedure refers to the procurement of commodities (section 2.65 of the Procurement Guidelines). Commodities are often bought over a period of time, and purchases are best made to take advantage of price fluctuations. In these cases, a list of pre-qualified bidders is built up to whom invitations may be sent when occasion arises. The procurement of commodities should be made at a current or previous price; and bid validity should be as short as possible. A single currency should be specified in the bidding documents; and bids may be telexed or faxed if no bid security is required, or if standing bid securities have been supplied as part of pre-qualification.

Although the World Bank generally recommends international competitive bidding as the best method of procurement, it does allow some other methods, which are set out in section 3 of the Procurement Guidelines. Such exceptions, and the financial limits to them, will be stated in the loan agreement. One such procedure Limited International Bidding

(LIB) is recognised, which is really ICB without open advertisement, and without allowances for domestic preference. This is allowed if contract values are small, or if there are few suppliers or for "exceptional reasons". A similar process is called National Competitive Bidding (NCB), in which advertisement can be limited to the national press, local currency is generally used for payment and bidding, and the local language is employed in the bidding documents. Foreign bidders are allowed to take part, although NCB is generally allowed specifically for contracts that will not attract foreign competition.

International and National "Shopping" are other possible procedures, but these have been much less frequently permitted in recent years. At least three different bidders must quote (from two different countries in the case of International Shopping), and the method is deemed suitable for small value orders of off-the-shelf goods. Standard World Bank documentation is not necessary or even laid down, but the Bank requires that the entire process should follow "sound public or private sector practises".

Very occasionally single-sourcing is permitted, but only as an extension of a previous order, or to standardise equipment or spares, or if there can be only one supplier, or if the equipment is required as a response to a performance guarantee.

Construction by the borrower's own staff using their own equipment is also permitted, but rarely. Borrowers would have to satisfy the Bank that "force account", as it is called, is the only practical method.

4. SOME KEY PROBLEMS WITH WORLD BANK PROCUREMENT PROCEDURES

Having considered in outline the procurement procedures laid down by the World Bank, we can now turn to consider some of the main problems that have been created by these procedures and their application in practice.

4.1 Failure to evaluate contractor and project performance

A first, and fundamental, criticism that can be made is that the World Bank has turned its back resolutely on evaluating the performance of its projects and using this information to any great extent in awarding future contracts. As explained above, while really poor performers may, in theory, be excluded from contracts, relative performance in previous contracts is not taken into account in considering different consultants for the award of future contracts. It appears that this is because there would be too large a subjective element in that process, because of the practical complexities of setting up a vendor rating system and also because it would limit the clients' choice.

As a result, bidders are encouraged to submit proposals that cannot necessarily be complied with. This is frequently a problem in the area of consultancy projects. For example, one common practice is to list an expert team to operate the consultancy that the provider knows will not be present to implement it, and later to substitute other people. The firm will be marked for the excellence of the original team, and is rarely held to later by the client state for failure to supply that team (and this is a matter which the World Bank largely leaves to the client). The problem is exacerbated by the fact that delays to the project start date in any case mean that the consultant cannot be contractually held to the original team. In addition, for many projects, the cost that would be involved in preparing a thorough and realistic proposal, including site visits, deters firms from doing so. There is also, in the author's experience, a tendency on the part of many firms not to be wholly truthful in the factual statement in their proposals – for example, in indicating the true qualifications and experience of proposed personnel. The fact that, in reality, past performance is of limited relevance to future success means that practices of this kind are able to flourish.

Although the World Bank does have a register of consultants, the DACON Register, which it encourages clients to use, the Bank states that: "When firms register with DACON, they provide information that may be useful to borrowers and the Bank in the preparation of short lists and review of qualifications of firms proposed by borrowers. The Bank does not verify or endorse the information provided."[4]

4.2 The inappropriate aggregation of requirements

Another problem is the World Bank's general preference for its clients to purchase in bulk. This arises because of the belief that bulk purchases will generally produce lower prices, and also the fact that a few large contracts are more cheaply and easily administered than many smaller ones.

An example of the consequences of this approach is shown in Table 8.1, taken from a recent example of international competitive bidding in which the author participated. In this example, column A represents the lowest price offered by all responsive bidders, and column B the price that had to be paid to the bidder who won according to World Bank rules. The difference of DM161,437 represents an increase of 39 per cent over the sum of the lowest individual prices.

Since most laboratory equipment manufacturers are specialists, and are therefore unable to quote for the full range of laboratory goods, the absence of a provision for bids to be submitted for only one or some of the lots meant that the original manufacturers, who are those most likely to give the best prices, were thereby excluded. In addition, a bidder who wins a contract of this size has to be prepared to raise the finance to cover the cost of supplying, in addition to the considerable cost of preparing the bid, and this is difficult for many firms.

Had each item in this example been tendered for separately, or with the possibility of dividing the contract into lots, a saving to the World Bank's client of over 39 per cent would have been made. The Bank does permit a method of procurement that it calls "International Shopping", which would have allowed procurement of each item separately (see previous page).

---

[4] *Guidelines – Use of Consultants by World Bank Borrowers and by the World Bank as Executing Agency* (1997).

Table 8.1 Comparative costs of environmental laboratory equipment

	Cheapest bids (DM)	Winning bid (DM)
Chromatograph	50,093	112,580
Titrator	26,612	36,520
Spectrophotometer	47,409	88,995
pH meter	3,649	3,649
Electronic precision balance	4,248	4,248
Electronic analytical balance	8,850	8,850
Autoanalyser	175,343	175,343
TOC analyser	44,529	80,581
Water purification system	22,966	23,098
Autoclave	9,380	11,682
Water pump	15,919	21,558
Pump generator	3,005	6,336
Total	**412,003**	**573,440**
Difference in DM		161,437

This example is by no means unusual. Many World Bank purchases of goods by International Competitive Bidding are of a more diverse nature, and may contain goods as varied as pumps, computers and electronics, diesel engines, fertiliser, warehouses, lifts and vegetable seed. In these instances, the only possible vendors are middlemen, and frequently a greater price difference than that shown above could be expected.

The problem here does not in general lie with the World Bank's guidelines themselves. It is quite possible under these guidelines to divide larger contracts into lots and allow bidders either to bid for one or more individual lots or to bid for the whole requirement. The problem lies in the practice of bundling together large and diverse requirements and the Bank's reluctance in practice to allow bidding for small lots because of the perceived administration and control costs. However, in the author's experience the costs of the Bank's rigid approach greatly outweigh the benefits in terms of administrative savings and improved control, and in any case many of these problems could be avoided if the Bank were to install proper sampling techniques into its relatively small internal auditing department.

4.3 Application of the rules on specifications

Other problems that arise relate to the application of the World Bank rules on specifications. One frequent scenario where problems occur is when a buyer is asked to purchase an item of equipment by a specific manufacturer. There may be extremely good reasons for wanting a particular manufacturer's item: for example, the client may want to concentrate his stocks of spares or that manufacturer's machine may be the only type in the country. Many private sector buyers would specify for supply of the particular manufacturer's equipment in such a case, but, as explained above, the World Bank rules on specifications generally do not permit this, but require design-based or performance-based specifications to be used as a general rule. As a result, a client will often end up with a machine he does not want, an extra training bill and shelves full of unnecessary spares. The consequences of this are more extreme in developing countries than it would be in the West. By their nature, the countries served by the World Bank are remote, and the costs of getting technicians to train staff and service machinery can be very high. The point can be illustrated by reference to a case in which the author was involved in the Sudan, concerning the purchase of pumps. The Sudanese did not want modern high-revving pumps, as these had a very short life in the gritty conditions on the edge of the desert, but something old-fashioned, slow running, and which they knew how to repair. However, a World Bank expert rejected the possibility of using a specification from a particular manufacturer which had been found to work well in the past. It was held that a properly neutral specification should only specify the output, the height to which the water would be lifted and the depth from which it must be raised. The specification finally approved by the Bank put a bias towards specifically those types of machine which were not suitable: there may have been more manufacturers, and they may have been cheaper, but they would have had a very short life.

In theory, the World Bank rules allow for the additional costs of training, spare parts and so on to be taken into account in running the procurement, in particular by providing for any additional costs to be built into the bid evaluation criteria, or by requiring firms to provide and price these additional requirements in their own bids. It is also true that the World Bank approach, of using broadly based functional specification and then providing for additional costs to be taken into consideration in other ways, is the one preferred by many advanced purchasing systems. However, the practical reality of procurement carried out in the context of the World Bank is that frequently the very high costs involved are not properly anticipated and provided for, with the result that the purchaser does not obtain best value for money. From the author's experience, a more satisfactory outcome would normally be achieved in practice for these procurements if the purchaser were to be given greater latitude to adopt a slightly stricter approach in the drafting of the basic specification.

Another problem, which has been experienced in many other national and international procurement systems that attempts to maintain a balance between efficient purchasing and openness and transparency, concerns the possibility for obtaining supplier input into the design of contract specifications. A client attempting to draw up specifications on developing world contracts is very much in the position of a government department in the United Kingdom attempting to specify its next computer system. It is in no position to do so, unless it is itself a computer department, as it will not have the technical knowledge. Such a department depends very much on the advice of its suppliers. To confer at length with a variety of possible vendors is widely considered legitimate in the private sector, but is regarded with great suspicion by the World Bank. Naturally this suspicion in turn makes it difficult to produce workable, up-to-date specifications, or gives rise to the production of specifications so wide that a good choice for purchase is difficult to make at the time of bid evaluation. Frequently a bad choice will be made, although the rules will have been followed precisely.

4.4 Excessive reliance on advertisements to find interested suppliers

A further peculiarity of the World Bank's procurement regulations is a rigid belief in the value of advertisement as a method for locating suppliers: advertisement is considered to be neutral, while it is felt that direct invitation can lead to sweetheart deals.

Advertisement may be effective when the goods required are of one type, all capable of being supplied by a single manufacturer. However, particularly because the Bank sees International Competitive Bidding as a method of bulking requirements together, goods in a competitive bidding shopping list can very rarely be capable of being manufactured by one maker. Furthermore, there are few manufacturers who employ staff to read advertisements.

The firms who do get business through perusing advertisements are middlemen. In whatever country the World Bank has been operating for a number of years, one is sure to find clusters of firms of middlemen. In some ways, they do a good job. They answer advertisements where no one else would apply, and they will find suppliers where none had been thought to exist. However, they add a sizeable cost margin. Furthermore, collusion is common: firms of middlemen, apparently competing with each other, will allocate the contracts from a project among themselves. Judicious grouping of lots inside international competitive bids, or, better still, the use of International Shopping as argued above, can, when combined with the use of direct invitation to known suppliers, avoid these problems.

4.5 Inadequate long-term planning and training

Another problem with World Bank procurement is that insufficient attention is given to the need to ensure that the client is able to procure efficiently in connection with the project once the immediate involvement of the World Bank has ceased. This problem is exacerbated by the use of advertisement as a method of finding suppliers and the consequent participation of middlemen, which often result in a situation where the normal mechanisms by which a purchasing office operates do not exist.

For example, to order spares for equipment supplied three years pre-viously it is necessary to find out who supplied the original equipment. Let us suppose coulters for ploughs are required. In this case every contract placed during the years when the ploughman thinks the plough was supplied has first to be examined. When eventually the papers concerning the supply of ploughs are found, the manufacturer's name will often have been removed from the documentation, and the middleman will be unable or unwilling to name the original manufacturer. This is one reason why so often expensive and nearly new equipment has to be abandoned for lack of spares in developing countries.

More generally, recipients of World Bank funds, having been trained to satisfy the Bank's procurement regulations, are often ill-equipped to survive on their own. They have never been trained to source suppliers, to make lists of previous suppliers, to list costs, to classify spares or even to file documents in any meaningful way.

4.6 Excessively bureaucratic procedures

Another serious problem is that aspects of Bank procedures aimed at open competition and transparency can create a disease that is worse than the cure, seriously inhibiting a purchaser's ability to obtain value for money as well as involving high administration costs.

This can be illustrated by a real life example experienced by the author, concerning procurement of fish fingerlings on the Third Fisheries Project in Bangladesh. The basic principle of the Third Fisheries Project was to breed carp fingerlings by the hundreds of tonnes, and then to insert these fingerlings into selected rice fields just as Bangladesh flooded at monsoon time. The rice seedlings and the fish fingerlings benefited each other, and then when the water subsided, both rice and fish were harvested.

Despite excellent technical arrangements laid on by the University of Stirling combined with high-quality project management, which struck this layman as the best he had ever worked on, the project was severely damaged by the World Bank's procurement arrangements. The Bank's Staff Appraisal Report for this project written in 1990 stated: "The Project is designed to support a sectoral development process aiming at increasing incomes, particularly of the poor",[5] a statement repeated on another page of the same document.[6] The benefits of the project were expected to "include increased net incomes to subsistence and professional fishermen, shrimp farmers, pond owners, women, nursery and hatchery owners and their families".[7]

However, a study written four years later, prepared under the auspices of the World Bank and the Government of Bangladesh said: "Considerable social impact and damage is repeatedly being caused upon the unprepared fishing communities with the sudden upsurge in the value of resources. The stocking programme has benefited the non-fisherman community often disproportionately leaving the genuine fisherfolk marginalised. Although the production and economic parameters have substantially proven positive, the distribution element is far from satisfactory. This has resulted in some sections of the community becoming worse off."[8] Another report, published in the same year, said "The Staff Appraisal Report 1990 assumed

---

[5] World Bank Staff Appraisal Report #8392-BD (2 May 1990).
[6] *Ibid.*, p. 14.
[7] *Ibid.*, paragraph 6.08.
[8] Bangladesh Centre for Advanced Studies, *A Study of Enhanced NGO Intervention in the Third Fisheries Project*, p. 2 paragraph 2.

the economic cost of fingerlings supplied to the Third Fisheries Project would fall in spite of the increased amounts required each year from Tk75/kg in 1992 to Tk45/kg in 1994 ... Clearly anticipated contractual stocking cost in 1994 of Tk110–140/kg is 60–100 per cent higher than projected in the Staff Appraisal Report ... It is generally believed that fingerling supply to the Third Fisheries Project has been acquired at high cost." The same study makes the point that "such high fingerling costs pushes the project to the very limit of economic sustainability".[9]

The problem was that the strict procurement regulations imposed by World Bank officials. They decided that the fish fingerlings had to be bought internationally, though it was impossible that any seller of fish fingerlings could be anything but Bangladeshi for technical reasons. This meant that all bidding documents had to be in English, thus excluding most of the less rich breeders of fingerlings. Further, faced with the possibility of dealing with large numbers of contracts, since only small contracts would be of a size manageable by those poorer people they intended to help, the Bank's staff limited the maximum number of contracts for the supply of fingerlings each year to nine for the whole country, meaning that only the wealthy could bid. Further, each year, before they could tender, each bidder had to pre-qualify in English in a detailed 40-page document, asking what fish-breeding equipment each potential bidder had, and requiring cash flows to be stated and balance sheets to be presented. This seemed particularly unnecessary in view of the fact that the document also asked bidders whether they were willing to supply even if they had none of the equipment. Pre-qualification was required every year for every supplier, whether they had pre-qualified in a previous year or not. Having pre-qualified, bidders wishing to enter the International Competitive Bidding process were then required to answer an advertisement, and on payment of a sum, to complete, in English, a further 40-page document. After the usual bid-opening, contracts were awarded, the bidders being divided into two by size of contract.

The actual costs of producing fish fingerlings were well known,[10] and though market costs before the arrival of the Third Fisheries Project were Tk63.75/kg, they were expected to drop to Tk45. Instead they rose to Tk110–140/kg, so that the total price paid nearly doubled. Thus the price that Bangladesh will have to repay to the Bank has also doubled, and interest will have to be paid as well. The reason for this rise was that fish producers in smaller businesses were not able to quote; the only people able to do so, both for financial reasons and because they were able to master the documentation, were the *mastans* or "musclemen". These people, many with armed retainers, acted as middlemen and were able to fix prices with selected fingerling producers and produce a price cartel.

---

[9] BCEOM/BCAS, *Study on Cost Recovery in Floodplain Fisheries in Bangladesh – Final Report*, 3 February 1994.
[10] *Ibid.*

As an experiment, one year the management of the Third Fisheries Project admitted a third grade of supplier without informing the Bank. These fish breeders did not have to pre-qualify, but were selected locally by Department of Fisheries officers and were allowed to bid to supply smaller quantities per bidder. As expected their prices were the lowest and their quality the best. The Third Fisheries Project management subsequently informed the Bank as to what they had done, and asked if, in view of the improved results, procurement could be decentralised, the number of contracts increased, and the supply of smaller quantities per supplier made the norm. However, the Bank forbade the practise thereafter.

5. RECOMMENDATIONS FOR REFORM

In World Bank procurement, wastage of money, poor projects and the supply of expensive goods hits the world's poorest. Clearly, this is a cause for concern. It is submitted that there is therefore an urgent need for the Bank to give its attention to several issues, relating both to specific procurement practices and some more general matters.

First, the bank should depart from its current refusal to apply the concept of vendor rating, whereby consultants (and suppliers) are graded according to performance and this grading taking into account in awarding future contracts. The Bank should take on board this concept, which is a standard best practice commercial technique. If encouragement were given to good performers, the standard of future projects would rise.

In relation to consultants, it can be noted the Bank's Consultancy Guidelines state that the Bank "maintains information concerning the capabilities and experience of a large number of consulting firms. This information is also used when the Bank prepares lists of suggested consulting firms for borrowers ... However, the information on any one firm may be limited or, in some cases, non-existent ... The fact that the Bank has been supplied with information about a firm does not indicate that the Bank has verified the accuracy of the information provided, that it has endorsed the firm's qualifications in general, or that it will approve the firm's appointment for any specific project. The Bank has no list of 'approved' consulting firms." However, further on we read: "The Bank evaluates and records the performance of consulting firms on ... Bank-financed contracts." Surely, so far as consultancy contracts are concerned, it would be useful for the Bank to connect the two sets of records?

Secondly, the Bank should place less reliance on advertisement as a method of obtaining suppliers. For the reasons that have been explained above, this would produce beneficial results for particular procurements in which the Bank is involved. In addition, it would mean that clients would be introduced from the beginning of each project to the skill of directly sourcing suppliers. Even four years ago in the remotest countries, this task could be achieved by trawling the commercial offices of the various embassies. Now it can be done electronically. The arguments for the wholesale use of advertisement as a means of tracing suppliers, weak as they always were, are less than ever.

Knowledge of the market as a way to locate suppliers and a shift away from placing advertisements should also encourage the Bank to switch from International Competitive Bidding to International Shopping. The latter is a method more suited to the smaller-scale projects now in fashion; the method is considerably faster than competitive bidding and can target suppliers more accurately. Lower prices should therefore be obtained.

What about the problem of corruption? Fear of corruption and the making of sweetheart deals lie at the heart of many of the Bank's rules. They are also the basic reason for much US government procurement regulation to which the Bank's rules are so similar. Professor Kelman has suggested[11] that the task of fighting corruption in procurement should be shifted to police skills, the technology of which has improved so much recently. However, since the World Bank operates largely in countries in which police investigation is still very basic and cruel, this solution is not possible in the case of the Bank's projects.

In this instance, we can start with the observations, first, that one person on his own cannot be corrupt; and, secondly, that there is a very widespread belief in the West that to survive in the developing world, a degree of sharp practice is essential. When that idea is general, corruption follows. In the author's experience, some firms behave on Bank contracts in a manner they would not countenance in their own countries. Such firms often do this reluctantly because they believe they must and because they know they will not be penalised for this at home. Third Word aid is of such importance, however, that corruption and sharp practice must be punished. If that is not possible through the courts, then it is not impossible for firms to be shamed into disciplining errant employees. Certain firms mooted a voluntary code of conduct a few years back. It is unclear what has happened to it, but it should be improved, publicised and enforced. Only those who subscribe to the code should be allowed to bid on most aid contracts. It should not be voluntary, and it should have international backing.

John Linarelli argues in chapter 7 that the US Foreign Corrupt Practices Act has a very limited effect in deterring corruption,[12] but it would be considerably more effective if the United States were not the only country with such a law. A recent Recommendation of the OECD Council has called upon all OECD members to bring into effect laws to tackle the problem of corruption by their national firms on foreign contracts. If the World Bank were to require the existence of such a law as a prerequisite for inclusion in the list of countries whose firms are eligible to compete on World Bank contracts, the effect could be dramatic.

More generally, a problem that is characteristic of the World Bank is the in-grown nature of its staff in most fields. Dissent, debate and ideas are discouraged. This is equally true of the Bank's procurement staff, who appear to have grown up knowing nothing of other systems of procurement. Existing staff, whether in Washington or in the field, should be

---

[11] S. Kelman, *Procurement and Public Management* (AEI Press, 1990).
[12] See chapter 7, section 3.1.

exposed to the best of modern systems of supply, both in industrial firms and in universities. Supply specialists should be brought in from outside. Auditors of Bank projects should also be external, and should programme their work independently of Bank staff.

The reforms proposed above may arouse some controversy. It appears to be an article of faith in the Washington headquarters that the Bank's procurement systems are nearly perfect, and that there is no alternative to them. The difficulties of reform are exacerbated by the fact that knowledge of the World Bank's procurement regulations is a meal ticket for many. There are also colleges and training courses that teach these systems.

On the other hand, there are signs that more generally the World Bank is paying attention to the criticism that it has received. At long last it seems that the Bank is beginning seriously to monitor the results of its investments as a Bank should. If we can dream of a time when the World Bank and the International Monetary Fund receive general approval rather than their present censure, then it will be all the more important that the Bank's buying philosophy and methods should also be transformed. To buy badly and slowly is bad enough when so many projects are suspect, but to do so for good projects will be worse. Poor countries cannot afford it.[13]

---

[13] Some World Bank sites on the World Wide Web are: the World Bank: http://www.worldbank.org; the International Rivers Network: http://www.irn.org; the Development Gap: http://www.igc.org/dgap; the Berne Declaration: http://www.access.ch/evb/bd; Alop: http://www.alop.or.cr; and Christian Aid: http://www.oneworld.org//christian aid.

Part III
Current Issues in Procurement Regulation

9. Information and Communication Technology Issues in International Public Procurement

*Auke Haagsma**

1. INTRODUCTION: THE INFORMATION AND COMMUNICATION TECHNOLOGY REVOLUTION

Globalisation has been occurring in the European private sector for at least a decade and is now also starting in earnest in public procurement. Some evidence that this is happening in the European Union can be found in the "Single Market Review" which was recently undertaken for the European Commission.[1] One of the findings of this study was that the "Europeanisation" of public purchases has occurred in a limited number of sectors, such as telecommunications and transport. In other sectors, however, and in particular in procurement by public sector authorities, import penetration is still alarmingly low. No similar studies have been undertaken at the international level, but the statistics compiled by the parties to the World Trade Organisation Government Procurement Agreement[2] (which are not public) do not seem to reveal a high degree of "foreign" participation in procedures covered by the Agreement.

While it is still uncertain to what extent globalisation has yet to take place in public procurement, to many the information and communication technology (ICTs) revolution, in particular in public procurement, is even farther removed from daily realities. It is submitted, however, that this is a misunderstanding. Even today and even in Europe ICTs already play a very important role in the procurement process, albeit in a manner which few would characterise as revolutionary. Indeed, since the inception of the European Community directives on public procurement new technologies

---

* Head of Unit DG-XV, Commission of the European Communities.
[1] For an accessible version of the findings of the review, see D. Buchan, *The Single Market and Tomorrow's Europe, A Progress Report from the European Commission* (Luxembourg and London, 1996).
[2] Agreement on Government Procurement, Marrakesh, 15 April 1994, concluded on behalf of the European Community by the Council by its decision of 22 December 1994 (94/800/EEC), OJ 1994, No. L336/1 of 23 December 1994.

such as personal computers, telex and facsimile machines have slowly but surely been introduced. Their use has become so widespread that they are hardly thought of as applications of ICTs. We have now reached a stage, however, where further logical steps, as small as they may sometimes be, require formal changes to the legal regime. These changes, when presented in an isolated manner and not as one element in a broader amendment, often meet with scepticism or even outright opposition.

Although ICTs have slowly crept into almost every aspect of our lives, their acceptance in the procurement area is problematic. The reason for this is that the regulatory system, both in the European Community procurement regime and under the World Trade Organisation Government Procurement Agreement (GPA) is fairly detailed up to the point of laying down which means have to be used for transmitting messages and for broadcasting tender notices, and indeed which procedures should be used for acquiring certain products and services. Hence even small and relatively unimportant changes in procedures often require legislative changes.

This chapter does not deal with sociological nor with political aspects surrounding the reluctance to accept such changes, or indeed any change at all in the procurement regimes. Nor is it proposed to list all of the (many) changes which are required to various Articles in the European directives to make possible even small steps forward towards a more efficient procurement regime.

The purpose is rather to set out two broad options, which are not mutually exclusive, for moving forward in relation to the problem of ICTs under international procurement rules. The first option would be to make those changes which enable new ICTs to be used within the current procedures in order to increase the efficiency of those procedures. Secondly, one could consider whether entirely new ways of procuring goods and services, made possible only because of the new ICTs, should be allowed. In both cases it is also necessary to consider whether a co-existence of both the new and the older technologies should be permitted or whether the legislator or the purchaser in a particular case can impose just one set of procedures – that is, one that operates either with or with-out the new ICTs. Finally this chapter will look at the role the law should play in the age of electronic procurement, and in particular whether the legislator still can or should lay down detailed procurement procedures, or whether EU or international procurement law should only set the broader principles such as transparency and non-discrimination and leave the development of the actual procurement procedures to "the market".

2. THE FIRST OPTION: USE OF ICTS TO FACILITATE CURRENT PROCEDURES

2.1 Limitations imposed by the general rules of the EC Treaty

The European Community's procurement regime as well as the GPA lays down detailed procedural requirements only for contracts above certain monetary thresholds. Legal issues relating to the use of ICTs should therefore only arise with regard to such contracts. However, in relation to the Community's procurement regime one might ask whether the position for other contracts is affected by the all-important non-discrimination principle which is enshrined in the EC Treaty, in particular in Article 30 of the EC Treaty guaranteeing free movement of goods and Articles 52 and 59 of the EC Treaty on freedom to provide services and freedom of establishment. These provisions are not limited in application only to larger contracts, but apply to all public procurement. Do these articles affect the power of public purchasers to require suppliers to use procedures which are in practice accessible only from certain countries? This question may arise, for example, if a French purchaser were to run a procurement procedure over the "Minitel" system which is in practice only accessible from France.

Although this particular example will soon be only hypothetical (since the French government recently announced that it would terminate the Minitel system) it is submitted that the general principle should be that the non-discrimination principle would not allow public purchasers to require the use of such a system.

It is difficult to define the exact limits of such a position, however. Even though the internet is accessible from all EU Member States (and indeed from all GPA parties) limitations in the telecommunications infrastructures may be such as to exclude important file transfers for some areas or Member States over the internet. Does this mean that *requiring* the use of the internet for purchases of certain goods or services is not possible unless every Member State is able to offer such access? This seems too restrictive a position even though one might find support for it in the case law of the ECJ. In the milestone *Dassonville* case the ECJ held that the requirement by a Member State for a certificate which was *less easily obtainable* for some products than for others was in breach of the Treaty provisions on free circulation of goods.[3-4]

If one were to apply a similar test to a requirement to use the internet might this then also be found to violate the non-discrimination principle of the Treaty? Some people would indeed argue that this is a means which is less easily accessible to suppliers from one Member State than by those from another. However, in this case it is not so much the accessibility which is a problem, as the internet can be accessed over regular phone lines. The problem results from the *quality* of the telephone networks.

[3-4] Case 8/74, *Procureur du Roi* v. *Dassonville* [1974] ECR 837; [1974] 2 *Common Market Law Review* 436. In the exact wording of the ECJ: "the requirement by a Member State of a certificate of authenticity which is *less easily obtainable* by importers of an authentic product which has been put into free circulation in a regular manner in another Member State than by importers of the same product coming directly from the country of origin constitutes a measure having an effect equivalent to a quantitative restriction as prohibited by the Treaty".

Difficulties of this nature are not really a reason not to allow the exclusive use of the internet, however. Even the communication means now allowed under the directives may pose similar problems. In particular there are, or have been in the past, major differences in the quality of postal services between Member States. One has to admit, however, that where regular mail services cannot be used, because of their slowness, a strike or for any other reason, alternatives still exist. The imposition of electronic procurement, using only the internet as a means of communication would in principle exclude alternatives.[5]

It seems hard to give a steadfast rule at this stage. Whether or not unlawful discrimination exists will have to be determined on a case-by-case basis but it seems likely that in a limited number of cases, such as in the Minitel example, the imposition of particular technologies is not yet possible because it would lead to discrimination prohibited by the Treaty. Whether such a general problem exists with regard to imposing the use of the internet seems unlikely, although there may be specific cases where even the internet cannot be used on an exclusive basis. This question will be returned to later.

Similar problems do not exist in the context of the multilateral General Agreement on Tariffs and Trade (GATT). The GATT exempts "procurement by governmental agencies of products purchased for governmental purposes" from the application of the national treatment provision.[6] The general international trade rules do not, therefore, impose any national treatment or requirements on government purchases. However, for purchases which are covered by the GPA the situation may be comparable to that under the directives, since a national treatment requirement does exist under Article III of the GPA. Whether this requirement goes quite as far as the non-discrimination principle in the EC Treaty remains to be seen, but it is submitted that, using a system such as Minitel as the required vehicle for, *inter alia*, submitting bids for procurements covered by the GPA, would clearly violate the national treatment principle, even if that requirement would be *de jure* the same for all potential suppliers.

2.2 Limitations imposed by the award procedures of the European Community directives

Leaving aside for the moment these more general issues, we can now turn to the use of ICTs in the application of the detailed award procedures laid down in the directives and in the GPA. At various stages of the procurement cycle the regulatory system created by these instruments requires,

---

[5] It would be possible, of course, to impose the use of the internet unless for an objectively justified reason the use of this means would not be available to a supplier from within the Community or another GPA member country.

[6] General Agreement on Tariffs and Trade, Article III(8)(a).

inter alia, the exchange of data between different actors. It is obvious that in a system which has the ambition of spanning the entire Community, or indeed the entire world, such exchanges of data may take place over large distances. Traditional means of communication often require significant time-periods for transmitting data or involve a substantial loss of quality. It is therefore particularly in this area that important benefits can be achieved from the use of ICTs. These new technologies not only increase the speed with which the actual data exchanges take place, they also improve the quality of the data, in particular by allowing better control by the sender of the entire dataflow. Of particular importance in the multi-linguistic environment which exists in the EU, and even more so within the WTO framework, are the possibilities of automatic translations.

The current legal regime in the European Community does not merely ignore these possible mechanisms, it often makes their use impossible. An interesting example can be found in Article 9(5) of Directive 93/36/EEC on public supply contracts.[7] According to this Article the various notices which have to be published in the *Official Journal* must be sent to the Publications Office in Luxembourg as rapidly as possible and by "the most appropriate channels". This would seem to allow the use of e-mail, as it is normally the most speedy and most reliable means. However, when contracting entities want to apply the *accelerated procedure*, the especially shortened version of the restricted procedure that applies in cases of urgency, the directive requires that the notices be sent by telex, telegram or telefax. Apparently e-mail is excluded in this case, even though it may be the most rapid means.

Although the rules are therefore not always suitably adapted to the emerging new technologies, one should not exaggerate the impact of this problem. Certainly it would be somewhat surprising if a court were to suspend or annul a tender procedure on the sole grounds that the tender notice for an accelerated procedure was sent by e-mail. In any case, the European Commission, which is administratively in charge of the Publications Office in Luxembourg, could make it known that in addition to the means mentioned in the directives it would also accept and therefore publish tender notices for accelerated procedures sent by e-mail.[8]

The example given is just one in a series of, perhaps minor, problems. What they all have in common is that they are the result of the high level of detail of the directives. Indeed, as is already clear from the above example, the European Community's procurement directives provide a level of detail

---

[7] Council Directive 93/36/EEC of 14 June 1993 (OJ 1993, No. L199/1 of 9 August 1993) co-ordinating procedures for the award of public supply contracts. Similar or identical provisions can be found in the other procurement directives, dealing with the award of public works and services contracts in the European Community.

[8] In its SIMAP project the Commission does, of course, allow contracting entities to send notices electronically, including for accelerated procedures.

rarely found in legislative (as opposed to regulatory) acts.[9] Another example of this can be found in Article 11(4) of Directive 93/36/EEC. According to this provision, requests to participate in restricted or negotiated procedures may be made by letter, by telegram, telex, telefax or by telephone; if one of the last four means are used, the request must be confirmed by letter. One could argue that e-mail messages sent over the internet or otherwise are sent "by telephone". However, it is hard to see why such transmissions, which do provide for printed confirmation of receipt, where needed, should be "confirmed" by letter (which apparently does not even have to be sent by registered mail).

Another interesting question relates to the *Official Journal*. According to the directives the various notices must be published by the contracting entities in the *Official Journal* and normally also in the *Tenders Electronic Daily* (TED) database.[10] Can this requirement be said to be fulfilled if the supplement to the *Official Journal* in which such notices tend to be published appears only as an on-line version on the internet? The directives do not seem to exclude this. Indeed, they do not provide that the *Official Journal* shall be published on paper, nor is there any other legal instrument requiring that the *Official Journal* be available on paper. One can argue, however, that the *Official Journal*, in which binding, directly applicable Community legislation is also published, should be available to any citizen without difficulty. The question then becomes whether a subscription to the *Official Journal*, which costs a certain amount of money every year, is more accessible than the one-time purchase of a personal computer with a modem, combined with a subscription to an internet provider. In monetary terms the latter will probably be cheaper if one takes a medium-term view. This is even more true for suppliers also interested in tenders from other GPA countries. Indeed, more and more countries, including the US, Japan, Canada and even many non-GPA members, advertise their procurement opportunities for free on the internet.

A supplementary argument may be found in the thresholds of the directives, in that any supplier or person who is aspiring to win a contract above the thresholds provided for in the GPA and/or the directives will normally already possess a personal computer.

The main argument against stems from the fact that a decision to allow the publication of the *Official Journal* as an exclusively on-line medium might have implications beyond the publication of procurement notices. Simply put this argument states that it should not be legally possible for directly applicable legal texts to bind ordinary citizens if they can only learn of the existence of those texts by consulting the internet.

---

[9] This may come as a surprise, particularly in a directive which is intended to leave some scope to the addressees, namely the Member States. It is even more surprising for directives which claim to be not about laying down harmonised procedures but only to co-ordinate national rules.

[10] See, for example, Directive 93/36/EEC, Article 9(6) and (7).

Although this argument would seem to apply much more to the validity of such a directly applicable legal instrument than to the nature of the *Official Journal*, it is this argument which is used for the time being to require that all procurement notices be published in a version of the *Official Journal* supplement, which is available either or paper, or at least as a CD-Rom.

The general conclusion has to be that in various respects the procurement directives do not take into account the new ICTs. However, their use can in most cases be allowed through a flexible but realistic interpretation of the directives. The Commission could play a role in favouring such an interpretation by issuing appropriate statements and by developing the necessary tools. The latter is currently being done mainly through the SIMAP project (*Système d'Information sur les Marchés Publics*)[11] which will be considered in more detail below. On the whole, however, the Commission seems to favour legislative amendments over bold interpretations. Thus it decided to include a provision in its proposals for amendments to the directives following the adoption of the GPA to deal with some of the problems mentioned above.

Thus, according to a provision included in the directive recently adopted by the European Parliament and the Council:[12]

requests for participation in contracts and invitations to tender must be made by the most rapid means of communication possible. When requests to participate are made by telegram, telex, telephone or any electronic means, Member States may require them to be confirmed by letter dispatched before the expiring of the time limit.

The solution provided by this provision raises a number of interesting questions. Indeed, it appears that under this provision the decision whether or not confirmation by letter of an e-mail message is necessary is neither taken at Community level, nor is it left to the contracting entity concerned. Instead it is for each Member State to take this decision, apparently in its implementing measures. This means that new differences between the legal regimes are created which may lead to important problems. Indeed, it is easy to imagine a supplier established in a Member State which does not require confirmation who forgets to confirm when wishing to participate in a tender procedure in a country which does. It is hoped common sense will result in all Member States deciding not to require confirmation.

The newly adopted directive also contains another interesting provision, which is designed to align the directives with Article XIII of the GPA:

---

[11] See further at http://simap.eu.int.

[12] Directive 97/52/EC of 13 October 1997 (OJ 1977, L328/1). This directive amends the three directives for the "classical" sectors, i.e. Directive 93/36/EEC, OJ 1993, No. L199/1, Directive 93/37/EEC, OJ 1993, No. L199/54 and Directive 92/50/EEC, OJ 1992, No. L209/1. A separate directive amending the so-called Utilities Directive 93/38/EEC was adopted as Directive 98/4/EC on 16 February 1998, OJ 1998, L101/1.

Tenders shall be submitted in writing directly or by mail. Member States may authorize the submission of tenders by any other means making it possible to ensure:

- that each tender contains all the information necessary for the evaluation of the tender;
- that tenders remain confidential pending their evaluation;
- that, where necessary for reasons of legal proof, such tenders are confirmed as soon as possible in writing or by dispatch of a certified copy;
- that tenders are opened after the time-limit for their submission has expired.

Once again the decision to allow the use of "any other means" provided it satisfies the four criteria is not taken in the directive but is left to the Member States. If a Member State allows e-mail as a matter of principle, this will in practice only be possible for purchasers who are able to receive e-mail messages while guaranteeing that the above conditions are met. The wording chosen does not seem to allow Member States (or their contracting entities) to require that *only* e-mail is used to submit tenders.

It is interesting to note that the directive does not amend the provisions relating to the publication of notices in the *Official Journal*. Thus, for the time being it seems that notices will have to continue to be published in a paper or CD-Rom version of the *Official Journal*.[13]

2.3 Limitations imposed by the award procedures of the Government Procurement Agreement

The situation is fairly similar for the GPA, although there are some differences. Exactly like the directives, the GPA does not take into account the existence of the new ICTs in its procedural rules. Thus it contains a provision[14] very similar to the one included in the directives requiring that requests to participate in restricted procedures (referred to in the GPA as selective tendering) may be submitted by telex, telegram or facsimile. The GPA requires furthermore that "tenders shall normally be submitted in writing directly or by mail".[15] Where tenders "by telex, telegram or facsimile are permitted" it is required, *inter alia*, that they should be confirmed "promptly by letter or by the despatch of a signed copy of the telex, telegram or facsimile". The same provision specifically excludes tenders presented by telephone. The latter rule is interesting as it might be argued that it excludes the use of the internet's e-mail facilities when these are accessed over regular phone lines. However, such an interpretation would seem to be too restrictive as facsimile messages *are* permitted.

---

[13] Recently the European Parliament expressed its discontent with the amount of money spent on the Supplement. It reduced the budget for OJ "S" for 1998 by a significant amount which undoubtedly increases the pressure to eliminate the paper version. Hence the Commissiion decided to discontinue the publication of the paper version as from 1 July 1998. The Official Journal Supplement will continue to be available as a CD-Rom.

[14] GPA, Article X(4).

[15] GPA, Article XIII(1)(a).

However, the GPA contains another interesting provision indicating that the GPA does acknowledge the existence of IT and its potential importance in the area of government procurement. Article XXIV(8) reads as follows:

With a view to ensuring that the Agreement does not constitute an unneccessary obstacle to technical progress, Parties shall consult regularly in the [WTO Government Procurement Committee] regarding developments in the use of Information Technology in government procurement and shall, if necessary negotiate modifications to the Agreement. These consultations shall in particular aim to ensure that the use of Information Technology promotes the aim of open, non-discriminatory and efficient government procurement through transparent procedures, that contracts covered under the Agreement are clearly identified and that all available information relating to a particular contract can be identified. When a Party intends to innovate, it shall endeavour to take into account the views expressed by other Parties regarding potential problems.

This provision currently forms the basis for discussions among the parties to amend the GPA in order to adjust it to the opportunities offered by ICTs. Although at the time of writing it is too early to predict how the GPA will be amended, it is clear that at the very least these discussions will need to deal with the provisions mentioned above.

3. THE SECOND OPTION: ALLOWING NEW PROCUREMENT PROCEDURES

The discussion so far has been based on the assumption that the actual procurement procedures are left untouched. Even the changes to the directives which have recently been adopted[16] only result in allowing the use of ICTs in the application of the three known types of procedure: the open procedure, the restricted or selective procedure, and negotiated or limited tendering procedures. It is obvious that ICTs can make those procedures more transparent, more accessible and more efficient. However, the benefits of ICTs can go much further. Indeed, the three existing procedures were developed with "old" communication technologies in mind. The new ICTs will reach their full potential only if procedures are developed which take full advantage of all the possibilities offered.

Currently for contracts above the thresholds, the GPA and the procurement directives impose the three procedures. It is not possible for covered entities and authorities to apply different procedures, even if the latter ensure that the ultimate objectives of the directives are met more effectively and more efficiently. The reason for the limitation to just three procurement procedures, of which one (the negotiated or limited tendering procedure) can be used only in exceptional circumstances, is that suppliers might be reluctant to participate in tender procedures, in particular across borders, if that would mean that they would have to get used to too many types of

---

[16] See note 12 above.

procedures. This is a perfectly valid reason for limiting the number of procedures, but does not explain why they have to be shaped the way they are.

Real life practices do not let themselves get caught that easily by rules and regulations, however. As long as the required procedures make economic sense they will probably be followed, but if and when other procedures emerge which make more economic sense, ways and means will be found to apply them. This has happened in particular in the United States which has been trying since 1994 to move to *electronic commerce* in federal procurement. Although the optimistic expectations voiced at the beginning have not yet been realised, it is interesting to look at the experiences thus far. These can probably be summarised as follows:

(i)   Electronic commerce is seen as a much less complicated alternative to the often complex "traditional" procedures. This is why it is applied first and foremost to small contracts where the traditional procedures have a prohibitive impact on transaction costs.

(ii) Where ICT was applied in the traditional procedures, purchasers quickly discovered that these needed to undergo certain adjustments in order to avoid practical difficulties. US agencies which started advertising tender notices on the internet and made it possible to submit bids by e-mail, sometimes received thousands of tenders. The traditional procedures simply could not cope with such massive responses. Hence, suggestions were made to allow for increased use of selective tendering procedures, with a view to reducing the number of potential tenderers.

(iii) Several options, the use of which became possible through the application of ICTs, resulted in shifting important aspects of the procurement process from the purchaser to the supplier. This was true in particular for electronic catalogues, payment cards etc., which are being used increasingly in the United States. In the traditional procedures the purchaser defines its needs to which the supplier can then respond. In the case of electronic catalogues as well as with purchase cards, which allow purchasing officials to shop for products and services at a supplier or catalogue of their choice, this is different. In this case the supplier defines its offers in general and not with a particular procurement in mind. The purchaser than chooses from among these predefined offers, without having to write down its needs in complex technical specifications. The result is that the latter are defined by the suppliers, rather than by the purchasers.

These experiences cannot be simply transposed to the European context. For a variety of reasons, some of them linguistic or cultural in nature, the Single European Market is still not as integrated as the US market. Furthermore the use of ICTs, and in particular the internet, is more widespread in the United States than in European Community Member States. Some of the lessons learned in the United States example may nevertheless be interesting to the Community.

Because actual market integration is much lower in the European Community than in the United States, the number of responses to calls for tender from another Member State is still relatively low. This is why it is unlikely that we will see the numbers which were seen in the United States if submission of tenders over the internet becomes possible. However, even if the numbers remain in the hundreds, rather than in the thousands, the current procedures will still be unable to cope with this. Like the United States, the European Community will therefore have to think about ways of solving this problem.

In the discussions in the Government Procurement Committee of the GPA in Geneva, one of the suggestions made was to allow more selective tendering to take place in order to reduce the number of companies who can actually participate in such electronic procurement. It may be difficult, however, to find the right criterion or criteria to reduce the number of tenderers in a non-arbitrary manner and without reducing the degree of competition. It is submitted that purchasers will have to define their tender specifications in such a manner that suppliers who objectively speaking do not stand a chance of ever winning the contract, because they are simply not able to provide the product or service of the quality and at the price which the purchaser wants will not participate. This is easier said than done, however. Indeed, defining their requirements well is one of the most difficult things for purchasers to do. It is therefore precisely here that there is a great need for help to purchasers and suppliers alike. The challenge for ICT is to provide this help in a cost-efficient and user-friendly manner.

ICT should in particular increase transparency of market circumstances. This requires first and foremost a much higher rate of publication of Contract Award Notices (CANs). Rapid calculations using TED data leads to the conclusion that CANs are published in less than 50 per cent of all cases in which contract advertisements are published.[17] Reluctance to publish CANs often results from the wish not to divulge sensitive information. It is for this reason that the US federal authorities do not publish all such information in a detailed manner on a contract-by-contract basis. The Federal Procurement Data Center[18] collects data on all federal procurement and publishes only certain of those data. The remaining data are published in an aggregated manner.

The Community directives also do not require that all information on awarded contracts is published in an individual manner and this is true for

---

[17] Such statistics are very difficult to compile. Our methodology consisted simply of taking the number of tender notices published in the *Official Journal* in 1996 and comparing it with the number of CANs published that same year. This is a far from satisfactory method, given that some tender notices may never lead to an award of contract, while others may lead to several, in particular where breaking up the contract into different lots, awarded to various companies, is possible. The time factor also complicates things. Indeed, CANs for tender procedures launched in 1996 may very well be published only in 1997 or even beyond. The generally low number of CANs remains a fact, however, and is confirmed also by other studies, including the study referred to in note 1 above.

[18] Created as part of the Office of Management and Budget by Public Law 93-400, now part of the US General Services Administration (GSA).

utilities covered by directive 93/38/EEC.[19] Thus entities which benefit from the exception in Article 3 of that directive, which provides a derogation from the detailed rules of the directive for certain entities in the oil, gas and solid-fuel sectors, still have to provide the Commission with "information relating to the award of contracts". Such information is kept by the Commission, but not published on an individual basis. The Commission could decide to publish aggregated data on these contracts on a Member State basis. If this proves to be a useful way of providing market information, similar aggregated information could be published on other "markets" as well.

It may well be that such a "policy" might make it easier for contracting entities to provide contract award information. On the basis of CANs and such aggregated information, ICT tools could then provide an idea of the type of products or services bought by particular purchasers more generally within certain regions or Member States, the prices paid, the (average) number of submissions etc. If a supplier realises that his prices are generally higher than the average paid in another Member State or by a particular purchaser, it would not make a lot of sense to submit a bid. On the other hand it could attract efficient suppliers to areas or Member States where prices paid are relatively high.

As this last comment suggests, the publication of these data may reduce the number of bids in certain cases, while in other cases, in particular where average prices paid in certain Member States are fairly high, they may also result in an increase in the number of bids. If entities have indeed been paying too much in the past this probably demonstrates that their purchasing skills are not very refined. In such a case their ability to cope with high numbers of tenders will therefore probably not be impressive either.

This leads us to an important conclusion with regard to ICTs. They can increase transparency, facilitate the job of purchaser and supplier alike, but they cannot replace the human element on both sides of the marketplace. The tremendous increase in information which ICTs will undoubtedly bring about will place higher demands on purchasers and suppliers. As a result their purchasing skills will need to be strengthened. Whereas the larger purchasers and suppliers have already heeded this advice in the majority of cases, smaller authorities and small and medium-sized suppliers may not always be able to meet the challenge. It is particularly here that information brokers and other "intermediaries" will need to play a larger role.

In certain Member States and sectors such intermediaries have already emerged. ICTs will not reduce the role that such intermediaries may play, but will almost certainly change it. These intermediaries will have to focus less on finding the actual information, and more on the need to offer the information together with other elements as a value added service. A fairly

---

[19] Council Directive 93/38/EEC of 14 June 1993 (OJ 1993, No. L199/84 of 9 August 1993) co-ordinating the procurement procedures of entities operating in the water, energy, transport and telecommunications sectors, hereinafter referred to as "the utilities directive".

simple survey carried out on behalf of the Commission a few years ago revealed that suppliers feel they need a large variety of additional information before they can be induced to prepare a bid for a purchaser they do not know, in a market they do not know.

Thus the role of these intermediaries can range from simply presenting the required information to the purchasers, to actually purchasing for or on behalf of their clients. Such "outsourcing" of the procurement function, or parts thereof, raises interesting legal questions. If the intermediary purchases on behalf of a covered authority, it will have to apply the procedures laid down in the directives. The situation is less clear, however, if it purchases the products and services itself and then sells them on to the authority. In the latter case one might argue that the only contract which has to be awarded according to the directives is the one between the authority and the intermediary. Once that contract has been awarded correctly through a tender procedure, the purchase of possibly huge quantities of products and services "for" the authority can then take place outside the framework of the EU rules.

This situation would be very similar to the conclusion of a "framework contract", which is specifically recognised and regulated in the Utilities Directive 93/38/EEC.[20] If this conclusion is right, the other Community directives applying to the public sector, which do not currently provide for such contracts, may have to be amended to allow for them. At this stage one can only state that the increased use of intermediaries, to which ICTs almost necessarily lead, will result in more framework contracts or similar legal relationships and therefore to less "traditional" tender procedures. Whether this is good or bad remains to be seen. If the contract between the authority and the intermediary is concluded after fully transparent and really competitive tendering and if, in addition, appropriate benchmarking procedures apply, the net result may well be positive. In this case one needs to ensure, however, that suppliers are fully informed of the framework contract and of the conditions under which they can "hope to" sell to the intermediary. Some legislative initiative to cover these situations and ensure that they are handled in a non-discriminatory, transparent and open manner may well be required.

One can take matters a step further, however. Would not a very similar situation exist if the intermediary is operating *on behalf of* the authority and has been selected in the same competitive manner as in our example above? Is there still a need to follow the rules of the directive if the contract between the intermediary and the authority specifically states that the procurement shall be done based on economic principles, purchasing the best product or service at the best price? To put it slightly differently, could a situation arise where exemptions from the full regime of the directives

---

[20] See note 18 above. Article 1(5) defines such contracts as an agreement between a contracting entity and "one or more suppliers, contractors or service providers the purpose of which is to establish the terms, in particular with regard to the prices and, where appropriate, the quantity envisaged, governing the contracts to be awarded during a given period".

were made possible on terms very similar to those of Article 3 of the Utilities Directive? Article 3 allows the Commission to give a derogation for certain energy sector utilities which are required to compete under market conditions for licences to operate and thus are exposed to competitive conditions. Entities taking advantage of the derogation are exempt from the detailed requirements of the directive (as has already been noted above) but must still, however, follow general principles of competitive and non-discriminatory procurement. An intermediary which has won its purchasing contract in a competition under the Community directives, and which is also subject to a contractual obligation to adopt a competitive and non-discriminatory approach to procurement, may be seen to be in a similar position to entities which are exempt from the Utilities Directive's detailed rules under Article 3.

In the present state of Community law, an exception for such situations does not exist.

A series of other issues will probably also come to the fore. These may apply to the use of intermediaries, but also to other situations where no intermediary is used. The increased transparency offered by the new ICTs may well lead to situations where the traditional tendering system is completely obsolete. If the internet provides 100 per cent transparency concerning the products offered, their price and other sales conditions, does a public purchaser still have to go through the motions of a full tender procedure, or is it enough if it can demonstrate that it really purchased e.g. the lowest-priced computer with a given configuration?

It is too early to respond to these questions. However, it is clear that they exist and that answers need to be given fairly soon. Those answers will almost certainly challenge the entire tendering system. This does not mean that the current rules and procedures are obsolete in all cases. However, if they are found to be so in certain cases, the solution will already mean that the days of "one procedure fits all" are over. That in itself may already be a revolution for purchasers and suppliers alike.

4. A BRIEF DESCRIPTION OF THE EUROPEAN COMMUNITY'S SIMAP PROJECT

The European Community's SIMAP (système d'information pour les marches publics) project on information technology issues in public procurement has already been referred to above. Although the "S" in SIMAP stands for system, it is probably much more correct to speak of a project, which will not replace but has the potential of bringing about substantial changes to the existing procurement rules and practices in the European Community and beyond. Originally started as an initiative to increase the level of information about the realities in procurement throughout the Community, including on the degree to which the rules and procedures were complied with, it has been transformed into a project which has the purpose of making procurement much more efficient through the use of ICT.

SIMAP can be subdivided into four aspects, which – somewhat mis-leadingly – are each called "projects". The first of these intends to improve the *notification* phase. As part of this sub-project, a series of activities were undertaken, ranging from developing "standard forms" on paper for all notices required by the different directives, to establishing a tool and a communication system for electronically creating notices and submitting them to the Office for Official Publications (EUR-OP) in Luxembourg.

This tool has now been tested. This was originally done with 75 author-ities throughout the European Economic Area (EEA), and the number is now being gradually increased to cover, potentially, all contracting entities in the EEA. Although the pilot has demonstrated that it is feasible to run an electronic "notification" system of this type, a major question has sprung up, which has not yet been resolved. One of the objectives of this part of the project was to improve the quality of the notices. In the past EUR-OP had developed a policy of informing procuring entities which sent in notices which did not contain all the information required by the directives. How-ever, if no or insufficient corrections were received from the entity within the 12-day period at the end of which EUR-OP has to publish the notice,[21] it would publish whatever it had, provided, at least, that a very limited number of essential elements were included. In very broad terms these minimum requirements can be said to include the name and address of the contracting entity, a description of the goods or services required and the deadline by which offers should be submitted. Interestingly, EUR-OP feels compelled to publish within the given time-period, although one could argue that this obligation only exists for those notices which comply with the directives. Thus it can be argued that the obligation to mention the Classification of Products by Activity (CPA), the Central Product Classifica-tion (CPC) and General Industrial Classification of Economic Activities within the European Communities (NACE) codes should be complied with as well as that to draw up the notices "in accordance with the models annexed to the directives".[22]

The decision to publish anyway was founded on the belief that it was more important to ensure at least some publication of tenders and not to create a disincentive to publication. The fear was that a refusal to publish a notice unless near perfect would result in most cases in a decision by procuring entities simply not to comply with the directive at all. However, there was a great deal of dissatisfaction with the lack of detail and sometimes the apparent inaccuracy of the notices. Hence the notification sub-project of SIMAP included the purpose of improving the quality of the notices. However, in doing so, this part of SIMAP ran into the same difficulties as before. Several entities, which the SIMAP project calls Data

---

[21] See, for example, Article 9(8) of Directive 93/36/EEC which provides that EUR-OP "shall publish the notices not later than 12 days after their dispatch". In the case of the accelerated procedure this period is reduced to a mere five days, according to the same provision.
[22] See, for example, Article 9(1) and (4) of Directive 93/36/EEC.

Entry Points (DEPs),[23] decided to abandon their participation in SIMAP and return to the old practices of submitting notices by fax. Notices which were refused by the SIMAP software as being incomplete, were published by EUR-OP if submitted by fax or regular mail. Apparently this is another example where the level of detail provided by the directives does not coincide with the needs and wishes of those who are regulated by them.

The second SIMAP sub-project deals with the improvement of the *dissemination* of notices. According to the directives, this is to take place through publication in the supplement to the *Official Journal* and in TED. However, neither of these were considered very user-friendly and both were rather expensive to the Community taxpayer, to the subscriber or to both. SIMAP's purpose was to improve both instruments, while adding to their usefulness by providing information on related aspects not covered by the directives. Given the reluctance to publish what is required by the directives, as just discussed, an attempt to add even further information seems quite ambitious. In an early pilot project SIMAP tested a single tool to access existing below-threshold databases. Even though such databases exist in several Member States, only two decided to participate in the pilot, one from Greece and one from Spain. The other Member States felt that providing information on below-threshold contracts went beyond the Community's powers or was unacceptable as long as reciprocity was not guaranteed. Both views are wrong, both in fact and in law. Any supplier can subscribe to these databases, even if sometimes through a local subsidiary or an importer. Attempts to limit access to such databases only to nationals would be clearly incompatible with Community law. Another problem resided in the fact that both participating databases were available only in (one) national language. In the case of the Spanish database this may not have been an insurmountable problem, but the Greek data could not even be displayed on the screens used in the other Member States without adaptations to the software.

Fortunately the SIMAP project was helped by technological developments and in particular by the emergence of the internet. More and more companies and authorities offering databases feel compelled to offer access over the internet. Even if the original idea comes from the wish to satisfy national subscribers, the worldwide character of the internet ensures accessibility to users from throughout the Community and beyond. Because of the heavy bias of this medium towards the English language, a decision is often made to offer access to at least general information in English. Finally, the present state of the internet still favours free of charge access over paid access.

---

[23] The SIMAP project distinguishes three different types of DEPs: those which only submit their own notices; those which submit notices for other contracting entities in addition to their own (for example, a province submitting its own notices and those of the municipalities on its territory); and DEPs which submit notices from contracting entities, without themselves being such entities (this is the case of some Euro Info Centers, for example, in Portugal and the Netherlands).

All of these elements combined now offer a completely different perspective for future developments in the dissemination of procurement data in Europe and for our major trading partners. Indeed, if all information about procurement opportunities and related data is increasingly offered over the same medium, solutions can be developed which draw the full benefits from this. In August 1997 the Commission launched a tender procedure, the technical specifications of which can be found in the "Archives" section of the Commission's SIMAP website. According to these specifications the Commission has sought, *inter alia*, "to develop the dissemination part of SIMAP (pilot project '2') into a high-performance system able to offer millions of potential suppliers in the EU and beyond user-friendly access, ideally through a single interface, to tender information offered both centrally by the EU and in a decentralised manner through websites which can be accessed without cost".

In plain language this means that what the Commission seeks to achieve is a situation in which persons and companies looking for procurement data need no longer go to each individual database in order to find the information. Instead, they should be able to search a variety of databases through the "single interface" the Commission would like to see developed and would be offered the results, possibly without even knowing where the information was retrieved from.

It is hard to overestimate the importance of this development, if it succeeds. When the Commission launched its call for tender, TED (Tenders Electronic Daily) was available on the internet, though not as a database which can be accessed without cost. At the time of writing it seems almost certain that TED will be offered free of charge over the internet from 1 January 1999. This means that the "single interface" can search TED as well as a growing number of other databases. If this can be done successfully, it is hard to see why the single interface would be limited to searching only the existing databases. Technically nothing would exclude the possibility of searching a large number of websites, including those which are maintained by procuring entities themselves. That this is already on the Commission's mind may be reflected in the suggestion, also on the SIMAP website, for contracting entities to provide procurement information in a so-called "purchaser profile".

The third sub-project in SIMAP deals with *monitoring the procurement markets*. This is the part which most closely reflects the origins of the project, namely, to offer a system which allows Member States and the Commission to obtain a better picture of how and to what extent the procurement rules are being complied with. In practice, however, this part of SIMAP has been very slow to come off the mark and has still not produced significant results. This is partly due to substantial criticisms from the Member States of this aspect of "big brother is watching procurement", and also to a change in focus by the European Commission itself; the Commission has sought to change SIMAP from a "control mechanism" to an instrument which makes procurement more efficient for all involved. Market surveillance can and must form an important part of such a system, however. Purchasers will need information on products and services offered and purchased on the public procurement market, as well as in private markets. Suppliers need to know what types of products and services particular purchasers are interested in, the prices paid, the award criteria usually applied and so on. Several of these elements require better compliance with the obligations in the directives to publish contract award notices or CANs.[24] As we have already noted above, the rate of publication of such CANs as compared to the number of tender notices published is, however, disappointingly low. In addition these award notices seldom contain the type of information which is required to offer real insights into procurement markets.[25]

A second theoretical source of information about the application of the directives is also hardly available in practice. The directives as well as the GPA require the provision of statistical data in a detailed manner and partly on an entity-by-entity basis.[26] This information is collected "[i]n order to permit assessment of the results of applying" the directive and the GPA. It can, however, also provide useful market information for both purchasers and suppliers. One of the purposes of the third sub-project of SIMAP is to facilitate the collection of these data.

As indicated, this part of SIMAP has so far hardly been developed. However, it is potentially one of the areas with electronic purchasing where SIMAP has the most to offer. The other parts of SIMAP have the objective of finding ways and means of doing more efficiently what is already done today anyway. In the area of this third sub-project it must be acknowledged that real transparency of the actual procurement markets in terms of products and services bought and prices paid does not exist currently. The challenge for SIMAP is therefore significant. At the same time the results will come almost automatically as a "by-product" of the other parts of SIMAP. Indeed, if all procedures are carried out electronically and through the SIMAP system, the collection of data will not require any additional activity on the part of the Member States, nor the procuring entities. Statistics can be compiled by the system itself. The transparency this will offer may lead to a market which is much more competitive than is currently the case. If indeed procuring entities are able to obtain information in an easily accessible manner on sales conditions including price from any company throughout the EEA and even the entire GPA area, all these companies will effectively compete against each other.

The fourth and final sub-project of SIMAP conceals the most fascinating aspect, that is, electronic tendering, behind a rather uninspiring title: *exchanges between purchasers and suppliers*. It is true, of course, that in

---

[24] See, for example, Article 9(3) of Directive 93/36/EEC: "Contracting authorities who have awarded a contract shall make known the result by means of a notice."

[25] The directives provide for exemptions to the information which the CAN should include: "However, certain information on the contract award may, in certain cases, not be published where release of such information would impede law enforcement or otherwise be contrary to the public interest, would prejudice the legitimate commercial interests of particular enterprises, public or private, or might prejudice fair competition between suppliers."

[26] See, for example, Article. 31 of the Supplies Directive which requires annual reports which provide a series of detailed statistics on contracts "awarded by each contracting authority".

electronic tendering many or even all of the exchanges between the purchaser and its supplier(s) should take place electronically. However, the title already highlights that the original thinking in the SIMAP project did not include challenging the current tender procedures. Electronic purchasing was still limited to electronic tendering and it was envisaged that the tender procedures would be essentially those of the directives and the GPA.

Since then it has become clear that the introduction of electronic procedures in the procurement process will necessarily lead to a reflection on the entire procurement procedure. As indicated above, this may well lead to a greater variety of procedures and to a much more active role for the supplier, in particular for purchases of low-value off-the-shelf products. In the framework of the SIMAP project two studies have so far been carried out, the second of which should lead to a strategy proposal for developing a pan-European procurement area. As a first step towards the implementation of such a strategy a pilot should be launched sometime in 1998.

5. A DIFFERENT ROLE FOR THE LAW IN THE AGE OF ELECTRONIC PROCUREMENT?

For the reasons mentioned above the directives create a sort of superstructure of rather detailed procurement procedures on top of the directly applicable free circulation or non-discrimination provisions of the EC Treaty. The situation is similar for the GPA, although this combines both the detailed procedural rules and the underlying principles in one instrument. It is certainly possible to develop electronic tools which are based on the procedures laid down in the directives and the GPA. Several ICT companies have already done so and the European Commission, through its SIMAP project, is doing the same.

The decision to lay down detailed procedural rules rather than limit the regime to defining broad principles as the EC did in the area of competition policy and free circulation of goods (except where exceptions to those principles are allowed[27]) leads to certain problems. These relate, in particular, to the degree to which such procedures are adjusted to the specific needs of a particular procurement or a particular purchaser. A balance had to be drawn between the need to limit the number of procedures in the interest of transparency and to avoid difficulties in determining which procedures applied in which cases on the one hand, and the need to take account of the specificities of each procurement on the other hand. In practice this has led, as we saw, to limiting the procedures to just three.

---

[27] Such exceptions are possible under Article 36 of the EC Treaty as well as under the ECJ's jurisprudence following the *Cassis de Dijon* case (C-120/78 [1978] ECR 649). The so-called "new approach" to harmonisation of legislation limits detailed provisions to those cases where essential requirements allow Member States to block free circulation of products.

The use of ICTs might change the situation, however, by shifting the balance in favour of greater flexibility but without immediately bringing about the dangers which existed previously whenever too many possibilities were allowed. This is because ICTs do not have to be limited to defining the actual procurement procedures, which they can do very well, but can also provide the necessary help in applying these, either through a built-in help function or "on-line", by allowing users to contact a "help desk" through electronic means. The SIMAP project has created both such a help-desk and "built-in help". Although currently available only to a limited number of participants in the "notification" pilot project and not yet fully in all official languages, this help desk could develop into a more sophisticated service.

It is doubtful whether the Commission will ever succeed in running such an operation itself. This is the reason why it has organised workshops and conferences through which it has invited private companies to develop the "business opportunities" which the SIMAP project had indicated existed. The important conclusion for our purposes is, however, that whoever provides such assistance, its very availability to users of the procurement rules would make it possible that a much higher number of types of procurement procedures could be allowed.

Thus it would be possible to take into account many or even most of the differences which might exist between Member States. It would also allow for different procedures for procuring widely varying things such as a completely electronic procedure for purchasing fairly simple off-the-shelf products, while more traditional procedures would be maintained for tendering for a public works contract such as for building a bridge.

In this multi-solution purchasing environment the scope for detailed procedural requirements laid down in provisions which can be amended only through difficult and time-consuming procedures may well be very limited. Yet, the need to ensure that those procedures are indeed non-discriminatory and transparent and that their variety does not in itself make things discriminatory or non-transparent is all the more important.

This may call for legal instruments which are less detailed, but at the same time better adhered to. Ensuring that such solutions can be found is a major challenge for the next decade.

10. The Scope for Post-Tender Negotiations in International Tendering Procedures

1. INTRODUCTION

Tender procedure is now to a large extent governed by public international administrative law, conforming with or departing from national legislation on public administration. Tender procedures are also part of national contract law in as far as the formation procedure is based around the three elements establishing the final contract between the public entity and the private contractor: the tender *documentation*, the *tender bid* and the ultimate *acceptance* of the tender bid succeeding the preparatory decision to award the contract. There are some differences, but in general the tender is a qualified irrevocable *offer* to perform the services or deliver the goods according to the specification at prices set out in the bid, and the award communication to the successful tenderer is the legally binding *acceptance* which establishes the contract between the parties.[1] European Community procurement law and that of many other international regulatory systems seems to be based on the assumption that the contractual position is in principle not subject to supranational mandatory rules or regulations and remains a matter for national law.[2]

---

* University of Bergen, Norway.

[1] UN 1980 Convention on Contracts for the International Sale of Goods (CISG 1980), Part II on formation issues would be applicable in public contracting where a non-resident contractor is selected for a supply contract; *cf.* the Anglo-Continental compromise provisions on qualified legally binding offers stated in the Article 16 exception to the main rule that unilateral non-accepted offers are not binding, thus: "However, an offer cannot be revoked: (a) if it indicates, whether by stating a fixed time for acceptance or otherwise, that it is irrevocable."

[2] Thus, whether a contract position acquired is affected by preceding internal infringements of the procurement law provisions (national or international) is primarily a matter for national legislation or case law to decide. Many systems – like the Nordic – insist that contract positions are unaffected by possible procedural errors both in cases where the contract has become more favourable than it should have been and in the opposite situation where a contractor gets a contract which should have been awarded to a competitor. The compromise solution available by the remedy rules is the rejected candidate's claim for damages.

A private party may conduct its contract negotiations relatively freely. However, international law principles or national law may impose limitations. For example, in EC law abuse of a dominant market position – even in public contracting – may attract competition law sanctions under Article 86 of the EC Treaty. Provisions such as the Nordic *generalklausul* may be invoked when the contents of contracts are unreasonably balanced, including in commercial transactions.[3] The refusal to contract with someone for reasons of nationality may amount to discrimination within the scope of Article 6 of the EC Treaty or could be treated as an infringement of provisions on free movements for goods and services such as for instance Article 59 of the EC Treaty. There may also be situations where pre-contractual non-disclosure of relevant information or undue influence (duress, fraud etc.) respectively could affect contractual liability.

National and international principles applicable to pre-contractual relations often do not distinguish between contracting within the private sector and contracts within the public or semi-public areas. Thus, internationally adopted standards for equal and competitive access to public commitments, such as the EC procurement directives and World Trade Organisation Government Procurement Agreement (GPA) fit into a wider perspective of international contract law. This includes the possible consensus on some of the general principles of international commercial contracting presented by Unidroit in 1994.[4]

The international law perspective on the regulation of pre-contractual activities deals with the decision-making process leading up to the award and signing of public, semi-public or utility contracts. These international rules (including, for example, those of the EC and the GPA) have supplemented and, to an extent, replaced previous national systems for the pre-contractual management of major public contracts.

The aim of this chapter is to consider one particular problematic area of contract formation under the European rules, that is, the extent to which these rules limit the possibility for post-tender negotiations with firms. The analysis focuses on the rules applicable under the European Community procurement rules (which are also applicable to the European Economic Area (EEA) nations of Norway, Liechtenstein and Iceland) and the GPA. Similar problems might, however, arise under other international procurement regimes that emphasise the concept of transparency as an underlying principle. It is argued that the restrictions that exist in EC law on post-tender negotiations are unduly strict, failing to recognise a number of commercial problems, and that the more flexible approach of the GPA is to be preferred.

---

[3] Scandinavian courts would be hesitant to apply pure "reasonableness" tests on commercial contracts outside the consumer area, but all Scandinavian Supreme Courts have stated clearly that the *generalklausul* may apply. For a well-known case demonstrating the limits for judicial "soft law" intervention in the commercial area, see the *Ula* case reported in Nordiske Domme i sjøfartsanliggender (ND) 1990.204 (Norwegian arbitration award in an offshore joint venture contract dispute).

[4] *Unidroit Principles of International Commercial Contracts* (Rome 1994); *cf.* O. Lando and H. Beale (eds.), *Principles of European Contract Law* (1995), Part I, prepared by a Commission on European Contract Law. The former contains extensive regulation on formation issues such as negotiations in bad faith, duty of confidentiality, battle of forms etc.

2. TRANSPARENCY VERSUS TAILORING THE CONTRACT TO THE ENTITY'S NEEDS

The well-established principle of formal open or restricted tender procedure as the main rule for public contracting is stated in the three EC public sector directives: Article 7(1) of the Works Directive;[5] Article 6(1) of the Supplies Directive;[6] and Article 8 of the Services Directive.[7] A different rule applies in the Utilities Directive (Article 20(1))[8] which allows a choice between the two formal tender procedures or negotiated contracting. There are certain exceptions to the main rule even outside the utility sector, and experience shows that public entities will press for maximum flexibility up to and even beyond the limits set in the procedural provisions on contract awards, often to a degree which causes doubt as to whether the rules are applied in the way they are supposed to apply. This does not necessarily mean that these authorities are acting inefficiently or deliberately undermining the directives. Many entities may experience the shortcomings of the public procurement legislation in situations where one is forced to find better solutions than provided for in the directives' regimes. In turnkey contracts and in the area of public services, the general experience seems to be that a ban on negotiations is being compromised by a practice of *ad hoc* communications with the intention of tailoring the contract to the actual needs of the entity. The directives themselves do not in plain words restrict negotiations. However, the implication is that a *main rule* on tender procedure as opposed to *exceptions* authorising negotiated contracts for some cases mean *some* restrictions in situations where the entity wants to combine the best of these two worlds. The ban on negotiation assumption was adopted and confirmed *ad hoc* by the Commission through "soft law" statements on how to read the procurement directives.[9] The Commission's position is that any negotiation with candidates or tenderers on fundamental aspects of the contract – "variations in which are likely to distort competition, and in particular on prices" – are to be ruled out. Without discussing the legal significance of the Commission's unilateral *ex post* declaration regarding the authentic interpretation of the directives' provisions, it may suffice to say that the understanding of the tender procedure concept voiced by the Commission in its communication probably will coincide with the position in many legal systems within the EC and the EEA. ECJ judgments seem to confirm the assumption. Thus in Case C-243/89, *Commission* v. *Kingdom of Denmark (Storebealt)*,[10] the ECJ stated that since the entity's negotiation with the selected consortium took place on the basis of a tender which did not comply with the tender conditions, Denmark had violated Community law.

---

[5] Directive 93/37/EEC, OJ 1993, No. L199/54.
[6] Directive 93/36/EEC, OJ 1993, No. L199/1.
[7] Directive 92/50/EEC, OJ 1992, No. L209/1.
[8] Directive 93/38/EEC, OJ 1993, No. L199/84.
[9] OJ 1989, No. L210/ 22; OJ 1990, No. L297/48; OJ 1994, No. L111/114; *cf.* also S. Arrowsmith, *The Law of Public and Utilities Procurement* (Sweet & Maxwell, 1996), pp. 247*ff* and p. 520.
[10] [1993] ECR I-3353.

Since the negotiated procedure operates as a complete exceptional procedure from the tender procedure, the idea must be that one cannot *combine* the formal tender procedure, based on transparent written communication in the form of a final "take it or leave it" irrevocable tender bid based on a tender contract documentation, with a situation where the entity treats the bid as a tactical opening for further bargaining on quantities to be delivered, unit pricing, contract conditions etc. This ban on negotiation has its parallel in a very blunt provision in the UNCITRAL Model Law, Article 34(1)(a) ("No change ... shall be sought, offered or permitted").[11] Similar restrictions are found in the World Bank Guidelines.[12]

The approach of the GPA on the other hand seems to be far more flexible, structured so that an entity may choose a method of procurement in which the entity decides for itself whether the procedure is to be open or selective and whether or not it will involve negotiations. Article XIV of the GPA states:

1. A Party may provide for entities to conduct negotiations:
    (i)   in the context of procurements in which they have indicated such intent, namely in the notice referred to in paragraph 2 of Article IX (the invitation to suppliers to participate in the procedure for the proposed procurement); or
    (ii) when it appears from evaluation that no one tender is obviously the most advantageous in terms of the specific evaluation criteria set forth in the notices or tender documentation.
2. Negotiations shall primarily be used to identify the strengths and weaknesses in tenders.
3. Entities shall treat tenders in confidence. In particular, they shall not provide information intended to assist particular participants to bring their tenders up to the level of other participants.
4. Entities shall not, in the course of negotiations, discriminate between different suppliers. In particular, they shall ensure that:
    (i)   any elimination of participants is carried out in accordance with the criteria set forth in the notices and tender documentation;
    (ii) all modifications to the criteria and to the technical requirements are transmitted in writing to all remaining participants in the negotiations;
    (iii) all remaining participants are afforded an opportunity to submit new or amended submissions on the basis of the revised requirements; and
    (iv) when negotiations are concluded, all participants remaining in the negotiations shall be permitted to submit final tenders in accordance with a common deadline.

---

[11] UNCITRAL, *Yearbook* (1994), vol. XXV, pp. 307*ff.*

[12] World Bank, *Procurement under IBRD Loans and IDA Credits* (1995, as revised) (hereinafter the World Bank Guidelines), p. 24: "Except as otherwise provided in paragraphs 2.61 and 2.62 of these Guidelines, bidders shall not be requested or permitted to alter their bids after the deadline for receipt of bids. The Borrower shall ask bidders for clarification needed to evaluate their bids but shall not ask or permit bidders to change the substance or price of their bids after the bids opening. Requests for clarification and the bidders' responses shall be made in writing." See also FIDIC Tendering Procedure Cl 5.3.

This GPA provision departs from previous EU and EEA law in two respects. First, the distinction between tender procedures and negotiated procedures is blurred. Secondly, the principle of transparent decision-making based on the tenders alone seems to be abandoned in principle. The EC has recently adopted a directive to adjust the public sector directives to align them with the GPA.[13] However, this directive contains nothing on post-tender negotiations: there is no express confirmation of the Commission's statements that post-tender negotiations are not permitted; neither is there any attempt to broaden the possibility of negotiations under the EC rules to accord with the more flexible position under the GPA. The latter is hardly surprising since in general the new directive is concerned simply to reduce the obligations in the directive when they are more stringent than those of the GPA.

The principle stated by the Commission in 1994 and widely accepted in national procurement law on the matter will probably remain in EU and EEA contract situations.

The relationship between the GPA and EC directives in the matter of negotiations seems to be that the EC rules in the area will prevail over the GPA negotiation principles expressed in Article XIV. Is this, however, desirable?

3. NEGOTIATIONS AS PART OF PUBLIC CONTRACTING: POLICY ASPECTS

Why is the EC law on public contracts so reluctant to prohibit otherwise normal commercial negotiations in the establishment of contracts? In a global historical setting, the danger of corrupt procurement justifies contracting procedures which leave as little room for discretionary decision-making as possible on the negotiating level. The World Bank Guidelines rule out unwarranted alterations of bids, and also require the Bank's prior concurrence before entering into negotiations even with the lowest evaluated bidder.[14] The UNCITRAL Model Law reflects this in its suggested preference for extremely rigid and formalistic procurement arrangements, with the purpose of preventing abuse in the exercise of public office in contracting with private parties.[15]

The overriding formula for getting best value in the spending of public money may be better served by recognising and accepting the public buyer's potentially strong market position. In the private sector, competition law restricts the abuse of a dominant market position (Article 86 of

---

[13] Amended Proposal for a Directive Amending Directives 92/50/EEC, 93/36/EEC and 93/37 EEC (COM (96) 623 final of 13 December 1996; OJ 1997, No. C-111/1/97 of 9 April 1997, p. 000) and Amended Proposal for a Directive Amending Directive 93/38/EEC (COM (96) 598 final of 20 November 1996; OJ 1997, No. C-28/97 of 29 January 1997, p. 4).

[14] World Bank Guidelines, Item 2.45, 2.61 and 2.62.

[15] UNCITRAL Model Law, Article 18. See Guide to Enactment of the UNCITRAL Model Law Procurement (A/CN.9/403).

the EC Treaty), but in the balancing of public interests in negotiations, one could find reasons for going as far as saying that the squeezing of potential contract candidates to bring performance up and price down does *not* amount to abuse within the competition law perspective.

Similarly, the basic "call for competition" requirement for promoting equal opportunities for obtaining the contract in question is not necessarily in conflict with the idea of negotiated contracts. On the contrary, the results achieved in dialogue with one candidate might very well prompt an even better contract from a competitor. The Commission's statements ruling out use of tender negotiations are ambiguous in this respect. The statements can *either* be understood as an assertion that *all* negotiations on fundamental aspects of contracts will necessarily distort competition (and thus prevent both equal treatment and "best value") or as banning only negotiations which in fact have a distorting effect in the particular case. Since competition may take place also in conjunction with or in prolongation of tendering procedures, and is actually practised in many markets which allow for negotiations, it is somewhat hard to accept that the implication of parallel negotiations with contract candidates necessarily must distort competition. This is particularly so if one assumes an honest intention on the part of the entity to really go for best value.

If the rules of the game are that the tender must be prepared as the contractors' one-shot chance to win the contract, negotiations may violate reasonably legitimate expectations in the arena of competing tenderers. But then on the other hand, if the entity makes it clear *ex ante* that the tenderers may have to adjust or amend their offers before final award at a later stage (such as in the cited GPA provision), following discussions on price, contract scope and performance aspects, then the rules of the game have been set and the argument based on frustrated expectations fails.

Combining opening tender bids with subsequent time-consuming negotiations might contradict economic standards for the amount of time and resources reasonably to be spent in public contracting activities. That argument, however, cannot in itself be decisive.

The only two valid objections to negotiations as a manner of acquiring public contract commitments lie either, first, in the risk for covert abuse of discretion as a means for awarding access to public contracts or, secondly, in the possibility that the actual national preference or conduct otherwise contrary to Community policy in decision-making on part of the entity will necessarily become more difficult to detect and review. In other words, it seems as if the true basis for a ban on negotiations is the need for effective *transparency* in the step-by-step decision-making process leading up to the final award. The process of such a negotiation, as in private commercial matters, may take place partly in meetings, partly in the exchange of letters, faxes and e-mails, and partly over the telephone. Effective review of this fragmented decision-making in such circumstances is next to impossible. Since combating covert or preferential treatment is an important objective for EC law, it seems as if the genuine objection to negotiated contracts lies in the risk that entities may try to conceal unacceptable reasons used in the final selection of the contract candidate, such as, for instance, an award preferential to domestic industry or an award contradicting the rule of "most advantageous tender". In this respect, negotiations may violate expectations of equal treatment of the competing contract candidates.

4. EXCEPTIONS AND MODIFICATIONS

No modern public contract regime can do without negotiated procedures, at least as a limited exception to the main rule on the use of open or restricted tender procedures. The cases covered by the EC exceptions generally refer to different failures to find a suitable contract candidate (for example, in Article 7(2)(a) and (3)(a) of the Works Directive 93/37/EEC) or alternatively contracts of a kind where tendered procedures are manifestly unsuited for the purpose, for example because only one contractor can do the job (Article 7(3)(b)), or where there is no time to initiate the full tender procedure (Article 7(3)(c))[16] or because the work in question naturally has to be done in connection with an existing contract.

As mentioned, a negotiated procedure preceding the award of a contract is justified in cases where an already conducted tender procedure has failed to bring up a tender or candidate to the entity's satisfaction. Provisions authorising negotiations are found in Article 3(a) of the Works Directive, requiring as a condition "the absence of tenders or of appropriate tenders in response to an open or restricted procedure". It is a well-known problem that entities may seek to terminate a tender procedure by *not* awarding the contract to any of the tenderers and then subsequently initiate negotiations by invoking the principle stated in the cited provision. Blatant circumvention of the requirement to conduct a tender procedure without parallel negotiations should be ruled out, but it causes some problem to define the exact limit between dishonest adaptation of the "negotiated procedure" provisions like the one cited and *bona fide* negotiations in the situation at which the exception is directed.[17]

The general and largely valid objection to Community law in these matters is that the present exceptions are far too narrow. For major turnkey construction works or for extensive technological projects (such as in the field of information technology) and other contracts requiring a joint *ex ante* exploration of the possible progress, time schedule, performance or regulation of adverse unpredictable contingencies, the market has since long advocated that it is impossible to create a satisfactory contract relationship based only on the pre-contractual documentation prepared by the entity (which may not have the expertise or experience to draft a suitable

---

[16] Case C-318/94, *Commission* v. *German Federal Republic* [1996] ECR I-1949.

[17] In practice, one might require some time between the termination of the prior tender procedure before initiating negotiations. In Danish practice six months has been deemed acceptable. One may also require some change in the contract object since the idea is to make an effort to achieve something less costly by negotiating with the already known contract candidates. The Works Directive, Article 7(3)(a), however, states as a condition that the contract should *not* be substantially altered (obligation to report to Commission upon request).

contract). Similarly, for complicated services outside the works and supplies sectors, the view is that the tender procedure prevents a sensible tailoring adjustment of the contract to the needs of the procuring entity. The liberal approach adopted in the procurement principles of the GPA can be seen from this perspective. The question is the extent to which demands like these can be reconciled in practice with a fair competitive setting for a competition between two or more possible candidates for the contract in question. The Norwegian experience within the oil and gas sector, where pre-contractual negotiations succeeding the conclusion of a tender procedure have been practised since the 1970s, seems to prove that the problem may be solved with common sense.[18]

5. IMPLICATIONS OF THE BAN ON NEGOTIATIONS

Let us assume that the ban on negotiations stands as the main principle and is likely to do so in the future for public contract law. The principle has a range of necessary implications which are not dealt with explicitly by the Commission in the communicated statements. There is the question of distinguishing between commercially well-founded clarification of a tender bid and negotiations. There is also the question of how to deal with "errors" in bids which may be accidental or may be deliberately "planted" tactical discrepancies in tenders. Such errors may manifest themselves in various forms including miscalculations, ambiguities, inconsistencies within the bid, apparent misreading of contract documentation (which may or may not be inherently ambiguous), or leaving out items which will inevitably necessitate extras under variation orders. The issue is the tenderer's right and also the entity's right or even duty, to "correct" or amend the bid in a clarification or quasi-negotiation scenario.

Ruling out negotiations means in practice also a ban on amendments of tenders. If one allows the tenderer to require or the contracting entity to effectuate (unilaterally or upon the tenderer's request) amendments which might alter the basis of comparison between the tenders, this would affect the tender procedure negatively. Correcting the legal contents of an offer unilaterally on the part of the procuring entity may result in subsequent objections if the amendments extend the obligation actually contained in the offer (for example price, or scope of obligation), even if the amendments mean that the offeror succeeds in acquiring the contract. From another perspective, after opening the bids it is of vital importance that the tenderers are not allowed to continue their competitive efforts with newly acquired knowledge of competitors' figures and sums. For example, by

---

[18] One solution seems to be the increase of non-tendered joint-venture partnering arrangements which by definition fall outside the scope of the EC utilities directives, such as the present Norwegian NPA 96 Project Alliance Contract under preparation; *cf.* K. Kaasen in MarIus 209 (1995) (Isle of Man seminar report, Scandinavian Institute of Maritime Law, Oslo: 1995).

reducing the scope of their apparent offer, or by invoking mistakes or misunderstanding a bidder's post-tender adjustments might get him the contract as the most favourable tenderer. It is also important to exclude the temptation for the entity to achieve an even better contract by suggesting amendments which in fact could mean that one rearranges the order of the existing bids.[19] The procuring entity is entitled neither to press the successful tenderer to lower his price, nor to introduce new aspects in order to bring a tender which was not the most favourable into an improved position by suggesting or demanding alterations in price or scope of contract performance. In Case T-19/85 *Adia Interim SA* v. *Commission*,[20] the European Court of First Instance stated:

It follows that, even though the [entity] detected the presence of a systematic calculation error, it was unable to ascertain its exact nature or cause. In those circumstances, any contact made by the [entity] in order to seek out jointly with it the exact nature and cause would have involved *a risk that other factors taken into account in order to establish the tender price ... might have been adjusted, and this would have entailed ... an infringement of the principle of equal treatment to the detriment of the other tenderers*, all of whom, in common with [the tenderer in this case], are under an equal duty to take care in drawing up their tenders.[21]

The post-tender scenario involves some aspects of importance. One has to bear in mind the utmost importance of precision and clarification of the documentation which is supposed to be the final one-shot basis for tender pricing. Ambiguities and sources for misunderstandings brought about by professional errors on the part of the entity (in practice by staff or independent consultants) must normally be treated at the risk of the entity, for instance in the interpretation of a specific tender which apparently is based on an intelligible misunderstanding of the information supplied in the contract documentation. One expects documentation which is clear and exact in all respects. Time for preparing a tender bid is always short and the misunderstanding of the documentation on the part of the tenderer leads to the question whether the documentation was well prepared, sufficiently

---

[19] Even negotiating with the lowest or most advantageous bidder – assuming that he has actually already won the contract – might be unacceptable, not because it affects the "call for competition", but because it is a breach of the "rules of the game" which seem to be inherent in a tender system where the tenderers are advised that their offer will be treated as *final*. The situation dealt with by S. Arrowsmith, *The Law of Public and Utilities Procurement* (Sweet & Maxwell, 1996), pp. 249–50 ("Negotiations with the most favourable bidder") seems to be aimed at amendments after the signing of the contract or possibly in the interval between the actual selection of the successful tenderer and the signing of the contract. The selection, however, is only made notorious by communicating the award decision to the tenderer. In my view, there is no room for accepting options for the entity to introduce improvements in price, scope or contract conditions in the post-award pre-contractual stage of the process. After concluding the contract, the situation is different. Either there is a dispute on the correct legal interpretation of the contract – or there is a constructive variation order (see below at section 7).

[20] [1996] ECR II-321.

[21] Emphasis added.

precise and so informative that the tenderer only had to price the unit elements in the documentation.

There is also the issue of the extent of an entity's control in checking the tender bids. Blatant calculation errors must by rectified[22] and the checking will also include the possibility that the bid deviates from the tender documentation, for instance by reservations or modifications, by suggested alternatives to the product or function asked for, or by reference to contract clauses which do not conform to the entity's invitation. Where a bidder has submitted a variant bid, this might necessitate a pecuniary conversion of contract clauses into an operative "price" tag in order to enable an effective and rational comparison of the bids.[23]

Under the European rules, abnormally low tenders are dealt with in provisions such as Article 34(5) of the Utilities Directive, Article 27 of the Supplies Directive, Article 30(4) of the Works Directive and Article 37 of the Services Directive. The assumption is that the contracting entity is entitled to reject such a tender after having required in writing the constituent elements of such a tender for subsequent verification, and taking account of the explanations received. The provision obviously deals with final price tender bids. The problem of abnormally low unit prices seems not to be covered.[24]

The discovery of discrepancies, misunderstandings, deviations etc. may lead to the *rejection* of the tender in cases where it is totally out of line with the specification, that is, where it is not a variant but a non-conforming bid. Since one cannot bring the tender back in line through direct communication, rejection seems to be the only workable alternative.[25] When discrepancies or ambiguities affect minor matters, both Commission state-

---

[22] The condition is that (i) the error is apparent and (ii) it is equally apparent what should have been the correct figure or specification. If the tender is vague or ambiguous, it must be *rejected* as unsuited for the subsequent tender bid comparisons to come. Even an apparent calculation error may lead to rejection: if one figure composed of separate unit prices under one item does not correspond to the sum of each of the single elements of the specified units, this could mean *either* that the final calculation is wrong *or* that the accumulated price is correct but the composite single units are miscalculated. A tender like this must be rejected since a clarification would necessarily create an option for the tenderer to "correct" the price at its discretion, in other words something which is beyond the limits for clarification of the bid according to Commission's statements.

[23] There is no prohibition against filing a tender which deviates from the tender documentation as long as it is possible to do a sensible comparison and as long as all tenderers are given the same and equal access to information on how to prepare their tender (assuming that the final acceptance is in accordance with the award criteria and there is no unlawful discrimination). In contract law, the tender is the *offer* which the entity may accept or not accept. In some systems, and in particular for complicated technical projects, it would be wise to invite alternative suggestions for products or solutions.

[24] As pointed out by McCrudden in chapter 12 in this volume, the abnormally low price provision may affect the "soft" value impact of sex discrimination, potential social dumping or of competition due to child labour or other working conditions generally unacceptable under universal international public policies. There is also an issue of state aid under Article 92 in cases where the reason for an abnormally low tender bid is the fact that the contract has been subsidised.

[25] See the *Storebaelt* case [1993] ECR I-3353.

ments and generally accepted legal and ethical standards for tender procedures allow for clarification to achieve increased precision. This could be the situation where the tender bid could mean alternatively A or B, but where the choice has no impact on the price or order of the tender bids. Such minor clarifications are fully acceptable in EC law, and under the GPA (even when the entity has *not* given a notice of its intention to allow for negotiation according to Article XIV of the GPA), and often in national law as well.

Another issue is the possible mis-pricing of elements in the documentation due to misunderstanding or otherwise. Prices might be more or less apparent to the entity in its scrutiny of tenders. Discrepancies may appear through the tender in question and other tenders submitted by competitors in the package of competitors. It may for instance be clear from the figures that elements which were meant to be included and which are in fact included by the majority of the tenderers have been omitted by one or more tenderers. Normally the *pacta sunt servanda* principle would entitle the entity in good faith to rely on the wording of the contract offer, but there may be cases where discrepancies lead to the inevitable conclusion that there *must* be some mistake. What are the options in a case like this? Relying on the tender and awarding the contract with presumed knowledge that the unit pricing really does not express the offeror's real intention means that the issue becomes a matter of contract interpretation affected by the fact that the entity invoking the figure has not acted in good faith.[26] Allowing the entity to reject the tender bid without any communication with the tenderer is not advisable; the entity cannot know for sure whether there really is a mistake or not. Who knows whether this tenderer – whom one cannot approach directly – has a genuine possibility to offer the items at a fraction of normal market price reflected in the other bids? Approaching the tenderer with the question "Are your unit price quotations *really* meant to be as listed?" opens for tactical speculation since the tenderer is by now fully aware of the price range in his competitors' bids. If the tenderer is safely ahead of his competitors and optimistic of winning the contract, the answer to the question will be "sorry, they are not" and the entity will have to pay a higher price to the selected contractor. If the margin is narrow, the answer to the question might be "yes indeed they are" since this may be the only way to get the contract, knowing that the competing bids are very close.[27] This is

---

[26] Which in Nordic law at least would prevent that party from relying on the wording of the contract. This might open the way for rather extensive discretionary innovative "law-making" by the court or arbitrators applying customary principles on contracts not expressed or implied *in casu*, including the above-mentioned "reasonableness" test under the Uniform Scandinavian Formation of Contract Act, section 36. Scandinavian contract law tradition accepts to a large degree the idea that the judge makes the contract in the absence of genuine good faith consent between the parties, maybe to a larger extent than in UK common law. Similarly, law by customary established principles for the contract category in question will easily be relied upon.

[27] Subsequently under contract performance the answer "yes" may turn out to be a disaster for the private contractor: the entity may employ contract options for variation orders exploiting the unit price by heavily increasing quantities of that particular item.

unacceptable unless one opens up the prices for full equal negotiations with all tenderers. However, if that is the case, the whole procedure to a large extent fails to function in the way it is meant to.

6. REMEDIES FOR INFRINGEMENTS

Violation of the ban on negotiations may lead to action at the European level through the European Commission or under the EEA through the EFTA Surveillance Authority.[28] However, the procurement remedies regime in this respect is less directed to active intervention than, for example, the much more extensive options within competition law. Rather, in procurement, the key role is played by those whose interests are harmed by violations, namely, aggrieved firms.

The remedy options on a private level operate primarily within national law based on the two remedies directives, the Public Sector Remedies Directive 89/665/EEC and Utilities Remedies Directive 92/13/EEC. The two ECJ cases *Lottomatica* and *Walloon Buses* demonstrate that ECJ intervention orders under Article 186 of the EC Treaty may prevail over national litigation and dispute procedures,[29] but normally a procedural violation of the ban on negotiations, as expressed by the Commission and in national procurement law, will appear as issues either in connection with a request for corrective measures or injunctions under the remedies directives or in connection with claims for economic loss by bidders.[30]

Under the Public Sector Remedies Directive the provisions require a possibility of correcting procedural illegalities by *setting aside* decisions taken unlawfully or removing unlawful provisions, in contract documents or other documents relating to the contract award procedure (Article (2)(1)(b)). Unlawful amendments or alterations to the tender as a result of negotiations with one or more tenderers would fall within this. The sanctions are available to the tenderer which was pressed to negotiate, and also to competing candidates contesting negotiated changes in the basis for comparative evaluation of the tenders, for example where another tenderer originally ranked as second or third according to the contract award criteria has, as a result of negotiated amendments to the price or nature or scope of the contract now been promoted to the first place. The striking-out of such alterations would protect the original first-placed candidate. It is of some importance to note that the approach is to require options and legal avenues for corrections specified by functions and not by reference to

---

[28] The EFTA Surveillance Authority (ESA) has treated a few cases dealing with unlawful negotiations: see *Annual Report 1995*, p. 53. Compare the *Annual Report 1996*, p. 33 which, however, seems to have no reference to unlawfully negotiated contracts.

[29] Case C-272/91R, *Commission* v. *Italian Republic (Lottomatica)* [1992] ECR I-457; and Case C-87/94R, *Commission* v. *Kingdom of Belgium (SRWT – Walloon Buses)* [1994] ECR I-1395.

[30] The question of horizontal private law disputes between the competing contract candidates is not dealt with in WTO or EC law. Whether or not a claim for damages can be raised in this connection is a matter for national law.

traditional public administrative law remedies such as the cancellation of entire decisions. The directive allows national law to limit corrective measures to the stage of the procedure up until contract conclusion and to deny such relief thereafter.

In the utility sector, under Article 2(1) of the Utilities Remedies Directive, the question of corrective measures is left to the national legislator. Norway, for one, has availed itself of the option and ruled out corrective injunctions as well as judgments setting aside decisions or documents. The issue of negotiations in award procedures has reduced interest in the utilities area since, under Article 20 of the Utilities Directive, entities are allowed to select freely whether to operate formal tender procedures or negotiated procedures. However, a breach might still come about, for example in neglecting to notify that negotiations will take place, or possibly by unlawful combination of tender procedures with subsequent negotiations. The fact that corrective measures are available neither for the tenderer subjected to negotiations nor for competing tenderers affected by third party's negotiations with the entity means that the remedy of damages remains as the principal sanction.

The issue of damage is dealt with in Article 2 of both Remedies. The first provision does not specify how causation or loss are to be dealt with (except for Article 2(5) leaving the option for national legislation requiring the setting aside of a decision before damages can be awarded). However, Article 2(4) of the Utilities Remedies Directive specifically provides, in addition to the general provision on damages:

7. Where a claim is made for damages representing the costs of preparing a bid or of participating in an award procedure, the person making the claim shall be required only to prove an infringement of Community law in the field of procurement or national rules implementing that law, and that he would have had a real chance of winning the contract and that, as a consequence of that infringement, that chance was adversely affected.

This is without prejudice to any general right to claim damages for loss of the contract that is given by the directive or by national law. Thus, a tenderer who succeeds in establishing sufficient evidence which proves that he would actually have gained the contract if negotiations with his competitor leading to a rearrangement of the existing tender bids had not taken place, may claim damages for a *loss of the contract* and not only the costs.

The reference to having lost a real chance of winning the contract also does not exclude the possibility of claiming loss in cases where the tenderer did *not* have such a chance, but it is still established that he would not have participated in the tender procedure if one had informed him that the entity really never intended to "play by the rules". Extensive Norwegian case law deals with the "negative contract" costs and the legislator's assumption in connection with entering into the EEA agreement had been that pre-EEA law in this matter was to continue unaffected by the EEA. On the other hand, if the entity succeeds in proving that the tenderer would have participated anyway, in spite of established proof of procedural irregularities, then the chain of causation is broken and the affected tenderer may find himself without a claim against the entity.

If the unlawfully negotiated contract becomes effective as a result of the final award, there is the possibility that the affected tenderer (now the contractor) may claim damage for losses incurred because the contract has become less favourable to him than if the entity had played by the rules. This situation is complicated by the fact that the contractor in question might not have acquired the contract if the entity had acted according to the procedural requirements. At any rate, the more probable remedy in a situation like this – at least under Nordic law – would be to contest the legal effect of amendments and alterations introduced into the contract by way of unlawful pre-contractual negotiations, asking a court or arbitrators to set the provisions aside in the interpretation process, as explained below.

7. THE CONTRACTUAL POSITION OF AMENDMENTS INTRODUCED BY UNLAWFUL NEGOTIATION

The law of procurement relates to the *pre-contractual* stage. After the award decision a contract will be concluded and one passes into the realms of contract law.

The overall picture on the stages leading up to contract formation and subsequent contract is shown in Figure 10.1. The stages preceding the conclusion of a contract are shown in the left part of the figure, namely the limited options for *ex ante* clarification of potential ambiguities in the tender

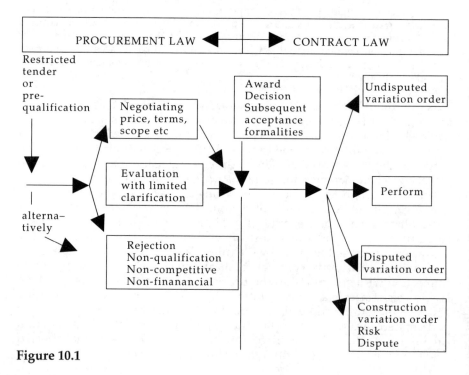

Figure 10.1

bid or the tender contract documentation. The right part of the figure shows that these issues will come up as matters of interpretation of the overall risk picture of the contract, which will be discussed below.

In Nordic contract law, the perspective is the relationship between the unilaterally legally binding offer in the form of the tender bid on the one side and the actual acceptance of that offer on the other. The "mirror rule" as reflected in Article 19(1) of the Convention on the International Sale of Goods[31] is paralleled in provisions on the establishment of mutual obligations in 1918 Scandinavian Formation of Contract Law, section 6, first paragraph. The acceptance in tender procedures is established by the written or oral notice addressed to the successful tenderer that he has been selected.[32] Once the contractor has entered into the contract, many of the issues mentioned above in the context of post-tender negotiations will reappear, but now as disputes over the validity of, or alternatively the proper interpretation of, the contract in connection with disputed variation or change orders. This means that the actual physical performance of the contract takes place according to the public customer's overriding acceptable and binding demand under the optional character of the contract. The exercise of a formal variation order option will include units or items allegedly *not priced* in the bid (or alternatively priced specifically as variation order extras) and thus places the extras outside the scope of the tender bid.[33]

Under contract law traditions following the common law "parol evidence" rule, the parties may be faced with procedural problems in pleading evidence from the tender procedure stage. In other legal traditions – such as the Scandinavian – it is evident that the contract must be viewed

---

[31] Compare United States Uniform Commercial Code, section 2-207.

[32] A conclusive acceptance by ordering the commencement of activities under the contract may amount to an acceptance, as might the instruction to start checking contract quantities against contract documentation (Norwegian *massekontroll*), *cf.* Norwegian Supreme Court decision reported in Rt. (Norwegian Supreme Court Reports) 1994.1222 (*Sjøen*). It is a disputed issue whether calling in the tenderer for meetings which the tenderer reasonably believes to be equivalent to a final award can also be treated as such. The question is crucial when it appears during the meeting that the entity really wants to negotiate contract terms and prices: would the reasonable expectation of winning the contract be protected in contract-law-based principles on quasi-acceptance with the same effect as a formal conclusion of the contract? In Norwegian law, the distinction must be drawn between actions in tort ("negative" costs) on the one hand and contractual obligations on the other. The entity may on the other hand accept conditions such as reserving the possibility of financing the contract or acquiring the necessary political consent, for instance local government finalising of the project (Norwegian Supreme Court decision reported Rt. 1985.1066). Negotiations may take place to extend the time limit for acceptance of existing tender bids. Such quasi-contracts raise some particular problems since the tenderer may wish to ask for some remuneration in addition to the price originally offered.

[33] The situation must not be confused with agreements which *alter* or *amend* the contract. The important distinction must be drawn between variation order options to order extras *under an effective contract* on the one side and to renegotiate and extend the contract by amendments on the other, the point here being that (real or constructive) variation orders are within the scope of an existing contract but (most often) outside the price tendered for.

and interpreted in the light of the pre-contractual activities.[34] A provision such as section 32 of the 1918 Scandinavian Formation of Contract Law has proven important in these matters; a party cannot rely in bad faith (actual knowledge or culpable or inexcusable ignorance) on conditions and terms which he, by the time of concluding the contract, knows or should have known did not reflect the real intention of the other party.[35] In the "error" situation, the obstacles for clarification prior to the signing of the contract and the fact that tenderers, due to shortage of time, depend on an unambiguous specification ready for pricing often result in disputes of this kind.

The contract will often contain clauses ranking the different elements in the contract documentation. The tender might for instance prevail over (or be subordinate to) the tender documentation. However, clauses like this will not necessarily clarify the legal position. In Nordic law, the law emphasises supplementary principles such as (i) the presumption that the tender bid is in conformity with the contract documentation presented by the entity; (ii) the risk on the entity for culpable ambiguities in contract documentation which may excuse misinterpretations and misunderstandings on the part of the tenderer; (iii) the risk of the tenderer in pricing units and elements without having read the documentation in a thorough and professional way; (iv) the risk of obscurity in interpretation caused by the contracting entity's negligence in clarifying potential errors in the tender bid listing of price quotations of units and items.

Failure to clarify elements in the bid may result in ambiguities being imported into the subsequent contract. This could be the case where the entity accepts a tender bid knowing that there are open ends in the interpretation of it. Alternately, it could be the case that hidden discrepancies later give rise to disputes over the correct understanding of the contract. The focus in the sale of goods law on "defective" products is not necessarily paralleled with similar problems in public contracts. The normal procedure would often be to accept the entity's request for the actual physical performance and leave the question of contract interpretation to a "disputed variation order" procedure. In other words, failing to clarify the exact extent of the contract obligations in view of the documentation and corresponding tender bid, the issue becomes one of deciding the exact scope of

---

[34] Generally, and in principle, as compared to common law, Scandinavian legal method seems far more open to relying on preparatory material both in the interpretation of statutory law (preparatory ministerial documents) and in looking at the context in the interpretation of contracts.

[35] Statutory law even allows the court to take into considerations information acquired at a later stage, provided there is a short interval of time, strong reasons for revocation and a counterparty which has not yet acted according to the otherwise binding offer (or contract) – the Roman/German law inspired principle of *re integra* as stated in the Norwegian 1918 Formation of Contract Act, section 39. The principle will, however, probably not apply to filed public contract tender bid offers, which must be treated as irrevocable from the expiry of the tender bid time limit.

the tender unit price for the performance.[36] This modern procurement law variant of the well-known contract law "battle of forms" scenarios is a dispute where the contractor asks for extras in performing according to the entity's requirement, whereas the entity asserts that the physical execution is *within* the documentation tendered for. The balance of market power may have an impact on this. In a buyer's market, the trend will be to attempt a maximum shift of risks for hidden price "torpedoes" to the detriment of the contractor. At the same time, the tenderer will be tempted to plant similar price torpedoes in the tender bid by failing to disclose apparent discrepancies in the contract documentation, so that the pricing of the listed units *must necessarily result in subsequent variation orders due to the lack of foresight on part of the client*. The overall tactics involved in such scenarios can be illustrated by Figure 10.2.

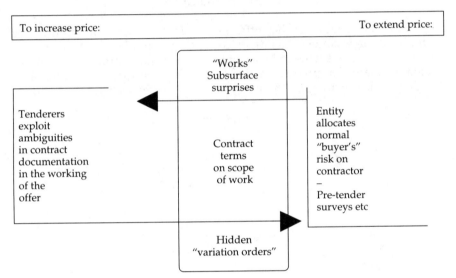

Figure 10.2

---

[36] The author has participated for many years in informal professional panels offering extra-judicial opinions in relation to construction contracts and public procurement for supplies and services in general. A majority of tender procedure issues raised in these cases deal with the problems mentioned in the text: discrepancies between the entity's intention concerning the contract's scope and the tenderer's understanding of the scope asked for in the tender documentation. In many cases, the problem originates in a failure to adopt correctly computerised standard references for separate elements in a construction or fabrication contract. It also happens that technical drawings differ from written specifications, or that the documentation contains internal ambiguities or discrepancies. In a "buyer's" market (where entities attempt to place a maximum of risks for functions and unexpected extras on the contractor) low tender prices are often compensated for by the planting of hidden "price bombs" in the tender, for instance by the contractor not informing the entity about shortcomings which must be rectified during the contract by extras under a variation order. In contract law, it would be difficult to prove fraud or professional negligence by reference to principles governing the duty to render pre-contractual information to the other party.

The left part of the figure illustrates the contractor-to-be's efforts to limit units and price quotations so that a subsequent inevitable variation order (VO) will increase the profit of the contract.[37]

Efforts to solve these problems by negotiations exceeding the limits for lawful acceptable pre-contractual clarification may result in a court judgment or arbitration award putting the contract back to "zero", disregarding the negotiated positive amendments as part of the effective binding contract between the parties. In other words, instead of leaving the detailed design and performance parameters to the parties which jointly possess the experience and expertise, the issue is left to subsequent litigation or arbitration discretion.

8. CONCLUSION

Transparency enabling the efficient review of the enforcement of Community law policies has its price. In simple public purchase of commodities the price seems to be acceptable. In major commercial contracts which normally require the parties' joint efforts to foresee contingencies the EC public procurement regime's price may have been set too high.

---

[37] This will be particularly apparent if the variation order is to be paid in the fashion of reimbursement of actual costs incurred on part of the contractor. Modern sophisticated contracts, however, often state in the contract itself that both undisputed and disputed variation orders are to be remunerated on the basis of the general price level set in the contract, so that the overall cost–benefit picture of the contract is left unchanged. Whether the contractor alternatively may claim remuneration by invoking liability for *culpa* in negligent design and cost supervision activities on part of the procuring entity therefore becomes an issue of great importance since an arrangement for loss coverage might lead to dramatically different results as compared to an arrangement where any performance under the contract is to be paid according to the price level of the priced tendered in the bid. The point illustrates and emphasises the consequential aspects of the ban on negotiations in complicated contract situations where planning and design really should be dealt with in thorough pre-contractual joint scheduling between the parties. Added to this is the possibility that the expertise and experience may be found on the contractor's side and not – or at least not only – in the consultants' ability to foresee the progress of the performance under the contract.

11. Environmental Issues in International Procurement

Peter Kunzlik*

1. INTRODUCTION

When considering the extent to which environmental factors can be taken into account in the procurement process it is important to distinguish between three key concepts. First, a contracting body may wish to impose "product-related" environmental requirements relating to the post-procurement environmental performance of the product. Such requirements specify the desired characteristics[1] of the product[2] being procured and, as such, form part of the definition of the subject matter of the contract. Secondly, at the other end of the spectrum, bodies may wish to adopt an "affirmative purchasing" approach to pursue broad environmental goals not specifically connected to the subject matter of the contract. In such cases they would like to use their market power to encourage providers to act in an environmentally responsible way generally. Here, because the policy in question takes account of conduct unconnected with the contract, it is properly regarded as a "secondary policy".

A third category of requirement lies somewhere between product-related requirements and secondary policy. It comprises so-called process and production methods (PPM) requirements which arise when contracting bodies impose requirements as to the process and production methods used in producing the supplies to be procured.[3] From an environmental

---

* Nottingham Law School.

[1] For example, as to energy use, discharges into water and land and emissions into the atmosphere; and specifications as to recyclability, reuse and disposal after completion of the product's operational life.

[2] The term "product" is used to describe supplies, works and/or services except where the context is more specific. Similarly, the terms "contracting body" and "provider" are used to describe respectively public authorities and/or utilities and providers of supplies, services and/or works.

[3] In the trade-environment context generally, the concept of PPMs refers to measures adopted by states to regulate process and production methods. In the present context, the phrase is being borrowed to describe contracting bodies' requirements as to the process and production methods used in respect of products which they wish to procure.

point of view, it seems obvious that the acceptability of a product cannot be ascertained only by reference to its environmental performance during or after its operational life, but should instead take account of the product's environmental performance throughout its whole "life cycle", including the production stage.[4] In fact, however, it is the thesis of this chapter that, although both the procurement regimes of the World Trade Organisation Government Procurement Agreement (GPA) and the European Community, accommodate product-related requirements and neither accepts the admissibility of secondary environmental policy, they differ in their treatment of PPMs. Although the GPA regime expressly permits contracting bodies to take account of PPM requirements, the EC regime appears not to do so. It seems that PPMs and secondary environmental policy cannot figure as part of the procurement process under the EC regime,[5] a position which seems inconsistent with the Community's own environmental policy. It is intended to demonstrate these points by reference to the three key stages of the procurement process: specification, selection of tenderers and contract award.

2. THE GATT 1994 CONTEXT

In order to put the GPA regime into context, it is helpful to consider the general treatment of environmental factors under GATT 1994 which effectively constitutes a regime of free trade rules subject to possible derogation on environmental grounds.[6] Articles I and II ban discrimination against products originating in another state party by respectively requiring

---

[4] Taking account, for example, of use of natural resources, energy consumption, discharges and emissions into the water, land and atmospheric environment and minimisation of production of waste, all during the production process itself.

[5] Although, as we shall see, non-discriminatory contractual conditions relating to PPMs and secondary policy may be included in the contract, they may not be considered in the procurement process itself. See section 6.2.3 below.

[6] For the interrelation between environmental protection and the GATT 1994 regime generally, see T.J. Schoenbaum, "International Trade and Protection of the Environment: The Continuing Search for Reconciliation" (1997) 91 *American Journal of International Law* 268; H. Ward, "Common But Differentiated Debate, Environment, Labour and the World Trade Organization" (1996) 45 *International and Comparative Law Quarterly* 592; M. Hession and R. Macrory, "Balancing Trade Freedom with the Requirements of Sustainable Development" in E.O'Keefe (eds.), *The European Union and World Trade Law After the GATT Uruguay Round* (Wiley, 1996); Z. Makuch "The WTO and the GATT" in J. Werksman (ed.), *Greening International Institutions* (Earthscan, 1996); J. Garvey, "The GATT/WTO Committee on Trade and the Environment – Towards Environmental Reform" (1995) 89 *Australian Journal of International Law* 423; P. Sands, *Principles of International Environmental Law* (1995, Manchester University Press), vol. 1, chapter 18; R.B. Stewart, "Environmental Regulation and International Competitiveness" (1993) 102 *Yale Law Journal* 2039; E.B. Weiss, "Environmentally Sustainable Competitiveness: A Comment" (1993) 102 *Yale Law Journal* 2123; and K. Anderson and R. Blackhurst (eds.), *The Greening of World Trade Issues* (Harvester Wheatsheaf, 1991). See also "About Trade and Environment in the World Trade Organization" (WTO Secretariat, 1997) (http://www.wto.org/environm.htm); and *The Report of the WTO Committee on Trade and Environment*, Press/TE 014, 18 November 1996 (http://www.wto.org/french/environf/teo14f.htm).

the parties to confer most-favoured-nation and national treatment on "like products" from such states. Furthermore, Article XI prohibits national measures restricting imports or exports between state parties.

The general exceptions in Article XX(b) and (g) do, however, allow derogations for certain national measures having an environmental character, namely those "necessary to protect human, animal or plant life or health" and those "relating to the conservation of exhaustible natural resources if such measures are made effective in conjunction with restrictions on domestic production or consumption", provided that they are not "applied in a manner which would constitute a means of arbitrary or unjustifiable discrimination between countries where the same conditions prevail, or a disguised restriction on international trade".[7]

Clearly, these derogations permit states wishing to protect the environment to prescribe product-related environmental requirements so long as they do not discriminate against imported products, and provided that the technical regulations in question do not constitute "unnecessary obstacles to international trade" and are not "more restrictive than necessary to" achieve the environmental objective in question.[8] They do not, however, permit states parties to prescribe PPMs relating to production or harvesting methods used in the manufacture of a product in another state since such requirements were held incompatible with Article III of GATT 1994 in the well-known *Tuna/Dolphin I* and *Tuna/ Dolphin II* cases. These concerned a US ban on imports of certain tuna from countries permitting fishing with purse seine nets (and from other states importing the tuna from such countries). The ban had been imposed in order to protect dolphins which were being killed by the nets, but the Panels found it to be incompatible with Article III of GATT notwithstanding the argument of the US that the GATT only prohibited discrimination between "like products", and that tuna caught according to the regime established for domestic fishermen should not be regarded as a "like product" to that caught by countries sanctioning the use of purse seine nets.

The *Tuna/Dolphin I* Panel[9] held that both bans were incompatible with the Article III of GATT since, in determining whether US produced tuna, and tuna from the other states concerned were "like products", only the characteristics of the tuna "as a product" could be taken into account, not the different production methods. Furthermore, the US legislation effectively amounted to an attempt by the US to impose its environmental regulations on other states. The Panel held that Article XX(b) of GATT did not permit the US to take measures to protect animal life outside its territorial jurisdiction and that to allow each contracting party unilaterally to prescribe "the life or health protection policies from which other contracting parties could not deviate without jeopardising their rights under [GATT]" would negate the multilateral nature of GATT, and would mean that it could "provide

---

[7] As to which, see "United States – Standards for Reformulated and Conventional Gasoline Appellate Body Report" (1996) 35 *International Legal Materials* 63.
[8] Agreement on Technical Barriers to Trade, Article 2.2.
[9] United States – Restrictions on Imports of Tuna, DS21/R, 3 September 1994.

legal security only in respect of trade between a limited number of contracting parties with identical internal regulations".[10] In *Tuna/Dolphin II*, the Panel (which also found the bans incompatible with GATT) differed from the earlier Panel in that it accepted that states were permitted to protect natural resources and animals outside their territory but only as against those (such as its own nationals, corporations and vessels) who would be subject to their jurisdiction under international law. Thus, as Cheyne has explained,[11] GATT (and GATT 1994) permits states to take measures for the protection of the environment outside their territory but not extra-jurisdictionally.

National environmental measures prescribing PPMs in respect of trade in goods from other states parties will therefore infringe GATT 1994.[12] The position is, however, different under the GPA itself which takes a more liberal approach.

3. THE WTO AGREEMENT ON GOVERNMENT PROCUREMENT: BASIC RULES

The World Trade Organisation (WTO) Government Procurement Agreement (GPA) is one of the plurilateral trade agreements annexed to the Agreement Establishing the World Trade Organisation.[13] It is part of the WTO Agreement only for those members which have accepted it but is binding upon them *inter se*.[14]

The preamble of the GPA makes no reference to environmental protection. This does not, however, mean that contracting entities are precluded from taking account of environmental factors in defining

---

[10] Paragraph 5.26.

[11] I. Cheyne, "Environmental Unilateralism and the WTO/GATT System" (1995) 24 *Georgia Journal of International and Comparative Law* 433.

[12] See also "United States – Standards for Reformulated and Conventional Gasoline" Panel Decision, WTO Doc. WT/DS2/R, 29 January 1996 and (1996) 35 *International Legal Materials*; and Appellate Body Decision, WTO Doc. WT/DS2/AB/R, 29 April 1996 and (1996) 35 *International Legal Materials* 603. As to which, see M.D. Shent (1996) 90 *Australian Journal of International Law* 669. See also D.A. Reid, "Trade and the Environment: Finding a Balance: the EC Approach" (1996) *European Environmental Law Review* 144; R.J. Zedalis, "Product v. Non-Product Based Distinctions in GATT, Article III Trade and Environment Jurisprudence: Recent Developments" (1997) *European Environmental Law Review* 108; and T.J. Schoenbaum, "International Trade and Protection of the Environment: The Continuing Search for Reconciliation" (1997) 91 *American Journal of International Law* 268 at 288. *Cf.* the EC Commission's view stated in Communication on Trade and Environment (COM (96) 54 final) noted by M. Montini, "The First Ministerial Conference of the WTO (Singapore 1996): A Summary of the EC Commission's Views on Trade and Environment" (1996) 5 *Review of European Community and International Environmental Laws* 262.

[13] See generally "Overview of the Agreement on Government Procurement" (WTO Secretariat) (http://www.wto.org/govt/over.htm); Report (1996) of the WTO Committee on Government Procurement (GPA/8 of 17 October 1996) (http://www/wto/govt/repgp.htm); and S. Arrowsmith, "Developing Multilateral Rules on Government Procurement: A New Approach in the WTO?" (1996) 5 *Public Procurement Law Review* CS145.

[14] Agreement Establishing the World Trade Organization, Article II(3).

specifications, or in deciding upon criteria for qualification of tenderers and/or in framing contract award criteria. They must, however, do so within the GPA framework which lays down two basic rules:

3.1 National treatment and most-favoured-nation treatment

The fundamental rule of the GPA is that "with respect to all laws, regulations, procedures and practices regarding government procurement" (so far as they are covered by the GPA) each party is to provide to products, services and suppliers of other parties treatment no less favourable than that accorded to domestic products, services and suppliers and that accorded to those of any other party.[15]

3.2 Non-discrimination

This is supported by a prohibition on discrimination against locally based suppliers on the basis of degree of foreign affiliation and ownership or on the basis of the country of production of the good or service being supplied (provided that the country of production is a party to the GPA).[16]

4. THE PROCUREMENT PROCESS UNDER THE GOVERNMENT PROCUREMENT AGREEMENT

The GPA also regulates the procurement process in the various ways considered below.

4.1 Technical specifications[17]

Article VI(1) provides that:

Technical specifications laying down the characteristics of the products or services to be procured, such as quality, performance, safety and dimensions, symbols, terminology, packaging, marking and labelling, *or the processes and methods for their production* and requirements relating to conformity assessment procedures prescribed by procuring entities, shall not be prepared, adopted or applied with a view to, or with the effect of, creating unnecessary obstacles to international trade.[18]

This provision clearly assumes that both product-related requirements and PPMs may in principle be included in specifications, a view confirmed by Article VI(2) which provides, *inter alia*, that "technical specifications" shall, where appropriate, be based on international "standards", where they

---

[15] GPA, Article III(1).
[16] GPA, Article III(2).
[17] For an example of governmental advice on green product specifications, see "Green Product Information – Criteria, Specifications and Applicable Standards" (Canadian Federal Government, March 1996) (http://www.epi.ca/spec.htm). See also Enviro-Spec (http:/www.epi.ca/essamp.htm).
[18] Emphasis added.

exist, or otherwise on national "technical regulations" or "recognised national standards". The terms "technical regulations" and "standards" are defined[19] respectively as referring to mandatory documents "which [lay] down characteristics of a product or a service *or their related processes and production methods*" and to non-mandatory documents "approved by a recognised body ... for common and repeated use [which provide] rules, guidelines or characteristics for products or services *or related processes and production methods*".[20]

In each case the document,

may also include or deal exclusively with terminology, symbols, packaging, marking or labelling requirements as they apply to a product, service, process or production method.[21]

Thus it seems that technical specifications may in principle deal with PPMs and may also require the use of symbols, labelling and marking which might, for example, reflect environmental performance. "Eco-labelling" of goods reflecting their friendliness to the environment comes within this category. Similarly, the prescription of specifications as to labelling could include labelling as to contents or as to optimum or safe conditions of use, reflecting environmental or health concerns. Packaging requirements might also specify environmental conditions as to the methods used in the production of the packaging, as to the reusability or recyclability of packaging or as to the supplier's obligation to take back packaging for reuse etc.

The GPA does, however, limit the use of environmental (and other) technical specifications in two ways. First is the requirement that "where appropriate" technical specifications should be based on international standards, where they exist, or otherwise on national technical regulations, recognised national standards, or building codes. Secondly, specifications shall "where appropriate" be prescribed "in terms of performance rather than design or descriptive characteristics".[22] If the word "performance" were to be taken as referring to the level of "performance" of the product or service while *in use*, or to its performance *as a product*,[23] then this (reflecting the approach taken in the *Tuna/Dolphin* cases) might preclude the use of PPMs. Such an interpretation would, however, be inconsistent with the definition of "technical specifications" which, as we have seen, expressly including PPM requirements. The "performance" of a product or service should therefore be taken as including its wider "environmental performance" from cradle to grave. Quite apart from that, however, it is surely arguable that even if "performance" were to be narrowly construed, it would not be "appropriate" to specify environmental requirements in such narrow terms given the environmental legitimacy of life-cycle analysis of environmental impact.

---

[19] By Article VI(1), footnotes (1) and (2).
[20] Emphasis added.
[21] *Ibid*.
[22] GPA, Article VI(2)(a).

In conclusion, therefore, the GPA allows technical specifications to include PPMs provided, of course, that they do not discriminate against products from other parties since such discrimination would infringe Article III(1) of the GPA. To this extent it seems to depart significantly from the general approach under GATT 1994 taken in the *Tuna/Dolphin* cases.

4.2 Selection

Article VIII bans discrimination between domestic providers and those of other parties (or between suppliers of other parties) at the selection stage and provides that:

Any conditions for participating in tendering procedures shall be limited to those which are essential to ensure the firm's capability to fulfil the contract in question.[24]

Since the selection conditions must relate to the tenderer's capacity to deliver the contract as specified, it follows that, if the contract specifies both product-related environmental conditions and PPMs, the tenderer's capacity to fulfil both types of condition may be taken into account. This is because, if the contract itself requires the successful tenderer to meet specified environmental requirements in delivery of the contract, then such qualification requirements would be "essential to ensure the firm's capability to fulfil the contract in question"; and any technical qualifications or further information relating to environmental performance (for example, history of prosecution or other proceedings for infringement of environmental laws) which might be required might well be "necessary for establishing the ... commercial and technical capacity of suppliers" as required by Article VIII(b) of the GPA. Capacity might be measured by reference to international environmental management systems (EMSs) such as that under ISO 14001 (approved in January 1996).[25] On the other hand, if the contract does not itself require a specified level of environmental performance, then it would not appear permissible to exclude contractors on the basis of their lack of environmental credentials. To do so would hardly be "essential" to ensure the contractors capability "to fulfil the contract in question". Nor, arguably, would it be "necessary" to establish the commercial or technical capacity" of the contractor. This seems to preclude the exclusion of tenderers on the grounds that they do not satisfy requirements of the contracting body's environmental secondary policy.

---

[23] That is, its ability to serve the specific purpose for which it is procured to the level of performance specified.

[24] Emphasis added. GPA, Article VIII(b). See also Article VIII(c).

[25] *Cf.* the Environmental Management and Audit Scheme based on EC Regulation 1836/93/EEC (operational from 1995). Other ISO standards being developed concern eco-labelling, environmental performance evaluation and life-cycle assessment. See generally P.M. Thimme, "Environmental Management – ISO 14001 and EMAS" (1996) 5' *Review of European Community and International Environmental Laws* 267; and E.S. Howard "Environmental Management – ISO 14001 Approved" (1996) 5 *Review of European Community and International Environmental Laws* 340.

4.3 Invitations to participate, tender documentation and award criteria

Where entities wish to include environmental conditions or specifications they must observe the GPA's procedures. Except in cases of limited tendering, for example, entities are required to publish "invitations to participate" in respect of intended procurement.[26] These must contain "any economic and technical requirements, financial guarantees and information required from suppliers".[27] In selective tendering cases entities must publish annually a notice stating, *inter alia*, "the conditions to be fulfilled by suppliers with a view to their inscription on lists [of qualified suppliers] and the methods according to which each of those conditions will be verified".[28] These provisions cover the environmental specifications and qualifications (whether product-related or PPMs) which we have examined. Such information must also be included in the tender documentation since this must state "any economic and technical requirement, financial guarantees and information or documents required from suppliers",[29] and "a complete description of the products or services required *or of any requirements including technical specifications*",[30] and the award criteria, including "any factors other than price that are to be considered in the evaluation of tenders".[31]

It is essential that the desired environmental specifications and qualification conditions are stated in these documents since awards are to be made in accordance with the criteria and essential requirements specified in the tender documentation[32] and (unless in the public interest an entity decides not to issue a contract), it "shall make the award to the tenderer who has been determined to be fully capable of undertaking the contract and whose tender, whether for domestic products or services, or products or services of other parties, is either the lowest tender or the tender which in terms of the specific evaluation criteria set forth in the notices or tender documentation is determined to be the *most advantageous*".[33] It is important to note that, unlike the EC regime, the GPA does not limit the non-price criteria to "most *economically* advantageous" tender, merely to the "most advantageous" in terms of the criteria stated in the tender documentation. This means that in applying such environmental criteria it is not necessary for a contracting body to demonstrate any economic advantage in the application of the criteria, still less any economic advantage of direct benefit to itself. It is submitted that this is an appropriate approach since the principles underlying the GPA – transparency and non-discrimination – are not threatened by allowing contracting bodies to apply published award

---

[26] GPA, Article IX.
[27] GPA, Article IX(5) and 6(f).
[28] GPA, Article IX(9)(b).
[29] GPA, Article XII(2)(f).
[30] GPA, Article XII(2)(g).
[31] GPA, Article XII(2)(h).
[32] GPA, Article XIII(4)(c).
[33] GPA, Article XIII(4)(c).

criteria which reflect values such as environmental values, which though objectively verifiable may not always be easily expressed in terms of economic benefits to the bodies concerned.

4.4 Derogation

Article XXIII(2) provides that:

> Subject to the requirement that such measures are not applied in a manner which could constitute a means of arbitrary or unjustifiable discrimination between countries where the same conditions prevail or a disguised restriction on international trade, nothing in this Agreement shall be construed to prevent any Party from imposing or enforcing measures necessary to protect ... human, animal or plant life or health.

If, as we have seen, entities are entitled under the general GPA rules to take account (in a non-discriminatory way) of some environmental factors in defining specifications, conditions for the qualification of tenderers and award criteria, there seems to be little need for this exception. The general rules would, after all, only be infringed if selection criteria were adopted which were not "essential" to ensure the firm's ability to fulfil the contract, if such definition were done in a discriminatory way or, in the case of specifications, if they were defined "with a view to, or with the effect of, creating unnecessary obstacles to international trade".[34] In such circumstances, however, the exception could not apply since the practice in question would amount to arbitrary or unjustifiable discrimination or a disguised restriction on trade. The exception, therefore, only makes sense when it is understood to refer not to the practices of contracting entities themselves but (as expressly stated) to preserve the rights of any "Party" to impose or enforce the requisite "measures". Thus, the exception in Article XXIII is not intended to preserve the rights of entities to adopt specifications etc. having an environmental justification but, *for the avoidance of doubt*, to preserve the right of the states party to the GPA to take and enforce mandatory "measures" to protect human, animal or plant life or health which might otherwise to considered to infringe the GPA.

5. EC ENVIRONMENTAL POLICY CONTEXT

Environmental factors are relevant under general Community law in two ways. First, they may justify Member States derogating from freedoms enshrined in the EC Treaty.[35] Secondly, the Treaty endows the Community with its own environmental mission. It provides that the "task" of the

---

[34] GPA, Article VI(1).

[35] For example, derogation under Article 36 of the EC Treaty for "the protection of health and life of humans, animals and plants" or under the *Cassis de Dijon* doctrine on grounds of environmental protection more generally; Case 302/86 *Commission* v. *Denmark* (*Danish Bottles*) [1988] ECR 4607.

Community includes, by implementing stated policies, the promotion of "sustainable and non-inflationary growth respecting the environment".[36] The policies in question include "a policy in the sphere of the environment".[37] In addition, Article 130R(2) of the EC Treaty provides, *inter alia*, that:

Environmental protection requirements must be integrated into the definition and implementation of other Community policies.

Furthermore, Community environmental policy is developed within the context of Environmental Action Programmes approved by the Council and representatives of the Member States meeting within the Council. The current programme is the Fifth Environmental Action Programmes, entitled "Towards sustainability: a Community programme of policy and action in relation to the environment and sustainable development".[38] This states a number of underlying principles and, in particular, stresses the "shared responsibility" of all economic "actors" in protecting the environment. The actors in question are all of those whose decisions may affect the environment; the Community, Member States, public authorities, business undertakings and individuals (whether as voters or consumers). "Shared responsibility" requires that environmental factors should in particular be integrated into:

economic and sectoral policies, in the decisions of public authorities, in the conduct and development of production processes and in individual behaviour and choice.[39]

Furthermore:

administrations need to critically analyse their own operations, for example public services, siting of offices, *purchasing policies*, choice of vehicles and equipment, energy conservation, environmental auditing.[40]

The Fifth Environmental Action Programmes does not impose legally binding obligations upon public authorities or utilities but its principles should, at the very least, be used as a guide to the interpretation of Community procurement legislation to ensure that environmental protection requirements are "integrated into the *definition and implementation* of other Community policies".

---

[36] Article 2 of the EC Treaty.

[37] Article 3(k) of the EC Treaty. The objectives of the policy are stated in Article 130R(1) of the EC Treaty.

[38] OJ 1993, No. C138/1; OJ 1993, No. C138/21.

[39] Executive Summary of the Programme, OJ 1993, No. C138/11, paragraph 4; emphasis added. For a manifestation of shared responsibility, see the Commission's Communication on Environmental Agreements, noted by Songaerts (1997) 6 *European Environmental Law Review* 84.

[40] Executive Summary of the Programme, OJ 1993, No. C138/11, p. 26 under the title "internal auditing"; emphasis added.

6. THE EC PROCUREMENT PROCESS

The EC regime[41] might be said to involve two elements. First, there are the general Treaty rules, freedom of movement of goods, workers, of establishment and so on, as they apply in the context of procurement.[42] Secondly, there are the specific public procurement rules laid down by directives. In the Community hierarchy of norms, the Treaty rules are the most important and the directives cannot derogate from them.[43] We have seen that the Treaty rules on the free movement of goods are subject to possible derogation on environmental grounds. The procurement directives, however, make no specific provision for environmental protection but contracting bodies may nonetheless further environmental objectives (to a limited extent) through the procurement process as the Commission's Green Paper, *Public Procurement in the European Union: Exploring the Way Forward*,[44] makes clear. After all, both as a matter of integration of environmental protection into the definition *"and implementation"* of Community procurement policy and as a matter of "shared responsibility" the pursuit of environmental objectives by public authorities in the procurement context is not only legitimate but also desirable. As we interpret specific provisions of the procurement directives we should do so with that clearly in mind.

The Green Paper acknowledges that it would be desirable to clarify the opportunities within existing Community legislation "for taking environmental concerns into account and, at the same time, to define more precisely the limits of these possibilities"[45] and identifies the following ways in which environmental factors may currently be taken into account:

6.1 Technical specifications

The Commission accepts that "environmental protection considerations" can be incorporated into technical specifications.[46] These, of course, are the

---

[41] For the interrelation between the EC and GATT trade and procurement regimes, see P. Eeckhout, "The Domestic Legal Status of the WTO Agreement: Interconnecting Legal Systems" (1997) 34 *Common Market Law Review* 11; M.E. Footer, "Public Procurement and EC External Relations" in E.O'Keefe (eds.), *The European Union and World Trade Law After the Uruguay Round* (Wiley, 1996); A. Appella, "Constitutional Aspects of Opinion 1/95 of the ECJ Concerning the WTO Agreement" (1996) *International and Comparative Law Quarterly* 440; D.D. Dingl, "Direct Effect of the Government Procurement Agreement" (1996) 5 *Public Procurement Law Review* 245; P. Trepte, "The GATT, GPA and three EC Public Procurement Rules: Realignment and Modification" (1995) 4 *Public Procurement Law Review* CS42; and C. Bovis, "Public Procurement within the Framework of the EC Common Commercial Policy" (1993) 4 *Public Procurement Law Review* 210.

[42] See S. Arrowsmith, "The Application of the EC Treaty Rules to Public and Utilities Procurement" (1995) 6 *Public Procurement Law Review* 255.

[43] Case C-21/88, *Du Pont de Nemours Italiana SpA Unita Santaria Locale No. 2 Di Carrera* [1990] ECR 899.

[44] Commission Communication of 27 November 1996, section VI.

[45] *Ibid.*, paragraph 5.47.

[46] Green Paper, p. 44, paragraph 5.49. On technical specifications generally, see R. Bickerstaff, "Applying the EC Rules on Standards and Specifications in Public and Utilities Procurement" (1994) 3 *Public Procurement Law Review* 153.

technical requirements relating to the characteristics of the works, goods or services being procured and do not relate to the environmental performance of the provider unconnected with the contract itself.[47] So far as specifications are concerned, two sets of rules apply. First, the Treaty itself requires that specifications must not be so drawn as to discriminate against goods, works or services (or providers) from other Member States[48] and, even if indistinctly applicable, must not restrict intra-Community trade.[49] Measures may be justifiable in the latter case, however, under the *Cassis de Dijon* principle which allows Member States to derogate from free movement of goods to protect "mandatory interests" recognised by the ECJ.[50] As we have seen, these include environmental protection so that such measures will be lawful provided they are proportionate. It would, therefore, be permissible under the Treaty to impose non-discriminatory product-related specifications as to the environmental performance of products, provided that those requirements are not already harmonised at Community level, provided that they truly relate to environmental justification, and provided that they are no more restrictive of intra-Community trade than necessary. It does appear that in the procurement context these rules imply a general principle that specifications must not be drawn up in such a way as to exclude products which meet the authority's performance requirements[51] so that environmental specifications, like others, should be expressed whenever possible in terms of performance or that, where specific products or processes are referred to, the specification should add "or equivalent".[52]

That being the case, an issue arises as to when a product will be said to be "equivalent" to that specified by the authority. Advocate-General Darmon in *Dundalk*[53] suggested that a product should be so regarded when it has been allowed onto the market in any Member State. This has been criticised as limiting "government's policy choices to an unacceptable degree".[54] That, with respect, is particularly true in the case of environmental specifications. If authorities are to embrace their "shared responsibility" for the environment they must be permitted to set high levels of environmental protection and not be forced to accept products, works or services which attain only lower standards accepted for general market access elsewhere in the Community.[55] At heart, perhaps, this question really concerns the scope

---

[47] They do, however, have an indirect effect on selection of the provider since "technical capacity" involves capacity to fulfil the contract *as specified*.

[48] Case 45/87, *Commission* v. *Ireland (Dundalk)* [1988] ECR 4929.

[49] Case C-359/93, *Commission* v. *Netherlands (UNIX)* [1995] ECR I-157.

[50] Case 302/86, *Commission* v. *Denmark (Danish Bottles)* [1988] ECR 4607.

[51] S. Arrowsmith *The Law of Public and Utilities Procurement* (Sweet & Maxwell, 1996), p. 583.

[52] Regulation 8(8) of the United Kingdom's Works Regulations (SI 1991 No. 2680), Supply Regulations (SI 1995 No. 201) and Services Regulations (SI 1992 No. 3228), however, prohibit specification of particular makes of product. *Cf.* Utilities Regulations (SI 1992 No. 2911), Article 12(10).

[53] Case 45/87, *Commission* v. *Ireland (Dundalk)* [1988] ECR 4929.

[54] S. Arrowsmith *The Law of Public and Utilities Procurement* (Sweet & Maxwell, 1996), p. 584.

[55] Particularly since Member States are themselves permitted by Article 130T of the EC Treaty to adopt higher levels of environmental protection than those laid down by Community legislation, so long as the measures are compatible with the Treaty and notified to the Commission.

for review of an authority's decision-making under Article 30 of the EC Treaty. If a product is to be deemed "equivalent" merely because it has been allowed onto the market elsewhere in the Community then a decision by an authority (or other emanation of the state) to exclude such products would infringe the principle of mutual recognition of goods and so Article 30 of the EC Treaty. As we have seen, however, it might then be justifiable under derogations under Article 36 or *Cassis de Dijon* but it seems inappropriate to put authorities into the position where they have to accept products not achieving the environmental performance they require or else face the prospect of court action.

It appears that under the Community's regime specifications may only lay down product-related requirements and not PPMs. This follows from the definition of "technical specifications" given in the directives. The Supplies Directive, for example, defines the term as meaning

the totality of the technical prescriptions contained in particular in the tender documents, *defining the characteristics required of a material, product or supply, which permits [it] to be described in a manner such that it fulfils the use for which it is intended by the contracting authority.* These technical prescriptions shall include levels of quality, performance, safety or dimensions, including the requirements applicable to the material, the product or the supply as regards quality assurance, terminology, symbols, testing and test methods, packaging, marking or labelling.[56]

Such definition, since it focuses upon a product's fitness for post-procurement use does not seem to encompass PPM requirements. This, as we shall see, also limits the extent to which PPM requirements can be taken into account at the selection stage. On the other hand, it might be argued that this provision should be interpreted in light of the "shared responsibility" and the policies enunciated in the Fifth Environmental Action Programme so as to permit PPM requirements to be included in specifications. Indeed the definition itself refers to some aspects of the production process when it refers to "quality assurance" and to "testing and test methods". On the other hand, these references do seem intended to allow the contracting body to ensure post-procurement performance rather than to regulate the production stage itself.

The directives' rules requiring that specifications be drawn up by reference to European specifications[57] apply in the environmental field as elsewhere. The Green Paper states that efforts should be made to develop European standards or common technical specifications and gives as an

---

[56] Directive 93/36/EEC, OJ 1993, No. L199/1, Annex III, emphasis added. Similar wording can be found in the definition of "technical specifications" in respect of public works (Directive 93/37/EEC, OJ 1993, No. L199/54, Annex III), public services (Directive 92/50/EEC, OJ 1992, No. L209/1, Annex II) and utilities (Directive 92/38/EEC, OJ 1993, No. L199/84, Article 1(8)) contracts.

[57] See Public Supply Directive 93/36/EEC, OJ 1993, No. L199/1, Article 8(2); Public Works Directive 93/37/EEC, OJ 1993, No. L199/54, Article 10(2); Public Services Directive 92/50/EEC, OJ 1992, No. L209/1, Article 14(2); and Utilities Directive 92/38/EEC, OJ 1993, No. L199/84, Article 18(2).

example the "European eco-label, complying with Community law" under Regulation 880/92/EEC.

6.2 Selection

6.2.1 Technical capacity

The Green Paper suggests that "*under certain conditions,* environmental protection objectives [may] be included among the criteria for selecting candidates"[58] but such criteria:

> are designed to test candidates' economic, financial and technical capacity and may therefore include environmental concerns *depending on the expertise required for specific contracts.*[59]

Accordingly, in the Commission's view, the EC public procurement regime, like the GPA, allows environmental factors to be taken into account in selection but only to the extent that they qualify as relating to economic and financial standing or technical capacity and only to the extent that they relate to the tenderer's ability to perform the contract in question. Many product-related environmental considerations may relate to contract performance itself and fall well within the concept of technical capacity.[60] In such cases contracting bodies can have regard to the capacity of the tenderers to meet such requirements. Since it appears, however, that PPMs may not be specified in the contract it follows that selection conditions may not be prescribed relating to the tenderer's process and production methods. This would exclude consideration of the technical capacity of tenderers to meet even non-discriminatory PPM requirements at the selection stage.

It is submitted, however, that, where contracting bodies wish to impose PPM requirements (or to pursue at the selection stage non-discriminatory secondary environmental policies properly so-called), they should be permitted to do so since that would allow them to embrace their "shared responsibility" by using their purchasing power to encourage beneficial environmental practices. Such an interpretation would ensure that Community environmental policy is integrated into the *implementation* of Community procurement policy as required by the Treaty itself.[61] Further-

---

[58] Green Paper, p. 44, paragraph 5.50; emphasis added.

[59] The selection grounds are limited in public contracts to those relating to "economic, financial and technical capacity". Utilities may, however, prescribe any "objective criteria and rules", as to which see below.

[60] Just as the ability to conform, during execution of a contract, with the contracting authority's health and safety policy was held to relate to "technical capacity" in *General Building and Maintenance* v. *Greenwich London Borough Council* [1993] IRLR 535, noted by S. Arrowsmith, "Restricted Awards Procedures under the Public Works Contracts Regulations 1991: A Commentary on *General Building and Maintenance* v. *Greenwich Borough Council*"(1993) 4 *Public Procurement Law Review* CS92 at 96.

[61] In the UK, section 17(1) of the Local Government Act 1988 (which prohibits certain authorities from taking account of a range of listed "non-commercial" matters in procurement) does not conflict with this policy as the listed matters do not include environmental performance policy or protection.

more, it would seem consistent with the judgment in the *Gebroeders Beentjes* v. *Netherlands* case[62] which held that the selection criteria listed in the directives (financial and economic standing, technical capacity) are not exhaustive. On that basis authorities would be free to take account of PPMs or secondary environmental policy at the selection stage provided that they did so in a way which did not infringe the Treaty (for example, in a non-discriminatory way). The Commission, however, takes the contrary view,[63] a view now supported by the decisions in *General Building and Maintenance* v. *Greenwich Borough Council*,[64] where the court held that the list of relevant selection factors was exhaustive, and in *R.* v. *Secretary of State for the Home Department ex parte the Mayor and Burgesses of the London Borough of Harrow*,[65] where it was held that selection could not take account of providers' ability to perform services of a type other than those required by the contract. Above all, it seems inconsistent with *Commission* v. *Italy*,[66] where the ECJ held that under the Works Directive the contracting authority could not take "local preference" factors into account at the selection stage because the only permissible factors were those expressly listed in the directive.[67]

The Utilities Directive differs from the public procurement regime in that it allows contracting entities to base selection on "objective criteria and rules" which they establish.[68] It is possible that this might give a utility a greater ability to take account of environmental factors either by insisting upon PPM requirements or even by pursuing secondary policy by applying criteria relating to the environmental performance of the tenderer's organisation in areas wholly unrelated to the contract in question. This would, of course, depend upon the meaning of the words "objective criteria and rules" If they merely connote criteria capable of being defined in the abstract without reference to the characteristics of particular tenderers then it would be possible to include both PPM requirements and secondary policy since both of these may be expressed in objective terms. If, however, the criteria must be objective not only in that sense but also in the sense that they must be objectively related to the characteristics of the product being procured *as a product* the position would be different. Neither PPM nor secondary policy criteria could be applied at the selection stage and the position would mirror that in the public procurement regime. The latter position would seem consonant with the Commission's position as stated in the Green Paper.

[62] Case 31/87 [1988] ECR 4635. See also H.K. Nielsen, "Public Procurement and International Labour Standards" (1995) 4 *Public Procurement Law Review* 94.
[63] See *Public Procurement: Regional and Social Aspects*, COM (89) 400 final, 22 September 1989.
[64] Note 60 above.
[65] (1996) 2 *Common Market Law Review* 524.
[66] Case C-360/89, *Commission* v. *Italy* [1992] ECR I-3401.
[67] As to which, see S. Arrowsmith, note 60 above.
[68] Articles 30(2) and 31(1).

6.2.2 Environmental crime or misconduct

The public procurement directives allow contacting bodies to exclude providers found guilty of an offence concerning their professional conduct or of grave professional misconduct.[69] Of course, for exclusion of tenderers on grounds of conviction to be an effective tool in promoting environmentally appropriate performance, the necessary environmental offences need to be on the statute book and national authorities need to have sufficient resources and the willpower to enforce them. In fact the extent to which environmentally polluting activity is a crime varies throughout the Community as, no doubt, does the extent to which enforcement authorities exist and are able to pursue systematic and rigorous enforcement policies.[70] Furthermore, with the exception of polluting activity, environmentally inappropriate conduct (such as, for example, inappropriate use of natural resources, energy consumption or development) is not of its nature likely to be criminalised.

Similarly, although the Commission suggests that a provider might be excluded on grounds of "grave professional misconduct" relating to the environment, it is hard to see how, except in wholly exceptional cases, a contracting authority would be in a position safely to conclude, in the absence of a conviction, that a provider has been guilty of such misconduct. In some cases professional bodies may themselves censure or expel members for breach of professional rules and such a ruling might strengthen the authority's hand. But very few industries, even heavily polluting industries, are subject to professional regulation of the type likely to produce such rulings. The position may be different, of course, for firms established in countries which maintain official lists, where registration depends on proof that grave professional misconduct has not occurred (in which case authorities must accept registration as evidence that the firm in question has not been guilty of such conduct). Professional regulation, even in sectors where it exists, will in any event only be relevant if the professional rules in question actually prohibit environmentally damaging conduct. Most professional rules, however, tend only to relate to the interests of the customer, to professional etiquette, fair dealing, technical competence, compliance with criminal law and, in some cases, health and safety. The "environment" as such is not generally regarded as an interest in respect of which professionals owe professional obligations.

6.2.3 Contract conditions relating to environmental performance

It appears from the judgment in *Beentjes* that, regardless of whether PPMs and secondary policies can be taken into account at the selection stage,

---

[69] See Public Supply Directive, Article 20(1)(c) and (d); Public Works Directive, Article 24(c) and (d); and Public Services Directive, Article 29(c) and (d). It is generally assumed that these factors fall within the "objective criteria" available at the selection stage under the utilities directive.

[70] For further difficulties in applying the "crime/misconduct" rule in the case of corporate groups, see S. Arrowsmith, note 51 above, p. 332.

contract conditions can nonetheless be stipulated (provided they are non-discriminatory) to impose such requirements and to further such policies. The Green Paper accepts that:

> purchasing entities can pursue environmental protection objectives through performance conditions imposed contractually on successful tenderers. [They] can require the supplier whose tender has been selected to perform the contract in accordance with certain constraints aimed at protecting the environment. Clearly, such performance conditions should not be discriminatory or in any way disturb the smooth functioning of the single market. The conditions should also be mentioned in tender notices or contract documents to ensure that bidders are sufficiently aware of their existence. Lastly, *verification of the successful tender's ability to perform the contract in accordance with the conditions should take place outside the contract award procedure.*[71]

This does seem, however, to assume that all environmental conditions are necessarily "secondary" whereas, to the extent that they relate to the performance of goods, works or services provided, they surely relate to the definition of the subject matter of the contract and are not secondary at all. If that is so, then, as we have seen, verification of the tenderer's ability to meet the conditions must be permissible at the selection stage as relating to technical capacity. Even in the case of PPMs and secondary environmental policy properly so called, however, it makes little sense to say that verification has to "take place outside the contract award procedure" because, although such a conclusion is consistent with the post-*Beentjes* case law, it could well make the environmental stipulation ineffective to deliver the envisaged environmental goals. The contract must, after all, be awarded in accordance with that very procedure and if the tenderers' ability to meet environmental conditions were not considered during selection the authority would necessarily have to impose them without regard to the tenderers' ability to comply. If the successful tenderer then proved unable to comply, the contracting body's only option would be to react after the event, perhaps by terminating the contract or suing for breach. Such an approach conflicts with the notion that the purpose of the selection stage is to assess to the ability of tenderers to deliver the contract and would be unlikely to add much in the way of environmental advancement.[72]

6.3 Contract award criteria

6.3.1 *Regulated contracts*

Regulated contracts must be awarded on the basis of either lowest price or to the "most *economically* advantageous" tender. Clearly, environmental factors have no part to play at the award stage when price is the sole criterion. As the Green Paper makes clear, however, they:

---

[71] Green Paper, p. 45, paragraph 5.5; emphasis added.
[72] See S. Arrowsmith's trenchant remarks to like effect in S. Arrowsmith, "Abolition of the UK Procurement Preference Scheme for Disabled Workers" (1994) 3 *Public Procurement Law Review* CS225 at 227 and note 10.

could play a part in identifying the most economically advantageous tender, *but only in cases where reference to such factors makes it possible to gauge an economic advantage which is specific to the works, supplies or services covered by the contract and directly benefits the contracting authority or contracting entity.*[73]

The words which have been emphasised indicate the limited role which environmental factors can play at this stage.[74] The restrictive approach which they indicate really arises from the word "economic" as it appears in the directives. There is no doubt scope for argument that "economic advantages" should be construed to include advantages of a general nature accruing for the benefit of society as a whole. On such a basis the avoidance of pollution (and consequent clean-up costs) might, for example, be said to produce "economic advantages"[75] even if the clean-up costs would not have fallen on the contracting body itself. Similarly, the preservation of landscape or the conservation of animals, plants and their habitats might be said to produce economic advantages by attracting tourists; or by improving quality of life and so attracting potential work force to an area. The Commission's interpretation is, of course, much narrower and even where it is possible to link environmental protection with economic advantage it may be impossible to say that the advantage is "specific" to the works, supplies or services covered by the contract, and that it "directly benefits" the contractor. That is not to say, however, that such conditions might never be satisfied. Recyclability or reusability of goods may confer economic advantages directly on users by reducing disposal costs; the energy efficiency of a building or piece of equipment may reduce running costs.

The Commission's approach, however, contrasts sharply with that under the GPA. As we have seen, the GPA does not require that non-price award criteria must relate to "economic advantage" at all. The GPA allows contracting bodies to chose non-price award criteria for themselves so long as they are published in the tender documentation. The Commission's approach, on the other hand, restricts the choices available to contracting bodies and the range of values which they may reflect purely to those resulting in economic benefits to themselves. This appears to encourage selfish procurement policy in a way quite inconsistent with the Treaty's integration principle and with the concept of "shared responsibility" Furthermore, it is difficult to see how such an approach can be justified in terms of the purpose of the directives themselves. Just as under the GPA, so long as award criteria are published in advance neither the principle of transparency nor of non-discrimination would be jeopardised if contracting bodies were allowed to take account of environmental criteria other than those which bring them direct economic advantages.

---

[73] Green Paper, p. 45, paragraph 5.51; emphasis added.

[74] See also the EC Commission's Guide to the Community Rules on Open Government Procurement OJ 1987, No. C358/1 at p. 36 which states that "only objective criteria may be used which are strictly relevant to the particular project". See further S. Arrowsmith, note 51 above, p. 238.

[75] The author is indebted to Professor Kai Kruger of the University of Bergen for comments made on this point during presentation of this paper.

6.3.2 *Non-regulated contracts*

In non-regulated procurements (for example, where the value of the contract falls below the threshold for application of the relevant directive), contracting bodies may go much further in greening their procurement policies. Environmental preferences may then be used as award criteria provided that they are non-discriminatory "and open to all tenderers in the Community on the basis of the mutual recognition principle".[76]

7. CONCLUSION

It is a shame that the EC procurement regime does not more fully embrace the implications of the concept of shared responsibility as enunciated in the Fifth Environmental Action Programme because, if that concept has any validity at all, it is precisely in the area of public and utilities procurement. After all the "actors" in those sectors might well be able to achieve significant environmental benefits through the power of their very considerable purses. Furthermore, the contracts with which they are concerned are often, by virtue of their size and subject matter, of particular environmental importance.[77] Authorities and utilities themselves seem willing to play their part[78] and the rules should allow them to do so fully. It would therefore be a major step forward if the Green Paper consultation process were to result in clarification to the effect that, at the very least, PPM requirements might (as under the GPA) be regarded as permissible in the specification, selection and award stages.[79] The present position, after all, makes little environmental sense. If a product's environmental impacts arise throughout the whole of its life cycle it is anomalous to allow contracting bodies to prescribe requirements as to the end of that cycle but not the beginning.

---

[76] Green Paper, p. 45, paragraph 5.51.

[77] For example, major infrastructure projects such as water or waste-treatment plants, hospital facilities, large municipal office blocks or housing schemes, etc.

[78] For illustrations of authorities' commitment to environmental protection, see the International Council for Local Environmental Initiatives, "European Environmental Procurement Initiative" (http://www.icki.org/europe/procura.htm). See also the Green Procurement Reporting Framework, Bureau of Real Property and Materiel, Treasury Board of Canada Secretariat (http://www.tbs-sct.gc.ca/tb/materiel/greenpro/gprfe01.html).

[79] Mr D. Reddonet, a spokesman for DG-XV of the Commission, however, informed the Public Procurement: Global Revolution Conference, University of Wales, Aberystwyth on 11 September 1997 that it was unlikely that the Commission would liberalise the rules to permit "affirmative purchasing" policies in the social and environmental fields.

12. Social Policy Issues in Public Procurement: A Legal Overview

*Christopher McCrudden**

1. THE ISSUE DEFINED

The focus of this chapter is on the following problem: how far, if at all, may a public body lawfully take "social issues" into account in the public procurement context? There is no shortage of examples of such an approach being taken. In many western European and North American countries there is a long history of public procurement being viewed as a potentially important mechanism for the achievement of "non-economic" goals.

Broadly speaking, we can identify at least seven (overlapping) "non-economic" goals served by using public procurement as a tool in the past:[1] achieving certain traditional foreign policy goals such as protecting national security, stimulating national economic activity in particular sectors of the economy, protecting national industry against foreign competition, improving the competitiveness of certain key industrial sectors, remedying regional disparities within the state, improving environmental quality, and securing human rights and employment standards nationally or internationally. Such uses of public procurement are not of merely historical interest. In particular, the last two goals (environmental and social) appear to be increasing in popularity, possibly as a result of greater globalisation, partly as a result of the limited effectiveness of other regulatory mechanisms.

This chapter will concentrate on the integration of "social" policies into public procurement. "Social issues" is meant to include such policies as tackling long-term unemployment, promoting fair labour conditions or other human rights internationally, promoting the use of local labour in economically deprived areas, prohibiting discrimination against minority groups, encouraging equality of opportunity between men and women,

---

* Reader in Law, Oxford University and Fellow, Lincoln College, Oxford. The author is grateful to participants in the International Law Workshop of the University of Michigan Law School for comments on an earlier draft of this chapter. The chapter is based in part on sections of a report prepared for the Commission of the European Community. They bear no responsibility for any view expressed.
[1] J.M. Fernández-Martín, *The EC Public Procurement Rules: A Critical Analysis* (Clarendon Press, 1996), chapters 2 and 3.

and promoting the increased use of the disabled in employment, to name but a few.

There are many recent examples of such policies. The Commonwealth of Massachusetts has recently passed a law prohibiting the award of state contracts to firms with operations in Myanmar, because of the country's dismal human rights record, and (with several other states) Massachusetts is considering similar legislation concerning Indonesia. The Canadian government has introduced preferential award of federal contracts to Native Americans. The South African government has recently published a report advocating the increased use of "targeted" procurement as part of its policy on social integration. And these are merely the tip of the iceberg. Several European countries have several different types of policies for achieving women's equality attached as requirements in the award of public procurement contracts. Indeed, in a recent Communication on public procurement, the European Commission "encourages the Member States to use their procurement powers to pursue" a range of social objectives "providing the limits laid down by Community law are respected".[1a]

What is the problem with the linkage between such social policies and public procurement? The problem which this chapter addresses is the apparent conflict with both the spirit and the letter of various public procurement codes, at both the national, regional, and international levels. Although these issues have been debated more in the context of the EC procurement rules at present, similar issues arise with the WTO Government Procurement Agreement (GPA). The discussion will therefore concentrate on the public procurement regime of the European Community, and (in less detail) on the WTO Government Procurement Agreement (the question of the compatibility of these types of policies with national law will not be considered, although in several countries interesting legal issues arise).

The question which this chapter considers is of more than academic interest. The legality of such schemes is a subject of current concern under both European Community law and under the GPA. Indeed, infringement proceedings have been brought against Germany by the European Commission because of a scheme operated by North Rhine Westphalia. The *Land* gave a preference in procurement awards to tenderers which had in operation an equal opportunity policy for women. The Commission concluded that this was contrary to the procurement directives. Most recently, the European Community has complained to the United States that the Massachusetts law relating to Myanmar is contrary to the GPA, and it is possible that this will result in a WTO disputes panel considering the matter.

2. TAXONOMY OF APPROACHES ADOPTED

Before we turn to consider the legality of such schemes under Community law and the GPA, it will be useful to set out more systematically the different ways in which public procurement may be harnessed to the achievement of

---

[1a] Commission Communication, Public Procurement in the European Union, XV/5500/98-EN, Brussels, 11 March 1998.

socio-economic ends, for the differences in approach taken, we shall see, considerably affect the legality of the scheme under both EC law and the GPA.

2.1 Stage of tendering process

The relationship between the social policy in issue and the stage of tendering process differs significantly in different programmes. In some, the programme adopts *qualification* criteria (and the process by which qualification is to be determined differs from programme to programme). Other programmes provide that the link between public procurement and the social policy aim is by depriving a tenderer of the opportunity to bid for contracts in the future as a *sanction*, additional to other legal sanctions, for failure to adhere to legal obligations of a social policy nature. In some programmes, the sanction is applied administratively, in some judicially. In some the programme adopts *contractual requirements* which the contractor must carry out in the course of the contract (the penalty for breach differs from programme to programme: in some it can include cancellation of the contract; in others contractual penalties; and in some the breach is used to evaluate the bidder's reliability in the award of future contracts). In some the programme considers the policy to be adopted during the course of *pre-award* negotiations. In some the issues are of relevance at the *award stage*.

The "award stage" approach also differs considerably between different programmes. In some, the approach taken is to establish a quota of contracts which is *set aside* for contractors of a particular type. In others there is a *price preference* for certain types of contractors whereby the bid which bidder A submits, though higher than that of tenderer B, is regarded as equal to that of B, if A undertakes a particular social policy. In others the approach taken is that the willingness or ability or past practice of the bidder is taken into account as a *tie-break* where otherwise equal tenders are in competition (in some programmes the social criterion is one among many to be taken into account where tenders are equal; in others the social criterion is determinative). In others, the procedure is to *offer back* to preferred tenderers, to allow them to match the lowest bid of their non-preferred competitors.

2.2 Content of the requirement or preference

Programmes also differ, crucially, in the *content* of the requirement or preference. Let us take the example of a requirement prohibiting discrimination on grounds of gender. In some contracts the obligation consists of an obligation not to discriminate, in others much more is required. For some programmes, the additional requirements are for firms to monitor the composition of their workforce; in others they are to appoint an equal opportunities officer; and in others they require firms to allow the contracting authority to inspect or to notify statistics to the contracting authority. In other programmes, yet more extensive forms of positive action are required, such as out-reach, the use of the tie-break, or preferential treatment of particular groups.

Requirements also differ considerably from country to country, in terms of their relationship to the legal obligations of employers generally. In some countries, these requirements are already required of all or most employers, whether contractors with the government or not, while in others the requirements are additional to those imposed on employers generally. Returning to the anti-discrimination requirement, the content of the requirements also differ from country to country in terms of the protected groups involved. In some, the programme is directed at racial and ethnic groups, in some at gender discrimination and women, in some at the disabled and in some at religious minorities. The relationship between the socio-economic requirements and general anti-discrimination legislation also differs markedly. In some, these requirements are a substitute or alternative to the imposition of obligations directly by law; in some, it operates in a parallel and independent way; and in others its role is supplementary.

2.3 Public bodies and private firms involved

The way in which social policies are linked to government contracts varies also in relation to which public bodies are involved. In some cases the programme is applicable to the contracts of central government departments; in some, regional governments are involved while others include local governments. Sometimes other public bodies are involved, sometimes not. What types of contracts are covered by the programme differ significantly. Some cover supplies, others works, others services. Some programmes are limited to contracts above a threshold amount, others not. For some the threshold amount is relevant for the type of requirement that is imposed: the larger the contract, the greater the set of obligations imposed. The type of firm is sometimes specified. Thus sometimes the programme only affects firms employing a certain minimum number of employees; while sometimes sub-contractors are covered and sometimes not. In some programmes, all the activities of the contractor, whether those employees are involved in carrying out the contract or not, are subject to the requirements; in others, only those activities of the contractor directly involved in carrying out the contract are covered.

2.4 Institutional mechanisms

There are also crucial differences between programmes as to what, if any, institutional mechanisms are established within the public administration to support and monitor the policy. For those programmes which have such institutional support, there are further differences in the function which it plays. In some cases the mechanism established is responsible for the enforcement of requirements in the contract. In other cases it is involved merely in monitoring. Sometimes it may be responsible for negotiating with potential or actual contractors, for setting the standards which contractors should comply with and/or in certifying that potential contractors have reached that standard. The status of the machinery vis-à-vis the administration also differs. It may be centralised within the administration of the contracting authority; it may be decentralised within the administration of the contracting authority; it may be situated outside the administration of the contracting authority; or it may be an independent public body. In others, the social partners (particularly the unions) are relied on to enforce the provisions. Lastly, programmes differ on the extent to which contractors are supposed to bear any costs of implementing the requirements, and in how much support is available to contractors to enable them to meet the requirements. In some cases financial subsidies are available, in other cases merely advice. State resources are also made available for identifying relevant members of the protected group(s).

3. EUROPEAN COMMUNITIES

Turning now to the legality of such schemes under European Community law, the issue is complicated by the interaction of the relevant Treaty Articles and the European directives on public procurement. With this caveat, let us consider as systematically as possible the legality under Community law of a provision which seeks to link procurement with the achievement of one or more such social policy goals. We begin with the main Treaty requirements,[2] and then consider the position under the directives.

3.1 Treaty Articles

3.1.1 *The four freedoms*

Several Articles of the EC Treaty are relevant, in particular Article 6 (prohibiting discrimination on grounds of nationality), Article 30 (free movement of goods), Article 48 (free movement of workers), and Articles 52 and 59 (freedom to provide services and the freedom of establishment). These provisions prohibit not only *direct* discrimination on the basis of nationality, but also treatment by a Member State which in *effect* discriminates against, or does not provide equal treatment to,[3] a person or entity from another Member State. The importance of these provisions is that they provide a binding standard against which to consider *all* public procurement decisions by public contracting authorities. Therefore, even if a particular contract does not fall within the coverage of the procurement directives, the non-discrimination requirement must still be satisfied.

In Case C-360/89, *Commission of the European Communities* v. *Italian Republic*, the ECJ considered the compatibility of two provisions of Italian legislation with Article 59 of the EC Treaty.[4] The first was a provision requiring that the main contractor for certain public works contracts should reserve a certain percentage of the work for undertakings whose registered office was in the region where the works were to be carried out. The Commission contended that this requirement was in breach of Article 59 of the EC Treaty in that its effect was discriminatory against entities established outside Italy, and this was accepted by the ECJ. The Italian government had

---

[2] I do not consider here issues arising out of state aids or competition requirements.
[3] Case C-243/89, *Commission* v. *Denmark* [1993] ECR I-3353, paragraph 37.
[4] Case C-360/89, *Commission* v. *Italy* [1992] ECR I-3415. See, in general, S. Arrowsmith, "Public Procurement as an Instrument of Policy and the Impact of Market Liberalisation" (1995) 111 *Law Quarterly Review* 235.

argued that the measures might be justified in terms of the exceptions to Article 59 for provisions concerning public policy, public security and public health which applied by virtue of Article 56 and 66 of the EC Treaty, in that the measure to which the Commission objected would promote the participation of small and medium-sized enterprises, but the ECJ rejected the view that these considerations fell within the scope of the exceptions.

A second provision of Italian law was also held to be in breach of Article 59 of the EC Treaty. In certain cases, in deciding which undertakings from among others should be invited to submit bids, authorities were required to give preference to consortia and joint ventures which involved undertakings carrying out their main activity in the area where the works were to be executed. The ECJ held this to be discriminatory in effect and not susceptible to being saved by the exceptions discussed above.

In *Commission* v. *Denmark*,[5] the ECJ held that a clause in a tender specification, which stipulated that "the contractor is obliged as far as possible to use Danish material, goods, labour and equipment" was incompatible with Articles 30, 48 and 59 of the EC Treaty.

3.1.2 *"Communitarisation"*

Common to all the Treaty provisions discussed is the obligation not to discriminate against actual or potential tenderers from other Member States, and not to adversely affect trade to a significant extent. For those contracts under the thresholds of the procurement directives, therefore, it will be important to develop mechanisms by which these pitfalls can be avoided while still retaining the freedom to link legitimate social policy goals with public procurement. One attractive possibility is to open up preferences to the enterprises of other regions by providing that similar preferences apply to those enterprises which can demonstrate that they too fit within the social criteria laid down (so-called "communitarisation"). Such arrangements would need to ensure that contracts were open to all in fact as well as in form. For that reason, the transparency of the process, the clarity of the criteria, and the extent to which information about the contracts is available equally throughout the Community, are all crucial.

3.2 Procurement directives and social policy goals

For those public contracts above the relevant financial thresholds, the tendering and award procedures must also comply with the terms of the Community's directives on public procurement.[6] The Treaty requirements are therefore necessary but not sufficient norms against which public

---

[5] Case C-243/89, *Commission* v. *Denmark* [1993] ECR I-3353, paragraph 23.
[6] The current directives are Directive 93/36/EEC on public supply contracts, OJ 1993, No. L199/1; Directive 93/37/EEC on public works contracts, OJ 1993, No. L199/54; and Directive 92/50/EEC on services contracts, OJ 1992, No. L209/1. Procurement in the sectors of water, energy, transport and telecommunications (utilities) are governed by the separate Directive 93/38/EEC, OJ 1993, No. L199/84; and remedies by Directive 89/665/EEC, OJ 1989, No. L395/83 (public sector); and Directive 92/13/EEC, OJ 1992, No. L76/14 (utilities).

procurement decisions must be tested. In addition, the directives apply a considerable range of procedural and substantive requirements to those public contracts above a certain value. We shall now turn to some particular elements of the procurement directives. The purpose will be to see to what extent, if at all, they permit social policy requirements to be imposed by the contracting authority.

3.2.1 Conformity to national legislation

The procurement directives provide generally (with the exception of the Supplies Directive) for the ability of contracting authorities to notify tenderers of the application of national legal requirements regarding employment protection and working conditions. Article 23(1) of the Works Directive, for example, provides that the contracting authority may state in the contract documents, or be obliged by a Member State so to do, "the authority or authorities from which a tenderer may obtain the appropriate information on the obligation relating to the employment protection provisions and the working conditions which are in force in the Member State, region or locality in which the works are to be executed and which shall be applicable to the works carried out on site during the performance of the contract". Article 23(2) further provides that the contracting authority "shall request the tenderers or those participating in the contract procedure to indicate that they have taken account, when drawing up their tender, of the obligations relating to employment protection provisions and the working conditions which are in force in the place where the work is to be carried out. This shall be without prejudice to the application of the provisions of Article 30(4) concerning the examination of abnormally low tenders."

In some respects, these provisions are unclear in their implications. Is, for example, legislation providing for non-discrimination on the basis of sex, race and religion included within the meaning of legislation "relating to employment protection ... and working conditions"? If so, it would appear to be justifiable to request tenderers to provide a guarantee that their future compliance with national anti-discrimination requirements had been included in the calculation of the cost of completing the contract. The implication of the provision goes somewhat wider, however, since it clearly envisages that contracting authorities are permitted to require that tenderers should comply with such obligations in the first place. It would thus appear to be justifiable to request tenderers to provide guarantees regarding their future compliance with national anti-discrimination requirements, although, if the contractor does so, little more can be done under this provision.

Such legislative provisions themselves, and the *methods* adopted by the contracting authorities for satisfying itself of future conformity, must not, however, be discriminatory against contractors from other Member States, either directly or indirectly. Since, however, the directives requiring non-discrimination between women and men apply throughout the Community, any national legislation which reflects the *requirements* of the Community equality directives could hardly be regarded as discriminating against contractors in any Member State, since all are bound by these provisions already. That freedom to require a promise as to future conduct is, however, quite limited.

3.2.2 Suitability and award criteria

Regarding the other provisions of the directives, we can distinguish between two different aspects of contractor selection laid down in the directives. We shall use the Works Directive as an example. The first involves determining the *suitability* of *potential* contractors. Suitability is to be determined by scrutinising those potential contractors (who have not been excluded under Article 24) in accordance with the criteria of economic and financial standing and of technical knowledge or ability referred to in Article 26 and Article 27 of the directive. In considering suitability, an authority is limited to considering only the general matters referred to in these Articles. The second aspect of the selection of contractors provided for by the directives is the actual *awarding* of the contract itself to one of the contractors considered suitable as determined at the first stage. This is to be done according to the criteria of lowest price or most advantageous tender stated in Article 30. It will be appropriate to consider further the issue of compatibility with the directives separately under these two aspects: *suitability* criteria and *award* criteria.

3.2.2.1 Suitability. The ECJ has given some attention to the issue of suitability criteria, and the permissibility of incorporating social criteria into the procedure of deciding on suitability. The second provision of Italian law, considered in *Commission* v. *Italy* and discussed above, was also contested by the Commission as contrary to Article 22 of the Works Directive.[7] The Commission argued that, in making a decision on which undertakings to invite to tender, an authority was limited by Article 22 to taking into account factors which could be deduced from the information referred to in Article 17(d).[8] This, it was argued, referred only to information relating to those factors mentioned in Articles 23–26.[9] This argument was accepted by the ECJ. The local preference factor provided for in the Italian legislation was not contemplated in Articles 23–26 and it *could not be taken into account* in selecting bidders.

From this we can conclude that the *suitability* criteria set out in the relevant provisions of the directive are exhaustive, and therefore, unless the social policy which a contractor wishes to pursue comes within these provisions, the contractor may not take it into account in excluding contractors from tendering and being considered. A contractor can be excluded from participation in the contract only in the limited respects specified in Article 24 of the Works Directive, and on the criteria of economic and financial standing and technical knowledge or ability,[10] using the rules for verification stipulated in Articles 26 and 27 of the Works Directive. It should be added that the means by which the contracting authority is

---

[7] Now Article 22(1), amended in non-material respects.
[8] Now Article 22(1).
[9] Now Articles 24–27.
[10] Article 15(1) of the Supplies Directive refers to "technical capacity".

satisfied that these criteria are met must also be non-discriminatory as between tenderers in different Member States.

To what extent do these provisions relating to suitability enable issues of social policy to be taken into account? There are two relevant provisions. Article 24(c) provides that a contractor may be excluded from participation in the contract where it "has been convicted of an offence concerning his professional conduct by a judgment which has the force of *res judicata*". Article 24(d) provides that a contractor may be excluded from participation in the contract who "has been guilty of grave professional misconduct proved by any means which the contracting authorities can justify".

3.2.2.2 Award. We will consider now the different question of which criteria may be used for the actual *award* of contracts. We shall begin with those provisions specifically set out in some or all of the directives, which stipulate that the award of contracts should be on the basis of lowest price or most advantageous tender. To what extent do these provisions permit socio-economic issues to be taken into account?

In its interpretation of this provision, the Commission has made clear its limitations in being used as an opportunity for introducing social considerations. Discussing an award criterion of whether the contractor was willing to employ unemployed persons, the Commission states that:

The various criteria [in Article 29 of the Works Directive] given as examples ... all relate to matters which affect the economic benefit to the contracting entity of the offer in question in the context of the subject matter of a particular works contract. A tenderer's capacity to employ long-term unemployed does not normally have any impact on the economic benefit of the contract to the procuring entity. Economic benefits which may result, for example, through the reduction of welfare payments or an increase in spending by those employed, are indirect and quite extraneous to the subject matter of the contract itself. Unless particular circumstances could be shown to exist under which employment of the long-term unemployed would improve the economic benefits of the contract to the procuring entity, this criterion would not be compatible with the directive. The same applies to other criteria which have nothing to do with the subject matter of a particular contract.[11]

However, that said, the notion of "economically advantageous" might be thought, at least, to allow risk criteria to be taken into account in the assessment of tenders in some cases.[12] This may be relevant, for example when a contracting authority considers that a contractor is clearly at risk of substantial damages in a pay discrimination claim, rendering the contractor unable to perform the contract conditions. This may justify assessing the tender submitted by that firm as less "economically advantageous" than one submitted by another tenderer not subject to such a risk. We may

---

[11] COM (89) 400, OJ 1989, No. C311/7 of 12 December 1989, at paragraph 48.

[12] "Risk assessment is a matter relating to economic advantage and may be given as one of the criteria where a contract is to be awarded on the basis of the offer which is most economically advantageous. Such assessment would involve a critical appraisal of contractor's safety policies and safe working systems.": M. Paddon, *Going Public in Europe: A Guide to the EC Public Procurement Directives* (Association of Metropolitan Authorities and the Local Government Management Board, July 1993), p. 66.

perhaps also note at this point that a contracting authority might itself be at risk, in some jurisdictions, of incurring liability (and thus an award of damages against it) as a principal if the contractor discriminated while carrying out a contract as agent for the principal. One significant problem with this argument, however, is how the contracting authority is to judge whether it or the tenderer is clearly at risk. For that reason alone, the argument should be treated with some caution.

A second potentially relevant argument may arise from the ability to reject "abnormally low" tenders. There are provisions allowing this in each of the directives.[13] It is relevant to consider whether this exception could be used to justify exclusion of contractors where the low tender is the result of discrimination against women contrary to Article 119 of the EC Treaty, and therefore gives rise to an unfair competitive advantage.

Some have argued that this approach is of dubious legality in light of the restrictive approach adopted by the ECJ to this exception in the *Costanzo* case.[14] In that case Italy adopted a provision which required the automatic exclusion from procedures for the award of public works contracts of tenders which were abnormally low, judged according to a mathematical criterion. The ECJ held that these provisions were contrary to Article 29(5) of Directive 71/305/EEC which required the contracting authority to examine each case, and to allow the tenderer to show that the bid is a genuine one. Trepte has argued that the justification for the approach adopted by the ECJ lay in its view that the procurement directive's aim "was to promote the development of effective competition in the field of public contracts". He continues:

It is always possible that certain tenderers may benefit from exceptional or particularly advantageous economic, geographical or labour market conditions, for example, to put forward an exceptionally low bid. These bids would be genuine and to reject them, simply because they appear to be abnormally low, would not only deprive the tenderer of his right to compete fairly with other tenderers by using the legitimate advantages presented to him but would also defeat the object of the tendering game, namely to get the best deal for the awarding entity.[15]

On this interpretation, it might appear that the judgment prohibits a national authority from interpreting "abnormally low" in the way suggested above. However, the *Costanzo* case hardly seems conclusive on this issue, particularly given that the ECJ stressed that what constitutes an abnormally low tender "is for the national legislature to determine".[16] A more limited interpretation of the case would appear more justified, namely, that each case should be treated on its merits, that there should be no automatic exclusion, and that tenderers should have the opportunity to rebut the case against them. If these conditions are satisfied, and the

---

[13] Article 30(4) of the Works Directive; Article 27 of the Supplies Directive; Article 37 of the Services Directive; and Article 34(5) of the Utilities Directive.

[14] Case C-103/88, *Fratelli Constanzo v. Commune di Milano* [1989] ECR I-1839.

[15] P. Trepte, *Public Procurement in the EC* (CCH Editions, 1993), pp. 166–7.

[16] Paragraph 45(1), p. 1860.

condition of non-discrimination is complied with, the approach suggested seems appropriate, and is indeed more apt than that considered in the previous paragraph as a method of capturing the concerns which underlie the proposal there considered.

An argument which is analogous to those made above has been considered in the United States in the context of decisions by commissions charged with regulating an area of business or commerce. The question has arisen whether, in deciding the level of rates that a utility may charge to its customers, the Federal Power Commission (whose central function is the regulation of the cost of electricity and gas to consumers) may take into account employment discrimination by the utility in making its decision as to what price the utility may charge the consumer. In an important decision approving the Federal Power Commission taking such factors into account, the Supreme Court held that, to the extent that illegal, duplicative, or unnecessary labour costs are demonstrably the product of a regulated party's discriminatory practices and can be or have been demonstrably quantified by judicial decree or the final action of an administrative agency, the FPC should disallow them.[17]

Lastly, Article 30(3) of the Works Directive provides that the requirements of selection according to lowest price or most economically advantageous tender "shall not apply when a Member State bases the award of contracts on other criteria, within the framework of rules in force at the time of the adoption of this directive whose aim is to give preference to certain tenderers, on condition that the rules invoked are in conformity with the Treaty". Article 32 of the Works Directive also requires Member States to inform the Commission of national provisions covered by Article 30(3) and of the rules for applying them. It would appear that no Member State has notified the Commission of such preferences operating which are relevant for gender equality purposes. Only the Utilities Directive has an equivalent provision (Article 35(1)), and since there is no reporting requirement, it is open to question whether such preferences are operated in this context; there is no evidence which would lead to the conclusion that any such preferences relevant for gender equality purposes do operate in this context.

Neither the Supplies Directive nor the Services Directive has an equivalent provision. An equivalent provision was included in the original Supplies Directive but is absent from the current consolidated Supplies Directive in the public sector. No such provision was included in the directive governing the award of public service contracts.

3.3 The *Beentjes* case

We turn now to consider whether there is any further scope beyond that found in the specific provisions of the directives which is relevant. In the *Beentjes* case,[18] the ECJ considered a request for a preliminary ruling

---

[17] *National Association for the Advancement of Colored People* v. *Federal Power Commission*, 425 US 662 (1976).
[18] Case 31/87, *Gebroeders Beentjes BV* v. *The Netherlands* [1988] ECR 4635.

made by a Dutch court.[19] The proceedings before the Dutch court concerned a decision to award a public works contract. Beentjes had submitted the lowest bid, but the contract had been awarded to another bidder. Several reasons were given for preferring the other bid, including that Beentjes was not able to employ long-term unemployed persons. The awarding authority had stated this as a necessary condition. Beentjes challenged the decision contending that the Works Directive precluded the contracting authorities from taking account of this consideration. The ECJ was asked whether the ability of contractors to provide work for the long-term unemployed could be taken into account by the national awarding authority under the Works Directive,[20] if in the invitation to tender no criteria of this type had been stipulated. The ECJ interpreted this question as raising two different questions: first, could such considerations be taken into account at all; and, secondly, if they could be taken into account, was the awarding authority required to notify them to bidders in advance?

3.3.1 Possible interpretations of the directives

Three possible interpretations were open to the ECJ in *Beentjes* regarding the first question. We shall consider each possible interpretation in turn, beginning with the narrowest. While the first, and narrowest, interpretation was not in fact adopted by the ECJ, it remains the preferred interpretation by some Member State public authorities. It is therefore important to consider the implications of such an interpretation.

The first interpretation is that Article 29 (now Article 30) of the directive regulates comprehensively the factors which may be taken into account by the authority in selecting the contractor: that the directive is a complete code. This interpretation would leave no room for authorities to take considerations into account in awarding the contract which were not specified in Article 29 of the directive. On this interpretation, Article 29 of the Works Directive laid down all the specific exceptions to the lowest price or most economically advantageous tender requirement. These included, in the old Article 29(3), a provision that these criteria "shall not apply when a Member State bases the award of contracts on other criteria, within the framework of rules whose aim is to give preference to certain tenderers by way of aid". Article 29(4) (now Article 30(4)) provides another exception allowing the rejection of abnormally low tenders. The new Article 31 further provided, until 31 December 1992, for exceptions relating to regional aid. These exceptions, but *only* these exceptions, would be permissible on the basis of the first interpretation. This is the approach which the Advocate-General adopted in the *Beentjes* case. Were this narrow interpretation to have been upheld in *Beentjes*, or be upheld subsequently, contracting authorities would be limited to relying on the provisions specifically included in the directives themselves and discussed above.

---

[19] For a discussion of this case, see S. Arrowsmith, note 4 above, pp. 274–5.
[20] Directive 71/305/EEC, now replaced by Directive 93/37/EEC.

A second possible interpretation is that where the authority lays down a social policy (such as equality between men and women) specifically as part of the *contractual conditions* which must be complied with by the contractor, this is permitted by the directive.

A third interpretation is similar to the second in that the directive is not regarded as providing a complete code. The authority may then decide not to award a contract to a contractor for a reason *other* than those specified in the directive. The authority may decide not to award a contract to a contractor for a reason *other* than failure to agree to a contractual condition. The function of the directive, on this interpretation, is to lay down mandatory procedural requirements relating to some aspects of the contracting process, but otherwise to leave discretion to contracting authorities as to whom to award the contract. Under this interpretation, contractors could be rejected, for example, because of anticipated failure to meet a desired policy aim specified by the contracting authority.

3.3.2 The Beentjes decision itself

The ECJ emphasised in its decision that the directive was not intended to regulate procurement exhaustively in the Member States. It is clear, therefore, that the ECJ rejected the first interpretation discussed above. The ECJ concluded that the condition relating to long-term unemployed persons was not precluded by the directive. However, the ECJ held further that the policy could only be lawful if it was consistent with Treaty principles, which excluded practices operating in a discriminatory manner. The ECJ did not itself decide whether the conditions taken into account did or did not discriminate, which was left to the national court.

There are, however, several major uncertainties concerning the meaning and implications of the decision of the ECJ. In particular, it is unclear whether the ECJ adopted the second or the third interpretation discussed above. On the one hand, it has been argued that Case 360/89, *Commission v. Italy*,[21] discussed above, implies that the second interpretation of the directive discussed above is correct; otherwise an inconsistency between it and the *Beentjes* case would arise. It should be noted also that it is the second interpretation which the Commission appears to advocate in its Communication following the *Beentjes* decision.[22] If the second interpretation is correct, several issues arise.

---

[21] Case C-360/89, *Commission v. Italy* [1992] ECR I-3401.
[22] COM (89) 400, OJ 1989, No. C311/7 of 12 December 1989, p. 12, paragraph 47: "The Court drew a distinction between the contractual condition concerning long-term unemployment on the one hand and the criteria for selection of firms and the criteria for the award of a contract on the other. The condition was not relevant to an assessment of the bidders' economic, financial or technical capacity to carry out the work. Nor did it form part of the criteria applied by the purchasing authority to decide to whom to award the contract. It was simply an obligation which the firm securing the contract would have to accept."

3.3.3 *Agreement to comply, or anticipated ability to comply*

First, may a contracting authority which specifies achievement of a social policy as a contractual requirement take agreement to comply with the contractual condition into account in deciding to whom the contract should be awarded? Secondly, may a contracting authority which specifies achievement of a social policy as a contractual requirement reject a tender where the tenderer agrees to carry out the conditions of the contract, but the contracting authority considers that the tenderer may be unable to do so?

Some have argued that the second interpretation only allows the determination of a contract once failure to comply with a contractual term is established, and not in anticipation of inability to comply. The Commission's Communication stressed that the *Beentjes* approach must not be interpreted as effectively allowing the application of a criterion of award not specified in the directives.[23] As Winter argues, "a careful analysis will be necessary to ascertain whether a contractual condition should in reality not be characterised as an unlawful criterion of award. This would be the case if the contract notice, rather than requiring the successful tenderer to employ a specific number of unemployed persons, would indicate that the contracting authority is to choose between tenders taking into account the proposals of tenderers to use unemployed persons in the performance of their contract *or their ability to employ* such persons."[24] On this interpretation, the sanction for failure to meet the condition specified will be not to award future contracts to that contractor. Indeed, failure to meet a contractual condition might well amount to professional misconduct sufficient to refuse to consider the tenderer in future.

3.3.4 *Technical capacity: suitability criteria revisited*

If the second interpretation is accepted, we need to consider also the implications of this approach for the earlier question of what may be taken into account in the context of suitability criteria. May these contractual conditions be taken into account in *selecting* contractors? In the light of what has been said above concerning suitability criteria, the answer would seem to be that they may not be taken into account in the context of suitability. However, we have not yet considered one element in the directive relating to suitability. The directive clearly envisages the rejection of contractors in the context of suitability who do not meet "technical capacity". "Technical capacity" relates to the ability to carry out the contractual conditions of the contract. If these contractual conditions include certain social policy objectives, then "technical capacity" might include the ability to carry out these social objectives. If so, contractors might legitimately be excluded

---

[23] Paragraph 47: "Nor did it form part of the criteria applied by the purchasing authority to decide to whom to award the contract."

[24] J. Winter, "Public Procurement in the EEC" (1991) *Common Market Law Review* 741 at 774; emphasis added. See also W. van Gerven, "General Report to the 14th FIDE Congress" in FIDE, *L'Application dans les Etats Membres des Directives sur les Marchés Publics* (Madrid, 1990), p. 333.

under selection criteria also for anticipated failure to meet such conditions, as well as in the context of the application of the award criteria. Otherwise, it might be said, we would be left in the position whereby it would be permissible to exclude for likely failure to meet a contractual condition when awarding the contract, but not at the stage of shortlisting potential contractors.

The major legal problem with this argument lies in the *Beentjes* case itself. For in its judgment the ECJ stated that the ability to comply with the condition relating to the long-term unemployed was not a matter of technical capacity.[25] It has been argued that this statement by the ECJ strengthens the argument that the third interpretation is the one which the ECJ intended to adopt. For if the ECJ were intending to permit such policies, however they were implemented (that is, whether or not by contractual requirement), then ability to comply would not be a matter of technical capacity.[26]

3.3.5 Transparency

The ECJ went on to consider the issue of the extent to which such selection criteria must be made known in advance. The ECJ held that the conditions relating to the contractor's ability to provide work for the long-term unemployed were required to be notified in advance to potential contractors. This is an extremely important point. It means that whether the second or third interpretation is adopted, the relevant criteria must be made clear to potential contractors from the start. There must be full transparency in the award criteria. The Commission also points out the advisability of discussing such conditions with it in advance.[27]

4. THE WTO GOVERNMENT PROCUREMENT AGREEMENT

Just as EC law does not answer clearly the question we have been concerned with throughout this article, the World Trade Organisation Government Procurement Agreement (GPA) is similarly open to interpretation. It is true that some questions which remain open under the Community directives are determined by the GPA. There is, for example, a specific exception for products derived from workshops for the disabled.

In addition, the national annexes of some countries clearly permit social policies which are more problematic under the Community directives. As under the 1979 Agreement, the predecessor to the current GPA, several countries sought exemptions from the coverage of the Agreement for

---

[25] *Beentjes*, note 18 above, paragraph 28.
[26] S. Arrowsmith, note 4 above, p. 276.
[27] COM (89) 400, OJ 1989, No. C311/7 of 12 December 1989.

particular social policies. Canada stipulated that as regards sub-central government entities, "[n]othing ... shall be construed to prevent any provincial entity from applying restrictions that promote the general environmental quality in that province, as long as such restrictions are not disguised barriers to international trade."[28] A similar provision was included by the United States.[29]

The United States continued to seek an exemption under the new GPA for those legislative policies which required that a percentage of public contracts should in certain circumstances be set aside in favour of tenderers from minority businesses.[30] The United States stipulated that the Agreement does not apply in respect of "set asides for small and minority businesses".[31] Canada was "unable to persuade the United States to moderate the terms"[32] of these programmes. "Consequently", according to an official Canadian Government report, "the Canadian federal government is not required to open up to Code members its procurement of high-technology communications, transportation-related construction and specified services."[33] Specifically, Canada included a minority and small business exception in its annex.[34] A similar exception for set asides for small and medium-sized businesses was adopted by Korea.[35] Regarding sub-central government entities, the United States also required that a provision be inserted that "[p]rocurements subject to programmes promoting the development of distressed areas and businesses owned by minorities, disabled veterans and women are reserved from coverage".[36] The exemptions granted to the United States in the new GPA apply both in relation to the provisions forbidding discrimination on the basis of nationality and to the rules on award procedures.[37]

Nevertheless, there are many national provisions attaching social policy requirements to public procurement which may appear to breach the GPA. Indeed, the argument has been made[38] that the GPA may be more restrictive of the use of social policies than the Community directives.

As mentioned earlier, this issue is now no longer a theoretical question. The issue has come to a head because of the increased popularity, in the United States, of state and local policies designed to restrict government contracts going to companies which deal with particular countries

---

[28] Canadian Annex to Appendix 1, Annex 2, note 2.

[29] United States Annex to Appendix 1, Annex 2, note 1.

[30] The United States had earlier taken a reservation stating that agreement obligations would not apply to set asides on behalf of small and minority businesses under the North American Free Trade Agreement, chapter 10, Annex 1001.2b, General Notes, Schedule of the United States, note 1.

[31] United States Annex to Appendix 1, General Notes, note 1.

[32] Industry Canada, *Industry and the Uruguay Round*, vol. 1, *Results of the Negotiations* (March 1995), internet edition.

[33] *Ibid.*

[34] Canadian Annex to Appendix 1, General Notes, note 1(d).

[35] Korean Annex to Appendix 1, Annex 1, note 3; Annex 2, note 3; and Annex 3, note 2.

[36] United States, Annex 2.

[37] US Annexes to Appendix 1, General Notes, note 1.

[38] Arrowsmith, note 4 above, p. 270.

regarded as breaching human rights standards. Such policies have been in existence in the United States since the late 1970s, when they were first devised as a technique for opposing apartheid in South Africa. Since then, the approach has broadened to encompass issues related to Northern Ireland. More recently, however, this approach has burgeoned (in part because of increased US press and consumer interest in human rights in parts of the world largely ignored until recently[39]), with actual or proposed state and local restrictions on the award of public contracts to businesses involved with Nigeria, Switzerland, China, Indonesia and (particularly) Myanmar.[40]

In 1996 the Commonwealth of Massachusetts enacted legislation limiting state agencies from signing new contracts or renewals of contracts with companies doing business with or in Myanmar.[41] The legislation was based directly on previous legislation which had regulated state contracts with companies which had South African links (indeed, the state legislator responsible for introducing the Myanmar legislation had previously been responsible for introducing the South Africa legislation). The Myanmar legislation provides for the establishment of a restricted purchase list, which includes persons doing business with Myanmar. Most state agencies may only procure goods or services from persons on the restricted purchase list if the procurement is essential and if elimination of that person would result in inadequate competition among bidders. Even then, it would seem that, where any procurement includes bidders who are on the restricted purchase list, the state authority may award the contract to a person on the list only if there is no "comparable low bid or offer" by a person not on the list. A bid by a person not on the list can be up to 10 per cent greater than a bid submitted by a person on the restricted list and still remain comparably low. Exceptions are provided for news organisations operating in Myanmar, and for the procurement of medical supplies.

---

[39] "Advocacy Group's 1997 World Report Shows Heightened Interest in Labor Rights" *BNA International Trade Daily*, 6 December 1996, reporting a study by Human Rights Watch. The group said that "perhaps the most potent force in support [of] labor rights is the growing consumer interest on guarantees that the good[s] being purchased are not the products of abusive labor conditions".

[40] K. Whitelaw, "The Very Long Arm of the Law. Is the World Ready for 7,284 Secretaries of State?" *US News and World Report*, 14 October 1996, p. 57; P. Blustein, "Thinking Globally, Punishing Locally: States, Cities Rush to Impose Their Own Sanctions, Angering Companies and Foreign Affairs Experts" *Washington Post*, 16 May 1997, p. G-01; G. de Jonquieres, "Business Worried by US States' Sanctions" *Financial Times*, 24 April 1997, p. 9; G.G. Yerkey, "Administration Still Has No Policy On State, Local Government Sanctions" (1997) 14 *International Trade Reporter*, No. 28, 9 July, pp. 1176–7; "A State's Foreign Policy: the Mass that Roared" *Economist*, 8 February 1997, p. 32; and P. Magnusson, "A Troubling Barrage of Trade Sanctions From all Across America" *Business Week*, 24 February 1997, p. 59. For an excellent analysis of the activities of pressure groups in the United States regarding Myanmar, see IRRC, *Social Issues Service, 1997 Background Report K:1* (18 February 1997); and for a detailed description of state and local selective contracting laws on Myanmar, see IRRC, *Multinational Business in Burma* (1997), Appendix F.

[41] An Act Regulating Contracts with Companies Doing Business With or in Burma (Myanmar), chapter 130, 1996 Session Laws.

In January 1997, the European Commission formally complained to the United States regarding this legislation, and threatened to invoke the WTO dispute settlement procedure if the issue was not resolved in a satisfactory way. The Commission's concern has been heightened by the likelihood of other similar legislation being enacted by Massachusetts and other states regarding other countries with a dubious human rights record. Already legislation is pending in Massachusetts prohibiting the award of contracts to those doing business in or with Indonesia.

So far the issue has not been settled diplomatically, despite consultations organised under the auspices of the WTO between the United States, the EC and Japan, another concerned party. Following this lack of success, in June 1997 the EC requested consultations with the United States under Article 4(4) of the Dispute Settlement Understanding (DSU).[42] Japan also requested to join these consultations under Article 4(11) of the DSU.[43] In a subsequent communication of July 1997, Japan also requested consultations on the same matter.[44]

The European Commission is of the opinion that the Myanmar legislation is in breach of the GPA in three respects.[45] First, it is alleged to violate Article VIII(b) of the GPA, on the basis that it imposes conditions on a tendering company which are not essential to ensure the firm's capability to fulfil the contract. Secondly, it is alleged to infringe Article X of the GPA because it imposes qualification criteria based on political, rather than economic, considerations. Thirdly, it is alleged to be contrary to Article XIII to the extent that the statute allows the award of contracts to be based on political instead of economic considerations. The request for consultations further states:

This measure also appears to nullify or impair the benefits accruing to the European Communities under this Agreement, particularly as it limits the access of EC suppliers to procurement by a sub-federal authority covered by the Government Procurement Agreement in such a way as to result in a de facto reduction of the sub-federal offer under the GPA.

The European Communities additionally consider that this measure has the effect of impeding the attainment of the objectives of the GPA, including that of maintaining a balance of rights and obligations.

In its request for consultations in July 1997 Japan formally complained to the United States, citing Articles III(2), VIII(b), X and XIII(4) of the GPA.[46]

There has been extensive publicity about these provisions in the specialist press in United States and Europe. However, much of the discussion has

---

[42] United States – Measure Affecting Government Procurement; Request for Consultations by the European Communities, WT/DS88/1; GPA/D2/1, 26 June 1997.

[43] United States – Measure Affecting Government Procurement; Request to Join Consultations; Communication from Japan, WT/DS88/2; 2 July 1997.

[44] United States – Measure Affecting Government Procurement; Request for Consultations by Japan, WT/DS95/1; GPA/D3/1, 21 July 1997.

[45] WT/DS88/1; GPA/D2/1.

[46] WT/DS95/1; GPA/D3/1. See also *Inside US Trade*, 25 July 1997, p. 14.

focused on the desirability of such legislation as a tool of public policy,[47] the extent to which the individual states are subject to federal foreign policy and the compatibility of the Massachusetts law with American constitutional law,[48] and the political implications of intervention by the WTO, rather than on the compatibility of such legislation with the GPA. Where compatibility with the GPA has been discussed, discussion has tended to focus on whether Massachusetts is bound by the GPA,[49] rather than analysing the legal position of the legislation if the state is bound by it. On this issue, many commentators assume the legislation to be incompatible with the GPA, but without detailed analysis of why that might be the case.[50]

For the moment, it seems unlikely that the United States government will take legal action against Massachusetts (or indeed any other state enacting similar legislation) under United States law. The indications, as at the time of writing, are that the federal Government supports Massachusetts in the formal complaint made by the European Community in Geneva.[51] The most that the federal Government appears willing to do is to advocate that states should avoid the potential legal problems under the GPA by attaching such policies to contracts below the thresholds for the GPA. Indeed, after intervention by the State Department, the Massachusetts legislature amended the Indonesia legislation to apply the conditions to contracts below the GPA threshold.[52]

Many of the most important issues will arise for decision if a WTO disputes panel is invoked over the Myanmar legislation, such as the meaning of "discrimination" in the GPA, and the scope of the public interest exceptions in Article XXIII(2). However, one important issue would not be considered, because of the method of linkage adopted in the Massachusetts legislation. This is the question of whether such policy goals could be attached as contract conditions.

---

[47] See, in particular, the testimony by various individual, companies and groups on the proposed Massachusetts Indonesia legislation. Those against included the Institute for Training and Development, Associated Industries of Massachusetts, the Alliance for the Commonwealth, United Parcel Service, the American Indonesian Chamber of Commerce. Those in favour included Professor Richard Falk, the Robert F. Kennedy Memorial Center for Human Rights. See M.S. Lelyveld, "Corporate Giants Take on State in Sanctions Fight" *Journal of Commerce*, 3 March 1997, p. 1A.

[48] G.G. Yerkey, "Administration Still Has No Policy On State, Local Government Sanctions" (1997) 14 *International Trade Reporter*, No. 28, 9 July, pp. 1176–7. In April 1998, the National Foreign Trade Council filed suit in the United States District Court in Boston, Mass. to enjoin state officials from enforcing the legislation. A copy of the briefs filed can be viewed at http://usaengage.org/background/lawsuit/lawsuit.html.

[49] The issue involves two interlinked questions: first, did the United States include Massachusetts in its offer to other countries as to what was included as a sub-federal entity; and, second, if the United States did so, did it do so legitimately under United States law?

[50] K.A. Elliott, "Backing Illegal Sanctions" *Journal of Commerce*, 6 August 1997, p. 8A.

[51] *Journal of Commerce*, 23 July 1997, p. 5A.

[52] Compare House Bill 3730, An Act regulating state contracts and investments with companies doing business with or in Indonesia, with House Bill 4575, An Act regulating state contracts and investments with companies doing business with or in Indonesia. The latter, which is the Bill favourably reported out of the Committee on State Administration in July 1997, inserted a provision limiting coverage of the legislation to contracts below the GPA thresholds in cases where the state agency is subject to the GPA.

The provisions of the GPA stipulating requirements (Articles IX and XIII) appear to envisage that contract conditions of this type may legitimately be imposed, provided they are non-discriminatory. Article VIII, indeed, appears to permit a similar approach to that permitted under the second interpretation of *Beentjes* discussed above. Arrowsmith disagrees: "the concept of 'capability' to fulfil the contract covers compliance with any legislative obligation which governs performance – for example, safety rules – whether or not referred to in the contract itself. It might also be argued that it covers requirements imposed merely under the contract, where these are of a secondary nature and relate to contract performance – for example to pay fair wages to those engaged on government work."[53] But she considers that this is not an acceptable argument, on the ground that it would be "odd if contractors could not generally be excluded for non-compliance with standards set by the authority, but could be excluded when these are prescribed in a contract term".

However, this argument appears to ignore the provisions of Articles IX and XIII quoted above, which appear to be very general indeed and do not appear to prohibit "exclusion for non-compliance with standards set by the authority". Arrowsmith's arguments also neglect the extent of discretion which also appears to be accorded to national authorities. As Hoekman and Mavroidis have written, "procuring entities have substantial discretion in judging the capacity of the tenderer to fulfil the contract and determining who best meets the evaluation criteria. The main constraint on such discretion is what is specified in the notices or tender documentation."[54] So too, Didier regards the provision as leaving "significant room for subjective evaluation".[55]

5. CONCLUSION

What conclusions can we draw from this brief overview on the legal questions raised? Under European Community law, the conclusion appears to be that some types of linkage between social policies and public procurement may be operated lawfully under Community law. There remains considerable uncertainty, however, concerning the manner and form in which socio-economic requirements may be implemented. With regard to the Government Procurement Agreement, the legal analysis is inevitably somewhat speculative, in the absence of any decisions of direct relevance. An interesting question of legal interpretation will arise when (or if) a disputes panel is called on to consider the issue: to what extent should the

---

[53] Arrowsmith, note 4 above, p. 281.
[54] B.M. Hoekman and P.C. Mavroidis, "Basic Elements of the Agreement on Government Procurement" in B M. Hoekman and P.C. Mavroidis (eds.), *Law and Policy in Public Purchasing* (University of Michigan Press, 1997), chapter 1, p. 14.
[55] P. Didier, "The Uruguay Round Government Procurement Agreement: Implementation in the European Union" in B.M. Hoekman and P.C. Mavroidis (eds.), *Law and Policy in Public Purchasing* (University of Michigan Press, 1997), chapter 7, p. 134.

approach taken to the interpretation of the procurement directives by the ECJ influence the approach taken to the construction of the GPA?

Leaving the legal questions aside, several policy issues come to the fore. In particular, is a relatively restrictive approach to the linkage between social policy and public procurement likely to advance or retard the ultimate goal of opening up public procurement markets, making them less discriminatory, and more transparent? Or will a restrictive approach to linkage serve only to provide an incentive to avoidance (such as increasing the use of the *"Beentjes* approach") and evasion, thus retarding the ultimate goals of the new regional and international procurement provisions?

13. Problems of Industrial Policy in High-Technology Collaborative Procurement

*Stephen Kahn**

1. INTRODUCTION

Industrial policy is a widely used and much abused term. In most cases where one comes across it, one could readily substitute the term "industrial politics" to achieve a clearer understanding of what is meant. For the purposes of this chapter the term is taken to mean any application of rules to the selection of contractors by a public procurement authority that does not restrict itself to either the cheapest price or to the best combination of price, or other factors relevant to the product and service itself, quality – that is, to best value for money. Notwithstanding the deviation from one of the most widely recognised general principles of public procurement law, the application of other rules aimed at industrial and economic objectives can be regarded as important, beneficial and even inevitable in some circumstances.

Non-selection of the best offer (or the exclusion of potential bidders to achieve this same result) for reasons of corruption, idleness, ignorance of applicable norms or a (usually misguided) conception that the rules are unnecessarily time-consuming, expensive and inefficient, does not fall under the category of policy and is not considered here. Avoidance of competition by single-source (direct negotiation) is also not treated, whether legitimate or abusive. Nor is it the purpose of this chapter to consider the inherent legality of the rules applying additional or other criteria. In some cases it will be legal, either through an explicit provision of law, or by an exemption. In other cases, particularly for some international organisations, it will be an unchallenged "rule of the game" which functions as a lubricant to the political and financial decision-making process between the Member or Contributing States. Indeed, some form of industrial return is so fundamental to many international co-operative projects that to challenge it would be futile – without such a policy there would be no project.[1]

---

* European Space Agency.
[1] There is an extensive discussion of the various forms of industrial, social and political procurement, and their legality under some of the international rules, in S. Arrowsmith, *The Law of Public and Utilities Procurement* (Sweet & Maxwell, 1996), chapter 16, pp. 799 to 845.

In considering industrial policy in this chapter, the emphasis is placed on such international collaborative projects, which are becoming an increasingly important area of activity. Many developments are now so costly that individual states are not, or hardly not, in a position to carry them out on their own. Typically, fields in which such projects occur are defence, civil aeronautics and space, and large civil engineering programmes. The benefits are not only derived from the sharing of costs; commonality of equipment is important in defence, and regional exploitation only makes sense for some projects relating to, for example, the use of water resources, electricity generation or satellite communication. The high costs of these projects, their industrial and technological significance and their political sensitivity add greatly to the difficulty, and the interest, of the associated procurements.

Assuming that the application of industrial policies within the procurement process can be legal, the question posed is how, in terms of good procurement practice, they can be applied in the best and most effective manner. It would seem important that, within the constraints of the policy:

  (i)   the best offers meeting the criteria are selected;
  (ii) the process is, within the constraints, as fair as it can be;
  (iii) bidders are not induced to waste time and resources in preparing bids that have no chance of success;
  (iv) the procurement process is not brought into disrepute; and
  (v)   any conditions in the resulting contract, and in particular those concerning responsibilities and liabilities, are not detrimentally distorted by the manner of selection.

In the following examination of the issues, the rules and practice of the European Space Agency (ESA, or the Agency) are widely cited. This is partly because of their familiarity to the author, but more because the Agency has explicit industrial policy rules which have been applied (with varying success) over a long period of time to a very large number of contracts, of great technical and contractual complexity, in an international and politicised context. At the same time, the end product – successful operating spacecraft – does not permit any compromise of the integrity of the technical work. This chapter is not, however, intended simply as an exposition of issues relating to ESA – the problems are in various forms common to many procurement authorities.[2]

---

[2] The industrial policy of ESA is at present under intensive consideration by the Executive and the Member States. The views expressed in this chapter are, even more than usual, purely those of the author. Much of the information relating to the practical implementation of industrial policy is unpublished and even unrecorded. The author would welcome comments from practitioners to widen the discussion.

2. VARIETIES OF INDUSTRIAL POLICY

Under the concept of industrial policy, as defined above, one can come across many variations:[3]

(i)   preference to contracts of nationals of the procuring authority[4] or of a (multi-state) region.[5] Under the World Bank and family related international development banks, this is expressed as price margin of preference.[6] This practice is recognised in the UNCITRAL Model Law on Procurement of Goods, Construction and Services, Article 32(4)(d);

(ii) preference to contracts partly performed by or giving employment to, nationals of the procuring authority;

(iii) national regional preferences;[7]

(iv) preference to industry of a particular scale, such as a small, or small and medium firm policy;[8]

(v)   preference to firms according to other social considerations, such as ethnic minorities, beginning entrepreneurs, the disabled, etc.;[9]

---

[3] "[Domestic policy goals] may be either explicitly prescribed in national legislations, for example prohibitions against the purchase of foreign goods or services or from foreign suppliers, preference margins, set-asides and offsets, or in the form of less overt measures or practices which have the effect of denying foreign products services and suppliers the opportunity to compete in domestic government procurement markets.": GPA – General Overview, introduction p. 1.

[4] GPA, Article V provides exceptions from the general rule of no national discrimination in favour of developing countries. It does this in two directions: developed countries should try to offer benefits in favour of the underdeveloped; and the underdeveloped may discriminate to some extent. Article XXIII gives exceptions for national security or national defence purposes, or in order to protect public morals, order or safety, human, animal or plant life or health or intellectual property; or relating to the products or services of disabled persons, or philanthropic institutions or of prison labour. This is a particularly extensive list, although within the classic mould. Offsets are specifically prohibited in the qualification and selection of suppliers, products or services, or in the evaluation of tenders and award of contracts (Article XVI). Developing countries may, however, having regard to general policy considerations, negotiate the use of offsets, but only for qualification to participate in the procurement process and not as criteria for awarding contracts (Article XV1(2)).

[5] See, for example, Inter-American Development Bank, Outlines for Procurement under IDB Loans, 3.8.g(ii), p. 22. For a discussion of domestic preference in Eastern Europe, see E.H.G. Huepkes, "Public Procurement in Central and Eastern Europe" (1997) *Public Procurement Law Review* 69.

[6] For a useful comment on this practice, see Guide No. 23, Improving Public Procurement Systems (International Trade Centre, UNCTAD/GATT, 1993), pp. 15*ff*.

[7] Apart from the classic "pork-barrel" approach of placing contracts within politicians' constituencies, there are understandable attempts to place work in areas of high unemployment or other economic disadvantage. In the ESA context, the German government has made efforts to have as much work as possible for those contracts allocated to German firms to be performed in the former East Germany.

[8] See G. O'Brien, "Public Procurement and the Small or Medium Enterprise (SME)" (1993) *Public Procurement Law Review* 82.

[9] See S. Arrowsmith, "Abolition of the United Kingdom's Procurement Preference Scheme for Disabled Workers" (1994) *Public Procurement Law Review* CS225–29.

(vi) a requirement for an international organisation for a *juste retour* whereby the value of contracts placed in each country corresponds to the budgetary contributions of the participating states. The organisation may be an *ad hoc* body for a particular project – something quite common in the defence field; or

(vii) other considerations specific to the procuring body.[10]

The application of these policies, and their success, can be measured in a number of ways. There may be a mere adding up of contract prices and a calculation of their distribution. There may be some weighting of the quality, economic or technical, of the contracts granted. There may be an effort to build up expertise, industrial skills, a manufacturing base, etc. or a reduction of unemployment figures, over a period of time.

3. THE ESA INDUSTRIAL POLICY

In order to understand the examples given of ESA practice, it is necessary to have a brief outline of the industrial policy rules that govern the Agency. ESA is an intergovernmental, convention-based organisation with 15 Member States (plus Canada as an associate member). Its membership is not identical to, but largely overlaps, that of the European Union, from which it is wholly independent. Its principle purposes are to carry out a space research and development activity on behalf of the Member States (science, earth resources, telecommunications, meteorology, manned space flight, launchers and basic technology), to harmonise the activities of the national space agencies of the Member States and to stimulate the competitiveness of the European space industry. It is not concerned with the commercial exploitation of spacecraft that it has developed, this being left to industry and other specialised agencies. While ESA has a staff consisting largely of specialist engineers, it is predominantly a procurement body, most of the work being carried out under contract by industry.[11]

The first and basic rule (Article 2 of Annex V to the ESA Convention) is that "in the placing of contracts, the Agency shall give preference to industry and organisations of the Member States". The Council of Ministers can authorise derogations. There is a standing derogation (Article 12(2)(a)(ii) of the Contract Regulations) which allows a potential bidder from a non-participating state to be invited if there is no other way of satisfying requirements or an unacceptable delay or cost would otherwise result. This relates particularly to certain high-technology components.

---

[10] Intelsat Procurement Regulations, Article IIB: "If there is more than one bid offering such a combination of quality, price and the most favorable delivery time, the contract shall be awarded so as to stimulate, in the interests of INTELSAT, worldwide competition." The EUMETSAT Contract Procedures and Instructions state categorically that "Geographical or industrial return shall not be considered" (paragraph 3 of the Principles of Procurement) though a recent Council resolution has weakened this categorical position.

[11] A detailed account of the procurement practices of ESA can be found in S. Kahn, "Advanced Technology Projects and International Procurement: the Case of the European Space Agency" (1993) *Public Procurement Law Review* 13.

The procurement process is regulated by the Contract Regulations, which have been approved by the Council. These state (Article 4 (Principles), paragraph 1):

The provisions in these Regulations and in any other instructions concerning the placing of contracts shall always be interpreted so as to insure the most economic and effective employment of the Agency's resources, *to implement the defined industrial policy and to guarantee a distribution of work among Member States provided in Article VII and Annex V of the Convention.*

Article 5 states that "open competition shall be the normal procedure for the placing of contracts" but restricted competition or non-competitive tendering may be used "if the Industrial Policy Committee [the Council Committee charged with approving procurement policy and individual large contracts] has given a directive or guideline to that effect to the Director-General" (Articles 5(2)(b) and 6).

The emphasis on open competition, and the detailed procurement procedures which are elaborated in the Regulation, are classic. The references to industrial policy refer to the Convention, and thus to a high-level formal agreement among the Member States. Article II of the Convention reads:

The purpose of the Agency shall be to provide for and to promote, for exclusively peaceful purposes, co-operation among European States in space research and technology and their space applications, with a view to their being used for scientific purposes and for operational space applications systems: ...

    d. by elaborating and implementing the industrial policy appropriate to its programme and by recommending a coherent industrial policy to the Member States.

Article VII reads:

1. The industrial policy which the Agency is to elaborate and apply by virtue of Article II(d) shall be designed in particular to:

    a. meet the requirements of the European space programme and the co-ordinated national space programmes in a cost-effective manner;

    b. improve the worldwide competitiveness of European industry by maintaining and developing space technology and by encouraging the rationalisation and development of an industrial structure appropriate to market requirements, making use in the first place of the existing industrial potential of all Member States;

    c. ensure that all Member States participate in an equitable manner, having regard to their financial contribution, in implementing the European space programme and in the associated development of space technology; in particular the Agency shall, for the execution of its programmes, grant preference to the fullest extent possible to industry of all Member States, which shall be given the maximum opportunity to participate in the work of technological interest undertaken for the Agency.

    d. exploit the advantages of free competitive bidding in all cases, except where this would be incompatible with other defined objectives of industrial policy.

Annex V to the Convention deals further with industrial policy. Article I(2) reads:

2. The Council shall keep under review the industrial potential and industrial structure in relation to the Agency's activities, and in particular:

    a.   the general structure of industry, and industrial groupings;
    b.   the degree of specialisation desirable in industry and methods of achieving it;
    c.   the co-ordination of relevant national industrial policies;
    d.   interaction with any relevant industrial policies of other international bodies;
    e.   the relationship between industrial production capacity and potential markets;
    f.   the organisation of contacts with industry;

in order to be able to monitor, and where appropriate, adapt the Agency's industrial policy.

Article VI of Annex V lays down the geographical distribution (also termed industrial return or *juste retour*):

The geographical distribution of all Agency's contracts shall be governed by the following general rules:

1. A Member State's overall return coefficient shall be the ratio between its percentage share of the total value of all contracts awarded among all Member States and its total percentage contributions.
2. For the purpose of calculating return coefficients, weighting factors shall be applied to the value of contracts on the basis of their technological interest.
3. Ideally, the distribution of contracts placed by the Agency should result in all countries having an overall return coefficient of 1.

It is not the purpose of this chapter to offer a full historical critique of the ESA industrial policy or its results, but some comments should be made.

First, much of the policy is not implemented directly through the procurement procedure, which is largely in this context an implementing tool, but through the selection of programmes and the setting up of supporting technology programmes. Much of this planning takes into account the views of the Agency, the Member States and the aerospace industry. Indeed, when operating within a clearly defined sector, a permanent dialogue, and even something of a symbiotic relationship, arises which removes some of the surprises and disappointments from contractor selection. As disciplines not purely related to space (such as complex software programming) become more important, firms from outside the "family" have become involved, and are sometimes less content with the existing rules of the game.

It can also be mentioned that in the early years, with an emphasis on pure science and the related technology, ample funds and a driving enthusiasm for a pioneering activity, strains in the procurement process were relatively rare. These factors are less evident in the present time. Active industrial policy occurred predominantly in the following areas. The first was by trying to ensure that for certain critical technologies there were at least two firms, where possible in smaller Member States, with skills and a capacity relevant to foreseen programmes. This was both to help in making it easier to place work of technical interest in the smaller countries, and to maintain competition.

The second was through an active encouragement in setting up consortia within Europe, which contained industry from all or most of the Member States, which covered all the necessary technologies, and which had a lifetime running over a number of programmes. These consortia were somewhat looser groupings than would usually be understood by the term, more in the nature of flexible strategic groupings. This was very successful, not only in maintaining competition with a satisfactory industrial return, but also in its beneficial effect on increasing international co-operation, with a mutual familiarisation and understanding of working methods, which has influenced other collaborations, particularly in the aircraft field.

Thirdly, the growth of commercial space applications, together with other factors not unique to aerospace, have led to a number of cross-frontier mergers, so that the number of potential prime contractors in Europe has been greatly reduced. Those that remain have acquired many smaller firms with specialist technologies, so that on the commercial market they can make complete and, it is hoped, cost-effective bids. This has clearly made the life of the Agency more difficult, both in maintaining some competition and in implementing the principle of equitable industrial return between Member States.

Fourthly, while geographical distribution has always played a major role, in the past the target figure for spreading work among states funding the Agency was relatively low (90 per cent) and it was accepted that the period over which it was measured before disparities were considered critical, was relatively long. Major distortions of smooth procurement and competition were rare. A price, or cost, had to be paid for such industrial return arrangements, which has never been properly quantified, but is often put at around 10 per cent. This price arises from the need to set up industrial groupings incorporating more participating firms than would be required by engineering criteria, leading to long management and communication chains, inefficient arrangement of the work, with complex interfaces, and sometimes the selection of a non-optimum (but always acceptable) sub-contractor. This price was considered worth paying for the benefits it gave in European co-operation. Over time, however, a number of factors changed. The Member States adopted the concept of optional programmes (in addition to the mandatory programme, essentially science and basic technology) and each programme required its own return coefficients. Some countries began to develop what seemed like endemic low returns, and national patience ran out. Member States began to look more rigorously at their share of the work, per contract, per programme and per phase of programme. The target return has been progressively increased at ministerial conferences and special financial methods adopted to correct the return figures. Technical excellence became less important, and many programmes suffered considerable delays in their early stages while efforts were made to find industrial structures that met the precise requirements of politicians. This has been a significant cause of the political crisis which the Agency has passed through in recent years.[12]

The Agency has recently made an intensive study of its industrial policy issues and has presented the Member States with far-reaching proposals that are currently under discussion. The main thrust, apart from trying to reintroduce some flexibility, is to ask Member States to make sufficient commitment to optional programmes to allow an effective start on definition and design, but then to attempt to match the final contribution scales to the industrial reality that stems from these activities.

4. PRACTICE AND PITFALLS

Where policy issues are permitted to influence contractor selection, it is still essential that the procurement be carried out in a fair and honest way, with the maximum possible role being given to competition. This is for precisely the same reasons that justify the regulation of public procurement in general: cost-effective expenditure of public funds, avoidance of corruption, achievement of excellence and the opening up of international markets on a fair and equal basis.[13] Any opening of the door to discretionary decisions can weaken a regulatory system, especially when the machinery for effective remedy is still in its infancy. The practical implementation of an industrial policy must therefore be particularly careful, indeed meticulous, if problems are not to ensue. The discussion below focuses on some of the most important practical issues that need to be considered to ensure maximum success in implementing industrial policy, with the minimum cost to other procurement objectives.

4.1 Transparency

Visibility of the procurement process by the participating parties is recognised as a major element in ensuring proper conduct. When criteria other than price, quality or other value for money criteria play a role, then it is imperative that potential bidders are made aware of this in advance. If the policy would exclude them completely, then they will not waste resources in preparing an offer. If it may reduce their chances of winning, then they can make a proper commercial judgment on whether to parti-cipate. If, in order to stand a good chance, they would have to take on sub-

---

[12] Anecdotally, a sub-contractor was recently declared bankrupt not long before delivery was due on an item critical to the schedule (and the cost) of a major programme. The obvious action to take was to find the most capable firm available to take over and complete the work. The national delegate of the bankrupt firm tried to insist that the work be passed to another firm in his country in order to maintain the geographical return.

[13] The continuing debate as to which are the driving motives for public procurement regulations seems a trifle sterile – different reasons can all point in the same direction. For once, economics and ethics seem to go hand in hand. On this issue, see further chapter 1 of this volume.

contractors from a particular source, they must have the time to make industrial arrangements. And, of course, where there is a system in force that allows them to challenge a policy, then this is best done early.

What constitutes sufficient notice to potential bidders will vary according to circumstances. In the past it might have been sufficient to rely on the background knowledge of industry, of the "rules of the game" for a particular procurement authority. With the general international opening up of public contracting, the usual assumption that the best bid will win can reasonably be relied on if there is no indication to the contrary. At a minimum, the notice of tendering, and the tender documents themselves, should be clear on the issue, with an indication how more can be found out, either by reference to public documents or by inquiry to the procurement authority.

Where the policy is more complex, more information is needed. ESA is, for example, obliged to put a variety of different statements in its invitations to tender depending on the type of work. For a spacecraft programme under the mandatory programme, it will give the current cumulative return coefficients, and targets for the spread of work which will partially correct any imbalances (total correction being impossible through one contract). Under an optional programme, both the participating states (a more or less absolute criterion) and the required percentages will be given. Technology programmes (with a large number of relatively smaller contracts) will have different statements according to the rules and requirements governing that programme. The requirements are spelled out in the covering letter to the invitation to tender (as stipulated in Article 10(j) and (k) of the Contract Regulations), and it is very rare indeed for firms to misunderstand the situation.

4.2 Early notification

The rules for early notification of future procurements are often at best skimpy and inadequate for complex projects. Potential bidders do not usually have, as of right, much prior information before the tendering documents are made available. Preparing a complex bid with advanced technology requires more time than is usually allowed, and the commitment of scarce and valuable resources. If there are industrial policy constraints, then more time is needed to find suitable partners. It is therefore good practice, indeed essential practice, for the customer in such circumstances to give as much advanced warning both of the procurement and the policy. Of course, within a specialist sector much of the information is known to the interested parties, who may even be indirectly involved in the early planning and decision process. They will also probably be in frequent contact with the customer through other contract work or sector organisations. Nevertheless, the earliest formal publication of intentions, and updating as needed, is vital to avoid misunderstandings. Open briefings to industry, with a presentation and questions answered, is another useful tool, especially as contact has to be highly restricted and controlled once the formal bidding period has started.

4.3 Addressing invitations to tender

If a procuring authority establishes its own list of potential tenderers and only sends prior notification or tender documents to those, then it can restrict bidding in accordance with its policy. Great care has to be taken so that the list is not restricted beyond the policy and thus violates basic principles. The ESA Contract Regulations (Articles 8 and 12) provide that, in general, lists of anticipated actions will only be sent to potential bidders within the Member, Associated and Co-operating States, and invitations to tender to those in the countries participating in the programme. For competitive actions, any firm meeting the nationality requirement is entitled to the documents.

Where tendering information is made accessible virtually without restriction via a database (such as TED or ESA's EMITS) attention must be paid to the design of the informatics so that any limitations on participation are evident.

4.4 Pre-qualification on the basis of nationality

Even if an interested firm understands the policy, it may not be clear as to how it applies to that bidder. When nationality is a qualifying characteristic, one must ask what determines the nationality of a bidder, and in a global economy this is not always easy to answer. This applies both in determining the nationality of a firm, and the origin of goods or services. So far as origin as goods are concerned, for example, the World Trade Organisation Government Procurement Agreement (GPA), in order to identify unlawful exclusion, states:

1. A Party shall not apply rules of origin to products or services imported or supplied for purposes of government procurement covered by this Agreement from other Parties, which are different from the rules of origin applied in the normal course of trade and at the time of the transaction in question to imports or supplies of the same products or services from the same Parties.
2. Following the conclusion of the work programme for the harmonization of rules of origin for goods to be undertaken under the Agreement on Rules of Origin in Annex 1A of the Agreement Establishing the World Trade Organisation ... and negotiations regarding trade in services, Parties shall take the results of that work programme and those negotiations into account in amending paragraph 1 as appropriate.[14]

The Inter-American Development Bank states that:

a good shall be considered to be of local origin if the cost of the local materials, labor and services used to produce the item constitutes no less than 40 per cent of its total cost ... a good shall be considered to be of regional origin if it originates in a country that is party to an integration agreement to which the borrower is also a party, and

---

[14] GPA, Article IV.

complies with the standards governing origin and other matters relating to trade liberalization programs established in the respective agreements.[15]

In other circumstances, such as procurement by international organisations, purely formal criteria become less and less important for the purposes of a meaningful industrial policy. ESA is not so much concerned either to exclude or accept participation of a particular firm or particular products or services, as to avoid objections from a Member State. For example, a country may wish to claim a firm as its national, although it has many non-national "characteristics", because it wants that firm to continue to invest in the country. Alternatively, it may wish to disclaim the firm, as only bringing in "non-noble" work in order to gain a political advantage. The ESA Convention (Annex V, Article II 2.3) provides that:

the question whether an enterprise should be considered to belong to one of the Member States shall be settled in the light of the following criteria: location of the enterprise's registered office, decision-making centres and research centres, and the territory on which the work is to be carried out. In doubtful cases the Council shall decide whether an enterprise shall be considered to belong to one of the Member States, or not.

In practice the authorities of the country in question will have the determining say, and will in reality base this on the interest to them or otherwise of gaining the contract. Increasingly the criterion that determines the issue is where the work is actually performed. For certain types of work this is not so obvious. Where services are out-sourced, the work may be performed in the country of the customer, the firm rendering the service may be incorporated in another country, and the individual staff can be of mixed and mobile origins. ESA takes account of this in its industrial return statistics by splitting the contract value between the countries of the firm and of the place of service.[16]

Issues of nationality are relatively infrequent with regard to the right or otherwise to participate. They are, however, a daily concern where statistics have to be compiled and regular reports on industrial return have to be made to political masters. In practice ESA has relied on the currencies utilised; ESA normally pays sub-contractors directly in their currencies. Recently, however, ESA has adopted the ECU for most contractual and accounting purposes, and this easy approach can no longer be relied on.

The underlying political support for a procurement activity, which is usually the basis for an industrial policy, is normally given, and known to participants, prior to the procurement activity. ESA has had, for some relatively minor activities, a problem whereby certain states have not wished to commit to a particular activity in advance beyond a general approval in principle. A firm from that state is therefore obliged, when submitting an offer, to include a statement that the national delegation will

---

[15] Guidelines for Procurement Under IDB Loans, pp. 21 and 22.
[16] For some reason British and Danish firms seem to have been particularly enterprising in following the geographical-return requirements and setting up matching subsidiaries.

support, and therefore fund, the contract. The scope for distortion of the process is clearly enhanced.

4.5 Advising the potential bidders

It sometimes happens that a firm approaches ESA to ask for help in finding suitable partners for a particular bid. On the one hand, a customer cannot involve himself in arranging relations between firms, and risk an accusation of favouring one or the other. On the other hand, nothing is gained by failing to do all that is fair and legal to get as many compliant bids as possible. Such requests for information rarely come from prime contractors, who tend to know the field. If there is a very special technology involved, they are usually made aware of it, and where the expertise is to be found, by technical reports being published by the customer or referenced in the tendering documents. It is less easy with requests from smaller firms, often new to the field.[17] A general inquiry can be answered by giving the names and contact points of the major industries. It may, however, be more specific. For example where ESA says that preference will be given to bids with sub-contractors from specific countries (see 4(g)(iii) below) guidance may be sought both from potential contractors and sub-contractors. The approach taken varies according to the precise circumstances and relies much on the good sense and discretion of the procurement officer. If there is a list of fixed bidders, then this can perhaps be communicated. The national delegation may be prepared to pass on details of firms in his country – subject, one trusts, to similar considerations of fairness and equality. There are sometimes publications listing firms and skills available. In practice, what a firm usually needs is a first push in the right direction. The usual marketing skills should then allow him to find his way further.

In order to enhance this process ESA has positively encouraged, politically and materially, an organisation called EUROSPACE, which represents the majority of aerospace companies in Europe whose interests it represents towards ESA. It also publishes directories of firms and specialisations.

4.6 Evaluation

In any procurement action for a contract of significant size, technological difficulty or industrial complexity, the process of evaluation takes on a major importance. The assessment of the quality against a range of criteria, with a large number of experts giving marks, is not only vital for the selection of a contractor, but is also useful for identifying weaknesses in the winning offer which will have to be corrected. There is a considerable – and natural – tendency for the technical evaluators to allow their knowledge of policy considerations to affect their technical judgment and procedures should be devised to avoid this. It is already common practice to separate

---

[17] It sometimes happens that an existing technology not previously used in space becomes relevant to space work. The firm is experienced in the technology but not the sector.

the technical evaluation from the price judgment – only balancing the two at a subsequent stage (and perhaps by another body) after final marking. This way the objectivity of the technical evaluation is preserved. Where industrial policy also plays a role in the selection, it is even more important that that element of the decision-taking be kept separate from the technical assessment. Unsuccessful bidders can, usually, live with a negative political decision, taken by an authorised political body, against clear rules or criteria. They are far more unhappy if they feel that the quality of their offered work has been misjudged in order to make a subsequent political decision easier or less transparent.

4.7 Sub-contracting

In the context of large and complex procurements, and an industrial policy that runs over a period of time and a number of procurements, it is most likely that the achievement of the policy depends not on prime contractor selection but on the spread of sub-contracting.[18] The way this is done raises issues fundamental to the conduct of the procurement.

4.7.1 *Responsibility of the prime contractor*

A prime contractor has to present a proposal incorporating an industrial structure, with tiers of sub-contracting, for which he is expected to take responsibility, technically and commercially. If he is given a prescribed distribution of work defined by, for example, countries, his choice may be drastically restricted. It is all very well for the customer to say, for example, 5 per cent of the work should be placed in country X. There may only be two identifiable coherent packages in the whole job that amount to 5 per cent, and maybe only one firm of country X has a capacity to perform one of these tasks. In effect, the prime contractor can make a reasonable case that a sub-contractor is being imposed on him. He will argue that he is not permitted to choose either the best technical solutions, the optimally efficient industrial structure or the lowest price. The responsibility for the performance of the sub-contractor and also of the prime contractor should at least be shared with the customer. The experience of ESA in these cases is that there has, indeed, to be a period of negotiation with the prime contractor where the structure of the consortium is manipulated to arrive at something that both parties feel is technically and commercially sound, and politically acceptable. The prime contractor is sometimes instructed to put his sub-contracts out to tender, and the offers will be evaluated in parallel both by the prime contractor and by the Agency. At least a common understanding of technical quality and realism of price is achieved. Some give and take on the negotiation of contract terms, prices, financial margins and incentives may be necessary. In the end the prime contractor does

---

[18] Very often there is no real choice of prime contractor, this being determined effectively on technical grounds, overall capacity or the predominance of financial contribution from one country.

accept full contractual responsibility, but some flexibility and goodwill is required of both parties in the subsequent contract management.

4.7.2 *Position of the sub-contractor*

A potential sub-contractor who finds that his technical skills and the policy requirements match is in a very advantageous position – virtually a monopoly. In most cases he can quote a price based not on the realistic value of the work to be done, but on the share of the total price he considers he can claim, that is the money available in the budget. The customer (prime contractor or ultimate customer) may suspect that he is not getting value for money but is in a weak negotiation position. A reduction in price will probably only result in an obligation to find more work to be placed, artificially or not, in the same country. Getting more, or better, work for the same money is somewhat easier, but the additional negotiation effort is a real burden.

4.7.3 *Abuse by sub-contractors*

ESA has had cases, in certain technology programmes, where there was pressure for some work to be placed in one of a small number of countries. Prime contractorship, on the other hand, could reasonably be let out to open competition, and due to its content would go to one of the larger aerospace companies. The danger arose that certain potential sub-contractors, due to their combination of capacity and nationality, could distort the competition either by playing the competing prime contractors against each other, or by refusing to submit a bid to one or more of them, thus destroying their chances. While ESA tender conditions prohibit collusive arrangements, such behaviour did not always fall under the terms, or could not be proven. The response by ESA was to put in the invitation to tender a requirement that, other things being equal, preference would be given to offers which placed sub-contract work in certain countries, or which demonstrated that reasonable, but unsuccessful efforts had been made to achieve this. The approach has had some success.

4.8 Phasing

The establishment of an industrial structure of companies to perform a major contract which both meets the policy requirements and makes technical and commercial sense is a dominating problem. One approach towards a solution is to make use of the concept of project phasing – a tool that has many other valuable applications as well. What is meant by project phasing is to split the contract, and the work, into phases over time. Each phase ends at a determined point which has to be satisfactorily achieved before the next phase can be released. Classical phases (terminology varies) are feasibility study, system definition, system design, detailed design, development, manufacture, exploitation and maintenance. If the policy requirements are treated lightly, or flexibly, in the early phases, requiring only a firm commitment when the technical details are frozen, the chances of success are considerably enhanced. There is more time to explore suitable sub-contracts, run competitions, identify critical areas and so on.

Indeed, there is no need to involve significant numbers of sub-contractors at all in the early phases, leaving the prime contractor (or contractors if there is still competition) to concentrate on the task of technical definition. This was by and large how ESA operated for many years. Recently, however, in some programmes there has been pressure to reflect the hoped-for ultimate industrial return in the sub-contract pattern in the definition and design stages. This means that a major effort in these phases is the management of a large consortium and the passing of reports between parties. Indeed, some sub-contractors receive only enough money to pay for them to attend meetings and study papers, without contributing anything themselves.

Recent thinking has been on the lines that participating states should declare their support at the beginning with a band-width of percentage financial contribution. When work has sufficiently progressed so that industry can commit itself to the design, price and industrial return, the participating states adjust their contribution to what is then offered. Industry and ESA is, of course, committed to figures within the bandwidths, but sufficient flexibility is, it is hoped, introduced to obtain a better and cheaper product without abandoning the policy.

4.9 Pre-development

An industrial policy does not suddenly appear out of nothing, and industry is necessarily organised at any particular moment so as to maximise its possible compliance. There is, therefore, scope both for procurement organisations and industry to prepare the ground in advance. Indeed such preparation is itself a form of industrial policy. It carries, however, a danger of carrying out preparatory procurements which themselves infringe regulations.

A procuring body can, for example, identify that a particular product or technology will be required for a number of future programmes and is within the capacity of its smaller Member States.[19] This capacity may have potential and require study or development work to be carried out. Ideally, a number of parallel development contracts would be placed in the candidate countries. Success of such a policy would presuppose both that there is sufficient budget to place several contracts and that there will be sufficient future work to provide a competitive market for more than one of the firms concerned. Creating monopolies does not improve overall effectiveness, even if it can solve an individual policy problem. In the present economic climate the availability of funds, development and

---

[19] Industrial return to the larger states is rarely a problem (though ESA has had an endemic difficulty with its Italian return coefficient). Smaller firms in larger countries do not usually carry the same lobbying power with their national representatives, unless they play a significant role in their country's internal industrial policy.

programmatic, is restricted, and such "seed-corn" development tends to depend on a particular country promoting one of its firms, and supporting the placing of a contract with it. Such a country will not necessarily be one of the smaller countries.[20]

Another form of pre-development is when a particular, specialised technology is identified as needed for a particular programme, rather than generally for the future. Good engineering and programmatic practice demands that work be done prior to the start of the main project. Only highly specialist firms come into question, and the choice of firm will have a powerful influence on the industrial policy of the future programme itself, perhaps having a cascade effect on other sub-contractor selection. This leads, almost inevitably, to a sole-source selection that will have to be justified.

Industry may, and often does, take its own steps in advance to meet the requirements of industrial policy. This may take the form of setting up a consortium which contains within it members capable of together making the final product and of meeting the policy constraints. In the early days of ESA there were three such aerospace consortia in Europe, with enough individual firms, enough potential prime contractors and enough programmes to maintain competition and an economic validity. Occasionally one firm would appear in more than one consortium bid, but this was not a general problem. Progressively all three elements of abundance have reduced. The major players have merged within countries and transnationally. Increasingly, rather than entering into fairly loose arrangements with the smaller (sub-system) suppliers, major players have taken them over or taken controlling interests. One of the major drives towards this is that ESA is no longer the sole or dominant (though still a major) customer in European space. To survive, an aerospace firm has to be competitive on the international market, bidding to customers who are commercially driven and not prepared to pay a price for an industrial policy and the complex industrial structure that it needs. Between the Scylla of European co-operation and the Charybdis of hard commerce, only the very big players seem to steer a survival course. The commercial customer tends to get lower prices, ESA tends to get monopoly suppliers.[21]

5. CONCLUSION

It is unrealistic to expect that large, costly, politically sensitive and international projects will be placed purely on the basis of open and equal competition. This should not mean, however, that good procurement practice and fair competition can be abandoned as soon as an industrial policy element enters into the procurement constraints. Inevitably, some

---

[20] The issue of state aids is a complex one and not addressed here.
[21] Another form of industry preparing itself for industrial policy problems is lobbying its national representatives. This is not the subject of comment here.

element of compromise will occur, but it becomes perhaps even more important than in conventional procurement actions that the good procurement rules and practices which are being directly or indirectly encouraged by the various codes and regulations of the last few years be applied with special vigour, rigour and professionalism.

14. Private Participation in Public Infrastructure: Some Strategic Issues

*John Linarelli**

1. INTRODUCTION

This chapter deals with selecting private firms (or consortia of firms) for the award of concession-type arrangements to build, operate and, in some instances, own public sector projects. It will identify some of the notable strategic and structural aspects of the concession process. The purpose of the chapter is to stimulate ideas about the legal norms and procedures that would produce good results in the procurement and regulation of concession-type projects. This chapter examines some of the basic issues that are related to the use of private finance, including a rudimentary examination of the economic theory underlying the legal rules and concession terms and conditions. In order to rest on a sound policy footing, the legal rules should be informed by the underlying economics.

The concession-type arrangements that are addressed in this chapter are the subject of various definitions. One concise and transaction-oriented definition is as follows:

> Privately financed infrastructure projects are transactions pursuant to which the national, provincial [or] local Government engages a private entity to develop, maintain and operate an infrastructure facility in exchange for the right to charge a price, either to the public or to the Government, for the use of the facility or the services or goods it generates.[1]

Concession-type arrangements are not traditional procurements, nor are they typical works or infrastructure projects. In the private financing of a public project, a government awards a concession or franchise to a project company, often with covenants guaranteeing exclusivity. What makes these arrangements different from typical works, goods or services procurement is their award of rights, and allocation of obligations, to a private concern

---

* Lecturer in Law, University of Wales, Aberystwyth.
[1] Privately Financed Infrastructure Projects: Draft Chapters of a Legislative Guide, UNCITRAL, A/CN.9/438, 18 December 1996, p. 1.

which will operate something that otherwise would be operated by a government agency or public enterprise. In addition, governments procure financing as well as the construction and operation of infrastructure. The selection of a project company is not strictly procurement, nor are governments involved strictly in the regulation of private firms:[2] such projects are hybrids between traditional procurement and full privatisation. Tirole and Laffont provide a description that illustrates the mixed nature of the arrangement: "we ... refer to procurement when the firm supplies a good to the government and to regulation when it supplies a good to consumers on behalf of the government."[3] The concession-type arrangements that are the subject of this chapter often meet both of these criteria. Another, perhaps overly simplistic, way of analysing the difference between procurement and regulation is that in procurement, "payments" are made pursuant to contract terms but, in regulation, "subsidies" are granted pursuant to regulations of a general nature.[4] In concession-type arrangements, monetary transfers may reflect both a payment for services rendered as well as a subsidy to deal with shortfalls in demand.

Concession-type arrangements can be used for a variety of infrastructure needs in water, electricity, natural gas, telecommunications, transportation and sanitation and sewerage facilities. They may also be used in areas that are considered outside the domain of government, such as in hotel operations. Finally, concession-type arrangements may provide governments with the ability to take advantage of the greater efficiency of the private sector in the operation even of traditional government operations, such as schools and prisons. The basic issue addressed in this chapter is in what circumstances would it be permissible for government to rely on concession-type arrangements rather than on pure market transactions. One substantial concern is the potential for subsidisation of private enterprise in situations where the marketplace without government intervention would be the more efficient provider of the good or service in question.

2. WHY THE RESURGENCE OF INTEREST IN CONCESSION-TYPE ARRANGEMENTS?

There are a number of reasons why private finance of public projects has evoked so much interest in recent years. Perhaps a major reason is the general failure of public enterprises, state-run monopolies and loans to the state sector to generate wealth. Indeed, lending to the public sector has impoverished countries. Public enterprises are inefficient and are

---

[2] It is a common method of legal analysis to examine the "regulation of procurement". The terms are used in a different context in this chapter. For the purposes of this chapter, a distinction is made between non-procurement-type regulation and pure procurement.

[3] J.-J. Laffont and J. Tirole, *A Theory of Incentives in Procurement and Regulation* (Cambridge, MA and London: MIT Press, 1993), pp. 8–10.

[4] *Ibid.*

susceptible to political influence.[5] The debt crisis of the 1980s has resulted in poor governments that are unable to create prosperity in their countries.[6] The Bretton Woods institutions were based on, among other things, the idea that large loans to state sectors could cause reconstruction and development. The trend today, however, is away from development banking, and toward merchant banking and hybrid structures, such as the European Bank for Reconstruction and Development, which can use only 40 per cent of its funds to finance state sector projects.

Concession-type arrangements reflect the fact that markets can also fail. In addition to uneconomic returns on sovereign debt, pure market transactions financed by traditional commercial debt will not fill the void for some of the large-scale infrastructure projects that are a critical necessity for developing countries. The economics literature shows that infrastructure has a significant effect on productivity and wage increases, as well as on economic growth and development generally.[7]

3. THE IMPLICATIONS OF THE MONOPOLY FRANCHISE

The concession-type arrangement will normally be part of a broader legal, economic and institutional framework.[8] Here again, there is a merger of procurement and regulatory subjects – this time between procurement planning and privatisation policy. The institutional issues will determine what is the appropriate scope of the project. Project "packaging" will essentially derive from the unbundling of government-run enterprises.[9] The planning stage is critical to the success of a government's plans for privatisation as well as to any one concession-type project. In this process, a government should endeavour to determine what should remain as monopolies because they meet (or come close to) the status of a natural monopoly. It is these "natural" monopolies that can be bid out using competitive procedures.[10] Procurement planning thus should be incorporated into the broader regulatory framework in which governments make privatisation decisions. Governments may examine public enterprises to assess which institutions, if any, may be subject to privatisation and which may be subject to a public concession-award regime.[11] Planning combines

---

[5] A. Shleifer and R.W. Vishny, "Politicians and Firms" (1994) Quarterly Journal of Economics 995.

[6] See T. Frankel, "Foreword: Why Did the Movement to Privatize Arise Recently?" (1995) 13 *Boston University International Law Journal* 295 at 297.

[7] B. Eichengreen, "Financing Infrastructure in Developing Countries: Lessons from the Railway Age" in A. Mody (ed.), *Infrastructure Delivery: Private Initiative and the Public Good* (World Bank, 1996), p. 107.

[8] P. Guislain, "The Award of Concession-Type Arrangements" (unpublished, 1996, on file with the author), p. 3.

[9] A. Mody, "Infrastructure Delivery: New Ideas, Big Gains, No Panaceas" in A. Mody (ed.), *Infrastructure Delivery: Private Initiative and the Public Good* (World Bank, 1996), p. xiii.

[10] *Ibid.*

[11] *Ibid.*

regulatory, economic and institutional disciplines to derive the appropriate scope for the development of concession-type arrangements.

Politics and special-interest groups may have a substantial effect on the choice of policies. A good deal of the literature assumes these issues away. The determination of when markets fail may be difficult to make in the bureaucratic and political spheres. Moreover, from market failure alone it does not necessarily follow that government intervention would produce a better result. A "careful comparative analysis of alternative institutional arrangements" would seem to be in order.[12]

The award of a concession-type arrangement will usually seek to create exclusivity to be provided to the franchiser. The result is the award of monopoly rights.[13] The basic inefficiency caused by monopoly concessions is what is referred to as "dead-weight loss".[14] In most cases, monopolies produce an output below that which is socially optimal, at a price greater than the socially optimal price. Although disagreement exists as to the magnitude of the loss, there is consensus that it does occur. Dead-weight loss may be substantial where firms have the opportunity to lobby for single-source concessions, and where governments are willing to create legal barriers to entry where such barriers are unnecessary for the furnishing of the good or service in question.

The choice that governments should make is between the government operation of the monopoly and private operation of it.[15] Two aspects of this choice merit discussion.

First, governments should bid out the right to perform a natural monopoly. Market failure should be a precondition for these projects; otherwise, governments could rely on pure market transactions. The distinction

---

[12] D.-J. Kraan, *Budgetary Decisions: A Public Choice Approach* (Cambridge: Cambridge University Press, 1996), p. 197.

[13] There are at least five ways that monopolies may arise: (1) As a result of innovation or entry into a new market. The innovation may have caused transaction costs to decrease sufficiently for the initial innovator to enter the market and to provide a previously unprovided service; (2) Firms may obtain monopoly power through the exit of other firms. Natural monopolies tend to fall within this category. The remaining firm may not be any more efficient that the exiting firms, but economies of scale may mandate that only one firm can exist in the market; (3) Firms may obtain monopoly power through regulation and through monopoly franchises granted by governments. This is the classic concession-type monopoly; (4) There may be economic or technological barriers to entry, such as fixed capital requirements and sunk costs, that may make entry of other firms difficult; (5) A monopoly firm may control a unique resource unavailable to other firms, which may be required for the production of consumer goods or services. R. Congleton, "Microeconomic Theory" (unpublished, on file with the author).

[14] A.C. Harberger, "Monopoly and Resource Allocation" (1954) 44 *American Economic Review* 77; G. Tullock, "The Welfare Costs of Tariffs, Monopolies, and Theft" (1967) 3 *Western Economic Journal* 224; R.A. Posner, "The Social Costs of Monopoly and Regulation" (1975) 83 *Journal of Political Economy* 807.

[15] There are actually four choices that governments can make: (1) private regulated monopoly; (2) private unregulated monopoly; (3) actual government operation; and (4) no project. The above analysis assumes that governments have ruled out choices (2) and (4). See O.E. Williamson, *Economic Organization: Firms, Markets and Policy Control* (Wheatsheaf Books, 1986), p. 185 for discussion of the first three choices.

between a natural monopoly, or market failure, and a government-created monopoly is important for determining whether the activities of the monopolist will result in socially desirable profit-seeking or socially wasteful rent-seeking. A government-created monopoly results in artificial or contrived scarcity created by a government. A natural monopoly results in real scarcity created by lack of markets. Rent-seeking is undesirable because it results in a misallocation of scarce resources from creating wealth through increased production to seeking differential advantages through government intervention. This misallocation results in a waste of resources on unproductive rather than productive enterprises.[16]

Second, the choice is to bid out the natural monopoly to the private sector, rather than having the government itself conduct monopoly operations through a public enterprise. If accomplished appropriately, this should result in efficiency gains.[17] Of course, private monopolies have their drawbacks, but self-regulated public monopolies have proven to be even less efficient than their private counterparts. Private monopolies may be regulated and subsidised through terms and conditions in the concession agreements and through promulgated regulation of a general character.[18]

Competitive bidding of monopoly franchises is desirable because it will reduce the rent of the winning firm. Competitive bidding "is a market solution that avoids many of the disabilities of regulation".[19] Competition will serve to ensure selection of the most efficient firm and hence the lowest-cost operator. Some have asserted that competitive bidding may help to alleviate dead-weight loss but may result in the expenditure of resources on competing for the monopoly rather than in real gains to consumers. Although there is disagreement over the mechanics of the bidding process, one clear point emerges: competition provides the best opportunities for an efficient outcome. In the absence of competition, the opportunities for rent-seeking and for the setting of rates which transfer too much from consumers to the concessionaire are significant. Government agents may not be adequately informed because they are less experienced, particularly with the sophisticated concession-type transactions that will be required.[20] Competition assists governments in overcoming information disadvantages.[21] The formality of the competitive procurement process limits the application of uninformed discretion by government officials.[22]

---

[16] J.M. Buchanan, "Rent Seeking and Profit Seeking" in R.D. Tollison and R.D. Congleton (eds.), *The Economic Analysis of Rent Seeking* (Edward Elgar, 1995), p. 51.

[17] Privately Financed Infrastructure Projects: Draft Chapters of a Legislative Guide, UNCITRAL, A/CN.9/438, 18 December 1996, p. 1.

[18] P. Guislain, *The Privatization Challenge: A Strategic, Legal, and Institutional Analysis of International Experience* (The World Bank, 1997).

[19] See O.E. Williamson, *Economic Organization: Firms, Markets and Policy Control* (Wheatsheaf Books, 1986), p. 263.

[20] R.C. Marshall and M.J. Meurer, "The Private Attorney-General Meets Public Contract Law: Procurement Oversight by Protest" (1991) 20 *Hofstra Law Review* 1 at 7.

[21] *Ibid.*; see F. Hayek, "The Use of Knowledge in Society" in *Individualism and Economic Order* (University of Chicago, 1949).

[22] R.C. Marshall and M.J. Meurer, "The Private Attorney-General Meets Public Contract Law: Procurement Oversight by Protest" (1991) 20 *Hofstra Law Review* 1 at 7.

In the concession context, exclusivity is a form of subsidy to the concessionaire, to make up for the imperfections of the market. But one of the fundamental tenets governing the production of any good is that there are always substitutes. Concession-type arrangements are not exempt from fundamental economic principles. Consumers will find substitutes, depending on the elasticity of demand for the product and the time in which they have to find or create substitutes. Toll roads have been circumvented through the use of clearly inferior local roads. One basic substitute for any good is simply not to consume it. People in developing countries, with limited economic means, can be ingenious in finding substitutes. Finally, exclusivity may be viewed as a trade-off or substitute for other "subsidies".

4. SOME REGULATORY PROVISIONS

Given the theory set forth in the preceding section, what are the procedures that governments may use to award concessions? There are a number of approaches that have been proffered, ranging from competitive sealed bidding to competitive negotiations to sole-source awards (i.e. awards to a selected provider made without competition). There appears to be some uncertainty as to the appropriate award procedures for these projects.[23] Although there is no "one size fits all" approach to award procedures for concessions, there are a number of parameters that can be applied. Several are examined here.

4.1 Award procedures

Governments should avoid single-source concessions. A single-source award would likely result in significant monopoly rents for the concession firm, which would result in higher prices and lower output. From a theoretical standpoint, competitive bidding has the potential to eliminate rent-seeking by converting concessions into private property rights.[24] This is just a more formal way of expressing the intuition that competition brings prices down. The monopoly franchise has posed problems for developing countries.[25] Some developers assert that a sound strategy from the perspective of the developer and other concession parties in the private sector, is for developers to be permitted to make unsolicited proposals that result in single-source awards. Unsolicited concessions are usually the most profitable.

This is not only an issue in developing and transitioning countries. In the European Community, there are requirements to publicise works con-

---

[23] D.A. Levy, "BOT and Public Procurement: A Conceptual Framework" (1996) 7 *Indiana International and Comparative Law Review* 95 at 96.

[24] J.M. Buchanan, "Rent Seeking and Profit Seeking" in R.D. Tollison and R.D. Congleton (eds.), *The Economic Analysis of Rent Seeking* (Edward Elgar, 1995), p. 55.

[25] A.O. Krueger, "The Political Economy of the Rent-Seeking Society" (1974) 64 *American Economic Review* 291.

cession contracts (in the sense of contracts that are wholly or partly remunerated by the contractor's right to exploit the work) but there are no requirements to use formal tendering procedures or even to use competitive negotiated procedures.[26] Professor Arrowsmith has criticised these gaps:

> There is no justification for this exclusion of concession contracts from the obligation to use competitive procedures. Even if special procedures may be appropriate for the award of certain concessions – for example, because of their complexity and the cost of bidding, or the need for an ongoing partnership between the authority and concessionaire in carrying out the project – in general such awards should be subject to much more stringent regulation than is presently the case.[27]

In the European Community, concessions for non-construction services are not subject to any procedural rules. The World Bank Procurement Guidelines offer little guidance, merely providing that international competitive bidding (ICB) or limited international bidding (LIB) should be used, "which may include several stages in order to arrive at the optimal combination of evaluation criteria".[28] What are the "several stages" in an ICB or LIB method of procurement? Perhaps a two-stage method of competitive tendering would be appropriate. An award procedure that provides for significant transparency would be preferred.[29]

There are no easy answers as to whether procurement rules should be substantially modified in favour of an auction similar to those conducted by the US Federal Communications Commission in the auctioning of radio spectrum licences, or whether more traditional procurement methods should be used.[30] Less information is passed to bidders in the traditional procurement methods such as two-stage tendering or the "request for proposals" method of procurement. Auction methods may not work in the award of a concession because a concession is not a homogeneous product, and the concession award is more like a purchase than a sale. A "Dutch auction" type procedure[31] may work in the "sale" of licences, but probably will not work in competitions for concessions. In competitions for concessions, governments seek innovative technical and financial solutions from bidders. The strategic behaviour of bidders caused by disclosure of the innovative solutions of their competitors may produce unfavourable results in that bidders would be given the wrong incentives. They would have the incentive to free ride on the innovation and proposal preparation

---

[26] S. Arrowsmith, *The Law of Public and Utilities Procurement* (Sweet & Maxwell, 1996), p. 358.
[27] *Ibid.*, p. 359.
[28] Guidelines Procurement under IBRD Loans and IDA Credits, Article 3.13 (January 1995, revised January and August 1996).
[29] P. Guislain, "The Award of Concession-Type Arrangements" (unpublished, 1996, on file with the author), p. 9.
[30] *Ibid.*
[31] See R. P. McAfee and J. McMillan, "Auctions and Bidding" (1987) 25 *Journal of Economic Literature* 699.

efforts of competing bidders, and to speculate only on price. This would create a significant disincentive to offer superior technical and financial solutions. For example, in a best value procurement, a free-riding bidder could merely promise to provide the best technical and financial solution offered by the highest ranked bidder at a marginally lower price.

4.2 Pre-qualification

Pre-qualification may be a prudent procedure to use in holding a competition for the award of a concession. There are two sides to this issue. On the one hand, it may be argued that, as competition increases, prices fall for a given quality and quantity of a good or service. On the other hand, it may be too costly for governments to evaluate proposals from numerous firms whose resources are ill-matched for concession awards.[32] The firms who form consortia to bid on concessions want a "fighting chance to win". If the field is too broad, investment by firms in proposal preparation may not be justified. Arguments that competition is "excessive" are often devices to create barriers to entry. Here, however, given the substantial transaction costs of competitive infrastructure bidding, the argument may have some merit in the context of concession awards. Pre-qualification creates an incentive to award firms that engage in a form of investment in a project.[33]

4.3 BOO or BOT?

The concept of BOO (Build-Own-Operate) refers to the case where the contractor retains ownership of the asset that is being exploited, while a BOT (Build-Operate-Transfer) is one in which the contractor transfers ownership to the government. In what circumstances should the transaction provide for eventual transfer back to the government or for renewal through competition in the future? Should a government recompete a concession? What are the differences between a concession arrangement and the more traditional privatisation of state enterprises?[34]

Some have asserted that concessions should be awarded competitively, and that concessions should be recompeted "to adjust for new, non-contracted for circumstances or to encourage entry of another, more efficient firm".[35] Although in theory recompetition would appear to be sound, in practice it may suffer from a number of drawbacks. Capital may

---

[32] R.C. Marshall and M.J. Meurer, "The Private Attorney-General Meets Public Contract Law: Procurement Oversight by Protest" (1991) 20 *Hofstra Law Review* 1 at 9–10.

[33] *Ibid.*

[34] See D.A. Levy, "BOT and Public Procurement: A Conceptual Framework" (1996) 7 *Indiana International and Comparative Law Review* 95.

[35] J.-J. Laffont and J. Tirole, *A Theory of Incentives in Procurement and Regulation* (MIT Press, 1993). The origins of this theory are in Edwin Chadwick, "Results of Different Principles of Legislation and Administration in Europe; of Competition for the Field, as Compared with Competition Within the Field of Service" (1859) 22 *Journal of the Royal Statistical Society* 381. A "modern" and extended treatment of the subject is in H. Demsetz, "Why Regulate Utilities?" (1968) 11 *Journal of Law and Economics* 55.

not be easily transferable to a new firm, and the incumbent's incentive to invest and maintain a facility may be decreased due to the allocation of temporary property rights to the incumbent.[36] Moreover, competitive renewals are costly to owners as well as bidders.[37] Transaction costs may impede or even preclude effective recompetition of a concession, resulting in effect in a sole-source award to the initial concessionaire. These are some of the basic strategic questions that may inform a government as to whether to structure the concession as a BOO or a BOT transaction.

A countervailing consideration to a no-follow-on competition policy is that it deprives the market of contestability, and may cause monopoly firms to engage in undesirable practices. Regulation of monopoly is important, but it is by no means perfect; regulators perhaps raise more questions than they provide answers. There is, moreover, the potential pitfall of "regulatory capture", where regulation does more to serve the private interest of the regulated firm than the public interest of the populace.[38]

4.4 Terms and conditions: transaction structure

Regardless of the award procedure used, concession arrangements inevitably will include subsidies to be provided to the concession firm. These subsidies may be provided through various means, in the concession documentation itself as well as in promulgated regulations.[39] The classic natural monopoly will operate at a loss, and thus subsidisation may be necessary in order to obtain financing.[40]

Some projects will use take-or-pay or off-take arrangements. As explained by UNCITRAL:

Another type of financial support may be an assurance by the host Government of a minimum revenue to the project company. When the Government or a governmental entity is the sole customer for the services or goods supplied by the concessionaire, the law sometimes provides that the Government or some governmental entity will be under an obligation to purchase such goods and services, at an agreed rate, as they are offered by the concessionaire. With regard to services provided directly to the public, the host Government sometimes undertakes to subsidise the project

---

[36] J.-J. Laffont and J. Tirole, *A Theory of Incentives in Procurement and Regulation* (MIT Press, 1993).

[37] *Ibid.*

[38] G.J. Stigler, "The Theory of Economic Regulation" (1971) 2 *Bell Journal of Economics and Management Science* 1; D.E.M. Sappington, "Principles of Regulatory Design" in A. Mody (ed.), *Infrastructure Delivery: Private Initiative and the Public Good* (World Bank, 1996), p. 79.

[39] P. Guislain, *The Privatization Challenge: A Strategic, Legal, and Institutional Analysis of International Experience* (World Bank, 1997), p. 258.

[40] For an explanation of this phenomenon in a standard economic text, see Walter Nicholson, *Microeconomic Theory: Basic Principles and Extensions* (Fort Worth: 6th edn, Dryden Press, 1995), pp. 628–9.

company, in the event that officially approved tariffs fall below the level provided in the project agreement. In other cases, the project company is paid a flat or variable sum directly by the host Government, on the basis of an estimated number of paying users of the facility arrived at in the course of the selection process.[41]

Some projects will require sovereign guarantees. Where a government's guarantee is insufficient, a World Bank guarantee may provide support (and in effect may be a substitute when a government has limited resources), and may serve as a catalyst for private financing. The types of guarantees may include guarantees that allow the revenue of the project to be converted into hard currencies, and guarantees against expropriation or nationalisation.[42] Governments may grant preferential treatment in the tax and customs areas,[43] or sometimes may take an equity stake in the project company. Even the non-recourse nature of the financing may be characterised as a subsidy as it is a concessional term designed to attract firms to engage in the project. With non-recourse financing, the government ultimately is accountable for the success of the project. However, it also increases risk to lenders, and thus lenders often want government guarantees.

4.5 Reserve price

Governments should consider using a reserve price in the procurement process. A reserve price may be particularly effective when the number of bidders is limited, such as where there is pre-qualification.[44] A reserve price is the "credible threat" often described in game theory. "A reserve policy establishes a minimum level of surplus or score that the best proposal must offer in order to receive an award. Simply put, beating the reserve is a necessary condition for winning an award. The strategy underlying the reserve is to compel firms to offer better terms."[45] However, if there is likely to be only one bidder, disclosure of a reserve price may be imprudent.[46]

5. TRADE AND PRIVATE FINANCE

There are no trade agreements in the GATT/WTO that deal explicitly with private finance of public projects. There are several, however, which may apply, depending on the project.

---

[41] Privately Financed Infrastructure Projects: Draft Chapters of a Legislative Guide, UNCITRAL, A/CN.9/438, 18 December 1996, p. 13.
[42] F. Agusti, "Build Operate Transfer ('BOT') Transactions" (unpublished, on file with the author), pp. 9–11.
[43] *Ibid.*
[44] R.C. Marshall and M.J. Meurer, "The Private Attorney-General Meets Public Contract Law: Procurement Oversight by Protest" (1991) 20 *Hofstra Law Review* 1 at 8.
[45] *Ibid.*
[46] P. Guislain, "The Award of Concession-Type Arrangements" (unpublished, 1996, on file with the author), p. 9.

It is unclear whether the WTO Government Procurement Agreement (GPA)[47] would apply. Which entity enters into a contract with a government? What is its nationality? What are the national origins of its goods and services? These issues make general conclusions about the applicability of the GPA impracticable, although some tentative generalisations can be made. Privately financed projects often involve a consortium of companies, sometimes multinational in character. The consortium may form a project company, which might typically enter into a concession contract with a government or government enterprise. A construction company, equipment manufacturer, developer and other parties may be the owners of the project company, while banks in syndication may be investors or even equity holders in the project company. These parties may themselves be from various countries and may be multinational in character, with only some of the countries in which they have their principal place of business as GPA contracting parties. Should the GPA apply to the concession agreement or to the construction contract between the project company and the construction contractor or to equipment contracts? The GPA presents a dispute waiting to happen.

Article I of the GPA sets forth a fairly broad scope for the GPA. Article I(1) provides that the GPA "applies to any law, regulation, procedure or practice regarding any procurement by entities covered by this Agreement, as specified in Appendix I".[48] Article I(2) continues by stating that the GPA "applies to procurement by any contractual means, including through such methods as purchase or as lease, rental or hire purchase ... including any combination of products and services".[49] The term "procurement" is not defined in the GPA. The reference to "by any contractual means", when read in conjunction with other GPA provisions, may be interpreted to cover privately financed projects.

Notably, Article I(3) provides that: "Where entities, in the context of procurement covered under this Agreement, require enterprises not included in Appendix I to award contracts in accordance with particular requirements, Article III shall apply *mutatis mutandis* to such requirements."[50] Article III of the GPA sets forth the basic national treatment and most-favoured-nation principles of the GATT. Article I(3) should be read in conjunction with Annex 5 of Appendix I for many of the contracting parties to the GPA. Annex 5 defines a "construction services contract" as "a contract which has as its objective the realisation by whatever means of civil or building works, in the sense of Division 51 of the Central Product Classification".[51] The GPA was broadened during the Uruguay Round to cover construction. Many of the privately financed projects which are the

---

[47] References to the Uruguay Round Agreements may be found in the US Trade Representative Publication, *Uruguay Round of Multilateral Trade Negotiations General Agreement on Tariffs and Trade* (15 April 1994).

[48] *Ibid.*, Annex, p. 18.

[49] *Ibid.*

[50] *Ibid.*

[51] Division 51 is a comprehensive list which identifies many of the types of infrastructure projects which could be the subject of private finance.

subject of this chapter will involve substantial construction. A privately financed infrastructure project may well fall into this requirement. Article 1 thus seems to say that a privately financed project could be subject to the basic national treatment and most favoured nation requirements of the GATT, but not to the tendering and other procurement disciplines of the GPA. This is not a controversial obligation. The position illustrates the nature of privately financed projects as a mixture of procurement of goods, services and works and investment of capital.

In addition, it is necessary to consider any derogations in Appendix I. Although Article III of the GPA sets forth the basic WTO national treatment and most favoured nation obligations, Appendix I sets forth a significant list of derogations from these principles, reflecting the bargaining of the parties. Appendix I would have to be read and applied to specific facts in order to provide a definitive answer as to whether the GPA applies. A few examples will illustrate the point. Annex 3 for Austria covers entities that "exercise as a principal activity, the provision or operation of fixed networks intended to provide a service to the public in connection with the production, transport and distribution of drinking water, and electricity".[52] Austria also extends the GPA to certain entities in the transport sector. In the notes to Canada's annex, it states: "Procurement in terms of Canadian coverage is defined as contractual transactions to acquire property or services for the direct benefit or use of the government ... It does not include non-contractual agreements or any form of government assistance, including but not limited to ... loans, equity infusions, guarantees, fiscal incentives, and government provision of goods and services."[53] Canada excludes European Community contractors from some contracts in the fields of drinking water, energy, transport and telecommunications. The examples could continue.

If the GPA applies to concession-type arrangements, then the tendering and other procurement disciplines set forth in the GPA would apply. If the GPA does not apply (or in the situation set out in Article I(3) of the GPA), other GATT provisions may apply to a concession-type arrangement. Perhaps the most obvious is the Agreement on Trade-Related Investment Measures (TRIMs). The TRIMs Agreement does not provide much protection; it is at its roots simply an affirmation that basic GATT most-favoured-nation and national treatment principles apply to some investment requirements.[54]

The WTO Agreement on Subsidies and Countervailing Measures may restrict the ability of governments to agree to subsidies for project companies when the product of the concession has the potential to be exported. Suppose that the economics of the situation mandate that the only way an electricity provider could obtain sufficient economies of scale would be for the concessionaire to export electricity. This may be critical to project

---

[52] *Ibid.*, Appendix 1.
[53] *Ibid.*
[54] M.J. Trebilcock and R. Howse, *The Regulation of International Trade* (London: Routledge, 1995), p. 292.

success where there is insufficient demand for electricity by industrial users within the borders of a country. As explained in the previous section, governments may have to provide subsidies to concessionaires in order to be able to use private finance. These subsidies may be actionable under the GATT or even prohibited *per se* if they are tied to export performance. Many concession-type projects are just assumed to address domestic demand for a product, and this may be the case for roads, airports, and other fixed assets. But where the assets are used to produce a product that can be transported across borders, the trade aspects of the arrangement will become important.

Concession-type arrangements have the potential to renew the significance of provisions of the GATT that deal with state trading and monopolies. The Uruguay Round Understanding on Article XVII of the General Agreement on Tariffs and Trade 1994 sets forth the following "working definition" of state trading enterprises:

Government and non-governmental enterprises ... which have been granted exclusive or special rights or privileges, including statutory or constitutional powers, in the exercise of which they influence through their purchases or sales the level or direction of imports or exports.[55]

As explained above, the concession-type arrangement may be a legally sanctioned monopoly in which a concession company is granted exclusivity of some sort over a valuable product. Governments may give concession companies exclusive rights, or exclusive rights may result due to market structure. Concession-type arrangements may trigger the GATT's notification and substantive requirements governing state trading enterprises. This is a somewhat bizarre result – privatisation that results in the application of provisions intended to govern activities in non-market economies. But the concession-type arrangement is not pure privatisation, and government involvement in the economy will still occur in these projects.

Finally, the General Agreement on Trade in Services (GATS) may apply to at least portions of the infrastructure projects that are the subject of this chapter. The GATS is a complex set of general and specific commitments with respect to services, and a detailed treatment is beyond the scope of this chapter. Two points, however, merit brief attention.

First, Article XIII of GATS exempts government procurement from its coverage in a roundabout way: government procurement is exempt from most-favoured-nation treatment (Article II) of services generally, from the national treatment obligations which are imposed on scheduled market access commitments which are not subject to most-favoured-nation treatment, and from any other additional commitments. The parties agree in Article XIII(2) to conduct multilateral negotiations on government procurement in services in the future.

---

[55] *Uruguay Round of Multilateral Trade Negotiations General Agreement on Tariffs and Trade* (15 April 1994), p. 27.

Secondly, Article VIII of the GATS sets forth a host of requirements with respect to "monopolies and exclusive service suppliers" which will have to be addressed in the planning of an infrastructure project. Article VIII(1) sets forth the basic obligation that: "Each Member shall ensure that any monopoly supplier of a service in its territory does not, in the supply of the monopoly service in the relevant market, act in a manner inconsistent with that Member's obligations under Article II [most-favoured-nation treatment] and specific commitments."[56] Where a monopoly supplier enters into a market outside of its exclusive rights, and which is subject to the WTO member's specific commitments under the GATS, the member "shall ensure that such a supplier does not abuse its monopoly position to act in its territory in a manner inconsistent with such commitments."[57] It is unclear what these provisions mean in the various domestic implementations which are bound to result from them. An abuse of a monopoly position is a question of domestic competition law. An abuse of a monopoly position may mean something different in the US than it would mean in Japan, for example. In addition, it is unclear whether GATS has the ability to be used to stop monopoly concessions. Article VIII(4) of GATS requires a WTO member to provide notice to the WTO Council for Trade in Services when a member "grants monopoly rights regarding the supply of a service covered by its specific commitments",[58] and GATS provisions concerning modification of schedules will come into play. Therefore, WTO members could exclude areas in which they might want more discretion in awarding concessions from GATS coverage, or subsequently modify their GATS coverage.

6. EFFORTS TO IMPROVE DOMESTIC LEGAL FRAMEWORKS

UNCITRAL is currently deliberating on the preparation of a legislative guide on privately financed infrastructure projects. The guide's purpose would be "to assist national Governments and legislative bodies in reviewing the adequacy of laws, regulations and decrees and similar legislative texts relating to transactions for the private financing, construction and operation of public infrastructure facilities".[59] In 1996, the United Nations Industrial Development Organisation (UNIDO) published its *Guidelines on Infrastructure Development through Build-Operate-Transfer (BOT) Projects*. It is unclear what UNCITRAL will produce that is distinct from the UNIDO product. It appears that the UNIDO text focuses on accomplishing the transactions, while the UNCITRAL focus is on guidance to governments on

---

[56] *Ibid.,* pp. 291–2.
[57] *Ibid.*
[58] *Ibid.*
[59] Privately Financed Infrastructure Projects: Draft Chapters of a Legislative Guide, UNCITRAL, A/CN.9/438, 18 December 1996 at p. 13.

drafting laws concerning concessions and private finance of public projects. Some countries already have concession laws on the books, although these laws may be inadequate.

The fundamental question concerning the work of UNCITRAL in this area will be whether the organisation will generate a coherent set of principles that will provide precise guidance to governments. UNCITRAL as an institution is subject to a number of constraints, including the requirement of consensus from experts from a broad spectrum of countries.[60] UNCITRAL's work product tends to vest broad discretion in the government users of it (legislatures, executives and courts).[61] Two of UNCITRAL's significant works, the UNCTIRAL Model Law on Procurement of Goods, Construction and Services and the Convention on the International Sale of Goods (CISG), illustrate these constraints. As for the CISG: "Many key provisions are open-ended, while others contain internal contradictions that permit decision-makers to reach whatever result they wish."[62] The more detailed nature of the UNCITRAL Model Law on Procurement may be due in part to the nature of public procurement regulation in developing and transitioning countries, which is the primary focus of the Model Law. Still, the Model Law contains 11 award procedures. To UNCITRAL's credit, however, the Model Law is significant in its attempt to promote accountability of governments and the role of competition in the procurement process.

7. CONCLUSION

Private financing of public projects is not a new trend; it is a reversion to nineteenth-century approaches to financing infrastructure. American and Indian railroads were built using private capital raised in the London capital markets and subsidised with such devices as land grants and government guarantees.[63] Mexican railroads were built on borrowed US capital and promoted substantially by Ulysses S. Grant; the interest in Mexican railroads derived from the need for ore and minerals located in Mexico. Utilities also were constructed using private money in the nineteenth and early twentieth centuries.

This chapter does not attempt an exhaustive analysis of the issues by any means. One area that may merit future research is whether the evolution of governments involved in public legislation, and in the regulation of

---

[60] See P.B. Stephan, "Institutions for International Economic Integration: Accountability and International Lawmaking: Rules, Rents and Legitimacy" (1997) 17 *Northwestern Journal of International Law and Business* 681.

[61] *Ibid.*

[62] *Ibid.*

[63] C.D. Jacobson and J.A. Tarr, "No Single Path: Ownership and Financing of Infrastructure in the 19th and 20th Centuries" and B. Eichengreen, "Financing Infrastructure in Developing Countries: Lessons from the Railway Age" in A. Mody (ed.), *Infrastructure Delivery: Private Initiative and the Public Good* (World Bank, 1996), p. 79.

economic activity, caused a substitution of public capital for private capital in infrastructure investment. It is not that we should seek to recreate the state of legal and economic affairs that existed in the nineteenth century. There is a great deal that has been learned about the operations of governments and monopolies and about procurement procedures that can be adapted to attempt to at least mitigate the undesirable aspects of the concession. What was implausible in the past may well be pragmatic in the future.

Index*

International Economic Development Law

1. J.J. Norton, T.L. Bloodworth and T.K. Pennington (eds), *NAFTA and Beyond. A New Framework for Doing Business in the Americas.* 1995
ISBN 0-7923-3239-3

2. N. Kofele-Kale, *International Law of Responsibility for Economic Crimes.* Holdings Heads of State and Other High Ranking State Officials Individually Liable for Acts of Fraudulent Enrichment. 1995
ISBN 0-7923-3358-6

3. Hani Sarie-Eldin, *Consortia Agreements in the International Construction Industry.* With Special Reference to Egypt. 1996 ISBN 90-411-0912-9

4. J.J. Norton and Mads Andenas (eds), *Emerging Financial Markets and the Role of International Financial Organisations.* 1996 ISBN 90-411-0909-9

5. B. Sodipo, *Piracy and Counterfeiting.* 1997 ISBN 90-411-0947-1

6. J.J. Norton and Mads Andenas (eds), *Emerging Financial Markets and Secured Transactions.* 1998 ISBN 90-411-0675-8

7. J.A. McMahon, *The Development Co-operation Policy of the EC.* 1998
ISBN 90-411-0744-4

KLUWER LAW INTERNATIONAL – LONDON, THE HAGUE, BOSTON